The Essential Criminology Reader

edited by

Stuart Henry

Wayne State University

and

Mark M. Lanier

University of Central Florida

A Member of the Perseus Books Group

Find us on the World Wide Web at www.westviewpress.com

Westview Press books are available at special discounts for bulk purchases in the United States by corporations, institutions, and other organizations. For more information, please contact the Special Markets Department at the Perseus Books Group, 11 Cambridge Center, Cambridge, MA 02142, or call (617) 252-5298 or (800) 255-1514, or e-mail special.markets@perseusbooks.com.

Library of Congress Cataloging-in-Publication Data

The essential criminology reader / edited by Stuart Henry and Mark M. Lanier.
p. cm.
Companion vol. to: Essential criminology / Mark M. Lanier, Stuart Henry. 2nd ed. 2004.
Includes bibliographical references and index.
ISBN-13: 978-0-8133-4319-8 (paperback : alk. paper)
ISBN-10: 0-8133-4319-4 (paperback : alk. paper) 1. Criminology. I. Henry, Stuart. II. Lanier, Mark. III. Lanier, Mark. Essential criminology.
HV6025.E77 2006
364—dc22

2005013373

The paper used in this publication meets the requirements of the American National Standard for Permanence of Paper for Printed Library Materials Z39.48-1984.

10 9 8 7 6 5 4 3 2 1

Contents

Preface and Introduction: Beyond Theory Textbooks

One may ask, why another reader on criminological theory? We respond that this book is designed to meet the need for a brief, accessible, "readable" companion volume written by active theorists that fills the gap between textbook summaries, encyclopedic works, and the standard reader/anthology.

In 2000, the late criminologist Richard A. Wright declared the 1990s a "golden era of theorizing" in criminology, and that the Renaissance had been chronicled by a "plethora of criminology texts" (Wright 2000, 179). As authors of some of these Renaissance-era theory textbooks in criminology and deviant behavior (Einstadter and Henry 1995; Lanier and Henry 1998, 2004; Pfuhl and Henry 1993), we are aware of their value and their limitations as teaching aids. At their best, textbooks provide the instructor and reader with a comprehensive survey of the field, even if the depth in any given area is insufficient to do full justice to the theory it is attempting to convey. A good text must be concise, yet it must also provide a sufficiently detailed synopsis of the ideas it is representing so that the student/reader is able to comprehend what is said without being confused. Ideally, the book should leave the student with a desire to find out more. At the same time, the synopsis of a particular theory, or set of ideas, should be as neutral as possible. Here, "neutrality" refers to representing the position that is being summarized in an unbiased fashion and as if the writer accepted the theorists' arguments. In other words, what is required of a textbook is clear prose, simplicity of understanding, conveyance of each theory's perspective as though one were an ethnographer rather than a commentator, and a measure of objective assessment.

Only after having presented the core ideas of a theory is the textbook writer allowed the freedom of criticism; it is only then that he or she can represent the ideas of those critical of the position taken by the advocate of the theory. Ultimately, the role of the textbook writer is to light a passion for "the intrinsic joy derived from theoretical creation and disputation," which, as Wright acknowledges, is an immense challenge for criminological theory textbook writers (2000, 200).

Inevitably, textbooks have their limits. However comprehensive and complete a text, it is not going to represent every theorist's ideas accurately, not least because its author(s) may distort the content, if not by simple omission, then through personal bias. Another tendency is to minimize or exaggerate differences among theories or to allow biases to creep through in the selection and conveyance of key points.[1] How many texts end with an author's favorite theory? How many authors contrast each theory with their favorite?[2]

In the end, however, there is likely to be an inevitable difference between the role of the textbook writer(s) and some of the theorists whose work is under discussion. This is well captured by the opening paragraph of Hirschi and Gottfredson's contribution to this volume:

> Authors of theories about the causes of crime and delinquency are likely to be uneasy about textbook accounts of their work. Textbooks are designed to appear to provide even-handed descriptions of the virtues and limitations of theories. The more theories they consider, the broader their appeal, and they consequently tend to describe a variety of perspectives. The more criticisms they provide of individual theories, the greater their apparent scholarship or coverage of the literature, and they consequently tend to emphasize problems and limitations. Commonly now in criminology, textbooks also list the public policy implications of each theory, apparently because they hope to provide students with another basis for choosing among them. Most textbooks judge the validity of criticisms by the frequency with which they are encountered. They often advocate putting theories together in a reason-

> able way, suggesting that the whole of the criminological enterprise is greater than the sum of its parts. Along the same lines, textbooks have a decided tendency to minimize the differences among theories.
>
> Theorists, in contrast to all this, tend to advocate particular ideas and to stress the differences among them. If their logic and reading of the evidence led them to conclude that every idea enjoyed the same modest support in the data, and that all or most could be satisfactorily combined into one perspective about crime, there would be no point in going forward. If they believed that critiques of theories cannot be answered or taken into account, they would again abandon their efforts. (Hirschi and Gottfredson 2005, 111–112)

It is for these reasons that we believe students should not rely on textbook accounts alone. It is our view that, although they provide a functional introduction to basic ideas, textbooks must be complemented by original readings written by the theorists themselves. Herein lies a serious challenge. Most theorists are writing works for the professional criminologist, not for the inquisitive student. As a result, their work is a huge leap for students who have just grasped the key idea and have a developing sense about the place of the theory among the totality of ideas about crime. Then, to appreciate a theorist's work, the student would need to read more than one article or book for each theorist's position. With at least twelve distinguishable positions in the criminological literature—each with its own subtheorists, empirical studies, and critics—instructors teaching the average semester-long criminology course would find this demand on students impossible to achieve.

There are several ways to solve this problem. One extreme is to abandon textbooks completely and have students focus on the original works of a selected group of theorists. The opposite extreme is to abandon the attempt to have students read original works, leaving that for subsequent senior level or graduate-level classes. However, many criminology instructors seek a compromise. Their solution is to provide a comprehensive textbook together with an anthology of original articles written by criminological theorists. The predominant approach is to produce an anthology of previously published articles edited for student consumption (e.g., Francis Cullen and

Robert Agnew, *Criminological Theory: Past to Present-Essential Readings*, 1999; Joseph Jacoby, *Classics of Criminology*, 2004; Suzette Cote, *Criminological Theories: Bridging the Past to the Future*, 2002; Einstadter and Henry, *The Criminology Theory Reader*, 1998). Although this works to some extent in that it provides students with a taste of the real thing, it also suffers from several limitations. First, most of the selections are prepublished, so they indicate the author's *past* criminological thinking rather than his or her *current* thought. (Indeed, several of the papers presented in this volume provide insight into the theorists and how they have changed and evolved in their ideas about crime causation.) Second, the articles were originally written for professional criminologists, not students, and so lack readability and simple prose. Third, in trying to simplify these works through editing, the editors are often unable to do justice to the original ideas.

In *The Essential Criminology Reader* we attempt to address each of these concerns. The text contains thirty original articles on current developments in criminological theory written to complement one of the twelve or more theoretical perspectives that form chapters in most theory texts, including our own *Essential Criminology* (Lanier and Henry 2004). Each perspective has up to three contributors. The authors, who come from a variety of disciplines or fields, including biology, psychology, sociology, criminology, and interdisciplinarity, were selected from those prominent in the development of a particular theory. Contributors also range across institutional hierarchies: from graduate students to professors, and from department chairs to a vice chancellor. Together they provide a window on the latest developments in the range of criminological theories. (For similar approaches, see Cordella and Siegal 1996; and Paternoster and Backman 2001.)

Each chapter addresses aspects of the following issues: (a) a brief summary of the ways a theory has been misinterpreted/distorted, (b) criticisms by others of the theory and how the author has responded, (c) a summary of the balance of the empirical findings, (d) the latest developments in a given theoretical position, and (e) the policy implications/practice of the theory and addressing the questions "Where do we go from here?" "What would the world look like if we took these ideas seriously?" and "How might the author see further theoretical development?" Each of the thirty-nine contributing authors wrote or co-wrote their article as a stand-alone piece in the manner of an encyclopedia entry: clear, concise, and devoid of unnecessary jargon.

It is conventional in anthologies to provide an introductory statement summarizing the works included in the text. Given that this book is designed to go beyond the textbook to the words of the original authors, further summarizing or editorializing by us would be not only unessential but also contradictory to our goal for this volume. In other words, it would be redundant, even tautological, for us to summarize what we present when we allow the actual authors to do so here. Instead, we let the authors speak for themselves. We do, however, provide short chapter introductions summarizing, in general, each of the theoretical perspectives to which the authors in this volume have made major contributions.

We would like to thank the students who have challenged us over the years, primarily with criticism about how dull theory is! This text shows theory to be anything but dull. We also should like to acknowledge the contributors to this volume who took valuable time away from their numerous other important projects to write one more piece about their particular theoretical perspectives. We believe they have written valuable contributions that will enhance your appreciation of criminology and the study of crime. Finally, we thank the Westview editorial team, who have astounded us with their ability to bring a manuscript to a published book in less time than a journal typically takes to publish its quarterly volumes. For their contribution to this accomplishment, kudos go to our original acquisitions editor, Jill Rothenberg; our current editor, Steve Catalano; and to Jennifer Blakebrough-Raeburn, who is quite simply the best copy editor we have ever had.

Note

1. Indeed several contributors to this text show how we inadvertently did just that in *Essential Criminology*.

2. What modest success we have enjoyed with *Essential Criminology* (1998, 2004) has been attributed to our ability to partially overcome this tendency to advocate for our favorite theory. We each come from very different educational

and cultural backgrounds. We view "realities" such as science differently. It is rare for criminologists with so many differences to speak to one another, much less collaborate! Thus, we were able to write a somewhat balanced account, or so we have been told, and we try to continue that balanced approach in this book.

References

Cordella, Peter, and Larry Siegel. 1996. *Readings in Contemporary Criminological Theory*. Boston: Northeastern University Press.

Cote, Suzette. 2002. *Criminological Theories: Bridging the Past to the Future*. Thousand Oaks, Calif.: Sage.

Cullen, Francis, and Robert Agnew. 1999. *Criminological Theory: Past to Present—Essential Readings*. Los Angeles: Roxbury.

Einstadter, Werner, and Stuart Henry. 1995. *Criminological Theory: An Analysis of Its Underlying Assumptions*. Fort Worth, Tex.: Harcourt.

Henry, Stuart, and Werner Einstadter. 1998. *The Criminology Theory Reader*. New York: New York University Press.

Hirschi, Travis, and Michael Gottfredson. 2005. "Social Control and Self-Control Theory." In *The Essential Criminology Reader*, edited by Stuart Henry and Mark M. Lanier. Boulder: Westview Press.

Lanier, Mark M., and Stuart Henry. [1998] 2004. *Essential Criminology*. 2d ed., Boulder: Westview Press.

Paternoster, Raymond, and Ronet Backman. 2001. *Explaining Criminals and Crime: Essays in Contemporary Criminological Theory*. Los Angeles: Roxbury.

Pfhul, Erdwin, and Stuart Henry. 1993. *The Deviance Process*. 3d ed. Hawthorn, N.Y.: Aldine de Gruyter.

Wright, Richard A. 2000. "The Chronicles of the Renaissance: Recent Textbooks in Theoretical Criminology." *Journal of Criminal Justice Education* 11: 179–201.

1

Classical and Rational Choice Theories

So-called classical ideas about crime and justice, originating in the eighteenth-century writings of European philosophers, are important for several reasons. First, they laid the foundations for many justice systems around the world, including the most expensive and largest system in the United States. This set of ideas then indirectly led to the scientific study of crime when positivist theorists subsequently criticized classical scholars for "armchair theorizing" and for ignoring the facts of crime; the irony here is that the earlier versions were not theories at all but simply philosophies about how crime should be addressed by society. Finally, classical thought about crime and justice is still relevant today, not least because so many correctional and behavioral strategies employed by justice systems are based on the set of principles that these ideas embodied.

The basic idea underlying classical theory is that humans are economic actors and that crime is a rational choice that people make from a range of behavioral options; in this way, people choose what they perceive to be in their best interests. Consequently, the underlying assumption is that humans, as rational goal-directed beings, conduct a cost/benefit analysis before engaging in behavior. Whether the key early thinkers of the classical period, such as the Italian marquis Cesare Beccaria and the British philosopher Jeremy Bentham, actually made such simplistic assumptions about human behavior is debated by contemporary criminologists. Indeed, when these ideas were implemented during the French Code of 1791, it was recognized that not everyone had the same ability to reason, and this modification to "pure" classicism was labeled "neoclassicism."

From the classical perspective, the general role of law (as well as specific laws) is assumed to be based on a consensus among the population. The social contract—that we all give up some liberties in exchange for an ordered and secure society—is another integral component. Those who break the law do so for hedonistic, selfish reasons and thereby violate the interest of the wider society.

Most of the criminal justice policies modeled on the classical perspective revolve around the idea of due process and include what are now considered basic individual "rights." These rights include the sovereignty of the individual, the presumption of innocence, efficiency of crime detection and law enforcement, restraint on the power of government, and fairness in the administration of justice. These rights became crucial because the ideas were developed in response to brutal, unfair, and cruel systems of justice found in the preclassical period in Europe. Following the early impact of classical ideas, scientific discoveries concerning the origins of crime led to several criticisms. For example, clearly we are not all created equal; this acknowledgement led to concepts such as limited rationality, imperfect rationality, and reduced capacity.

Contemporary classical theories, called neoclassical or, more recently, rational or situational choice theories, recognize that there are limits to the freedom of individuals to behave fully or perfectly rationally. They have gone beyond the framework of general laws and penalties to provide a disincentive to crime and have provided concrete policy and practice initiatives designed to reduce crime; these initiatives are based on analyzing and manipulating the costs, risks, opportunities, incentives, and provocations to crime, known generally as "target hardening." Rational choice and routine activities theorists focus on design, security, and surveillance measures that reduce the rewards of crime. This approach transcends the early focus of classical theorists on the law, legal systems, rights, and government. The new focus also places some responsibility on the potential victim as well for creating and maintaining crime-free environments.

1.1

Free Will *and* Determinism?

Reading Beccaria's Of Crimes and Punishments *(1764) as a Text of Enlightenment*

PIERS BEIRNE
University of Southern Maine

Written by the Italian lawyer and Enlightenment philosopher Cesare Beccaria (1738–1794) and published anonymously in 1764, the short treatise *Of Crimes and Punishments* is traditionally heralded as the first text in the history of premodern criminology. Incontestably, it was a groundbreaking humanist tract that opposed capital punishment, judicial arbitrariness, and judicial interrogation by torture, and that championed the rule of law, deterrence, and incarceration. The proposals for the reform of criminal law made by *Of Crimes and Punishments* were an instant and dazzling success, appealing to a large cross-section of intellectuals, politicians, and lawyers throughout Western Europe and colonial America.

Today, nearly every criminology textbook contains a stock of complacent assumptions about Beccaria's intentions, chief among them that *Of Crimes and Punishments* transformed the practice of eighteenth-century criminal law and justice. Since then, many commentators have inferred that the work (1) was primarily a humanist project, inspired by French philosophy and motivated by the author's humanitarian opposition to judicial barbarism; and (2) had as its chief objects (a) the reform of judicial irrationality and (b) the institution of a utilitarian approach to punishment based on a calculus of pleasure and pain.

In concert, these assumptions have led to the view that Beccaria was the founder of classical criminology; his thinking is characterized by a rational calculus based on the doctrine of the social contract and the belief that human action results from the exercise of free will by reasoning individuals.

Various authors have chipped away at this comfortable consensus on *Of Crimes and Punishments*. In particular, Foucault (1979, 73–103) has argued that neither Beccaria's classical criminology nor its effects were the projects of genuinely enlightened or humanitarian reform but were two among many artifacts peculiar to a new disciplinary power. Others have contradicted the view that Beccaria was a radical pioneer. He has been described as far more conservative, pro-aristocratic, and pro-capitalist than other Enlightenment theorists because he deliberately equivocated on dangerous issues such as materialism and spiritualism. Beccaria's intervention in criminal jurisprudence, for example, continues to be regarded as "humanist" because it opposed the barbaric practices of the ancien regime, or "revolutionary" because it was in the vanguard of the Italian Enlightenment in exposing religious intolerance, or "conservative" because it did not embrace materialism as did others. Even Beccaria's intervention in judicial history has been dismissed as a fairy tale, his humanism ridiculed because he did not know that the process of abolishing judicial torture had already been initiated through a decisive transformation of the medieval law of proof (Langbein 1976; Hirst 1986).

Of Crimes and Punishments shares with many Enlightenment treatises a certain lack of clarity. The vivid humanism in its forty-seven rambling chapters is a mask behind which some of Beccaria's other arguments lie hidden; these can be discerned only with some difficulty and not a little speculation. Accordingly, neither the structure nor the content of Beccaria's discourse should be taken at face value. To understand how and why this is so, some indication must be given of the conditions of the work's production as an Enlightenment text.

The Influence of the "Science of Man"

First, reflecting contemporary eighteenth-century thought, some of the arguments in *Of Crimes and Punishments* employed a deterministic discourse that is diametrically opposed to the classical notion of free will commonly attributed to it. Among Enlightenment thinkers, this scientific discourse was variously referred to as "geometry," "moral geography," "political arithmetic," "number," and the "science of man"—terms and principles that Beccaria also used. Several key features of this new science are plainly recognizable in *Of Crimes and Punishments*, including the doctrines of utilitarianism, probabilism, associationism, and sensationalism.

Utilitarianism is the idea that punishment is justified by the end result, which must benefit the wider society. The doctrine of utilitarianism operated for Beccaria as a core justificatory argument for the state's right to punish, and it is positioned prominently at the beginning of his text. With it, Beccaria attempted to forge linkages—as had the Scottish philosopher Francis Hutcheson before him—among the rule of law, justice, and the economic marketplace. In doing this, Beccaria employed probabilism, associationism, and sensationalism throughout the book, and he wielded these three doctrines in concert as mechanisms with which to advance his chosen strategies for punishment. To understand Beccaria's thinking, one must explore each of these concepts in some depth.

Probabilism: Rationalizing and Clarifying Law and the Administration of Justice

Beccaria's attempt to apply "probability" and "number" to matters of punishment reflects his dependence on the ideas of wise governance by contemporary authors of the period, such as the British philosopher John Locke. Beccaria also drew inspiration from the English statistician and physician Sir William Petty (1623–1687). Petty's staunch criticism of physical punishments was one of his many contributions to science. In his *Treatise of Taxes & Contributions*, Petty urged that pecuniary fines, made over to the Commonwealth as "reparations," were far better than physical punishments, which not only deprive the state of useful labor but benefit no one. Beccaria also drew on Hutcheson's utilitarianism, which was explicitly formulated in mathematical and economic terms: "Action is best, which procures the greatest happiness for the greatest numbers." Hutcheson meant this literally and mathematically; the original title of Hutcheson's *Inquiry* contained the words "with an attempt to introduce a mathematical calculation in subjects of morality," and when he attempted to calculate the precise incidence of "perfect virtue" and "moral evil," he did so strictly by way of algebraic equations (1725, 187–193).

Near the beginning of *Of Crimes and Punishments*, Beccaria asserted his intention of "going back to general principles" to uncover the rampant political and judicial errors "accumulated" over several centuries. He abhorred uncertainty, objected to "arbitrary notions of vice and virtue" (Beccaria 1764, 4), and sometimes complained that "despotic impatience" and "effeminate timidity" transform "serious trials into a kind of game in which chance and subterfuge are the main elements" (1764, 24). He also derided "the errors and passions that have successively dominated various legislators" (1764, 15), including the useless tortures "multiplied" with prodigious and useless severity; the punishment of crimes that are "unproven"; and the horrors of a prison, "augmented" by "uncertainty"—"that most cruel tormentor of the wretched" (1764, 4). At the same time, Beccaria bemoaned the unhappy fact that it is impossible to prevent all disorders in the universal strife of human passions because they increase at the compound rate of population growth and the intertwining of public interests; these, in turn, cannot be directed toward the public welfare with geometric precision. In political arithmetic, one must substitute the calculation of probability for mathematical exactitude (1764, 14).

Beccaria's advocacy of probability extended to each stage of the criminal justice system, including the clarity of the law itself; judicial torture; witnesses and evidence; jurors; and sentencing practices. Here, his remarks were partly addressed to enlightened lawmakers, "the legislator who acts like the good architect, whose role is to oppose the ruinous course of gravity and to bring to bear everything that contributes to the strength of his building" (1764, 15).

On the Clarity and Certainty of Law

Beccaria urged that only a fixed, understandable, and predictable law could provide citizens with personal security, reduce the number of crimes based on ignorance and uncertainty, and liberate them from judicial arbitrariness. The law itself must be unambiguous because only with "fixed" and "immutable" laws can citizens "calculate precisely the ill consequences of a misdeed" (1764, 12). Moreover, he stated that fixed law that is enforced, strictly interpreted, and universally applied removes many from the petty tyrannies of judges and lawyers.

In addition, for minor and less heinous crimes, there should be a statute of limitations that relieves citizens of "uncertainty" regarding their fate; but such time limits "ought not to increase in exact proportion to the atrocity of the crime, for the likelihood of crimes is inversely proportional to their barbarity" (1764, 56).

On Judicial Torture

Beccaria's support of probabilism also explains how *Of Crimes and Punishments* viewed judicial torture. On humanist grounds, Beccaria opposed the practice of interrogating an accused with methods of torture. However, he was not opposed to the infliction of physical pain on others because he vigorously supported noncapital corporal punishment "without exception" for crimes against persons and for crimes of theft accompanied by violence (Beccaria 1764, 37, 40). Yet he insistently opposed judicial torture because of its inefficiency as a method of establishing the "probability" or the "certainty" of the guilt or innocence of the accused. Accordingly, "the problems of whether torture and death are either just or useful deserve a mathematically precise solution" (1764, 23). The outcome of torture, then, is a matter of temperament and calculation that varies with each in proportion to hardiness and sensitivity: The robust criminal might resist, yet the feeble innocent might confess (1764, 31). Instead of judicial torture, Beccaria recommended the "real trial, the 'informative' one, that is, the impartial investigation of facts which reason demands" (1764, 34).

On Witnesses

In respect of witnesses and evidence, Beccaria argued that more than one witness is necessary in determining the guilt or innocence of a defendant; this is because if one witness affirms the guilt and another denies it, "there is no certainty" and the presumption of innocence prevails (1764, 24). Elsewhere in *Of Crimes and Punishments*, Beccaria extended to magistrates his idea of the relation between the number of concurring witnesses and the certainty of a verdict. Thus, he wrote about the body administering law that the "greater the number of men who constitute such a body, the less the danger of encroachments on the law will be" (Beccaria 1764, 78). A witness is credible if he is "a rational man" and his credibility increases if his reason is undisturbed by a prior relationship with either the defendant or the victim; "the credibility of a witness, therefore, must diminish in proportion to the hatred or friendship or close relationship between himself and the accused" (1764, 24). The credibility of a witness also diminishes significantly as the gravity of the alleged crime increases or as the circumstances of the crime become more "improbable" (1764, 24–25). However, and somewhat inconsistently, Beccaria also held that to the degree that "punishments become moderate, that squalor and hunger are banished from prisons, and that compassion and humanity pass through the iron gates . . . the law may be content with weaker and weaker evidence to imprison someone" (1764, 54).

On Evidence

For Beccaria there exists a "general theorem" that is most useful in calculating with certainty the facts of a crime, namely, the "weight of evidence." He argued that (1) when different pieces of factual evidence are substantiated only by each other, the less certain is any one fact; (2) when all the proofs of a fact depend upon one piece of evidence, the number of proofs neither augments nor diminishes the probability of the fact; and (3) when proofs are independent of each other, then the probability of the fact increases with each new witness (1764, 25). Moreover, Beccaria considered it ironic that the most atrocious and the most obscure crimes, "those that are most unlikely," are the most difficult to prove. These crimes are typically proved by conjecture and by the weakest and most equivocal evidence; it is as though "the danger of condemning an innocent man were not all the greater as the probability of his innocence surpasses the likelihood of his guilt" (1764, 58). That is not to say that certain crimes, also difficult to prove, are not frequently committed in society—such as "adultery" and "pederasty"—and, in these cases, "the difficulty of establishing guilt takes the place of the probability of innocence" (1764, 58). Finally, because the respective probabilities of "atrocious" crimes and of lesser offenses differ greatly, they must be adjudicated differently. For atrocious crimes, the period of judicial examination "should decrease in view of the greater likelihood of the innocence of the accused . . . [b]ut with minor crimes, given the lesser likelihood of the innocence of the accused, the period of judicial investigation should be extended, and, as the pernicious consequences of impunity decline, the delay in granting immunity from further prosecution should be shortened" (1764, 57).

On Juries and Sentencing

Finally, Beccaria offered some brief comments on jurors and sentencing practices from the perspective of probabilism. About jurors he wrote that when a crime has been committed against a third party, "half the jurors should be the equals of the accused and half the peers of the victim" (1764, 27). About sentencing practices, he warned that "certainty" ought to be required for convictions in criminal cases, and that if geometry "were adaptable to the infinite and obscure arrangements of human activity, there ought to be a corresponding scale of punishments, descending from the most rigorous to the slightest" (1764, 15).

Many of the strategies in Beccaria's penal calculus, including his key concept of deterrence, are derived not from geometry or probabilism as such but from the doctrines of associationism and sensationalism. To these related doctrines in the "science of man" we now turn.

Associationism: On the Connection Between Crime and Punishment

Beccaria's penal calculus rested on the view that it is better to prevent crimes than to punish them. This can only occur if the law forces potential criminals to make an accurate "association" of ideas between crime and punishment. "It is well established," Beccaria claimed, "that the association of ideas is the cement that shapes the whole structure of the human intellect; without it, pleasure and pain would be isolated feelings with no consequences." Following David Hume, Beccaria urged that associated ideas must be in a position of constant conjunction and that they must comprise a relation of cause and effect. Beccaria characterized the nexus of the desired association between crime and punishment in many ways, such as "deterrence," "intimidation," and "dissuasion" (1764, 33, 23, 29). The key properties of the association between crime and punishment are condensed in the following formula, which is the concluding sentence in *Of Crimes and Punishments*, now appropriately enshrined as the original statement of the principle of deterrence: "In order that any punishment should not be an act of violence committed by one person or many against a private citizen, it is essential that it should be public, prompt, necessary, the minimum possible under the given circumstances, [and] proportionate to the crimes" (1764, 81).

Elsewhere in his text, yet still within the context of an associationist framework, Beccaria expanded on several items in this formula, most notably on the need for prompt, mild, and proportionate punishment.

On Promptness of Punishment

Beccaria believed that the shorter the time between a crime and chastisement for the crime "the stronger and more permanent is the human mind's association of the two ideas of crime and punishment, so that imperceptibly the one will come to be considered as the cause and the other as the necessary and inevitable result" (1764, 36). Delay severs the association between these two ideas. Moreover, the temporal proximity of crime and punishment is of paramount importance if one desires to arouse in "crude and uneducated minds the idea of punishment in association with the seductive image of a certain advantageous crime" (1764, 37).

On Mildness of Punishment

Beccaria argued that to achieve its intended effect, the intensity of a punishment should exceed the benefit resulting from the crime, and that in its application punishment should be "inexorable," "inevitable," and "certain" (1764, 46–47). Cruel punishments, insofar as they destroy the association between law and justice, undermine the aim of deterrence.

On Proportionality of Punishment

Beccaria warned that "the obstacles that restrain men from committing crimes should be stronger according to the degree that such misdeeds are contrary to the public good and according to the motives that lead people to crimes" (1764, 14–15). This is so because when two unequally harmful crimes are each awarded the same punishment, would-be miscreants will tend to commit the more serious crime if it presents the greater advantage for them. If punishments are disproportionate to crime by being tyrannical (i.e., excessive), then popular dissatisfaction will be directed at the law itself—"punishments will punish the crimes that they themselves have caused" (1764, 16). For this reason, Beccaria suggested that some punishments might even be considered as crimes (1764, 17); for example, "It appears absurd to me that the laws . . . commit murder themselves . . . [and] command public assassination" (1764, 51). Further, in arguing that "punishment . . . should conform as closely as possible to the nature of the crime" (1764, 37), Beccaria implicitly attempted to link the argument about the proportionality of crime and punishment with the desired association among the ideas about the type of crime (e.g., theft), the form of punishment (penal servitude with forced labor), and the virtue of industriousness.

On Capital Punishment

Beccaria opposed capital punishment as a penal strategy not because he thought it cruel, which he did, but because it did not serve the new penal objective of deterrence. Beccaria argued, instead, that a life sentence is a sufficiently intense substitute for the death penalty and includes all the necessary ingredients needed to deter the most hardened criminal: "Neither fanaticism nor vanity survives among fetters and chains, under the prod or the yoke, or in an iron cage . . . a lifetime at hard labor" (1764, 50). For Beccaria, it is thus not the severity of punishment that has the greatest impact on a would-be criminal, but its duration.

> If someone were to say that life at hard labor is as painful as death and therefore equally cruel, I should reply that, taking all the unhappy moments of perpetual slavery together, it is perhaps even more painful, but these moments are spread out over a lifetime, and capital punishment exercises all its power in an instant. And this is the advantage of life at hard labor: It frightens the spectator more than the victim. (1764, 50)

Sensationalism

A third hallmark of the "science of man" engraved in *Of Crimes and Punishments* is the doctrine of sensationalism. In his discussion of the nature of honor and on the fluctuating and confused concepts of morality, for example, Beccaria refers to the human mind as "driven by the winds of passion" (1764, 19), which is why morality needs simple, abstract, and clear guidelines.

This reflects the doctrine of sensationalism, which, in the course of his book on aesthetics, Beccaria explicitly acknowledged having taken from works by Locke and Etienne Bonnot de Mably de Condillac (Beccaria 1770, 81–93). Locke's sensationalism tended to suggest that all things painful are by definition bad and all things pleasurable good. Condillac (1715–1780) developed Locke's doctrine of sensationalism, positing that, at birth, the human mind is a tabula rasa that operates through sensations. Like Locke, Condillac championed the rigidly materialist conclusion that "man" is simply what he has acquired through his sensations.

It is hard to imagine a doctrine more seemingly hostile to the doctrine of free will than sensationalism. When Beccaria applied it to criminal justice, sensationalism effectively displaced the free-will subject of Catholic theology and, thereby, denied an active role in human society for the Supreme Being. Beccaria was so fearful of the censor precisely because his text implicitly suggested that human agents are no more than the products of their sensory reactions to external stimuli. His text, replete as it is with probabilism, associationism, and sensationalism—all directed to the new objective of deterrence—is resolutely opposed to the notion of free will. *Of Crimes and Punishments* contains a concept of volition, it is true, but it is a determined will rather than a free will. Thus, "sentiment is always proportional to the result of the impressions made on the senses" (Beccaria 1764, 25). As a result of this, the penal recommendations in *Of Crimes and Punishments* are not at all predicated on the notion of a rational calculating subject who, when faced with inexorable punishment, will weigh the costs and benefits and choose to desist from crime. In this discourse, punishments ("tangible motives") have "a direct impact on the senses and appear continually to the mind to counterbalance the strong impressions of individual passions opposed to the general good" (Beccaria 1764, 7).

Sensationalism intersects concretely with Beccaria's chosen penal strategies in three ways. It appears, first, as an additional ground on which judicial torture must be rejected.

On Sensationalism and Torture

Beccaria insisted that, in their respective results, the only difference between judicial torture and other ordeals, such as fire and boiling water, is that the former appears to depend on the will of the accused, but the latter depends on a purely physical act. To this he responded that "[s]peaking the truth amid convulsions and torments is no more a free act than staving off the effects of fire and boiling water except by fraud. Every act of our will is always proportional to the strength of the sense impressions from which it springs . . . " (Beccaria 1764, 31).

On Sensationalism and Deterrence

In discussing the appropriateness of prompt punishment, Beccaria argued that "[t]hat gravity-like force that impells us to seek our own well-being can be restrained only to the degree that obstacles are established in opposition to it" (1764, 14), and that "remote consequences make a very weak impression" (1764, 64). Effecting a link with probabilism, he argued that "[e]xperience and reason have shown us that the probability and certainty of human traditions decline the farther removed they are from their source" (1764, 13); effecting yet another link, this time with associationist claims, he stated that "[s]tronger and more obvious impressions are required for the hardened spirits of a people who have scarcely emerged from a savage state. . . . But to the extent that human spirits are made gentle by the social state, sensibility increases; as it increases, the severity of punishment must diminish if one wishes to maintain a constant relation between object and feeling" (1764, 81).

On Sensationalism and Penal Strategies

Finally, Beccaria attached his belief in sensationalism to a variety of nonpenal strategies designed to manipulate and channel sense impressions into law-abiding actions. Penal strategies tend to operate swiftly and dramatically on their subjects, but these other strategies are designed as positive mental inducements that operate slowly and calmly at the level of custom and habit (i.e., socialization). Thus, Beccaria suggested that if crimes are to be prevented, "enlightenment should accompany liberty" (1764, 76–79), by which he possibly had in mind the importance of education, also emphasized by the French political theorists Montesquieu and Rousseau. Education, as opposed to mere instruction, would produce moral individuals who, as in the former Greek polis, understood the proper relationship between individual advantage and the general good and who, as citizens in a future enlightened republic, would feel a patriotic duty to obey the particular state that would defend the enjoyment of their natural rights. He warned that "the most certain but most difficult way to prevent crimes is to perfect education" (1764, 79). By "education," Beccaria likely intended a process the outcome of which, at least, was the gradual inculcation in the citizenry of such attributes as virtue, courage, and liberty—for the encouragement of which he recommended the distribution of prizes.

From the "Science of Man" to "Homo Criminalis"

It is fair to say, then, that in *Of Crimes and Punishments* Beccaria was throughout guided by the several new doctrines that lay at the heart of a wished-for "Science of Man" (Beccaria 1770, 71). To the mathematician Condorcet, Beccaria was one of a select group of scholars whose works, since the time of Locke, had advanced the moral (social) sciences through the application of the calculus of probabilities to the understanding of human societies. In 1771, Condorcet wrote letters to Beccaria in which he condemned the injustices of existing criminal jurisprudence, and he began to apply mathematics in the search for rationality in judicial decision-making. Later, he recommended to Frederick II of Prussia the application of the "calculus of probabilities" to Beccaria's ideas on capital punishment and on wise legislation. The influential English legal scholar Sir William Blackstone observed that Beccaria "seems to have well studied the source of human action." Blackstone emphatically placed Beccaria's "humane" reform proposals within the rubric of a new discourse of crime and penalty that emerged in Britain in the 1760s and that stressed the investigation of the "causes of crime," deterrence, and the correction of offenders (Blackstone 1769, iv, 17).

Attached to Beccaria's discourse on penal strategies, there is indeed present in *Of Crimes and Punishments* a rudimentary attempt to forge some key concepts, including "crime," "criminal," and "causes of crime," into an embryonic criminology. Beccaria understood "crime" as the harm done to society, and he attempted to identify "the criminal" as something other than a mere bundle of illegalities. This concept of "criminal" operates in concert with and is burdened by Beccaria's humanism and his advocacy of legal rationality, yet it marks a movement away from a single-minded focus on how to punish and towards a wider "criminological" concern with understanding the situation of "homo criminalis." An example of this movement occurs when Beccaria inserted the following words into the mouth of "a scoundrel":

> What are these laws that I must respect and that leave such a great distance between me and the rich man? . . . Who made these laws? Rich and powerful men who have never deigned to visit the squalid hovels of the poor, who have never broken a moldy crust of bread among the innocent cries of their famished children and the tears of their wives. Let us break these bonds that are so ruinous for the majority and useful to a handful of indolent tyrants; let us attack injustice at its source. (Beccaria 1764, 51)

Beccaria indicated several times that criminals and criminal behavior should be understood causally, in material and social terms rather than purely individualistic ones. He suggested, for example, that "[t]heft is only the crime of misery and desperation; it is the crime of that unhappy portion of humanity to whom the right of property . . . has left only a bare existence" (1764, 39). It is difficult to know precisely how much to invest in Beccaria's reasoning in passages such as these, other than to say that he seems keen to position illegalities in a quasi-social context.

Thus, he describes adultery as not only the problem of variable human laws but also "that very strong attraction which impels one sex toward the other" (1764, 58–59). He connects pederasty (sodomy, usually between a man and a boy) to "the sort of education that begins by making men useless to themselves in order to make them useful to others. It is the result of those institutions where hot-blooded youth is confined" (1764, 60). As another example of this protocriminological thinking, he describes infanticide with reference to limited choices that are shaped by context; that is, "one in which a woman is placed when she has either submitted out of weakness or been overpowered by violence. Faced with a choice between disgrace and the death of a creature incapable of feeling pain, who would not prefer the latter to the unavoidable misery to which the woman and her unfortunate offspring would be exposed?" (1764, 60).

Finally, *Of Crimes and Punishments* even contains allusions to a "dangerous class." Thus, Beccaria saw those who desire to overthrow government for anarchy as "the credulous and admiring crowd" (1764, 39), "a fanatical crowd" (1764, 47), "a blind and fanatical crowd, pushing and jostling one another in a closed labyrinth" (1764, 77) that "does not adopt stable principles of conduct" (1764, 7). In crowds there resides, for Beccaria, a "dangerous concentration of popular passions" (1764, 22) that is akin to the sentiments in "the state of nature . . . the savage" (1764, 74). In the following passage, Beccaria even indicated a stark contrast between an embryonic dangerous class, which looks for instant gratification, and the law-abiding citizenry, which prefers more long-term goals:

> Enslaved men are more sensual, more debauched, and more cruel than free men. The latter think about the sciences; they think about the interests of the nation; they see great examples, and they imitate them. The former, on the other hand, content with the present moment, seek a distraction for the emptiness of their lives in the tumult of debauchery. Accustomed to uncertain results in everything, the doubts they have about the outcome of their crimes strengthen the passions by which crimes are determined. (1764, 75)

Conclusion

It is clear from the analysis in this essay that the conventional textbook discussion of Beccaria's contribution as the introduction of rational cost/benefit calculus, crime as a free choice, and punishment as a deterrent is a gross oversimplification, and one that leaves out, not only contemporaneous ideas of science and sensation that influenced his writing and thinking, but also the ideas that shaped his protocriminology. Ultimately, *Of Crimes and Punishments* teases its audience with a presociological view of the relation between crime and social organization:

> Most men lack that vigor which is equally necessary for great crimes and great virtues; thus, it seems that the former always coexist with the latter in those nations that sustain themselves by the activity of their governments and by passions working together for the public good, rather than in countries that depend on their size or the invariable excellence of their laws. In the latter sort of nation, weakened passions seem better suited to the maintenance rather than to the improvement of the form of government. From this, one can draw an important conclusion: that great crimes in a nation are not always proof of its decline. (1764, 58)

Indeed, for all its contributions, Beccaria's *Of Crimes and Punishments* is ultimately a text of smoke and mirrors.

References

Beccaria, Cesare. [1770] 1984. "Ricerche intorno alla natura cello stile." In *Cesare Beccaria: Opere*, edited by Luigi Firpo. Reprint, Milan: Mediobanca.

______. [1764] 1986. *Of Crimes and Punishments*. Translated by David Young. Reprint, Indianapolis, Ind.: Hackett.

Blackstone, Sir William. [1769] 1978. *Commentaries on the Laws of England*. 4 vols. Reprint, London: Garland.

Foucault, Michel. 1979. *Discipline & Punish: The Birth of the Prison*. Translated by Alan Sheridan. New York: Vintage.

Hirst, Paul Q. 1986. *Law, Socialism and Democracy*. London: Allen and Unwin.

Hutcheson, Francis. [1725] 1973. *Inquiry Concerning Beauty, Order, Harmony, Design*. Reprint, The Hague: Martinus Nijhoff.

Langbein, John H. 1976. *Torture and the Law of Proof: Europe and England in the Ancien Regime*. Chicago: Chicago University Press.

1.2

The Rational Choice Perspective[1]

Derek B. Cornish
Wichita State University

and

Ronald V. Clarke
Rutgers University

Introduction

A pressing need for cash, and a lack of other practical alternatives, criminal or noncriminal, can make armed robbery an attractive option for some individuals. And knowing where to find cash-rich victims and how to overcome opposition can make the rewards well worth the risk and effort. For criminals doing their best to "get by" in their everyday lives, choices and decisions such as these play a significant role in determining the crimes they commit. The theoretical importance and practical benefits of investigating such decisionmaking are two of the main contributions of the rational choice perspective (Clarke and Cornish 1985; Cornish and Clarke 1986; Clarke and Cornish 2001) summarized in this essay. The rational choice perspective begins with the assumption that offenders choose crime because of the benefits it brings them; it treats offenders as decisionmakers who calculate where their self-interest lies and then pursue that self-interest. It also explains the conditions needed for specific crimes to occur, not just the reasons people become involved in crime. It draws few distinctions between offenders and non-offenders, and it emphasizes the role of crime opportunities in causation. Finally, it is as much designed to serve policymaking as criminological understanding.

First, we will describe the six basic propositions of the rational choice perspective. We will then outline the main points of difference between the rational choice perspective and other criminological theories. Last, we will discuss its policy relevance and give brief examples of its value in guiding situational crime prevention efforts.

Fundamentals of the Perspective

The six basic propositions of the rational choice perspective are summarized in Table 1.2.1 and explained in greater detail below.

TABLE 1.2.1 Six Basic Propositions of the Rational Choice Perspective

1. Crimes are purposive acts, committed with the intention of benefiting the offender.
2. Offenders try to make the best decisions they can, given the risks and uncertainty involved.
3. Offender decision-making varies considerably with the nature of the crime.
4. Decisions about becoming involved in particular kinds of crime ("involvement" decisions) are quite different from those relating to the commission of a specific criminal act ("event" decisions).
5. Involvement decisions comprise three stages—initiation, habituation, and desistance. These must be separately studied because they are influenced by quite different sets of variables.
6. Event decisions involve a sequence of choices made at each stage of the criminal act—for example: preparation, target selection, commission of the act, escape, and aftermath.

SOURCE: Adapted from Ronald V. Clarke and Derek. B. Cornish. (2001). "Rational choice." In Raymond Paternoster and R. Bachman eds., *Crime Theories*. CA: Roxbury, p. 24.

The Purposive Nature of Crime

In the rational choice perspective, criminal acts are never "senseless," but are viewed as purposive acts intended to bring some benefit to the offender. The benefits of theft are obvious, but the rewards of crime can also include excitement, fun, prestige, sexual gratification, and the defiance or domination of others. A man might "brutally" beat his wife, not just because he is a violent "thug" but also because this is the easiest way of making her do what he wants. "Senseless" acts of vandalism or gang violence might confer considerable prestige on the perpetrators among their peers. The term "joyriding" accurately conveys the main reason why cars are stolen—juveniles enjoy driving around in powerful machines.

It is tempting to exclude from rational choice analysis crimes that are driven by clinical delusions or pathological compulsions. But even here, rationality is not completely absent. For instance, serial killers who hear voices telling them to kill prostitutes might still take pains to avoid arrest—and might succeed in doing so for a long time. In any case, pathological crimes constitute a tiny proportion of all criminal acts and their exclusion from rational choice theory hardly weakens its claims to generality.

Limited or Bounded Rationality

The rational choice perspective takes the view of Simon (1990) that an individual's decisionmaking behavior is characterized by "limited" or "bounded" rationality. To use the technical term, their decisionmaking is "satisficing" rather than "optimizing"—it gives acceptable outcomes rather than the best that could be achieved. Criminal decisionmaking is always less than perfect because it reflects the imperfect conditions under which it naturally occurs. These conditions can be summarized as follows:

- Offenders are rarely in possession of all the necessary facts about the risks, efforts, and rewards of crime.
- Criminal choices usually have to be made quickly—and revised hastily.
- Instead of planning their crimes down to the last detail, criminals might rely on a general approach that has worked before, improvising when they meet with unforeseen circumstances.
- Once embarked on a crime, criminals tend to focus on the rewards of the crime rather than its risks; and, when considering

risks, they focus on the immediate possibilities of being caught, rather than on the punishments they might receive.

Much support for the rational choice perspective is found in ethnographic research in which offenders have been interviewed about their lifestyles, their criminal choices, and their motives and methods. Even Don Gibbons, a frequent critic of the perspective, has stated that studies of predatory offenders "provide considerable support for a 'limited rationality' view of offender decision making by lawbreakers" (Gibbons 1994, 124).

Like the rest of us, offenders often act rashly and fail to consider the long-term consequences of their actions. They may be encouraged to take risks by their peers, and their decisions may sometimes be made in a fog of alcohol and drugs. As a result, offenders can make foolish choices that result in capture and severe punishment. Mistakes and failures made by offenders contribute to the view that such behavior is irrational. To offenders, however, and to those taking a rational choice perspective on their crimes, they are generally doing the best they can within the limits of time, resources, and information available to them. This is why we characterize their decisionmaking as rational, albeit imperfect.

The Importance of Crime Specificity

Specific offenses bring particular benefits to offenders and are committed with specific motives in mind. Cash is the motive for bank robbery; whereas for rape it is usually sexual gratification or the desire to dominate women. Similarly, the factors weighed by offenders, and the variables influencing their decisionmaking, will differ greatly with the nature of the offense. This is especially true of event decisions because these are more heavily influenced by immediate situational factors. For example, the circumstances surrounding the commission of a mugging, and the setting in which it occurs, differ considerably from those of a computer fraud.

For these reasons, criminal choice cannot properly be studied in the abstract. Instead, descriptions of criminal choice in the form of simplified models, such as flowcharts depicting decision processes, must be developed for specific categories of crime. Broad legal categories such as auto theft or burglary are far too general to model because they include so many differently motivated offenses, a wide range of offenders, and a variety of methods and skills. For example, the theft of a car for joyriding is an offense very different from theft for temporary transport. And both are different from the theft of cars for selling to local customers or to overseas customers.

The Distinction Between Involvement and Events

Criminal choices can be divided into two broad groups: "involvement" and "event" decisions. Event decisions relate to the commission of a particular offense. They concern such matters as the choice of a particular target and ways to reduce the risks of apprehension. Involvement decisions are more complex and are made at three separate stages in a delinquent or criminal "career." Offenders must decide (1) whether they are ready to begin committing crime to obtain what they want; (2) whether, having started, they should continue offending; and (3) whether, at some point, they ought to stop. The technical terms used by criminologists for these three stages of involvement are initiation, habituation, and desistance.

It is easy to see why event decisions need to be understood and modeled separately for different kinds of crime. For example, the task of escaping apprehension is very different for a bank robber than for someone vandalizing a parked car. But crime specificity is just as important at the various stages of involvement. Thus, the issues faced by people deciding whether to become involved in particular crimes, and the background of relevant experience brought to bear, can vary greatly. The factors relevant to the decisions being made by juveniles from the ghetto when thinking about joining the neighborhood drug dealers, and those relevant to the decisions of bank employees when planning to defraud customers, are likely to be so different that they must be separately studied.

The Separate Stages of Involvement

Not only must involvement decisions be separately modeled for specific kinds of crime, so must each stage of criminal involvement—initiation, habituation, and desistance—because decisions at each stage are influenced by different sets of variables. These variables fall into three groups:

1. Background factors, including personality and upbringing
2. Current life circumstances, routines, and lifestyles

3. Situational variables that include current needs and motives, together with immediate opportunities and inducements

These are of differing importance at the various stages of involvement, as follows:

- At *initiation*, background factors have their greatest influence because they shape the nature of the individual's accumulated learning and experience as well as his or her current life circumstances.
- At *habituation*, current life circumstances, which now increasingly reflect the ongoing rewards of crime, may be of principal importance.
- At *desistance*, current life circumstances, together with the accumulating costs of crime, weigh heavily in decisions.
- During all stages, however, it is the immediate influence of situational variables, such as needs, motives, opportunities, and inducements, that trigger the actual decision about whether or not to commit a particular crime.

The Sequence of Event Decisions

"Crime scripts," which are step-by-step accounts of the procedures used by offenders to commit crime, can assist the analysis of event decisions (Cornish 1994). The scripts build on offenders' accounts of their criminal activities and treat crimes as stories involving a cast of characters, props, and locations that unfold in a purposeful sequence of stages, scenes, and actions. Table 1.2.2 provides one such script for residential burglary in the suburbs. Accounts like these help to identify the decisions that the offender must make at each step and the situational variables that must be taken into account if the rewards of crime are to compensate for the risks and effort involved. The stages also suggest intervention points for preventive efforts.

What Makes Rational Choice Theory Different?

A Theory of Both Crime and Criminality

Most criminological theories are geared to answering just one question: What makes certain people or groups of people more likely to become

TABLE 1.2.2 A Simple Crime Script: Residential Burglary in the Suburbs

STAGES	*ACTIONS*
1. Preparation	Get van, tools, co-offender (if needed)
	Take drugs/alcohol
	Select general area for crime
	Assume appropriate role for setting
2. Enter setting	Drive into development
3. Precondition	Drive around and loiter in development
4. Target selection	Scan for cues relating to rewards, risks and effort (e.g., potential "take," occupancy, surveillability and accessibility)
5. Initiation	Approach dwelling and probe for occupancy and accessibility
6. Continuation	Break into dwelling and enter
7. Completion	Steal goods
8. Finish up	Load up goods and drive away from house
9. Exit setting	Leave development
Further stages (if applicable)	Store, conceal and disguise goods
Further crime scripts (if applicable)	Market and dispose of stolen goods

involved in crime and delinquency? In current criminological language, the answer makes them theories of criminality. When it focuses on involvement, the rational choice perspective is also a *theory of criminality*, though one that gives a fuller role to current life circumstances, needs, and opportunities. But when the rational choice perspective focuses on the event and seeks to understand when and where offenders choose to commit particular offenses, or how they undertake them, it also becomes a *theory of crime*. This is one way in which it diverges from ostensibly similar approaches such as social learning theory (Akers 1990). It shares these dual preoccupations with crime and criminality with Gottfredson and

Hirschi's (1990) general theory of crime, but, unlike them, we do not think that offending is the result of low self-control. Different offenses require varying degrees of planning, and offenders of different ages, experience, and skills exhibit varying degrees of understanding and concern about the consequences of their actions.

The Dynamic Nature of Criminality

Preoccupied with explaining offending in terms of deep-rooted and relatively unchanging motivations, criminological theories have failed to capture its ever-changing contingent reality. Offenders' readiness to commit particular crimes varies according to their current needs and desires, and they constantly reassess their involvement in criminal activity. This assessment is deeply affected by their experience of committing particular acts and what they learn from the consequences; it can result in desistance from offending or concentrating on some new form of crime. In addition, the commission of a particular crime can bring in its wake the need or the opportunity to commit other crimes. Thus, a burglar might decide to rape a woman he finds sleeping in the house, or a prostitute might decide to rob a drunken client. The notion of the crime script was specially developed to explore extended sequences of criminal decision-making and links between crimes.

The Importance of Situation and Opportunity

With a few exceptions, such as routine activity theory (Cohen and Felson 1979), most criminological theories ignore or downplay the importance of situational factors in determining crime. But even though routine activity theory and the rational choice perspective are both described as opportunity theories, Clarke and Felson (1993) have enumerated important differences between the two approaches. Routine activity is a macro theory dealing with changes at a societal level that expand or limit crime opportunities. The rational choice perspective, on the other hand, is a micro theory dealing with the ways in which these opportunities are perceived, evaluated, and acted upon by individual offenders. Often, opportunities are sought and created. But they also play a more active role: They may tempt an otherwise law-abiding person into occasional transgressions. And the existence of easy opportunities in society might attract some people into a life of crime. These facts present important implications for prevention, and the rational choice perspective has proved invaluable in thinking about practical ways of blocking opportunities for crime.

The Normality of Crime

Unlike many other theories, the rational choice perspective makes no hard-and-fast distinction between offenders and the law abiding. It recognizes, of course, that for some people crime is more consistently chosen in a variety of circumstances than for other people. However, this is as much the result of their present material circumstances as it is of their backgrounds. Given a change in their circumstances, they might easily begin to choose legal means for meeting their needs and desires. Likewise, people who have generally avoided criminal choices might cease to do so in the face of overwhelming need or temptation. Many respectable bank clerks have resorted to fraud in the face of pressing financial need. On occasion, all of us will commit offenses when we think we can get away with them. Even the most respectable among us, those holding steady, well-paid jobs, will cheat on expense claims and pilfer employers' property. Indeed, the rational choice perspective is a general theory of crime—as much concerned with crime in the suites as in the streets; as much with incivilities and disorder as with organized crime; as much with property crime as with violent crime; and as much with crime committed by women as with crime committed by men. In short, there is no kind of crime in which reason, choice, and purpose play an unimportant part.

Compatibility with Criminal Justice

If crime is a result of social or psychological deprivation, which is the position of most theories, it seems irrelevant or unfair to respond with punishment. This explains why many criminologists are hostile to criminal justice and reluctant to become involved in policy studies. Law enforcement and criminal justice professionals often detect this hostility and, in turn, disparage criminology. This is unfortunate for both sides—and for society.

The rational choice perspective provides a more subtle view of this apparent dilemma. It recognizes that offenders from deprived backgrounds usually have fewer opportunities for meeting everyday needs than more privileged members of society. To this extent, their crime choices are, therefore, more readily understandable. However, only rarely are people forced to commit crime by virtue of background or current circumstances. Nor do all disadvantaged or deprived people turn to a life of crime. On the contrary, every act of crime involves a choice by the offender. If so, then a way is opened to influence such decisions by seeking to make criminal behavior less rewarding, more risky, and more difficult.

Policy Relevance

The rational choice perspective was explicitly developed to assist policy, and its most important policy application to date has been in the field of situational crime prevention—a broad set of techniques designed to reduce opportunities for crime (Clarke 1997). These are classified under the four rational choice objectives: (1) increasing the effort required by crime, (2) increasing the risks, (3) reducing the rewards, and (4) removing excuses for crime. More recently, a further objective—(5) removing provocation—has been added (Cornish and Clarke 2003). Many notable crime prevention successes have been achieved through using these techniques (Clarke 1997), including the virtual elimination of airline hijackings in the 1970s by baggage screening; the elimination of robberies of bus drivers in U.S. cities in the 1970s by the introduction of exact fare systems; and the virtual elimination in the 1990s of graffiti on New York City subway cars by systematic and prompt graffiti removal.

Situational prevention is vulnerable to the criticism that reducing opportunities merely results in crime's being displaced—for example, to some other target or location. The rational choice perspective has helped to show why displacement does not necessarily occur. Much crime is the result of easy opportunities, and offenders may be unwilling to incur the additional risks and effort involved following the implementation of situational measures. They can make do with less money and fewer drugs, or they can try to obtain these in noncriminal ways. In fact, one review found no evidence of displacement in twenty-two out of fifty-five crime prevention projects studied (Hesseling 1994). Some displacement was reported in the remaining thirty-three projects, but in every one there was still a net gain in preventive benefits. Accumulating evidence has also shown that, far from simply displacing crime with little real benefit, situational measures often reduce crime more widely than expected. Such a "diffusion of benefits" occurs because offenders often believe that situational measures are more far-reaching than they really are.

Conclusion

As Herrnstein (1990, 356) points out, rational choice theory "comes close to serving as the fundamental principle of the behavioral sciences. No other well articulated theory of behavior commands so large a following in so wide a range of disciplines." As far as the application of rational choice theory to criminology is concerned, we have yet to set out in detail all the components of this powerful perspective, or to explore its potential fully. But to be of practical utility, the rational choice perspective needs only to be "good enough" for the explanatory or policy purpose in hand. At the same time, it must be flexible enough to accommodate new needs. It is continually being refined, and if we were called upon to make a fresh statement of the theory some years from now, we believe this would incorporate new or more fully developed concepts. Otherwise, we will have failed in our objective of providing a useful tool, one capable of being honed and improved, to assist criminologists in thinking about the practical business of controlling crime.

Note

1. This paper is an abridged version of Clarke and Cornish (2001).

References

Akers, Ronald L. 1990. "Rational Choice, Deterrence and Social Learning Theory in Criminology: The Path Not Taken." *Journal of Criminal Law and Criminology* 81: 653–676.

Clarke, Ronald V., ed. 1997. *Situational Crime Prevention: Successful Case Studies*. 2d ed. Albany, N.Y.: Harrow & Heston.

Clarke, Ronald V., and Derek B. Cornish. 1985. "Modeling Offenders' Decisions: A Framework for Research and Policy." In vol. 6 of *Crime and Justice*, edited by Michael Tonry and Norval Morris. Chicago: University of Chicago Press.

———. 2001. "Rational Choice." In *Crime Theories*, edited by Raymond Paternoster and R. Bachman. Los Angeles: Roxbury.

Clarke, Ronald V., and Marcus Felson. 1993. "Introduction: Criminology: Routine Activity and Rational Choice." In vol. 5 of *Routine Activity and Rational Choices: Advances in Criminological Theory*. New Brunswick, N.J.: Transaction.

Cohen, Laurence E., and Marcus Felson. 1979. "Social Change and Crime Rate Trends: A Routine Activity Approach." *American Sociological Review* 44: 588–608.

Cornish, Derek B. 1994. "The Procedural Analysis of Offending and Its Relevance for Situational Prevention." In vol. 3 of *Crime Prevention Studies*, edited by Ronald V. Clarke. Monsey, N.Y.: Criminal Justice Press.

Cornish, Derek B., and Ronald V. Clarke. 2003. "Opportunities, Precipitators and Criminal Decisions: A Reply to Wortley's Critique of Situational Crime Prevention." In *Theory for Practice in Situational Crime Prevention*, edited by Martha J. Smith and Derek B. Cornish, vol. 16 of *Crime Prevention Studies*. Monsey, N.Y.: Criminal Justice Press.

———, eds. 1986. *The Reasoning Criminal*. New York: Springer-Verlag.

Gibbons, Don. 1994. *Talking About Crime and Criminals: Problems and Issues in Theory Development in Criminology*. Englewood Cliffs, N.J.: Prentice-Hall.

Gottfredson, Michael. R., and Travis Hirschi. 1990. *A General Theory of Crime*. Stanford: Stanford University Press.

Herrnstein, Richard J. 1990. "Rational Choice Theory: Necessary But Not Sufficient." *American Psychologist* 45: 356–367.

Hesseling, R.B.P. 1994. "Displacement: A Review of the Empirical Literature." In vol. 3 of *Crime Prevention Studies*, edited by Ronald V. Clarke. Monsey, N.Y.: Criminal Justice Press.

Simon, H. A. 1990. "Alternative Visions of Rationality." In *Rationality in Action: Contemporary Approaches*, edited by P. K. Moser. Cambridge: Cambridge University Press.

2

Biological and Biosocial Theories

With the advent of scientific methods and Charles Darwin's influential study of the evolution of species in the early 1800s, scholars studying crime and criminals began to rely on such positivistic methods as measurement, comparison, diagnosis, prediction, and treatment.

The original basic assumption of this theoretical approach is that people who break laws are different from those who do not; that criminals differ in significant ways from noncriminals. The goal of the scientific study of crime, therefore, is to compare the two by measuring a variety of features; the differences are then identified and catalogued so that explanations can be developed about how the differences between these "kinds of people" could lead some of them to commit crimes. Further, this approach would go on to distinguish the differences between various kinds of criminals—the mentally ill, for example, and offenders who commit crimes of varying degrees of severity—and how these patterns may persist or desist over time.

Individualized attention to the specific criminal, rather than to the crime, on the assumption that criminal offenders are different from members of the general population, and different from each other, eventually led to variations in how offenders were treated and in how the courts sentenced them. This differential treatment included indeterminate sentences and led to much greater discretion on the part of police, judges, and correctional officials.

Anthropologists were the first scientists to take advantage of these new strategies through an examination of criminals' physiology. These founders of scientific criminology, most notably Cesare Lombroso and his students, Enrico Ferri and Raffaele Garofalo, sought to identify physical differences between criminals and noncriminals. Initially, facial features and the shape of one's skull were used to identify the crime-prone, but later a wide variety of factors were identified, including those in the environment. The often simplistic and flawed study design and methods employed by the original researchers caused this approach to receive much criticism; it was eventually replaced by more sophisticated and rigorously designed studies and greater attention to factors that were "more than skin deep." Studies of twins separated at birth have provided some confirmation of the role that heredity plays in human behavior, as have studies of adopted children. As scientific techniques advanced, so did the range of differences found between criminals and noncriminals, including differences in genes, chromosomes, brain chemistry, brain development, hormones, and diet.

This scientific approach to crime via the study of criminals and their offenses remains relevant today, and it also provides an aid to policing. Popular television series such as *CSI* (Crime Scene Investigation) show how police agencies rely on physical evidence to identify criminals. Modern techniques can now examine a person's genetic structure, and most biological theorists argue that a genetic pattern interacting with the appropriate triggering environment may be responsible for an increased proclivity to antisocial and consequently criminal behavior. Sophisticated analysis of offenders' and potential offenders' brain patterns are explored through magnetic resonance imaging (MRI) and positron emission tomography (PET) scans. Contemporary sociobiological theorists acknowledge that the role of a person's environment in combination with his or her biological attributes can limit and channel the behavioral choices that the individual makes. The object of biological theories of crime is to examine the individual and social factors that make crime more likely so that interventions in the physiology and the environment of the individual can be made to prevent future crimes from occurring. Increasingly, this approach is being developed as an integrated biopsychosocial perspective.

2.1

Cesare Lombroso and the Origins of Criminology

Rethinking Criminological Tradition[1]

Nicole Rafter
Northeastern University

Cesare Lombroso (1835–1909) is widely recognized as one of the first scholars to bring scientific methods to bear on the study of crime. A physician, psychiatrist, and prolific author, Lombroso is best known as the founder of criminal anthropology, the study of the body, mind, and habits of the "born" criminal. Lombroso's theory of the atavistic offender dominated criminological discussions in Europe, North and South America, and parts of Asia from the 1880s into the early twentieth century. But critics attacked his theory even during his lifetime, and by the time he died, criminologists outside Italy had moved on to other explanations of crime.[2] Today, criminology textbooks continue to acknowledge Lombroso as the "father" of the field, but concerning the nature of his contribution they are vague; and in courses on criminology in the United States, Lombroso and his work are sometimes ridiculed.

Given the recent explosion of international studies on Lombroso, the time is ripe to reassess Lombroso's work and significance to the field. Although I have no intention of defending Lombroso as a researcher, I have spent the last decade immersed in the originals of his books; I have concluded that what we thought we knew about Lombroso differs in important respects from what he actually said. And because our view of his work has been unavoidably narrow and distorted, we have also reached some inaccurate conclusions about the nature of his contribution to criminology.

In what follows, first I summarize the view of Lombroso that has appeared over time in U.S. criminology textbooks. Then I identify the sources of this view, which was based on mistranslations and partial translations of Lombroso's work. Once misconceptions were established, they were passed through the academic generations, repeated without correction because correction was virtually impossible given the inaccessibility of the originals. I next explain how new research and fresh translations are making possible a more complete view of Lombroso and, in conclusion, I predict ways in which the new resources are likely to change contemporary (not just in the United States!) ideas about Lombroso's contribution to criminology.

The Traditional View of Lombroso

Using U.S. criminology textbooks published between 1939 and 2004,[3] I extracted a summary view of Lombroso. In this view, Lombroso formulated a biological explanation according to which criminals (or at least the worst of them) are doomed by their physical makeup to break the law. The main cause of this condition is atavism, a reversion to savagery. Criminals are throwbacks to a primitive stage in human evolution. A few textbooks mention another Lombrosian cause of crime, bad heredity, but without explaining how it relates to atavism. In addition, several mention in passing Lombroso's etiological interest in epilepsy and insanity, although again without explaining how Lombroso connected these conditions to other causes. Most of the authors refer to the stigmata of crime, the physical anomalies with which Lombroso expected the bodies of born criminals to be marked; and to their credit, most of the textbook authors resist going into detail about the stigmata—the silliest and most vulnerable aspect of Lombroso's work.

Several of the recent textbooks, perhaps sensitized by the current interest in women and crime, mention that Lombroso studied female as well as male offenders, although they are not always clear about what he said in this regard. According to one (Barkan 2001), Lombroso emphasized the female offender's passivity; according to another (Seigel 1995), he emphasized her masculinity. In addition, some of the books refer to problems with Lombroso's research. Vedder, Koenig, and Clark (1953) claim that Lombroso failed to use control groups, Jeffrey (1990) that he failed to use statistics. Vold and Bernard hold that he used control groups *and* statistics, and Jeffrey reports a secondhand rumor that Lombroso *sometimes* used control groups. Only Sutherland, Vold and Bernard, and Lanier and Henry, among the authors whose work I examined in detail, observe that Lombroso modified his theories over time.

The textbooks link Lombroso's significance to "positivism," though few explain the nature of that link or positivism's significance. One text seems to equate positivism with biological theories of crime per se, and another two imply that it has something to do with debates over determinism and free will. Only three of the works (Vold and Bernard, Beirne and Messerschmidt, and Lanier and Henry) locate the positivist endeavor in the historical perspective of efforts to apply principles of scientific investigation to an entirely new area of study, that of crime.

This summary of the traditional view, although it washes out some of the strengths of the better textbook coverage, reveals a deep uncertainty among authors of U.S. criminological textbooks as to the substance of Lombroso's criminology and its significance.

Sources of the Traditional View

The traditional view is understandably vague and halting: It was based on inadequate sources. Even though Lombroso's *L'uomo delinquente*, or *Criminal Man*, is widely acknowledged as a foundational text in the field, it has been available to English-only readers solely through two incomplete editions, both published in 1911. The first is a volume titled *Lombroso's Criminal Man*, produced shortly after his death by his daughter and translated by an unidentified party. This edition was reprinted in 1972 by Patterson Smith, but it is now out of print. Most of it seems to have been authored not by Cesare Lombroso but by his daughter, Gina Lombroso-Ferrero. For example, one passage reads: "It was these anomalies that first drew my father's attention to the close relationship between the criminal and the savage, and made him suspect that criminal tendencies are of atavistic origin" (Lombroso-Ferrero 1911/1972, 5). It is clear that these are the daughter's words, not the father's. But there is no way to tell from the book itself how accurately or completely Gina Lombroso-Ferrero presented her father's ideas.

The second English-language source is *Crime: Its Causes and Remedies*, a translation by Henry P. Horton, also out of print. In his "Translator's Note," Horton writes that he worked from a French edition of 1899, supplementing it with a German edition of 1902. He can only speculate on the relationship of these sources to the Italian originals and has no idea how the textual extract he has translated relates to Lombroso's *L'uomo delinquente* as a whole.[4]

Unless one compares these two English-language volumes with the Italian originals, one cannot possibly determine their relationship to Lombroso's own thought. Lombroso took *L'uomo delinquente* through five editions, the first a one-volume study published in 1876, the last a four-volume work published in 1896–1897. Are the English-language sources based on the first edition, the fifth edition, or on Gina Lombroso-Ferrero's vision of a text she wished her father had written? How did Lombroso's ideas evolve over time? Does our traditional view of Lombroso derive from the first edition, the last edition, both, or all five? Is it perhaps based, as is *Crime: Its Causes and Remedies*, on the translation of a translation?

Similar issues are raised by Lombroso's other major criminological work, *La donna delinquente*, co-authored with Guglielmo Ferrero and published in Italian in 1893. This work was translated into English in 1895 as *The Female Offender* and frequently reprinted thereafter, though it, too, is now out of print. The translation fails to mention that it covers only two of the original's four major sections. It also does not acknowledge that it has excised half of the original text, leaving out nearly all the material on "normal" women (the control group) and prostitutes. Nor does it mention that it switches the order of some chapters and bowdlerizes the original by cutting most references to female breasts and genitals and excising discussions of lesbianism and sexual deviance. Not only did the anonymous translator impose Victorian prudery on this book (which is a shame, because the study made one of the earliest contributions to the field of sexology); he or she rendered the original into literal but frequently incomprehensible English from which it is difficult to extract criminological concepts. In this work, too, then, it is impossible to test the traditional view of Lombroso against his text. The traditional view may be true or it may be false; one cannot tell.

New Resources

New resources are beginning to overcome the traditional inadequacy of our Lombroso materials. One consists of new studies in Italian: Over the past several decades, an outpouring of books and articles on Lombroso has emerged, including studies of his life and work (Bulferetti 1975; Villa 1985); his daughters' lives (Dolza 1990); his museum (Colombo 2000; Portigliato Barbos 1993); and his work on a particular criminal case (Guarnieri 1993). The new studies include a slightly fictionalized biography (Guarnieri 2000) and an intellectual history of Lombroso and criminal anthropology (Frigessi 2003). The French and Germans, too, have started to reexamine their involvement in criminal anthropology (Mucchielli 1994; Gadebusch Bondio 1995). In English, Gibson's *Born to Crime* (2002) provides a study of Lombroso's impact on Italian criminal justice practices before, during, and after fascism; Horn's *The Criminal Body* (2003) offers a history of Lombroso's idea that bodies themselves can testify to legal and scientific truths; and Cambridge University Press will soon publish *Criminals and Their Scientists* (Becker and Wetzell 2006), a collection of original essays examining Lombroso's influence on various fields and in various countries. Results of this international explosion of Lombroso scholarship will eventually filter through to working criminologists and their students; thus, knowledge of Lombroso's sociocultural circumstances, of his sources, and of his own research will improve and expand.

Another new source of material is fresh translations. Mary Gibson, an Italian historian at John Jay College of Criminal Justice, and I have prepared new Lombroso translations for Duke University Press. The first, which we have retitled *Criminal Woman* (a more accurate rendering of *La donna delinquente* than *The Female Offender*), appeared in 2004; our *Criminal Man* followed in 2005. Because one of our primary concerns is to make the texts accessible, and because accessible books must be not only readable but also affordable, we have condensed the works into a full view of Lombroso's originals that omits repetitions and unnecessary examples. The new *Criminal Man* includes passages from all five of Lombroso's own editions so that English-only readers can, for the first time, follow the development of his ideas over the two decades he spent working on this magnum opus. In addition, we have restored the references to sex and sexuality to *Criminal Woman*. Our extensive annotations and introductions are designed to clarify difficult passages, locate Lombroso in historical context, and show how his thought related to that of other major European intellectuals of the late nineteenth century. We have reproduced Lombroso's own notes so that readers can identify his specific sources; we have also reproduced many of his illustrations, including the bawdy tattoos.

These new translations should help correct misconceptions about Lombroso's work. Let me indicate just a small part of their potential by mentioning ways in which they contradict the traditional view of Lombroso.

Revisionist Views

Lombroso anticipated one of the most influential criminological ideas of recent decades, that is, the distinction between life-course persistent and adolescence-limited offenders (Moffitt et al. 2001), according to which some criminals continue to break the law for most of their lives while others desist after their teenage years. Lombroso's born criminal is equivalent to the life-course persistent offender, someone who continues violating the law into old age. Lombroso was not unique in formulating this concept of the lifelong recidivist, which also turns up in the work of several other late nineteenth-century criminologists, but he was the first to explore it in-depth and to make it the basis for a galvanizing popular image of the criminal. His typology, ranging from the biologically doomed born criminal through the salvageable criminaloid and on to the idealistic and essentially innocent political criminal, incorporates the idea of criminality as a continuum, a concept closely related to Moffitt's distinction between the biologically handicapped life-course persistent offender and the more adaptable adolescence-limited offender.

Lombroso also anticipated one of the most controversial theories in recent criminology: that of evolutionary criminology (e.g., Ellis and Walsh 1997), according to which personality structures conducive to crime are holdovers from an evolutionary period when rape and pillage contributed directly to male reproductive fitness. Regardless of one's opinion of evolutionary criminology, one can see a similar notion in Lombroso's idea of the criminal as atavism, a throwback to an earlier evolutionary stage when savage behaviors were more useful and social and personal controls had not yet developed. In this respect, then, Lombroso stole a march upon one of the major strands in current biological explanations of crime.

Lombroso further anticipated genetic explanations of crime. Although he died before the concept of genes became familiar, Lombroso's theory of degeneration, or an inherited tendency to devolve and become socially problematic, broadly resembles today's genetic theories. These theories argue that heredity interacts with environment to produce individuals with various potentials for offending. This is similar to what Lombroso said when he analyzed the ways in which social, hereditary, and environmental factors interact to produce criminals and crime. Thus, although some aspects of Lombroso's work are indeed outmoded today, others arguably offer examples of prematurity in scientific discovery (Hook 2002).

The new translations enable us to determine what Lombroso meant by "positivism." He called for the collection of "facts"—data about crime and criminals that could be verified and, ideally, quantified—and insisted on inductive reasoning from these facts, even though he often fell short of that goal himself. To follow him through the five editions of *Criminal Man* is to see him constantly searching for new data, adding cross-national comparisons, refining and elaborating his ideas. He identified fresh data sources, found and invented measuring tools to collect better information, and devised novel methods for displaying his data. Moreover, the new editions show Lombroso struggling to figure out how to apply his positivist principles, as when in studying female criminality, for instance, he tries to construct a control group of normal women (the first English translation left that part out). The overall lesson of the new editions is that, notwithstanding his many scientific shortcomings, Lombroso was central in, and crucial to, the development of the positivist tradition that remains fundamental to scientific criminology. Although he had predecessors, he was indeed the "father" of scientific methods in criminology. I would go so far as to suggest that Lombroso was the only figure in the history of criminology who might qualify for having produced one of those seismic scientific reorientations that the historian Thomas Kuhn (1970) labeled "paradigm shifts." Before Lombroso, the study of crime fell into the domain of metaphysicians, moralists, and penologists; Lombroso turned it into a biosocial science.

In retrospect, we can see that Lombroso often worked along major intellectual fault lines, contested areas where various trends in social thought collided. The tensions in his work—between feminism and antifeminism, liberalism and conservatism, protofascism and socialism, humanism and positivism—are as instructive as his attempted resolutions. Lombroso certainly had one of the most fertile minds in nineteenth-century Europe and he produced a body of work seldom equaled for its variety, richness, and influence. Subsequently mocked and forgotten, Lombroso is today being rediscovered. We are on the verge of new understandings that will, I think, help us better understand the origins of criminology itself.

Notes

1. My thanks to Mary Gibson of John Jay College of Criminal Justice for her help with this article.

2. Italian criminologists, reluctant to repudiate their famous countryman, continued to build on his work well into the 20th century (Gibson 2002).

3. In order of publication, I reviewed these texts: Sutherland 1939; Barnes and Teeters 1943; von Hentig 1948/1979; Vedder, Koenig, and Clark 1953; Barnes and Teeters 1959; Vold and Bernard 1979; Reid 1988; Jeffrey 1990; Seigel 1995; Beirne and Messerschmidt 2000; Barkan 2001; and Lanier and Henry 2004.

4. As Horton guessed, *Crime: Its Cases and Remedies* was based on the third volume of the fifth edition of *L'uomo delinquente*.

References

Baima Bollone, Pierluigi. 1992. *Cesare Lombroso: Ovvero: Il pincipio dell'irresponsabilità*. Torino: Societa editrice internazionale.

Barkan, Steven E. 2001. *Criminology: A Sociological Understanding*. 2d ed. Upper Saddle River, N.J.: Prentice-Hall.

Barnes, Harry Elmer, and Negley K. Teeters. 1943. *New Horizons in Criminology*. New York: Prentice-Hall.

______. 1959. *New Horizons in Criminology*. 3d ed. Englewood Cliffs, N.J.: Prentice-Hall.

Becker, Peter, and Richard F. Wetzell, eds. 2006. *Criminals and Their Scientists: The History of Criminology in International Perspective*. Cambridge: Cambridge University Press, forthcoming.

Beirne, Piers, and James Messerschmidt. 2000. *Criminology*. 3d ed. Boulder: Westview Press.

Bulferetti, Luigi. 1975. *Cesare Lombroso*. Torino: Unione tipografico-editrice torinese.

Colombo, Giorgio. [1975] 2000. *La scienza infelice: Il museo di antropologia criminale di Cesare Lombroso*. Reprint, Torino: Bollati Boringhieri.

Dolza, Delfina. 1990. *Essere figlie di Lombroso: Due donne intellectuali tra '800 e '900*. Milan: F. Angeli.

Ellis, Lee, and Anthony Walsh. 1997. "Gene-Based Evolutionary Theories in Criminology." *Criminology* 35: 229–276.

Frigessi, Delia. 2003. *Cesare Lombroso*. Torino: Einaudi.

Gadebusch Bondio, Mariacarla. 1995. *Die Rezeption der kriminalanthropologischen Theorien von Cesare Lombroso ini Deutschland von 1880–1914*. Edited by Rolf Winau and Heinz Muller-Deitz. Husum: Matthiesen.

Gibson, Mary. 2002. *Born to Crime: Cesare Lombroso and the Origins of Biological Criminology*. Westport, Conn.: Praeger.

Guarnieri, Luigi. 2000. *L'atlante criminale: la vita scriteriata di Cesare Lombroso*. Milan: Mondatori.

Guarnieri, Patrizia. 1993. *A Case of Child Murder*. Cambridge: Polity Press.

Hook, Ernest B., ed. 2002. *Prematurity in Scientific Discovery: On Resistance and Neglect*. Berkeley: University of California Press.

Horn, David. 2003. *The Criminal Body: Lombroso and the Anatomy of Deviance*. New York: Routledge.

Jeffrey, C. Ray. 1990. *Criminology: An Interdisciplinary Approach*. Englewood Cliffs, N.J.: Prentice Hall.

Kuhn, Thomas S. 1970. *The Structure of Scientific Revolutions*. 2d ed. Chicago: University of Chicago Press.

Lanier, Mark M., and Stuart Henry. 2004. *Essential Criminology*. 2d ed. Boulder: Westview Press.

Lombroso, Cesare. [1911] 1918. *Crime: Its Causes and Remedies*. Translated by Henry P. Horton. Reprint, Boston: Little, Brown.

______. 2005. *Criminal Man*. A new translation with an introduction and annotations by Mary Gibson and Nicole Hahn Rafter. Durham, N.C.: Duke University Press, forthcoming.

Lombroso, Cesare, and Guglielmo Ferrero. 2004. *Criminal Woman, the Prostitute, and the Normal Woman*. A new translation with an introduction and annotations by Nicole Hahn Rafter and Mary Gibson. Durham, N.C.: Duke University Press.

Lombroso, Cesare, and William Ferrero. 1895. *The Female Offender*. New York: D. Appleton.

Lombroso-Ferrero, Gina. [1911] 1972. *Criminal Man According to the Classification of Cesare Lombroso*. Reprint, Montclair, N.J.: Patterson Smith.

Moffitt, Terrie E., Avshalom Caspi, Michael Rutter, and Phil A. Silva. 2001. *Sex Differences in Antisocial Behaviour*. Cambridge: Cambridge University Press.

Mucchielli, Laurent, ed. 1994. *Histoire de la criminologie française*. Paris: Editions L'Harmattan.

Portigliatti Barbos, Mario. 1993. "Cesare Lombroso e il museo di antropologia criminale." In *Storia illustrata di Torino*, edited by Valerio Castronovo (pp. 1141–1160). Milan: Elio Sellino.

Reid, Sue Titus. 1988. *Crime and Criminology*. 5th ed. New York: Holt, Rinehart and Winston.

Siegel, Larry J. 1995. *Criminology*. 5th ed. St. Paul, Minnesota: West.

Sutherland, Edwin H. 1939. *Principles of Criminology*. 4th ed. Chicago: J. B. Lippincott.

Vedder, Clyde B., Samuel Koenig, and Robert E. Clark. 1953. *Criminology: A Book of Readings*. New York: The Dryden Press.

Villa, Renzo. 1985. *Il deviante e i suoi segni: Lombroso e la nascita dell' antropologia criminale*. Milan: F. Angeli.

Vold, George, with Thomas J. Bernard. 1979. *Theoretical Criminology*. 2d ed. New York: Oxford University Press.

von Hentig, Hans. [1948] 1979. *The Criminal and His Victim*. Reprint, New York: Schocken Books.

2.2

Integrating Findings from Neurobiology into Criminological Thought

Issues, Solutions, and Implications[1]

DIANA H. FISHBEIN
RTI International

Introduction

Over the past fifteen years, an explosion of research in the neurosciences has had direct implications for the study of criminology. Technological advancements, in particular, have led to significant increases in our ability to provide a more integrated perspective in the field of criminology. For the first time in the history of the behavioral sciences, possibilities for understanding linkages and interactions between genetic, biological, physiological, psychological, social, environmental, and economic factors are in sight. Researchers speculate that in another ten years we will have a more complete knowledge of factors that contribute to the developmental pathways that characterize various forms of antisocial behavior (Niehoff 1999).

Many challenges remain, however, in conducting integrated research that focuses on crime, delinquency, drug abuse, and violence. From a scientific perspective, it is necessary to become familiar with a diverse number of disciplines, some of which use highly technical and field-specific language and technologies. No unified theory or model has yet emerged to facilitate our understanding of these fields by tying together the perspectives, theories, concepts, terms, and methods of the many disciplines that would constitute integrated research. The relative isolation of these various behavioral sciences is unfortunate in light of widespread recognition that the only way to generate a comprehensive and accurate understanding of antisocial behavior is through the integration of relevant disciplines.

The many controversies that surround integrated scientific inquiry have alienated one discipline from another. There is fear that research into genetic contributions to behavior will undermine our conception of free will and will foster the idea that all behavior is caused by biological factors. Even more disturbing is the belief that the study of behavioral genetics is inherently racist and may reinforce racial stereotypes, prejudice, and discriminatory practices by the criminal justice system and society at large. Furthermore, some argue that the identification of genetic factors in antisocial behavior will lead to the elimination or low priority of social programs; an attitude of futility may arise and argue that if the problem is genetic, then it must be untreatable or unavoidable. Or, worse yet, according to opponents, we may increase reliance on pharmaceutical solutions or futuristic genetic engineering techniques to eliminate the problem of crime, drug abuse, and violence.

These scientific, moral, and social issues are discussed in this essay. And although no sure-fire solution is proposed, some direction is given for the eventual synthesis of the behavioral sciences as they relate to the study of crime. This essay promotes the idea that, with greater familiarity and understanding of the neurobiological sciences, many fears will be allayed so that safeguards can be put into motion. Moreover, increased attention to these issues will lead to informed scrutiny and input from investigators, practitioners, and policymakers; thus, the potential for ethical and effective applications of the research findings will be enhanced.

Integrating Scientific Disciplines

Numerous behavioral science subdisciplines, including molecular and behavioral genetics, neurobiology, physiology, psychology, cognitive neuroscience, endocrinology, and forensic psychiatry, provide substantial evidence that certain neurobiological functions contribute to an orientation toward the social environment that may increase risk for antisocial behavior. The vast range of studies from these disciplines on vulnerability to antisocial personality disorder, violence, and drug abuse can appear overwhelming at first, but several consistencies across studies reveal a pattern that may characterize vulnerable individuals. Findings indicate that vulnerability to antisocial behavior is partially a function of genetic and biological makeup that is expressed during childhood as particular behavioral, cognitive, and psychological traits, such as impulsivity, attention deficits, aggressiveness, and heightened sensitivity to rewards or stimulation. These traits have been associated with physiological and biochemical responses to environmental input; for example, cognitive function, heart rate, hormone and neurotransmitter levels, and EEG recordings are reportedly different in antisocial populations (Raine 1993). These various biological differences, however, do not function in a vacuum to increase risk; instead, they interact with a multitude of social and environmental conditions in a constantly evolving and changing dynamic to contribute to or protect from social dysfunction. In other words, basic genetic or acquired biological traits are thought to contribute to biochemical and physiological conditions that in turn may predispose individuals to a combination of particular behavioral and psychological outcomes that may occur, or be suppressed, in various environmental settings.

Specifically, evidence is mounting to suggest that several neurobiological systems may be involved in sensation-seeking, impulsivity, negative temperament, and other cognitive and behavioral correlates of antisocial behavior. These systems perform somewhat differently between individuals as a result of genetic factors and social experiences. The particular way they function in an individual determines the level of activity within areas of the brain that are responsible for motivation, emotion, and experiences of pleasure and pain. Although there is a wide range of variation in brain function that is considered normal, the variation itself contributes to personality and temperamental differences between people. Some of these "normal" traits can be associated with either prosocial or antisocial behavior, but the deciding factor depends on environmental conditions. For example, the trait "sensation-seeking" can be related to highly effective practices in the corporate or sports worlds or, conversely, to drug abuse, depending upon what sort of environment the individual was raised in.

On the other hand, when certain aspects of brain function occur outside the normal range, behavior and moods can become unusual and may be considered "pathological" in extreme cases. Deviations in brain function can be measured in physiological and biochemical processes that influence the behavioral and psychological outcomes. These biological factors are, in turn, influenced by socioenvironmental factors that can contribute either to the expression or to the inhibition of antisocial behaviors. In the presence of "negative" socioenvironmental conditions, such as poverty or poor parenting, the development of antisocial behavior becomes more likely. Called "stressors," these negative conditions act as triggers and offer one explanation for the disproportionate number of residents who are likely to indulge in antisocial behavior in lower income neighborhoods, where triggers are more prevalent (Moffitt 1997). Put simply, abnormalities in certain aspects of brain function can heighten sensitivity to negative environmental circumstances, increasing the risk for an antisocial outcome.

The resulting integration of research findings from various disciplines has direct implications for the study of crime and criminal behavior by providing a scientific foundation for philosophical viewpoints and should appeal to social scientists who hold widely divergent views and beliefs. This research compels the reader to acknowledge several decades of serious scientific criminological inquiry in psychology, psychiatry, and the neurobiological sciences. Findings account for intra-psychic and extra-psychic variables in their emphasis on the recent explosion of genetic and biological evidence that certain aspects of brain function may underlie violent and impulsive behaviors by sensitizing the actor to adverse social stimuli (Pallone and Hennessy 1996).

Several substantial works published in the past ten years provide contemporary research overviews and integrative perspectives with direct relevance to the field of criminology (e.g., Bock and Goode 1996; Fishbein 1996, 2000, 2004; Hillbrand and Pallone 1993; Pallone and Hennessy 1996; Raine, 1993; Raine et al. 1997a; Reiss et al. 1994; Rowe et al. 1998a, 1998b; Tarter and Vanyukov 1994; Volavka 1995). Although they acknowledge that biological research on various types of antisocial behavior is still in short supply, not always clearly enunciated, and rife with conceptual and theoretical issues not yet resolved, they also demonstrate that integrative works are actively in progress, report many consistent findings, and provide direction in potentially important and fruitful methodological approaches. This research has been instrumental in identifying aspects of brain function and environmental triggers that may relate to various antisocial behaviors warranting further investigation.

In spite of this progress, several limitations in the research remain. For one, many so-called "interdisciplinary" works tend to focus on biological factors and, rather than attempt to estimate relative influences, simply control for social variables. Also, many studies do not account for ongoing environmental influences on biological conditions but instead treat them as if they were fixed and uncorrectable. Furthermore, this body of research has not yet accounted for population or group-wide collective aggression and antisocial behavior or for the antisocial practices of corporations and political bodies. Further compounding the isolation of disciplines, there remains unfamiliarity with and resistance to interdisciplinary perspectives, and there has been a lack of communication among various branches of investigation. Unfamiliarity with genetic and biological terminology, methodology, and underlying mechanisms has hindered exchanges between social and biological researchers. These shortfalls, among many others, could be addressed by the behavioral sciences in more meaningful ways by incorporating the perspectives and methodologies of social scientists. More in-depth examination of this important research domain is essential for practitioners, academicians, policymakers, and social scientists who would greatly benefit from its knowledge (see Raine and Liu 1998).

Building Comprehensive Models in Criminology

There are many varieties of theories in the field of criminology, some of which are competitive with each other (e.g., conflict and differential association theories); others are considered to be "integrated" because they combine several criminological perspectives. The research addressed in this essay does not fall into either of these categories. Neurobiological research does reflect certain ways of thinking and modeling relationships between variables, but it should not be considered in terms of theories that are competitive with others in criminology. Instead, this research reflects a broad range of scientific perspectives and methods used to better understand human behavior, and these perspectives and methods are highly relevant to the questions posed by criminologists. Findings from the neurobiological sciences should, therefore, be viewed as having the potential to fill existing gaps in our knowledge relating to the development of antisocial behavior and eventually to be understood in the context of social forces that we have identified as significant players in this dynamic equation.

There are no exceptions to the assertion that all complex human behavior is the result of interactions between our genes and our environment. Even behaviors that are predominantly learned alter all future behaviors by modifying the way brain cells function and communicate, producing an essential feedback loop of information exchanged between neurological systems and the environment. This process is not, therefore, static or predestined. Throughout the life span, developmental changes reflective of age-related stages and differential experiences occur in a fluid way so that the pathway an individual follows can be altered, inadvertently or intentionally.

The field of criminology has concentrated on theories and concepts that revolve around experiential factors, whether they are system-wide, interpersonal, or individual. These theories do not, by nature, exclude the influence of genetic and biological conditions; rather, they simply do not provide a model that would accommodate their consideration. Thus, the next step in research is to address the ever-increasing body of neurobiological research and, subsequently, to fit models together to demonstrate their compatibility and complementary dimensions.

The prevention and treatment implications of this approach are significant: Given that antisocial behaviors tend to be fairly predictable and potentially understandable, they are a viable target for prevention (Patterson et al. 1989). Studies that focus on the interaction between genetic, neurobiological, and social factors further indicate that preventive interventions must be developmentally appropriate given significant changes in protective and vulnerability factors that occur during different stages of life. When researchers understand what underlies and stabilizes antisocial developmental paths, the opportunities for treatment and prevention improve the likelihood of successful alterations of that pathway (Nagin and Farrington 1992).

Shortcomings and Controversies

All fields of research are characterized by shortcomings and controversies, but some are uniquely targeted toward certain disciplines. Shortcomings refer to flaws in the research design, problems with the methods used to measure variables, inappropriate or improperly selected subject population, and misinterpretation of the findings. Controversies that arise from the type of research that is being done or from the way it is conducted usually revolve around social, legal, ethical, or political implications of the results. Both of these negatives must be addressed before the application of findings can proceed, particularly in criminology, where the results can directly affect people's lives.

Many of the "negatives" presented in this essay characterize various types of studies of human behavior and misbehavior in general. But several issues have arisen in response to neurobiological research specifically as a function of attempts to apply genetic and biological tools to the study of criminal behavior. Difficulties in definitions, the use of measurement tools, and interpretations often arise when collaborations are forged across disciplines that are unfamiliar with the techniques, limitations, and research nuances of others. And for reasons that are explained in the following sections, there are philosophical and scientific obstacles to understanding the roots of crime and criminality.

Limitations in Research Methods

Research findings from various behavioral sciences that are relevant to the criminologist must first be evaluated in the context of the conceptual framework and the extent to which it fits with frameworks currently used in criminology. The integrity of a study's findings is limited by the concepts chosen, how they are defined, and the relationships between them that are hypothesized and measured—these activities are the ingredients for a conceptual framework. Interpretations of findings that go beyond this framework are not considered valid and may be simply speculation or extrapolation.

One example related to the concepts selected for study involves the definition that is assigned to the behavior under study. In criminology and neurobiology, concepts often used to study criminal behavior vary widely between studies; and even when the same concept is chosen, it may be defined in different ways or different measurement methods may be employed. For example, surveys that measure aggression by using questions about hostile or negative attitudes do not measure aggressive behavior. Attitudes and behaviors do not reflect the same concept. Thus, it is critical that researchers recognize these differences and refrain from reporting that aggressive behavior is related to some biological trait or social condition when, in reality, only attitudes were measured.

Design of the study must also be appropriate to assess relationships that are hypothesized to exist, and the instruments (e.g., survey, behavioral tasks, etc.) employed to measure the variables must yield data that directly describe the concepts; this is the process of operationalization. This essay examines some of the weaknesses oft-cited in the neurobiological sciences specifically as they are applied to the study of crime, violence, and drug abuse.

Problems with Defining Concepts. When researchers from any discipline, including criminology, attempt to study criminal behavior, definitional problems often arise. But when investigators from other fields study criminal behavior, they may be even more unaware of the difficulties in defining the behaviors they intend to study. Neurobiologists are frequently not familiar with the operation of the criminal justice system (CJS), the plea bargaining process, the diversity of the subject population, and the nature of criminal behavior. The CJS is responsible for "criminalizing" certain behaviors, all of which are illegal by virtue of the label society gives them. But they vary dramatically with respect to the degree of severity, harm to others, and level of dysfunction they cause within the context of the social setting.[2] Focusing on criminal behaviors and crime, then, may really be more about the behavior of the CJS than of the offender. The plea bargaining process further contributes to this confusion because most offenders have the opportunity to "plea down" their charges. As a result, in these common cases, official records of their misconduct may not reflect actual behaviors engaged in during the crime. Or even more misleading, violent charges are sometimes reduced, resulting in convictions for nonviolent crimes. So it becomes unclear whether the researcher is studying violent or nonviolent offenders. If neurobiologists are to study criminal offenders and the CJS reliably and validly, it is critical for the researchers to become familiar with the unique properties of their subjects.

Compounding the study of the dependent variable further is the reality that offenders are not a homogeneous group, even within "crime categories." They vary tremendously with respect to behavioral predispositions and histories, family functioning, social experiences, personality and temperamental traits, and genetic constitutions. Examining the type of crime as the dependent variable completely ignores the diversity of behaviors and relevant traits that may act as contributors, aggravators, or triggers in the criminal behavior.

As a result of unfamiliarity with this population and the system, many investigators choose to focus on crime, criminal behavior, delinquency, violence, and other concepts that are, in large part, socially constructed and a function of the political climate. In other words, use of these concepts as dependent variables ignores the substantial contribution of social institutions and cultural norms to their definitions and to whom they are applied. And in this regard, it ignores the fact that definitions and their applications change over time in response to political movements, cultural events, and large-scale opinion shifts that have nothing to do with behavioral actualities. It is critical that studies concentrate on behavioral phenotypes that can be more reliably measured, can potentially be independently validated, and are not complicated by ever-changing social and systemic processes. Researchers are increasingly recognizing these shortcomings and altering their designs to include behaviors and traits whose definitions are less constructed by social forces, e.g., impulsivity, aggressiveness, sensation-seeking, and anxiety.

Related to these definitional problems, different conceptual and methodological principles are applied across studies, making it difficult to compare and contrast findings. Concepts such as psychopathy, antisocial personality, aggression, and criminal behavior are not consistently defined and measured in various studies. One investigator may use criteria for psychopathy to define antisocial behavior, but another may use the DSM-IV (APA 1997) criteria for Antisocial Personality Disorder. Are they measuring the same construct so that we can compare results across studies? The answer to this question is not always clear.

And finally, because boundaries for biological constructs are not often uniformly identified or operationalized, inconsistencies in findings can occur. Different measures of brain activity and different types of stimuli to evoke physiological responses, while attempting to measure similar constructs, do not produce similar measures and must be differently interpreted. Overall, measurement instruments differ among studies and interpretations of findings are variable.

Problems with Generalizability and Representativeness of Samples. Studies of incarcerated populations present obvious problems regarding the generalizability of findings, that is, the extent to which findings describe similar populations that were not directly studied. In these studies, an observed effect or correlation may be due to the effects of institutionalization rather than to the variable(s) of interest. Many studies that used institutionalized offenders as subjects did not attempt to measure or control for prison conditions and influences. We know, for example, that imprisonment can worsen behavioral problems and possibly further impair cognitive functions. So the question becomes: Which came first, the impairment or the imprisonment?

Also, prisoners are a selective group, and thus their study does not include individuals outside that population who also exhibit the trait of interest. Many offenders have their charges reduced through plea bargaining, as mentioned above. When studying prisoners only, there is no way to document what their crimes may have, in actuality, involved. And what about individuals who engage in the same behaviors but are never caught or are never incarcerated? The important differences between prisoners and other offenders need to be identified.

Many forms of bias in selecting subjects are also evident in some studies. For example, several studies that focused on criminal offenders ignored pervasive illegal and/or maladaptive behaviors in undetected samples. There is a strong possibility that apprehended or incarcerated subjects differ from those who avoid detection in terms of their characteristics and the impact of criminal justice procedures.

Lack of Proper Control Groups. The use of control subjects is, at times, either neglected or inappropriate. A viable comparison group, which is similar to the target group in demographics, risk status, and other relevant features, is essential in scientific research. A control group tells us (a) whether the characteristics of the offenders are unique to that group, (b) the extent to which the subjects differ from the general population, and/or (c) whether changes that occurred over time in the experimental group were in response to an intervention or might have occurred as a result of other factors. The use of control subjects who are not matched to the "clinical" group with respect to demographic characteristics or other relevant factors obscure the findings and make it impossible to compare the groups.

Unreliable Assessment Tools. Confidence in our data and findings comes from knowing that the tools we used to measure relevant variables are valid and reliable. Surveys, including questionnaires and interviews, are notoriously unreliable. They are likely to contain errors in judgment, memory, and truthfulness. On the other hand, they can be used with some acceptable degree of confidence if other measures supplement them; for example, including official reports and surveys together enables us to compare results from each measure and use them to corroborate each other. Behavioral tests are even more reliable, and should be used whenever possible. These tests actually simulate a real-world situation and challenge the subject to behave in response to the task at hand.

The terminology used to describe individuals exhibiting antisocial behavior is also often inexact, confusing, and inconsistent (Blackburn 1988). The literature suggests that offenders do not form a homogeneous group (Eysenck 1977; Hare and Schalling 1978; Raine 1988). Accordingly, reports of neurobiological differences between offenders and nonoffenders have disagreed depending on the definitions and selection criteria used (Devonshire et al. 1988). For these reasons, it is critical that, in addition to relying on self-report and paper-and-pencil measures, assessment tools use standardized criteria, provocative behavioral measures, and an integrated set of variables.

Overreliance on Animal Models. Although the use of animal models to provide direction and a priori hypotheses for human studies is critical, one cannot extrapolate from findings in animals to behavior in humans. Many of us do cite a variety of animal studies when providing support for a relationship that is being proposed between various biological markers and dimensions of antisocial behavior, but they are only informative, not definitive. Using the designs and methods from these animal studies, researchers began to examine human populations exhibiting various forms of psychopathology to determine whether these findings translated from monkeys to humans—we must be careful not to extrapolate from rats and monkeys to humans.

Narrowly Focused Research Parameters. Finally, the majority of so-called multidisciplinary studies have examined only a few variables in isolation; these studies have not accounted for the interactive effects between biological and socioenvironmental conditions. A truly collaborative research project that examines an extensive data set and incorporates the sophisticated methodological and statistical techniques of sociologists holds the promise of yielding more informative results regarding the nature of biosocioenvironmental influences on antisocial behavior.

Biological techniques provide a set of tools for dissecting broadly defined psychological and behavioral concepts such as attention deficits, impulsivity, and aggression, and may provide a reality check against excessive speculation and theory building (Evenden 1999). Nevertheless, there are problems in the way biological techniques can be applied to human subjects, and sometimes neurobiological theories of psychological or psychiatric phenomena lack good support from experimental data and/or animal models, although that issue is less true today. Also, not many biological scientists have adequate knowledge of the unique dimensions, characteristics, and issues that surround studies of criminal offenders. On the other hand, the development of knowledge in the biological sciences is driven by a different set of processes than that in behavioral sciences, and thus there are strong possibilities for progress through cross-fertilization.

Recommendations for Improved Research Designs

Barratt (2000) persuasively argues that there is a profound need for a *neutral interdisciplinary model* for studies on antisocial behaviors. A model of this type would help in the development of an effective mode of communication with other behavioral researchers and promote an understanding of the interactions and relative contributions of social and biological factors. Foremost among the steps necessary to achieve this goal is the creation of adequate and accurate assessments of behavioral phenotypes under study. Controversies over measurement techniques and the behaviors of interest are abundant in human research. For social scientists who study antisocial behavior, the controversy often revolves around whether we are actually studying the behavior of the individual, the criminal justice system, or society at large. For biological scientists, the question is whether we are measuring the behavioral phenotype, the underlying biological response, or the stimulus. An interdisciplinary model would potentially lead to agreed-upon techniques that enable investigators to examine all the interacting variables with a clear definition of what is being studied and what role each one plays in a total social, psychological, and biological environment.

The identification of the appropriate target behaviors for study is critical in creating a neutral model for understanding antisocial behavior.

Emphasis should be placed on the phenotypes or components of antisocial behavior that are measurable, stable, and consistent across cultures, such as aggression, impulsivity, or negative affect. The focus should not be on "crime," which is a legal abstraction, not a behavioral reality. Crime is usually secondary to these and other underlying problems that remain unattended when left unstudied.

Tarter (1998) outlined several research strategies that can be adopted for studies of human antisocial behaviors. These strategies can be viewed as the "next steps" needed to estimate the relative and interactive influences of biological and social factors, and they can determine the extent to which these influences contribute to various dimensions of antisocial behavior and, subsequently, the extent to which interventions can alter liabilities and improve outcomes. Future attempts to identify underlying generators of antisocial behavior must employ sophisticated modern designs and technologies that enable researchers to examine brain function and environmental triggers directly in relation to behavioral outcome.

1. Great precision is necessary to identify subjects who meet criteria for *chronic* antisocial behaviors, selecting for early childhood conduct disorders, persistent aggressiveness, ADHD, negative affect, and early onset of drug use. Single, isolated behaviors are generally a product of a situation rather than a pattern or orientation that may have biological origins. There is an obvious need for further longitudinal studies for wider availability of such subjects. Once subjects have been accurately classified, we can estimate the degree to which neurobiological factors influence offending, relative to and in interaction with social contributions.
2. Real-world conditions can be re-created to some degree within a laboratory setting by introducing a challenge or provocation during the collection of biological measures. Passive or "resting state" conditions do not generate the sorts of physiological and biochemical responses that are often associated with antisocial behavior.
3. To begin to tease out the relative influences of genetics and the environment, a concerted effort must be made to examine social and environmental experiences of subjects with greater care than most studies do at present. For example, the collection of genetically informative groups, such as twins and adoptive children,

permits estimates of relative gene-environment contributions. Molecular genetic approaches, on the other hand, assess static variations in neurotransmitter function; they carry the potential to identify precise brain mechanisms that characterize antisocial behavior. Used in combination with rigorous measures of socio-environmental influences, these contemporary techniques hold great promise for an integrated science.

4. To understand brain-environmental relationships, their underlying mechanisms, and ability to change them, the following questions must be answered:

   A. How can we assess environmental-neurobiological influences and then design interventions that impact at critical points in an individual's development to alter risk status?
   B. If the genetic complement and biological conditions set the stage for responses to information from the environment, can environmental interventions change the behavioral outcome?
   C. Can the environment be altered to improve brain function?
   D. And will the behavioral outcome of this impact be sufficiently measurable?

Controversial Issues

Critics of incorporating neurobiological findings into criminology research worry that, in looking for criminal predispositions, researchers rely on oversimplified views of genetic and biological influences and of criminal behavior. Critics also worry that even if this research is focused entirely on individuals and is apolitical on its face, it will be publicly perceived as supporting racial stereotypes and justifying repressive social policies. At the same time, some of the opposition to the research arises from a concern that these studies may be used in efforts to establish racial differences in genetic predisposition or to justify conservative programs of social control.

The issues that arise in discussions of biological mechanisms in criminal behavior fall into two categories: philosophical and scientific problems; and social, moral and ethical implications of the research findings.

Philosophical and Scientific Concerns. The philosophical and scientific issues that arise with this research involve, first, the potential that claims will be made for causal relationships between biology and crime. These problems raise questions about the ways in which the brain interacts with the physical and social environment. Which is a more powerful influence on our behavior—our biology or the environment? Does the social setting and our experiences change brain function and, subsequently, alter our perceptions of reality? Or does the brain determine how we respond to information from the environment and, perhaps, in turn alter the nature of information we receive from the environment? These questions all come to mind in debates regarding environment-biology interactions.

There are also fears about the prospects for explaining voluntary actions in terms of neurobiological processes. This is called biological reductionism, or reducing human behavior to the basic biological components and drives that motivate us. To what extent do we have the free will to choose our actions and determine our fate? Many who oppose this research fear that an understanding of brain function and genetic conditions may compromise our conception of what it is to be human, make decisions, and be responsible for our behaviors. Our criminal justice system is based on notions of free will, as are all the institutions within our society. Thus, determinism of any sort—environmental determinants or biological determinants—has been rejected in favor of voluntary actions.

Third, opponents of this research are concerned about the possibility of finding biological predispositions to behaviors that are, in essence, socially defined. For example, if a biological "cause" for violence is discovered, then would that invalidate all sorts of violent behavior? What about violence during war or as a defense or as the function of an intolerable political situation? Violence is largely a socially constructed concept that changes in response to political shifts, social trends, and legal responses. If a biological condition were found to explain violence, that would assume that violence is a static, cross-culturally defined phenomenon, which it is not.

Social, Moral, and Ethical Implications. The other set of issues concerns the social, moral, and ethical implications of research on biology and crime. Critics and proponents of this research set it against the backdrop of two very different legacies. On the one hand, humanity has a long, dark history of "discovering" sources of inferiority in certain individuals or groups, then of using the "discovery" to justify gross inequalities and coercive social programs. On the other hand, it has been a sign of progress and enlightenment to recognize that undesirable traits and behaviors often arise from biological or psychiatric problems rather than moral defects, and to offer humane treatments rather than to impose harsh punishments. Legal, ethical, and political obstacles to the acceptance and application of biological and medical information by the CJS are covered extensively elsewhere (Fishbein and Thatcher 1991; Jeffery 1985; Marsh and Katz 1985).

At the very least, care must be taken not to stigmatize or otherwise traumatize individuals or groups that are, as yet, innocent of a criminal or civil violation. As researchers, we must avoid applying labels to behaviors we do not fully understand. Even in the event that biological measures are shown to be reliable and valid predictors of behavior and mental status, several serious civil rights and constitutional issues demand careful consideration. What if we were able to identify individuals early in life who are at risk for antisocial behavior? Are we obligated to intervene—to provide an effective treatment? Do we mandate treatment? In cases in which a conviction is upheld, for example, forced compliance with a prevention or treatment regimen might result from findings that a biological abnormality played a role in an individual's antisocial behavior. In the absence of a proven violation of law, such forced compliance would raise some eyebrows in most societies. One must recognize the numerous legal and ethical concerns generated by such a strategy. To avoid these difficulties, a collaborative, multidisciplinary approach might be forged strictly to identify underlying sources of antisocial behaviors and minimize their occurrence in the population through a public health and mental health approach. Before someone has committed an offense, it is critical that the CJS does not become involved in detection or intervention efforts.

And the Debate Continues . . . Advocates of this research hope that its findings will be used to prevent crime and violence by recognizing the warning signs and intervening before its onset; in this way, potential perpetrators and potential victims alike will benefit. Critics fear that the research will lead to large-scale neglect and abuse. Its actual or reported findings may convince legislators that social and economic reforms are doomed to failure because they attempt to apply social solutions to a biological problem. Critics also believe that viewing crime as a medical problem to be treated, rather than as a response to oppressive social and economic conditions or as a matter of individual choice, may result in policies that are patronizing, disrespectful, and highly coercive. On the other hand, advocates argue that if we continue to examine only 50 percent of the equation (the social causes), then we will continue to mistreat the problem and support programs that have very low success rates.

Critics argue vehemently that biological research must be seen in the context of our racial history and racist attitudes. In our society, research that links criminal behavior to biological features may be mistakenly seen as implicating the African American community and contribute to its stigmatization. Many Americans see violent crime as a minority problem, in part because of the disproportionate number of African Americans in prison, and in part because of deep prejudices that make violent crime seem more characteristic of blacks than whites. Defenders of the research, however, deny that it must be captive to our racial history, and they argue that it will ultimately do far more to *alleviate* than to exacerbate racial tensions. Because this research focuses on biological deviations and adverse social circumstances that trigger the expression of existing vulnerabilities, it may highlight the profound impact that adverse environmental factors can have. More specifically, two hundred years or more of racial discrimination has resulted in the relegation of a large proportion of our African American citizens to impoverished and underserved communities. Nowhere do we see a greater concentration of "environmental triggers" and adversity than in these neighborhoods, and they contribute in substantial ways to maladaptive behaviors, irrespective of genetic or biological traits. Thus, we may eventually be able to concentrate on and alleviate those social problems that are differentially and disproportionately distributed throughout our society and that trigger underlying vulnerabilities and lead to an increased prevalence of various behavioral disorders (see David Wasserman's [University of Maryland] discussion from the 1995 Genetics and Crime conference in Maryland).

No study or body of research is without criticism. This reasoning does not excuse us from acknowledging these deficiencies or from attempting to rectify them. Instead, it reveals that in spite of the tremendous strides we have taken to understand human behavior, there is still much left unanswered and equivocal. It is clear, even so, that when we are able to break down disciplinary boundaries and work together in teams that represent many perspectives and technical skills, the answers will become more accessible.

Practical and Policy Implications

There is a growing awareness that if we begin to increase multidisciplinary research on antisocial behaviors, the strength and effectiveness of criminal justice (CJ) interventions will be substantially enhanced. To form a scientific and empirical foundation for emerging CJ policies and practices, it is critical that researchers incorporate findings from various subdisciplines within the behavioral sciences. Because CJ practitioners and scholars are instrumental in the design and implementation of criminal justice practices and policies, their involvement, familiarity, and scrutiny are critical to the field's development. Teams of researchers from relevant disciplines and practitioners from correctional and clinical settings can engage in a unique and powerful exchange between theory, empirical research, and practice.

For antisocial behavior to be understood, treated, and prevented, our beliefs about why certain behaviors occur and the rationale for the techniques we use should be backed by scientific evidence. Science must provide the bases for the development of effective treatment, prevention, and policy strategies. The fields of criminology and criminal justice are devoted to the study of human behavior and the "control" of antisocial behaviors that harm others. Findings within the behavioral sciences suggest that "control" is best achieved through effective means of preventing and treating those characteristics that underlie antisocial behaviors. Thus, an understanding of underlying mechanisms will lead to more effective and research-based targeted interventions.

Enhancing the Rigor of Assessments and Treatments

One overriding practical goal of this research is to develop assessment tools that can be readily used within correctional and clinical settings to identify individuals at high risk for various antisocial behaviors. Biological vulnerabilities, in interaction with adverse social conditions, may underlie these behaviors and are more prevalent within offender populations. Using multivariate assessment instruments, offenders can be triaged or subtyped on the basis of underlying disorders for targeted treatments. Because offenders who do not respond to conventional treatments often possess underlying susceptibilities, are subject to adverse social conditions that compound their problems, and are particularly at risk for persistent serious criminality and substance abuse, this subgroup requires more intensive and customized approaches. Accordingly, offenders will be better equipped to maintain control over their own behavior instead of requiring severe methods of external restraint that are terminated when they are released.

Treatment efforts that focus on the underlying mechanisms in antisocial behaviors will more likely succeed in reversing or redirecting these behavioral outcomes. Successful regimens attempt to make a comprehensive identification of the unique underlying mechanisms in an individual's antisocial behavior and may employ a combination of pharmaceutical, behavioral, cognitive, and family therapies. Nevertheless, although a clinical approach to treatment and prevention may be achieved with the knowledge of individual risks and vulnerabilities, global prevention and intervention programs that increase resiliency to prevailing risk factors in a population can now be implemented. Building safety nets, providing resources for those without opportunities, increasing the availability of alternative modes of behavior, revitalizing neighborhoods, assembling multidisciplinary teams to intervene, and enhancing community involvement could have an immediate impact on the problem by providing some protection for those who are particularly "vulnerable." Manipulations of the social environment may profoundly alter an individual's biological stamina, possibly improving impulse control and coping mechanisms.

Prospective Applications

Clinical approaches, based on the medical or mental health models, hold the most promise for the eventual application of treatments that result from biological and genetic research, with an understanding that they must be, for the most part, individualized and consented to by the "patient." Unfortunately, however, only those who are economically and opportunistically privileged in our society have access to clinical settings. Those who are less privileged face a variety of system-wide conditions that serve to deny them access, and they are often relegated to the criminal justice system instead. Although the criminal justice system has a notorious reputation for doling out tranquilizers and mood stabilizers, these medications have custodial (i.e., maintenance and security), not therapeutic, purposes. Cases with biomedical involvement, possibly genetic in origin, could instead be managed by the mental health system; within that system, those deemed dangerous could be held in secure facilities.

Clinicians may eventually be able to identify individuals at risk if they are armed with the knowledge of social, biological, and genetic traits that increase risk. With this information, more effective interventions, earlier in developmental stages, can be provided. Children will be better equipped to overcome disadvantages, social or genetic, and to reach their potential. Adults will be better equipped to maintain control over their own behavior rather than requiring external restraints such as jail or mental institutions. Research consistently indicates that far fewer crimes are committed when individuals are actively in treatment than when they do not receive treatment (see Fishbein 1991; Fishbein and Pease 1996). For drug users in particular, the length of treatment is negatively related to crime and drug use. If treatments or alternatives remain unavailable and ineffective, individuals at risk will likely continue to fall through the cracks.

The application of a clinical approach requires that legal professionals and ethicists scrutinize the research and create statutes to guide its application. The likelihood of abuse is greater if such research is not made public and regulated. Consent and compliance are also pertinent issues and related questions must be answered by legal scholars and ethicists before research influences policy. Can we enforce compliance with treatment? Will coercive treatments be effective? Many argue that treatment is much more humane than the techniques we currently resort to, including incarceration, solitary confinement, capital punishment, or even neglect for underlying precursors. We do not presently require consent for punishment or even execution. To what extent do we require consent for treatment? These questions must be addressed before we proceed.

The Public Health Approach

The public health model, which orchestrates global primary prevention programs aimed at populations at risk, stands in contrast to the medical approach. Based on the notion that interpersonal violence is a public health problem (Rosenberg and Mercy 1986), wide-scale manipulations may be implemented to prevent the development of a problem and to lessen the toll in illness, death, and quality of life without stigmatization. "The key to prevention may lie in greater understanding of the behavioral components that contribute to violence" (Spivak et al. 1988, 1341). One indicated public health approach would be to provide readily available prenatal care, particularly to populations without ready access to medical care. A public health approach strives to insulate vulnerable individuals from the effects of a criminogenic, high-risk environment and to increase resiliency by building safety nets and resources in a community. Such strategies are proposed to work regardless of the origins of behavior.

Contrary to popular belief, biological and genetic traits are not static and unchangeable; they can be altered in a social environment conducive to change. Thus, theoretically, large-scale social programs can lead to behavioral improvements, even in cases where the propensities are genetically influenced, by minimizing the impact of an environment that would otherwise be conducive to antisocial behavior.

Educational, social, economic, and behavioral programs all minimize the impact of an environment and a biological constitution conducive to antisocial behavior. Adverse interactions in the home such as physical abuse, parental absenteeism, and poor disciplinary practices exacerbate the child's innate liability to behavioral disorders. Also, association with peers who promote antisocial behavior is related to the combined influence of an innate negative affect and deficient parental monitoring. These findings indicate how, among high-risk individuals, adverse interactions with the social environment can leave the child at greater risk for a negative outcome. The quality of interaction between the person having a particular biological disposition and the social environment that determines the behavior response patterns and emotional reactions should be the focus of interventions.

Although the potential benefits are apparent, the public health approach also raises civil liberties issues pertaining to rights of privacy, freedom from unwanted disclosures, and ethical considerations concerning the wide-scale medical and social surveillance of select populations (Rosenfeld and Decker 1993). Such interventions may extend services to those who do not want them, have the potential to further victimize underprivileged classes, and may compromise personal freedoms (Hawkins 1989; Kittrie 1971; Marx 1985). Adverse consequences must be minimized by providing necessary safeguards for personal rights and liberties. On the other hand, "what rights and liberties [do the] beneficiaries of violence prevention programs currently enjoy [?]." Many of those "who would be directly affected by the interventions" cannot safely walk the streets and have already had many basic legal rights curtailed because they are under the control of the

CJS. "The issue . . . then, may not be whether their freedom will be endangered by violence prevention programs, but how such programs might improve their lives while they are under custody and reduce their risk for violence after they are released" (Rosenfeld and Decker 1993, 31–32).

Special Issues for the Criminal Justice System

Unlike other disciplines, results of research on offenders can have direct implications for the management and control of antisocial individuals. There are concerns in the field that neurobiological findings could lead to inappropriate or involuntary medical treatment in the criminal justice system and the possibility that individuals who are at high risk, but have not yet engaged in criminal behavior, may be prematurely targeted for these control measures. Hypocritically, however, tactics of the present criminal justice system that routinely incarcerates (with racial prejudice) the mentally ill and drug addicts who are desperately in need of treatment, not incarceration, have not been effectively challenged. Moreover, rather than intervening in cases where children's rights are visibly being violated (e.g., abuse or neglect) or special needs remain unattended (learning disabilities)—conditions known to increase risk for delinquency—society customarily waits until their problems have compounded and they are old enough to be incarcerated. Treatment of individuals with similar behavior problems in a clinical setting demonstrates that effective methods are available in many cases (see Fishbein 1999). It is considered malpractice to withhold effective treatment in the medical field, a dictate in marked contrast to practices of the criminal justice system. Treatments of many varieties, when appropriately dispensed, increase individual self-control rather than require the external restraints of the criminal justice system.

Criminal justice policies must be based on well-founded theories and findings that survive scientific scrutiny. The application of scientific findings to criminal justice programs that are well recognized and accepted by the discipline have more value than trial and error approaches in preventing or minimizing antisocial behavior. Although biological techniques in the assessment of human behavior are still under the microscope and definitive answers have yet to surface, the foregoing description of neurobiological foundations for behavior provides evidence of their applicability and value. By undertaking a collaborative strategy, we can develop more effective prevention and therapeutic programs as well as a legal system that reflects public consensus, meets human needs, and maintains an ethical and organized social structure.

E. O. Wilson, a leading figure in evolutionary approaches to the study of behavior, and one of the most distinguished scientific thinkers of our time, argues persuasively in favor of integration between the physical and social sciences by linking them with a single overarching theory (see Wilson 1998). As disciplines converge, he argues, we will develop the ability to solve many of the world's most dire problems. "Most of the issues that vex humanity daily—ethnic conflict, arms escalation, overpopulation, abortion, environment, endemic poverty, to cite several most persistently before us—cannot be solved without integrating knowledge from the natural sciences with that of the social sciences and humanities." Not coincidentally (nor inclusively), many of these problems contribute in substantial ways to antisocial behavior, from violent criminal offending to white collar crime. Bridging the sciences will yield answers to questions that have eluded the field of criminology for decades. As a result, practices and programs that incorporate findings linking environmental stressors to biological impacts and vice versa are likely to produce improvements in the integrity of social, psychosocial, and biological mechanisms. And more important, perhaps conclusions drawn from interdisciplinary research will promote the creation of socioenvironmental conditions that are more sensitive to basic human needs and, accordingly, conducive to prosocial behavior.

Summary and Conclusions

Biological and genetic research highlights the important role of the environment in modulating social and genetic instigators and can inform us of the value of primary prevention and public health strategies to curb antisocial behavior and violence. Interventions that are primarily social and educational can be employed to enhance environmental and biological insulators, as suggested above. It is not necessary to wait for biological and genetic research to demonstrate definitive causal influences. We have known for decades which social forces are protective against social and genetic risks and have neglected to provide adequate funding for programs that will provide insulation.

Conducting biological and genetic research does not excuse us from supporting social programs, particularly given the ability of social approaches to affect behavior positively no matter what the origins. Nevertheless, interdisciplinary research is crucial if we are ever to provide needed services and treatments for individuals with compelling biological and genetic disadvantages. Studies suggest that a subgroup of our population suffers from biological and genetic vulnerabilities that overwhelm the influence of any environment. Not only do these individuals stand to benefit greatly from the research, but the public may eventually give way to more tolerance of behavioral aberrations by understanding that behavior is not entirely volitional at all times in all individuals. Instead of waiting until a vulnerable child becomes old enough to be incarcerated, perhaps early assistance will enable us to avoid the personal and financial expense of criminal justice system involvement. There is little evidence that present tactics are effective; thus, we need to move forward into an era of early intervention and compassionate treatment that neurobiological research may help to advance.

Notes

1. A thorough description of neurobiological research in criminology and discussion of relevant issues can be found in Fishbein (2001).

2. Some social settings are more challenging than others and are more likely to lead to criminal behaviors for survival purposes—they may not be actually maladaptive or dysfunctional.

References

American Psychiatric Association. 1997. *Diagnostic and Statistical Manual of Mental Disorders*. Washington, D.C.: American Psychiatric Association Press.

Barratt, E. S., A. Felthous, T. Kent, M. J. Liebman, and D. D. Coates. 2000. "Criterion Measures of Aggression—Impulsive Versus Premeditated Aggression." In *The Science Treatment and Prevention of Antisocial Behavior,* edited by D. Fishbein. Kingston, New Jersey: Civic Research Institute.

Blackburn, R. 1988. "On Moral Judgements and Personality Disorders: The Myth of Psychopathic Personality Revisited." *British Journal of Psychiatry* 153: 505–512.

Bock, G. R., and J. A. Goode. 1996. "Genetics of Criminal and Antisocial Behaviour." *Ciba Foundation Symposium* 194. New York: John Wiley.

Devonshire, P. A., R. C. Howard, and C. Sellars. 1988. "Frontal Lobe Functions and Personality in Mentally Abnormal Offenders." *Personality and Individual Differences* 9: 339–344.

Evenden, J. L. 1996. "Varieties of Impulsivity." *Psychopharmacology* 146: 348–361.

Eysenck, H. J. 1977. *Crime and Personality*. Rev. ed. London: Routledge and Kegan Paul.

Fishbein, Diane H. 1991. "Medicalizing the Drug War." *Behavioral Sciences and the Law* 9: 323–344.

______. 1999. *The Science Treatment and Prevention of Antisocial Behavior: Applications to the Criminal Justice System*. New York: Civic Research Institute.

______. 2000. "Sexual Preference, Crime and Punishment." *Women and Criminal Justice* 11: 67–84.

______. 2001. *Biobehavioral Perspectives in Criminology*. Belmont, Calif.: Wadsworth.

______ 2004. *The Science Treatment and Prevention of Antisocial Behavior*. Vol. 2. New York: Civic Research Institute.

Fishbein, D. H., and S. Pease. 1996. *The Dynamics of Drug Abuse*. Boston: Allyn and Bacon.

Fishbein D. H., and R. W. Thatcher. 1990. "Legal Applications of Electrophysiological Assessments." In *Neuropsychology and the Law*, edited by J. Dywan, R. Kaplan, and F. Pirozzolo (pp. 135–163). New York: Springer-Verlag.

Hare, R., and D. Schalling. 1978. *Psychopathic Behaviour*. New York: John Wiley.

Hawkins, D. 1989. "Intentional Injury: Are There No Solutions?" *Law Medicine and Health Care* 17: 32–41.

Hillbrand, M., and N. J. Pallone. 1993. *The Psychobiology of Aggression: Engines, Measurement, Control*. New York: The Haworth Press.

Jeffery, C. R. 1985. *Attacks on the Insanity Defense: Biological Psychiatry and New Perspectives on Criminal Behavior*. Springfield, Ill.: Charles C. Thomas.

Kittrie, N. 1971. *The Right to Be Different: Deviance and Enforced Therapy*. Baltimore: Johns Hopkins University Press.

Marsh, F. H., and J. Katz, eds. 1985. *Biology, Crime and Ethics: A Study of Biological Explanations for Criminal Behavior*. Cincinnati: Anderson.

Marx, G. 1985. "I'll be Watching You." *Dissent* (Winter): 6–34.

Moffitt, T. E. 1997. "Neuropsychology, Antisocial Behavior, and Neighborhood Context." In *Violence and Child in the Inner City*, edited by J. McCord. Cambridge: Cambridge University Press.

Nagin, D. S., and D. P. Farrington. 1992. "The Stability of Criminal Potential from Childhood to Adulthood." *Criminology* 30: 235–260.

Niehoff, D. 1999. *The Biology of Violence*. New York: Free Press.

Pallone, N. J., and J. J. Hennessy. 1996. *Tinder Box Criminal Aggression: Neuropsychology, Demography, Phenomenology*. New Jersey: Transaction.

Patterson, G. R., B. D. DeBaryshe, and E. Ramsey. 1989. "Developmental Perspective on Antisocial Behavior." *American Psychologist* 44: 329–335.

Raine, A. 1988. "Psychopathy: A Single or Dual Concept?" *Personality and Individual Differences* 9: 825–827.

______. 1993. *The Psychopathology of Crime: Criminal Behavior as a Clinical Disorder.* New York: Academic Press.

Raine, A., P. A. Brennan, D. P. Farrington, and S. A. Mednick. 1997. *Biosocial Bases of Violence*. New York: Plenum Press.

Raine, A., and J. Liu. 1998. "Biological Predispositions to Violence and Their Implications for Biosocial Treatment and Prevention." *Psychology, Crime and Law* 4: 107–125.

Reiss, A. J., Jr., K. A. Miczek, and J. A. Roth. 1994. *Understanding and Preventing Violence*. Vol. 2, *Biobehavioral Influences*. Washington, D.C.: National Academy Press.

Rosenberg, M. L., and J. A. Mercy. 1986. "Homicide: Epidemiologic Analysis at the National Level." *Bulletin of the New York Academy of Medicine* 62: 376–399.

Rowe, D. C., C. Stever, J. M. Gard, H. H. Cleveland, M. L. Sanders, A. Abramowitz, S. T. Kozol, J. H. Mohr, S. L. Sherman, and I. D. Waldman. 1998a. "The Relation of the Dopamine Transporter Gene (DAT1) to Symptoms of Internalizing Disorders in Children." *Behavioral Genetics* 28: 215–225.

Rowe, D. C., C. Stever, L. N. Giedinghagen, J. M. C. Gard, H. Cleveland, S. T. Terris, J. H. Mohr, S. Sherman, A. Abramowitz, and I. D. Waldman. 1998b. "Dopamine DRD4 Receptor Polymorphism and Attention Deficit Hyperactivity Disorder." *Molecular Psychiatry* 3: 419–426.

Spivak H., D. Prothrow-Stith, and A. J. Hausman. 1988. "Dying Is No Accident. Adolescents, Violence, and Intentional Injury." *Pediatric Clinics of North America* 35: 1339–1347.

Tarter, R., and M. Vanyukov. 1994. "Alcoholism: A Developmental Disorder." *Journal of Consulting and Clinical Psychology* 62: 1096–1107.

Tarter, R., E. H. Moss, T. Blackson, M. Vanyukov, J. Brigham, and R. Loeber. 1998. "Disaggregating the Liability for Drug Abuse." *NIDA Research Monograph* 169: 227–243.

Volavka, J. 1995. *Neurobiology of Violence*. Washington, D.C.: American Psychiatric Press.

Wilson, E. O. 1998. *Consilience*. New York: Knopf.

3

Psychological Theories

Another scientific search for the cause of crime involves the study of the mind: how we think, how we process and react to inputs (visual, emotional, and cognitive information), and how the physical brain affects our cognitive processes. This constellation of theorizing is categorized as psychological explanations for criminal behavior. Psychological theories of crime explain abnormal behavior, of which crime is one category, as the result of mind and thought processes that form during human development.

Psychological thinking about crime has appeared in various forms, beginning with ideas about the mind that seek to show how individuals are different from each other. People have different personalities that produce variations in behavior, some of which is abnormal and some antisocial. Personalities are formed through socialization and developmental processes, particularly during the early years of childhood, that involve a series of mental, moral, and sexual stages. When this developmental process is abnormal or subject to traumatic events, personality disorders and psychological disturbances may become part of the individual's personality characteristics, or they may be constructed as an appropriate behavioral response under a particular set of emerging circumstances. Psychologists who look for differences in personality types rely heavily on scales, inventories, and questionnaires to identify and classify the differences between individuals who suffer from psychological disturbances and those who do not. Because what is "normal" must be differentiated from what is "pathological," measurement is thus a critical component.

As technology has advanced, so has the study of human behavior and the brain and how the brain integrates information from various senses and constructs meaning. Psychologists and psychiatrists have shown how humans learn, how emotions play a role in our behavior, and how chemicals, diet, hormones, and other substances affect our thoughts and subsequent behavioral patterns. Each of these factors has been applied to the study of crime, or, more specifically, to the behavior of those we classify as criminal.

Another significant component of the psychological approach to crime is the examination of how people are socialized into conformity or nonconformity during the developmental process. Just as personalities are formed in a variety of ways, so is behavior. Behavior is learned from rewards and punishments and from social learning by observing, that is, the behavior of others is modeled, including that of media images.

More recently, psychologists have taken the view that antisocial behavior is the result not of the personality and learning alone but of an interaction between a person's propensities, learning, and environmental and situational context. Here criminal or antisocial behavior is the outcome of an interactive process that develops over time. For example, social or environmental factors may trigger erratic or criminal behavior in those psychologically predisposed, and they may have developed particular learned scripts and thinking patterns that respond to certain situations, such as frustration, or barriers to achievement, that are antisocial as well as destructive to others and themselves.

Because criminal behaviors are influenced by environmental triggers and are seen to stem from abnormal developmental processes affecting the mind, some form of psychological treatment intervention is necessary to correct or to counteract those exhibiting criminal predispositions. Psychologists aim to change the process whereby these personalities are formed, to manipulate the conditions that might trigger antisocial behavior, and to correct thinking patterns that lead to antisocial behavior.

Moreover, criminal justice agencies employ some aspect of psychology. For example, all police recruits undergo psychological screening; the FBI has a behavioral unit and develops psychological profiles of offenders and terrorists. Some crimes are not "punished" but "treated" according to the psychological state of the defendant and, even while being incarcerated, many inmates are offered training in such therapies as anger management. As techniques and scientific aids improve, so will the role of psychology.

3.1

Forty Years of the Yochelson/Samenow Work

A Perspective

STANTON E. SAMENOW
Alexandria, Virginia

In 1970, two years after receiving a doctorate in clinical psychology from the University of Michigan, I joined Samuel Yochelson, a psychiatrist and psychologist, in his Program for the Investigation of Criminal Behavior located in Washington, D.C., at St. Elizabeths Hospital. Dr. Yochelson already had been working for nine years to understand the mental makeup of offenders and to develop a program that would help the participants become responsible adults. Serving as clinical research psychologist, I collaborated with Dr. Yochelson in what turned out to be a seventeen-year research-treatment study of career criminals. On his first trip out of town to speak about his work, Dr. Yochelson collapsed in the St. Louis airport and later died on November 12, 1976, at a nearby hospital.

Shortly after his death, CBS News's 60 *Minutes* broadcast a segment on our work during which Morley Safer reported that we had found that criminals, not the environment, cause crime, that there are patterns of thinking common to all hardcore criminals regardless of their backgrounds, and that Dr. Yochelson had developed a program whereby some criminals gave up crime, changed their thinking, and became responsible people.

Approximately 18 million people watched this program; in the aftermath, interest in our work became widespread. Volumes 1 and 2 of *The Criminal Personality* were published during 1976 and 1977 (the third volume not until 1987), enabling professionals to learn in detail what our work was all about (Yochelson and Samenow 1976; 1977; 1987). I received invitations to present the work to corrections, mental health, and law enforcement professionals; social workers; and educators. Later, interest was expressed by attorneys, judges, clergymen, educators, and substance abuse counselors.

The findings of the study were highly controversial, largely because they ran counter to pervasive thinking in the United States about the causes of crime. For decades, a deterministic view held sway. The prevailing thinking was (and still is in many quarters) that people are influenced or forced into crime by poverty, divorce, abusive parents, peer pressure, and other environmental factors. We found this not to be so. More critical than specific environmental factors is how human beings choose to deal with the environment in which they find themselves. Virtually every man in our study had at least one sibling who had overcome adversity or, at least, had responded to it without victimizing others. Critics deemed our work unscientific; they claimed we had taken a tiny sample housed in a psychiatric facility and generalized our findings about these inmates to speak about all criminals. They pointed out that we did not follow a scientific method and that we lacked a control group. And there was a polemic decrying our work as reflecting an opinion, not a real study.

If one looks at what Dr. Yochelson did, his work is comparable to what Sigmund Freud accomplished with neurotic patients. Freud had no experimental design. He did not operate by a strict scientific method complete with carefully formulated hypotheses and a control group. Freud was a student of the mind, and so was Yochelson. Plowing new ground, Yochelson used to say that he was engaged in a "search," not a "re-search." During his years of patiently searching for facts and of meticulously recording his findings (there were thousands of pages of dictated notes), he came to a new understanding of how criminals think instead of proving what he already thought to be true. It was a hypothesis-generating study rather than a hypothesis-proving study.

Samuel Yochelson abandoned the concepts and approaches that he had used successfully during decades of psychiatric practice in Buffalo, New York. This occurred gradually as he discovered that he was dealing with people radically different from his Buffalo patients, most of whom sought his help.

The assertion that we were voicing an opinion rather than reporting conclusions objectively arrived at suggested that we had proved nothing at all, only reinforced what we already believed. Nothing could be further from the truth. Chapter 1 of volume 1 of *The Criminal Personality* is titled "The Reluctant Converts." This referred not to the men in our study, but to ourselves—how reluctant we were to lead our sacred cows to pasture and slaughter them. Dr. Yochelson and I were psychoanalytically oriented by training. We were constantly confounded by what we were learning while engaged in a study of men for whom crime had been a way of life—murder, arson, rape, larceny, assault, and so forth.

We did not have a control group. What kind of control group would have made sense? Ours was a method of amassing clinical data and subjecting it to a content analysis that yielded core concepts and basic themes.

Then there was the contention that our subject base was far too narrow, that we had generalized from a group of patients who were in a hospital because they had been declared legally insane. The study was of 250 men. Approximately half were St. Elizabeths' patients and "not guilty by reason of insanity" (NGRI). The rest never were hospitalized for psychiatric disorders. They came to us through criminal justice, social service, and other agencies. Participating in the study were men who had committed hundreds of crimes but had never been convicted of one. They were referred to the program by noncriminal justice sources, and a few were referred by their own families upon hearing about our work.

Some critics were vociferously critical because they were wedded to a particular view of criminals and crime. Others had never read our work but, nonetheless, formed opinions and were vitriolic in their attacks. In the mid-1970s, cognitive work had not taken hold as firmly as it would later. We were accused of brainwashing, and our approach was compared to the notorious methods depicted in the classic Stanley Kubrick film *A Clockwork Orange*.

No sinister methods to force compliance were employed. Dr. Yochelson did not prescribe drugs; nor did he participate in administrative decisions or judicial proceedings that concerned participants in the study. In fact, to minimize any attempts the men might make to manipulate him, he avoided playing dual roles.

We were also accused of trying to impose our moral values while working with offenders. Our critics failed to consider that people from virtually all walks of life oppose stealing, murder, and other heinous acts by which innocent people suffer. Being moral is hardly synonymous with being white or middle class. How does one work with criminals and not take a moral stance?

Writers and commentators in the media have characterized me as conservative, tough on crime. This is because, rather than being an environmental determinist, I have emphasized the role of personal choice as contributing to criminal behavior. It is important in understanding who the criminal is not to confuse the victimizer with the victim. When held accountable, criminals often blame circumstances. And, if they don't come up with enough excuses for crime on their own, mental health and other professionals supply more.

A distortion consistent with portraying me as a conservative has been the assertion that I regard the environment as irrelevant to understanding criminals and crime. I have long stated that the environment can make it easier or more difficult to commit and get away with crimes by the presence or absence of deterrents. If firearms are easy to obtain, most people will not use them. If the criminal can readily have access to a gun, he may seek revenge in a more lethal manner than he would if the gun were not at hand. The issue is not the presence of the gun, but the psychological makeup of the user. Were a gun not available to a criminal, he'd use a different weapon.

Conservatives have claimed that I am a dewy-eyed liberal because I continue to advance the proposition that offenders can change and should be afforded that opportunity. After spending thirty-five years in this field, I continue to state what should be obvious—that every man, woman, and child who is locked up today eventually will be released, exceptions being inmates on death row or serving life sentences with no possibility of parole. Once the individual returns to the community, the criminal mind functions as it did before confinement and during incarceration. Therefore, it is in society's interest to find more effective ways to help offenders change.

Some critics dismissed our work out of hand by asserting that there is no such entity as a "criminal mind"—that under sufficiently adverse circumstances anyone can become a criminal. Although hypothetically this may be so, in reality this contention is glib and absurd. Men and women suffer through terrible adversities but cope with them constructively, even heroically. Consider a person laid off from his job whose family depends on his wages. Some unemployed workers become depressed, anxious, or resentful. Others become determined to do whatever they must to find a new job as quickly as possible. It takes a particular sort of mind to plot revenge and return to one's former place of employment and retaliate by shooting one's former supervisor. A significant difference exists between the psychological makeup of a person who struggles to improve his situation and that of an individual who focuses on proving that he will have ultimate control and prevail in any situation, no matter what the cost to others.

The youngster with the incipient criminal personality reacts to consequences differently from his responsible counterpart. Every boy who steals a candy bar does not become a one-man crime wave. For most young first-time shoplifters who are caught and punished, that is the end of the thievery. Not so for others, who conclude that the next time they need to be slicker to avoid detection.

Dr. Yochelson identified the "errors in thinking" that we all make from time to time. The individual who is extreme in these thinking errors pursues excitement by doing the forbidden and builds himself up at the expense of others. Human relationships are seen by these people as avenues for conquest and triumph. Any means to self-serving ends, including deception, intimidation, and brute force, are employed without considering the impact on others.

In critiquing our work, some people have professed that criminality is defined by laws, and thus the definition of a crime is relative. One can be a criminal today but not tomorrow if the laws change. However, the work I have been part of for all these years is not about laws but about minds! The men in the St. Elizabeths Hospital study, and hundreds of my clients since, would be "criminals" no matter what the laws, mores, or social customs. They have the mentality of the rapist who asserted, "If rape were legalized today, I wouldn't rape, but I'd do something else." For such an individual, to be "somebody" in life is to do whatever is forbidden. "Take my crime away, and you take my work away," declared one offender, citing what was most central to his life.

With the publication of *Inside the Criminal Mind* (Samenow 1984), this work became available to a much larger audience than the one that had plowed through the thousand pages of the first two volumes of *The Criminal Personality*. By 1984, I had been giving workshops throughout North America to professionals working with adult and juvenile offenders. I was hearing anecdotally from workers in the trenches (professionals who deal with criminals every day) that focusing on "errors in thinking" had a strong and positive impact on offenders. Moreover, one did not have to have a Ph.D. or an M.D. to do this work effectively. The concepts were clear. Errors of thinking and obstructive tactics were readily observable.

A hazard of developing a new approach is learning of its misuse. I recall a corrections worker asking, "Don't you have to be a psychopath yourself to do this work?" The notion was that one must out-manipulate the manipulator. Nothing could be further from the truth. One irresponsible person cannot teach another to function responsibly.

An initially dismaying distortion was that the Yochelson-Samenow approach is devoid of compassion, that it is "hardline" and unrelentingly confrontive and potentially destructive. One can be confrontive without being provocative or harsh. In fact, harshness will evoke anger in return. Compassion is expressed not by sympathizing with the criminal who has created his own predicament; instead, it is demonstrated by a dedication to work tirelessly with people whom many deem hopeless and prefer to incarcerate and forget.

During these many years, interest in the Yochelson-Samenow work has increased among men and women in a variety of careers who have contact with offenders. I have broadened the work in an effort to do more than pay lip service to early intervention and prediction. Not surprisingly, I have encountered criticism. Instead of devising an alleged diabolical plan to label youths and remove them from society, I have maintained that we know enough to identify expanding and intensifying patterns of destructive behavior before a boy or girl is immersed in crime. In *Before It's Too Late: Why Some Children Get Into Trouble and What Parents Can Do About It* (Samenow 2001), I have identified such patterns and discussed mistakes that parents and other adults make in failing to recognize and deal effectively with young people who are at risk.

Dr. Yochelson's contribution was to provide a phenomenological understanding of how the criminal sees himself and the world. The work spans nearly a dozen presidential administrations and has been, and remains, apolitical (even though combating crime often is a political subject). Dr. Yochelson did more than describe the criminal's patterns of thinking in meticulous detail: He piloted a program to help offenders change. By knowing their fears and vulnerabilities, a change agent can get his foot in the door and begin a constructive dialogue with an offender who long has sought to control others while regarding himself as the hub of a wheel around which all else revolves. Dr. Yochelson developed an approach by which that discussion can evolve into a process during which a criminal becomes increasingly fed up with himself and slowly begins to embrace a way of life that he has both envied and reviled.

Twenty-nine years after Dr. Yochelson's death, our work lives on, and interest in it is increasing. I have spoken in all but two states, Canada, England, and China. I have written more books and produced a series of nine videotapes with workshops ("Commitment to Change") that are being used in correctional facilities throughout the United States. Some international interest has been shown also because my books have been published in Japan, Taiwan, and Poland.

With the new millennium having begun, my challenge is to help others use this work during an era of diminishing resources and to assist professionals who continue to dedicate their careers to habilitating offenders.

References

Samenow, Stanton E. 2001. *Before It's Too Late: Why Some Children Get Into Trouble and What Parents Can Do About It*. New York: Three Rivers Press.

______. [1984] 2004. *Inside the Criminal Mind*. Reprint, New York: Crown.

Yochelson, Samuel, and Stanton Samenow. 1976. *The Criminal Personality*. Vol. 1, *A Profile for Change*. New York: Jason Aronson.

______. 1977. *The Criminal Personality*. Vol. 2, *The Change Process*. New York: Jason Aronson.

______. 1987. *The Criminal Personality*. Vol. 3, *The Drug User*. New York: Jason Aronson.

3.2

Contributions of Community Psychology to Criminal Justice

Prevention Research and Intervention

Sarah Livsey and William S. Davidson II
Michigan State University

Introduction

Community psychology "concerns the relationships of the individual to community and social structures. Through collaborative research and action, it seeks to understand and enhance community and individual well-being" (Dalton et al. 2001). Since the formal inception of their field, community psychologists have been concerned with a broad range of social issues, including those related to crime and delinquency. The multidisciplinary, nonterritorial nature of the field can make the specific contributions of community psychology to these areas difficult to pin down. It is easier, however, to identify the principles of community psychology and how these principles have been, or could be, applied to criminal justice. The purpose of this chapter is to highlight one of the central principles of community psychology, prevention, with a focus on new developments and current studies related to criminal justice and delinquency.

Prevention

The Swamscott Conference in 1965 laid a foundation for the emerging field of community psychology. A critical theme of the conference was the importance of prevention research and action. Although community psychology shares the principle of prevention with many other disciplines, prevention has remained central to the discipline.

IOM Report

Prevention research has advanced greatly since Swamscott, and particularly over the past decade. In 1994, the Institute of Medicine released a report titled "Reducing Risks for Mental Disorders: Frontiers for Preventive Intervention Research" (Mrazek and Haggerty 1994). The report contributed to the field in various ways, including the conceptualization of the "preventive intervention research cycle." The cycle included the five steps to be undertaken as a precursor for successful prevention research. Although the focus of the research cycle was mental health, the steps are equally applicable to research regarding crime and delinquency.

The first step in the cycle is to identify and define the desired outcome or problem to be averted. It is critical for measurement purposes that these definitions be specific and detailed. Step two involves searching previous literature in all relevant disciplines to determine the possible risk and protective factors related to the desired outcome and what prevention techniques have been previously tried. The actual creation and implementation of a pilot intervention effort comes at stage three. It is important to test prevention efforts within a smaller population before using them on a larger scale. Assuming that pilot interventions prove effective, step four instructs researchers to carry out field trials to test these interventions further in a broader setting and population; this step ensures that the interventions are transferable beyond the pilot population. Finally, step five involves actual implementation and further evaluation within the community. In following the five steps of the cycle, researchers are encouraged to value rigor and direct community implementation (Koretz and Moscicki 1999).

In addition to defining the research cycle, the report also distinguished between three levels of prevention: universal, selective, and indicated.

These levels of prevention differ according to the populations that receive them. Universal prevention efforts are those given to an entire population regardless of risk. Selective interventions, on the other hand, are appropriate for those at risk for a particular pathology. Finally, indicated prevention involves an effort to prevent the reoccurrence of a behavior in a population having already experienced it (Dalton et al. 2001). For example, if community psychologists were interested in preventing illegal drug use, they may choose to implement drug prevention programs in all elementary schools, provide targeted services for children of drug abusers or those living in high-risk neighborhoods, or provide treatment for criminals convicted of drug crimes. The choice would depend on the desired level of prevention. The following are three examples of recent delinquency-related community psychology prevention efforts at each level.

Universal, Selective, and Indicated Prevention Efforts

Zeldin (2004) argues in favor of engaging young people in their communities as a universal effort to prevent violence and delinquency. There is much research to support the negative effects on youth of social and community isolation. On the reverse side, there is also evidence to support the positive effects of involving youth in community decisionmaking. As such, Zeldin and others advocate various community- and policy-level efforts, including service-learning and extracurricular opportunities in schools and involving youth on community boards and in other community decisionmaking capacities.

Researchers have identified risk factors that are associated with an increased likelihood of delinquency. Such factors include a child's family, personality, school performance, and peer group. Yoshikawa (1994) focused on family factors to prevent delinquency. This selective prevention effort was targeted at young people with high family risk factors for delinquency. Results suggested success in preventing delinquency by using family support and educational groups for high-risk adolescents who had not yet committed a delinquent act.

Quinn and Dyke (2004) offer an indicated prevention effort for first-time juvenile offenders. Instead of traditional punishment-oriented probation, juveniles in this program participated in a multiple-family group intervention. As stated above, previous delinquency research has identified a link between various family factors and recidivism. The goal of this prevention effort was to strengthen the families of youth and provide critical community support and feedback through multiple family support and information groups. Four hundred and fifty-five total first-time offenders and their parents participated in a study of the effort. Two hundred and sixty-seven youths participated in the Family Solutions Program, a ten-session multiple-family group intervention. Results suggested that those first-time offenders who participated in the program were significantly less likely to reoffend than those who did not. As such, this program appears to be an effective indicated prevention effort.

In addition to focusing on different levels of prevention, community psychologists also distinguish between different levels of analysis. Unlike other subdisciplines in psychology and law, community psychologists do not focus exclusively on the individual or small group and they seek to avoid victim-blaming approaches to crime and delinquency (Seidman and Rappaport 1986). Instead, community psychology shifts the focus from individual to multiple levels of analysis. This does not mean the individual is not studied, or not considered important, when it comes to prevention, but individuals are studied within a broader context of influence.

Levels of Analysis

A discussion of the levels of analysis must begin with the work of Bronfenbrenner (1979). Bronfenbrenner identified three distinct levels of analysis, the individual, the microsystem, and the macrosystem. The first level, the individual, is studied by community psychologists to determine its relationship to the other levels. In other words, how do individuals influence their environments and how do environments affect individuals within them? The second level, the microsystem, includes systems with which an individual has a direct, personal, ongoing interaction. Examples would include families, support groups, school classrooms, and employment settings. Finally, macrosystems are large systems that influence a vast group of members. Societies, cultures, and governments are examples of macrosystems (Dalton et al. 2001).

In addition to Bronfenbrenner's three levels, community psychologists also work within two additional levels, organizations and communities.

These two levels can be thought of as positioned between the microsystem and the macrosystem. Organizations involve the merging of multiple microsystems. For example, a university can be viewed as an organization composed of numerous microsystems such as departments, housing units, and student clubs. A community, on the other hand, is usually defined in geographic terms (Dalton et al. 2001).

In addition to their differing prevention populations, the three studies cited earlier can also be thought about according to their level of analysis. The first study uses a universal prevention effort at the level of the individual (young people involved in the program), the community (service-learning and community involvement), and the macrosystem (policy-level goals). The second study involves the interaction between the individual (the youth) and the microsystem (the youth's family) and uses a selective prevention approach. Finally, the third study examines interactions between the individual (the youth), the microsystem (the youth's family), and the community (other families) and is aimed at an indicated prevention population.

Another example of prevention using multiple levels can be found in Banyard, Plante, and Maynihan (2004). Although the issue of sexual violence prevention has been well studied, these authors argue for a new approach. Much of the previous research has focused on the individual level of analysis and how people can avoid becoming victims or perpetrators. However, the problem goes beyond the individual and involves deeply rooted societal norms. As such, the authors propose a multilevel comprehensive approach in which all community members are educated about the societal factors related to sexual violence and taught appropriate bystander responses. They also provide support to violence survivors. The goal is that societal attitudes toward sexual violence will be altered and communities will better respond to the needs of survivors.

Future Directions for Prevention and Criminal Justice

Since the IOM report in 1994, various works have been dedicated to further strengthening the marriage between the fields of prevention and criminal justice. From the theoretical to the methodological, the following suggested tracks will take the fields far into the future.

The concept of "community justice" is introduced in an article by Karp (1999). As the name would suggest, community justice shifts the focus away from individual offenders and criminal acts; it identifies crime patterns, community level challenges associated with these patterns (such as poverty and mental illness), and community solutions to address these challenges. The central goal of community justice is to put the job of crime prevention directly in the hands of the local community. Karp outlines six elements of community justice: (1) it functions at the local level; (2) it is driven by information, not politics or rhetoric; (3) it involves problemsolving techniques; (4) it decentralizes authority; (5) it involves extensive citizen participation; and (6) it is process-oriented. The idea behind community justice is that prevention efforts and sanctions that come from the community will be relevant and more likely to be effective. In addition, community members will have a stake in the process and outcome of prevention efforts.

Biglan and Taylor (2000), in an article titled, "Why Have We Been More Successful in Reducing Tobacco Use Than Violent Crime?" argue in favor of applying the principles used in tobacco prevention to violent crime prevention. These factors include developing a clear consensus among the scientific community as to the causes of violent crime, organizing to determine policy and programming needs, and communicating effectively to policymakers and the community at large.

In their prescription for the development of prevention research, Koretz and Moscicki (1997) focus on a widely cited criticism of community psychology, that is, lack of good theory. They highlight the importance of comprehensive theories resulting in models that include biological and psychosocial factors leading to pathology. The goal of such models should be to "distinguish among risk factors, mediators, and moderators and to plot developmental trajectories toward or away from psychopathology over time" (1997, 192). Prevention designs should match such models and should take into consideration differential risk, intervention timing, and length; they should also be contextually flexible, allowing for cultural or other population differences.

Qualitative techniques, such as in-depth interviews and focus groups, should also be considered by prevention researchers. These methods can offer rich data that can help in the construction of contextually relevant measures and interventions. Dumka and colleagues (1998) used such techniques to construct a measure of parenting stress for low-income parents from three different ethnic groups. Qualitative methods were also used to guide creation of a family-focused delinquency prevention effort for these populations.

Summary and Conclusion

Prevention has been a central theme of community psychology since the birth of the field and has advanced greatly over the past several decades. Community psychologists have contributed to criminal justice by exploring and advancing the principles of prevention and applying them to such areas as violence, delinquency, and drug prevention. Working within different risk populations (universal, selective, and indicated) and at different levels of analysis, community psychologists have challenged individualistic, victim-blaming approaches. New theoretical and methodological techniques will continue to advance the field of prevention as it relates to criminal justice with community psychologists at the center.

References

Banyard, V. L., E. G., Plante, and M. M. Maynihan. 2004. "Bystander Education: Bringing a Broader Community Perspective to Sexual Violence Prevention." *Journal of Community Psychology* 32: 61–79.

Biglan, A., and T. K. Taylor. 2000. "Why Have We Been More Successful in Reducing Tobacco Use Than Violent Crime?" *American Journal of Community Psychology* 28: 269–303.

Bronfenbrenner, U. 1979. *The Ecology of Human Development: Experiments by Nature and Design*. Cambridge, Mass.: Harvard University Press.

Dalton, J. H., M. J. Elias, and A. Wandersman. 2001. *Community Psychology: Linking Individuals and Communities*. Belmont, Calif.: Wadsworth.

Dumka, L. E., N. A. Gonzalas, J. L. Wood, and D. Formoso. 1998. "Using Qualitative Methods to Develop Contextually Relevant Measures and Preventive Interventions: An Illustration." *American Journal of Community Psychology* 26: 605–637.

Karp, D. R. 1999. "Community Justice: Six Challenges." *Journal of Community Psychology* 27: 751–769.

Koretz, D., and E. K. Moscicki. 1999. "Core Elements of Developmental Epidemiologically Based Prevention Research." *American Journal of Community Psychology* 27: 463–481.

Mrazek, P. G., and R. J. Haggerty, eds. 1994. *Reducing Risks for Mental Disorders: Frontiers for Preventive Intervention Research*. Washington, D.C.: National Academy Press.

Quinn, W. H., and D. J. Van Dyke. 2004. "A Multiple Family Group Intervention for First-Time Juvenile Offenders: Comparisons with Probation and Dropouts on Recidivism." *Journal of Community Psychology* 32: 177–200.

Seidman, E., and J. Rappaport, eds. 1986. *Redefining Social Problems*. New York: Plenum Press.

Yoshikawa, H. 1994. "Prevention as a Cumulative Protection: Effects of Early Family Support and Education on Chronic Delinquency and Its Risk." *Psychological Bulletin* 115: 28–54.

Zeldin, S. 2004. "Preventing Youth Violence Through the Promotion of Community Engagement and Membership." *Journal of Community Psychology* 32: 623–641.

4

Social Learning and Neutralization Theory

Social learning theorists take the view that human behavior is the result of learning from others who already possess aspects, or "scripts," of such behaviors including what to value, what motives are appropriate, and how to behave. In social learning, humans adjust their behavior in response to the reactions of others, or they copy parts of others' behavior and reproduce it, often with slight modifications. Alternatively, they absorb adaptations and variations of the behavior and apply these to new situations. Neutralization theorists argue that some of the important things that are learnt and applied to new situations are the words and phrases that cancel out the moral and legal inhibition society creates against participating in a desired criminal behavior.

Social learning theories share the assumption that humans start out as social blanks who learn behavior as well as justifications, rationalizations, and reasons for engaging in a given activity—criminal or law-abiding. Consequently, these theories are considered sociological insofar as they go beyond the stimulus-response type of learning associated with psychological behaviorism. Their advocates reject personality theory with its claim that criminals are different (yet psychology has its own version of social learning that also involves learning not just from others but also from images presented via the mass media). According to social learning theorists, delinquents or criminals are no different from noncriminals. Criminals learn to commit crimes just as they learn any other behavior and just as anyone else learns any type of behavior. The primary learning mechanism occurs in association with others. Most responsible for learning are those we are in close association with, usually through informal small groups such as parents, family, friends, peers, or gangs. We learn through our interactions with these significant others and adapt to their social conventions. What is crucially different between lawbreakers and law abiders is the content of what is learned. Law abiders and lawbreakers are both socialized to conform to social norms. People are influenced, taught, and ultimately act upon what others around them expose them to, whether they are parents, peers, gang members, or cultural heroes. The norms that law abiders learn are those of conventional mainstream society, whereas the norms learned by delinquents and criminals are those of a delinquent subculture that adheres to values opposed to the larger society. Those who commit criminal acts acquire the knowledge, skills, motives, and techniques needed to commit their acts, along with the rationalizations that excuse or justify their behavior.

By contrast, neutralization theory takes a more active view of humans; it states that humans are not passive social actors or blank slates to be filled in with good or bad knowledge about how to behave but creative agents who can interpret their word and have a will to act. Nor does neutralization theory draw a stark contrast between conventional society and delinquent subcultures as the source of knowledge about delinquency. Instead, it argues that delinquency forms a subterranean part of mainstream culture. By learning one, people are exposed to the other. Instead of being immersed in and committed either to convention or to delinquency, individuals are socialized to behave conventionally, but they can occasionally be released from the moral bind of law to drift between these extremes. Neutralization explains how, when potential offenders are contemplating illegal behavior, excuses and justifications function as motives that free them from inhibitions and allow them to express their will to offend.

Because these theories involve interaction, group dynamics, behavior, and learning, their crime reduction policies are social psychological and educational in nature. Policymakers are urged to adopt programs that would identify potential offenders and provide education about behavioral alternatives, group therapy, counseling, or other interventions that will show offenders how to substitute legal behaviors for illegal ones. Furthermore, prevention involves exposing the reasons, rationalizations, or neutralizations for crime as incorrect, inaccurate, or misguided. The harm of crime must be made clear to the perpetrators.

4.1

Social Learning Theory

Correcting Misconceptions

CHRISTINE S. SELLERS
University of South Florida
AND
RONALD L. AKERS
University of Florida

It is inevitable that any theory of crime will be subjected to critique by academic criminologists. Although many criticisms are legitimately grounded in sound scientific principles, others arise from misunderstandings of the theory in question. Social learning theory is no exception. Throughout its history, social learning theory has been subjected to a wide range of criticisms, many arising from inaccurate interpretations of the theory, which have persisted despite numerous attempts to address and correct them (Akers 1973; 1977; 1985; 1996; 1998). In this essay, we briefly describe the full theoretical statement of social learning theory, review criticisms based on mischaracterizations of the theory, and correct these misconceptions.

Social Learning Theory

Social learning theory developed as a reformulation of Edwin Sutherland's (1947) differential association theory. Drawing from the symbolic-interactionist perspective, differential association theory proposes that criminal behavior is learned within the contexts of social interaction. Social interaction provides exposure to varying configurations of definitions; when definitions favorable to crime exceed those unfavorable to crime, criminal behavior results. Sutherland asserted that the learning process for criminal behavior involves the same mechanisms that all learned behaviors entail; however, he was virtually silent on precisely what those mechanisms were. Social learning theory was developed to address Sutherland's omission and to elaborate the means by which social interaction "produces" conforming and deviant behavior. To accomplish this task, social learning theory integrates Sutherland's symbolic-interactionist propositions with modern behavioral psychology. Social learning theory does not compete with differential association theory but complements it; thus, we are able to explain crime and delinquency more thoroughly.

Social learning theory has undergone some revision itself since its initial statement as "differential association-reinforcement theory" (Burgess and Akers 1966b). Originally drawing from the more radical operant behaviorism of B. F. Skinner (1953; 1959), the theory has moved closer to the cognitive learning theories of Albert Bandura (1973; 1977). This move toward "soft behaviorism" allows social learning theory to integrate behavioral learning more seamlessly into differential association theory's symbolic-interactionist framework.

Social learning theory proposes four concepts that are influential in the learning of deviant or conforming behavior. (1) *Differential reinforcement* refers to the balance of actual or anticipated rewards and costs, both social and nonsocial, that follow a behavior. (2) *Imitation* refers to engagement in behavior after observing similar behavior in others who have meaning to the individual. (3) *Definitions* refer to one's own attitudes that define the commission of an act as right or wrong, justified or unjustified. (4) *Differential association* refers to direct and indirect exposure, via associations with others, to patterns of behavior as well as to patterns of norms and values.

The groups with which one is in differential association provide the context within which all social learning mechanisms operate; they include—but are not limited to—family, friends, teachers, coworkers, neighbors, and churches. They are the social sources of reinforcers and punishers; their norms and values shape the individual's own definitions and provide the individual with discriminative stimuli, or cues, to expected or appropriate behavior in given situations; and they serve as models to imitate. Because one may associate with multiple groups displaying contradictory norms, values, and behaviors, it is the *relative balance* of reinforcements, definitions, and behavioral models provided to the individual that determine whether deviance or conformity will occur. The configuration of groups with which one is in differential association, and the patterns of norms, values, and behaviors to which one is exposed, are not random; they are influenced by elements of the social structure, including the social organization of the community and sociodemographic characteristics of the individual.

For almost forty years, numerous empirical studies have found strong evidence to support the social learning model. These studies, as well as theoretical articles and books on social learning, have been widely cited, reprinted, and discussed among criminologists; moreover, social learning theory is nearly always covered in major criminological textbooks and readers. Most of the tests and discussions of social learning have been accurate, appropriate, and well-reasoned. However, we find a persistent tendency by some to ignore, misstate, or misapply the theory. For example, early critics objected to social learning theory's reliance on behaviorism, but they ignored the sociological character of the theory drawn from its differential association roots. Social learning theory has also been inaccurately aligned with "cultural deviance" theories and then maligned for this affiliation despite the broader assertions of social learning theory compared to "true" cultural deviance theories. Yet others conceive of social learning theory as exclusively a "peer influence" theory; indeed, they accuse the theory of commandeering a variable that "belongs" to other theoretical explanations of crime. In the following section we examine these misconceptions.

Misconceptions of Social Learning Theory

The distorted images of social learning theory bring to mind the fable of the six blind men who were asked to describe an elephant by feeling only one part of the elephant's body. The blind man who felt the tail declared that an elephant was like a rope; the one who felt its trunk asserted that an elephant was like a snake. Similarly, social learning theory has often been mischaracterized because observers have focused too closely on a single feature of the theory and have turned a "blind eye" to the full theoretical statement.

"It's Just a Behavioral Theory"

In the early years of social learning theory's development, various criticisms were leveled against it for its infusion of behavioral principles into a sociological explanation of a social phenomenon. One criticism was that social learning theory was tautological, a problem that plagued all behavioral theories. By definition, reinforcement is any contingency that strengthens a behavior. Therefore, reinforcement cannot be used to predict a behavior because a behavior that proliferates *must*, by definition, have been reinforced. Burgess and Akers (1966a) tackled this criticism by recommending a propositional strategy that separated the theory's predictions from the definitions of key concepts: The presence of rewards that have followed criminal behavior in the past can be used to predict criminal behavior in the future.

More critical were those who doubted that behaviorism could be used to understand any social phenomenon. These critics falsely assumed that social learning theory had *replaced* (rather than *integrated*) differential association theory with behavioral learning theory. One error was the confusion of radical or orthodox behaviorism (Skinner 1953; 1959) with the "soft behaviorism" upon which social learning theory is ultimately based. Radical behaviorism evokes the image of a robot-like human, devoid of context and meaning. In the soft behaviorism foundation of social learning theory, however, operant conditioning allows for individuals to engage the environment actively rather than serve as mere passive recipients of stimuli. Soft behaviorism recognizes verbal behavior as a legitimate stimulus or response and acknowledges a role played by cognition in the learning process (Bandura 1977). Thus, there is nothing inherently contradictory about an integrated behavioral-sociological explanation of human social behavior.

A second error made by critics of social learning theory's behavioral component was their failure to recognize that the sociological framework of differential association theory had been retained in social learning theory. At the core of Sutherland's differential association theory is symbolic interactionism. Symbolic interactionism stresses the exchange of meanings communicated between human beings in face-to-face interaction through words and gestures. Of importance is the effect that this interaction has on the individual's self-concept and identity. Given the starkly contrasting images of humans between radical behaviorism and symbolic interactionism, it is easy to see possible contradictions should efforts be made to integrate the two perspectives. However, soft behaviorism, unlike radical behaviorism, is compatible with symbolic interactionism, and this is the integration represented by social learning theory. Behavior is indeed learned through its consequences in the environment, but the content of those consequences may be either concrete or verbal and symbolic. It is important to recognize, then, that social learning theory is *not* "just a behavioral theory" that dismisses all mentalistic concepts (Halbasch 1979) but rather a symbolic-interactionist theory that has incorporated behavioral principles. The image of the human being in social learning theory remains that of a thinking, feeling individual who operates reflexively with others in the environment.

"It's a Cultural Deviance Theory"

Perhaps no other mischaracterization of social learning theory has generated more controversy than the classification of social learning theory as a "cultural deviance" theory. Hirschi (1969) first identified differential association theory in the published literature as a cultural deviance theory (see also Hirschi and Gottfredson 1979; Gottfredson and Hirschi 1990; Hirschi 1996). Both Kornhauser (1978) and Costello (1997; 1998) vilified differential association and social learning theories on the basis of cultural deviance theory's faulty assumptions. Akers (1996; 1998) and Matsueda (1988; 1997) have been firm in their protestations against this mischaracterization of both theories.

The primary criticism leveled against cultural deviance theories is that they assume that socialization is "perfect." Therefore, deviant acts represent only conformity to the norms of the group to which one belongs; there are no deviant *individuals*, only deviant *groups* whose norms are internalized by the individuals who belong to them. However, critics fail to recognize that they impute to differential association and social learning theories a false dichotomy between the dominant culture and the deviant subculture. Sutherland and Akers are both explicit in their depiction of the groups from which definitions are learned. Some groups align with the dominant culture, others with a subculture, and some may straddle both at the same time. Each individual has a unique configuration of others from whom definitions are learned; even members of a delinquent subculture do not march entirely in lockstep because, aside from their associations with each other, each member may differ widely in his or her associations with other individuals.

Critics of the cultural deviance perspective mistakenly attribute to learning theories the assumption that individuals belong *either* to the dominant culture *or* to a deviant subculture. As a result, they also mistakenly conclude that in learning theories, deviance *must* occur from exposure to norms that explicitly *require* deviance rather than merely *allow* for deviance. However, social learning theory clearly specifies that the norms to which one is exposed may be positive (approving), negative (disapproving), *and* neutralizing. What matters is not *which* of these three sets of definitions one is exposed to but in *what ratio*. Thus, although deviance *may* occur from exposure to norms requiring deviance, it may also occur from exposure to norms tolerating or excusing deviance, even when norms prohibiting deviance are also present.

The debate over whether social learning theory can be criticized on the basis of shortcomings of cultural deviance theory has led to an inaccurate image that social learning theory is just a "norms-cause-deviance" theory. Although the exposure to others' definitions and the internalization of norms in the development of one's own definitions are certainly predictors of deviance in social learning theory, they are not the only ones. In addition to others' definitions (the normative component of the differential association variable in social learning theory), individuals are also exposed to others' behaviors (the behavioral-interactional component), which need not be identical to others' definitions. It is the configuration of attitudes *and* behaviors to which an individual is exposed, as well as the extent to which attitudes and behaviors are socially reinforced, that in combination predict whether deviant or conforming behavior will follow.

Thus, there is no assumption of complete socialization and internalization of any set of norms. Social learning is explicit in postulating deviance resulting from incomplete or failed socialization. Further, by referring to the operation of additional social learning variables such as differential reinforcement, the theory explains not only violations of the norms of groups to which one belongs, but also behavior in violation of the values to which one expresses allegiance.

"It's Just a Peer Influence Theory"

Other than one's own prior deviant behavior, the best predictor of the onset, continuance, or desistance of crime and delinquency is differential association with conforming and law-violating peers. Research findings also support reciprocal effects between peer association and delinquency (Akers and Lee 1996; Elliott and Menard 1996; Warr 2002). It is true that the mutual influences of peers and deviant behavior are central to social learning theory. No other general criminological theory has put as much focus on these peer factors, and no other theory is as strongly supported by the findings linking differential peer association with conforming and deviant behavior. Perhaps because of the importance of peer influence to the theory and the evidence that strongly validates it, social learning theory is too often mistakenly taken as *only* a theory of peer association, and, sometimes, as the *only* theory that incorporates peer influences. Nothing could be further from the truth. Certainly, self-control theory (Gottfredson and Hirschi 1990) denies any causal effect of peer relationships; and social bonding theory (Hirschi 1990) denies that the deviant or conforming behaviors or attitudes of peers make any difference to the adolescent's own behavior; however, both theories are contradicted by the consistent findings that peers' attitudes and behaviors do have a direct, nonspurious impact on one's deviant behavior. We do recognize that peers play a role in other theories (general strain theory, for instance), although the peer-delinquency relationship may be interpreted differently within these theories (Agnew 1995). What we take issue with are those instances in which the finding of a peer-delinquency correlation is reported in the literature but interpreted as supporting another theory without acknowledging the implications of the finding for social learning theory (see, for example, Osgood and Anderson 2004). Even more disconcerting are research reports declaring support for social bonding theory even when the best empirical model in the study includes a direct effect of differential peer association, which, as noted above, is contrary to social bonding but directly in line with predictions from social learning theory (Costello and Vowell 1999).

Although ignoring or misinterpreting the role of peers in social learning theory is troublesome, the opposite practice of reducing the entirety of the social learning model to *only* a peer-influence theory is equally problematic. In addition to peer association, the theory clearly refers to various primary and secondary group influences, especially the family. Yet one often sees reports of an empirical relationship between family variables and delinquency interpreted as supporting control theories *instead of*, rather than *in addition to*, social learning theory. Correlates of delinquency such as parental support, discipline, and supervision are, indeed, supportive of control theories, but they are also rightly and fairly seen as evidence in support of social learning theory. The family provides exposure to normative values, behavioral models, and differential reinforcement. Variables such as parental control, discipline, and management are clearly also measures of differential social reinforcement (rewards and punishments) for conforming or disobedient behavior.

The presumption in the literature that social learning theory is "only" a peer-influence theory is further documented by the scores of partial tests of the theory that routinely include a peer association variable, and possibly measures of definitions, but that exclude measures of associations with other primary groups, behavioral models, and differential reinforcement.

Further, empirical tests of theoretical models that "integrate" social learning with other theories typically include only the peer association variable; it is as if this one variable operationalized the entire theoretical model. Interestingly, Krohn (1999) suggests that this practice might be valid, given Akers's portrayal of differential association as an overarching concept that summarizes the other learning mechanisms in the theoretical model. Krohn's (1999) preferred strategy, however, is to exclude measures of differential association and retain measures of definitions, imitation, and differential reinforcement as a means of operationalizing the full social learning model without redundancy. As Akers (1999) has argued elsewhere, we do not advocate the separation of differential association from other learning mechanisms in the explanatory model because to do so would hamper our ability to better understand the learning process in the acquisition of deviant behavior. Social learning theory was created so that we could reach beyond Sutherland's differential association theory by specifying the learning mechanisms embedded within social interactions. To divorce one from the other would be a step backward.

Conclusion

Among the major social psychological explanations of crime and deviance, social learning is the most strongly and consistently supported by empirical evidence and also does well when judged by other criteria such as logical consistency, scope, and usefulness (see Akers 1998; Akers and

Jensen 2003; Akers and Sellers 2004). A large body of research demonstrates relationships of social learning variables to delinquency, deviance, and crime that are statistically significant and of substantial magnitude. Moreover, few empirical findings are contradictory or inconsistent with the theory. When social learning theory is tested against other theories or placed in statistical models combining variables from different theories using the same data collected from the same samples, the measures of social learning concepts usually (but not always) have the strongest main and net effects. Cross-cultural studies have found that social learning theory is also well supported (see a detailed review of the research in Akers and Jensen forthcoming).

Although social learning has been and continues to be among the leading theories receiving prominent attention in the field, it has also been challenged by critics over the years. Many of those challenges have been appropriate and useful to the further development of the theory; other criticisms, however, have been based on misconceptions about the theory. These misconceptions can be traced in large part to a failure to see the theory in its entirety. Although it (1) relies on behaviorism to elaborate the learning mechanisms inherent in social interactions; (2) allows for the transmission of subcultural norms and values; and (3) identifies peers as a primary group with which one differentially associates, social learning theory is not a purely mechanistic behavioral theory, should not be confused with cultural deviance theory, and must not be reduced to a simple peer correlate of delinquency. Instead, social learning theory is deeply rooted in a sociological, symbolic-interactionist framework that situates humans within social contexts through their associations with a variety of social groups. Behavior is acquired, maintained, and changed within these contexts through the operation of primarily cognitive learning mechanisms: social reinforcements and costs, imitation, and discriminative stimuli derived from exposure to attitudes and behaviors of others. The social groups that are the source of these learning mechanisms are numerous and variable for a given individual; individuals are influenced not by a single group but by the relative meaning that multiple groups hold for them. When social learning theory is viewed in this more holistic way, as it often already is in the literature, misguided criticisms are less likely to arise and more constructive challenges that move the theory forward are likely to result.

References

Agnew, Robert. 1995. "Testing the Leading Crime Theories: An Alternative Strategy Focusing on Motivational Processes." *Journal of Research in Crime and Delinquency* 32: 363–398.

Akers, Ronald L. 1973. *Deviant Behavior: A Social Learning Approach*. Belmont, Calif.: Wadsworth.

______. 1977. *Deviant Behavior: A Social Learning Approach*. 2d ed. Belmont, Calif.: Wadsworth.

______. [1985] 1992. *Deviant Behavior: A Social Learning Approach*. 3d ed. Belmont, Calif.: Wadsworth. Reprint, Fairfax, Va.: Techbooks.

______. 1996. "Is Differential Association/Social Learning Cultural Deviance Theory?" *Criminology* 34: 229–248.

______. 1998. *Social Learning and Social Structure: A General Theory of Crime and Deviance*. Boston: Northeastern University Press.

______. 1999. "Social Learning and Social Structure: Reply to Sampson, Morash, and Krohn." *Theoretical Criminology* 3: 477–493.

Akers, Ronald L., and Gary F. Jensen. 2003. "'Taking Social Learning Theory Global': Micro-Macro Transitions in Criminological Theory." In *Social Learning Theory and the Explanation of Crime: A Guide for the New Century*, edited by Ronald L. Akers and Gary F. Jensen. Vol. 11 of *Advances in Criminological Theory*. New Brunswick, N.J.: Transaction.

______. Forthcoming. "The Empirical Status of Social Learning Theory." In *Taking Stock: The Empirical Status of Criminological Theory*, edited by Francis Cullen, John Paul Wright, and Kristie R. Blevins. Vol. 15 of *Advances in Criminological Theory*. New Brunswick, N.J.: Transaction.

Akers, Ronald L., and Gang Lee. 1996. "A Longitudinal Test of Social Learning Theory: Adolescent Smoking." *Journal of Drug Issues* 26: 317–343.

Akers, Ronald L., and Christine S. Sellers. 2004. *Criminological Theories: Introduction, Evaluation, and Application*. 4th ed. Los Angeles: Roxbury.

Bandura, Albert. 1973. *Aggression: A Social Learning Analysis*. Englewood Cliffs, N.J.: Prentice Hall.

______. 1977. *Social Learning Theory*. Englewood Cliffs, N.J.: Prentice Hall.

Burgess, Robert L., and Ronald L. Akers. 1966a. "Are Operant Principles Tautological?" *Psychological Record* 16: 305–312.

______. 1966b. "A Differential Association-Reinforcement Theory of Criminal Behavior." *Social Problems* 14: 128–147.

Costello, Barbara J. 1997. "On the Logical Adequacy of Cultural Deviance Theories." *Theoretical Criminology* 1: 403–428.

______. 1998. "The Remarkable Persistence of a Flawed Theory: A Rejoinder to Matsueda." *Theoretical Criminology* 2: 85–92.

Costello, Barbara J., and Paul R. Vowell. 1999. "Testing Control Theory and Differential Association: A Reanalysis of the Richmond Youth Project Data." *Criminology* 37: 815–842.

Elliott, Delbert S., and Scott Menard. 1996. "Delinquent Friends and Delinquent Behavior: Temporal and Developmental Patterns." In *Delinquency and Crime: Current Theories*, edited by J. David Hawkins (pp. 28–67). New York: Cambridge University Press.

Gottfredson, Michael, and Travis Hirschi. 1990. *A General Theory of Crime*. Palo Alto, Calif.: Stanford University Press.

Halbasch, Keith. 1979. "Differential Reinforcement Theory Examined." *Criminology* 17: 217–229.

Hirschi, Travis. 1969. *Causes of Delinquency*. Berkeley: University of California Press.

______. 1996. "Theory Without Ideas: Reply to Akers." *Criminology* 34: 249–256.

Hirschi, Travis, and Michael Gottfredson. 1979. "Introduction: The Sutherland Tradition in Criminology." In *Understanding Crime: Current Theory and Research*, edited by Travis Hirschi and Michael Gottfredson. Beverly Hills, Calif.: Sage.

Kornhauser, Ruth Rosner. 1978. *Social Sources of Delinquency*. Chicago: University of Chicago Press.

Krohn, Marvin D. 1999. "Social Theory." *Theoretical Criminology* 3: 462–476.

Matsueda, Ross L. 1988. "The Current State of Differential Association Theory," *Crime and Delinquency* 34: 277–306.

______. 1997. "'Cultural Deviance Theory': The Remarkable Persistence of a Flawed Term." *Theoretical Criminology* 1: 429–452.

Osgood, D. Wayne, and Amy L. Anderson. 2004. "Unstructured Socializing and Rates of Delinquency." *Criminology* 42: 519–549.

Skinner, B. F. 1953. *Science and Human Behavior*. New York: Macmillan.

______. 1959. *Cumulative Record*. New York: Appleton-Century-Crofts.

Sutherland, Edwin H. 1947. *Principles of Criminology*. 4th ed. Philadelphia: J. B. Lippincott.

Warr, Mark. 2002. *Companions in Crime: The Social Aspects of Criminal Conduct*. Cambridge: Cambridge University Press.

4.2

Techniques of Neutralization

W. William Minor
Northern Illinois University

Gresham Sykes and David Matza's (1957) "Techniques of Neutralization" was written largely in response to Albert Cohen's (1955) *Delinquent Boys*. Cohen had argued that some lower-class boys were so frustrated by their inability to achieve success in middle-class terms that they deliberately rejected those values and embraced the values of an oppositional subculture. In Cohen's terms, they were *malicious, negativistic, and nonutilitarian*. That is, they stole things they didn't need (or even want) and destroyed property just for the fun of it. If they couldn't succeed via middle-class norms (e.g., punctuality, neatness, hard work, deference, delayed gratification), they would make a show of rejecting those norms through their delinquency.

Sykes and Matza challenged Cohen's thesis almost immediately, arguing that he had grossly overstated the differences between delinquents and nondelinquents. If delinquents actually *approved* of delinquent values, why did they feel it was okay to victimize some people but not others? Why did they express remorse when caught? And why did they express admiration for those who were "really honest," such as a pious mother or an upright priest?

In contrast to Cohen's imagery, Sykes and Matza argued that delinquents were in most respects like other youths. In particular, they embraced the same conventional set of values as other youths, that it was wrong to steal things, to hurt people, and to destroy property. The thing that set delinquents apart was that when the situation called for it, they could identify certain excuses that made the general rule inapplicable at the time. These excuses presented themselves *in advance* (a point we'll return to later); the delinquents were therefore freed from the restraining influence of the moral rule and from the guilt that could follow from violating it. Being thus free to violate rules in which they believed, delinquents could, in a sense, eat their cake and have it too.

Sykes and Matza called these excuses *techniques of neutralization*, and they identified five specific types. The *denial of responsibility* applies when a delinquent is able to argue that it wasn't his fault because he was not in full control of his actions, perhaps because he was drunk, for example. The *denial of injury* applies when the victim isn't hurt very badly, or if the victim can afford the monetary loss. The *denial of the victim* presents an image of a victim who "deserved it," perhaps because of some degraded status (e.g., drunk or homosexual) or because of some inappropriate behavior toward the offender, such as showing disrespect. *Condemnation of the condemners* refocuses attention on the behavior of those who would criticize the delinquent—discriminatory or brutal police, corrupt judges—thus mitigating the wrongfulness of the delinquent's behavior in comparison. Finally, the *appeal to higher loyalties* sometimes requires that delinquents violate the law when more important values are at stake, such as supporting one's family or being a stand-up guy in the eyes of the gang.

That's the theory as it was presented almost fifty years ago. How has it fared since then? This question can be addressed in four ways. First, have other scholars paid attention to the theory? Do they refer to it in their own works? Second, has the theory been incorporated into other theoretical perspectives? Third, has the theory been tested empirically, and if so, how has it been evaluated? And finally, have practical applications or policy implications been derived from the theory? I'll discuss each of these in turn.

Citation Support

By the first criterion above, attention from other scholars, the theory has been an unqualified success. It is one of the best known and most frequently cited theories in criminology (Wolfgang, Figlio, and Thornberry

1978), and by 2003 it had been cited more than seven hundred times in the scholarly literature (Maruna and Copes 2004). It has also been expanded beyond the realm of juvenile delinquency and applied to a wide variety of other behaviors. These include such major crimes as rape (Bohner et al. 1998), pedophilia (DeYoung 1988), and murder (Levi 1981); a variety of white-collar and occupational crimes (e.g., Benson 1985; Dabney 1995); and various lesser forms of deviance such as marijuana smoking (Priest and McGrath 1970), topless dancing (Thompson, Harred, and Burks 2003), Sunday shopping (Dunford and Kunz 1970), and entering one's young daughters into beauty pageants (Heltsley and Calhoun 2003).

Incorporation into Other Theories

Neutralization theory was never intended to be a complete theory in itself. Initially, Sykes and Matza (1957, 664) presented the theory to flesh out the "motives, drives, rationalizations, and attitudes favorable to the violation of law" that were a part of Sutherland's (1947) theory of differential association. Differential association has been updated as a more general learning theory (Akers 1985), and some authors (e.g., Lanier and Henry 2004) continue to treat neutralization as a component of such a learning theory.

However, like most authors (e.g., Akers and Sellers 2004; Lilly, Cullen and Ball 1995), I think it makes better sense to think of neutralization as part of a control theory of crime. Control (or social bonding) theories are those for which deviance is more of less taken for granted; after all, most forms of deviance (or crime) provide some sort of immediate satisfaction. *Conformity*, however, needs to be explained. Within this tradition, neutralization can be seen as part of the process that Reckless (1967) described as *norm erosion* (Ball 1966), or as a part of the element that Hirschi (1969) referred to as *belief* in the legitimacy of the dominant moral code. By far, however, the most comprehensive adoption of neutralization into a control theory framework is Matza's (1964) *Delinquency and Drift*.

In *Delinquency and Drift*, Matza continued the themes he and Sykes had previously outlined. In particular, he argued that subcultural perspectives account for "too much delinquency," that is, more than actually occurs. Matza corrected for this in several ways. First, he introduced the framework of *soft determinism*, in which behavior is neither fully determined nor fully free. Second, he changed the "delinquent subculture" concept to that of a "subculture of delinquency." The latter is a context in which delinquent acts can be contemplated and perhaps engaged in, but are not required. Third, he noted that the subculture of delinquency is one in which youths have a "shared misunderstanding." That is, each youth believes that the others are more committed than he is to delinquent norms, and this shared misunderstanding thus encourages and facilitates delinquency when the youths are together. Finally, Matza noted that delinquents' neutralizing verbalizations bear a striking similarity—he called it a "subterranean convergence"—to various excuses and justifications embodied in the criminal law, such as accident, self-defense, and insanity. In this sense, the law itself plants some of the seeds of its own neutralization.

Although neutralization fits best as a dimension of control theory, its insights have been incorporated into most other contemporary criminological perspectives (see Maruna and Copes 2004, 17–18). However, in one important perspective the potential of neutralization theory has been underdeveloped. Sykes and Matza relied in part on psychological literature (Redl and Wineman 1951), and Festinger's (1957) work on cognitive dissonance was published in the same year as Sykes and Matza's theory. Despite this, the linkages between cognitive psychology and neutralization theory have largely been ignored. Maruna and Copes (2004) explore this issue in some detail, and they make a strong case that psychologists and criminologists should have been reading each others' work over the last half-century.

Empirical Support

The concept of *cause* is not as popular in social science circles as it once was, but if we understand it in a probabilistic rather than an absolute sense, there is no need to abandon this useful concept. In any event, if we want to make a causal assertion that one thing (e.g., neutralization) causes another (crime or deviance, for example), we have to meet three criteria. First, there has to be a *correlation* between the two variables; that is, higher scores on one variable must be statistically associated with higher (or lower) scores on the other. Second, the *causal order* must be established; the cause has to precede the effect. Third, there cannot be a relationship between the two variables simply because both are related to some third variable that is causally prior to both; this criterion is referred to as *nonspuriousness*.

Studies based on interviews and personal narratives are numerous, but they have failed to meet these criteria. For example, Thompson, Harred, and Burks's (2003) interviews with topless dancers found verbalizations similar to those found in Sykes and Matza's techniques, but there was no indication that these verbalizations *preceded* the dancers' entry into a stigmatized occupation. Similarly, in their interviews with apprehended shoplifters, Cromwell and Thurman (2003) found widespread use of neutralization statements, but acknowledged that they were unable to tell whether these accounts were before-the-fact neutralizations or after-the-fact rationalizations. To my knowledge, the interview-based neutralization studies are all vulnerable to this criticism.

Surveys have fared little better. Most have been one-shot surveys relating acceptance of "neutralization" statements to variation in either self-reported or officially-recorded measures of some form of deviance. Because the behavior has already occurred at the time of the survey, these studies almost invariably reverse the appropriate causal order. One study (Thurman 1984) did establish the proper causal order by using estimates of *future* behavior as the dependent variable, but the accuracy of those estimates of future behavior was not verified.

Accounts are verbalized excuses or justifications that are offered when the appropriateness of one's behavior is challenged (Scott and Lyman 1968). By definition, accounts occur after the fact, but neutralizations, by definition, must occur *prior* to the behavior in question. Thus, as Lanier and Henry point out (2004, 174), the "timing" of account giving is crucial. The distinction is simple and fundamental, but many authors have ignored it when conducting research on "neutralization." For those who intend to do research in this area, Scott and Lyman's article should be required reading.

A few studies have attempted to maintain this distinction by using a panel design, in which the same respondents are studied at two or more points in time. Minor (1981; 1984) conducted a two-wave study of college students that related their acceptance of excuses at Time One to their reported misbehavior at Time Two. As a check against spuriousness, he controlled for the students' general moral evaluations of the behaviors in question and for their prior participation in those behaviors. The results were supportive of neutralization theory, but the relationships were not strong. Minor's studies satisfy the minimal criteria for causality discussed earlier, but they have been criticized for their use of a convenience sample (college students) and a short time lag (three months) (Maruna and Copes 2004).

A second panel study, this one based on a sample of incarcerated youths, was conducted by Shields and Whitehall (1994). The researchers found that those who recidivated a year later had achieved higher neutralization scores in the initial survey. However, when the analysis included other key variables measured at Time One (such as a measure of prosocial and antisocial sentiments), neutralization had no significant predictive effect.

The strongest study to date is Robert Agnew's (1994) research based on the second and third waves of the National Youth Survey (Elliott, Huizinga, and Ageton 1985). In this study, Agnew examined the effect of Time Two neutralization scores on Time Three violence, controlling for prior violence, delinquent peers, and approval of violence. Thus, he used an appropriate sample, got the causal order right, and controlled for other relevant variables. The effect of neutralization was statistically significant in the expected direction, but modest in size.

Practical Applications

There are two possible practical applications of neutralization: crime prevention and offender treatment. As a *preventive* strategy, neutralization theory would suggest a tactic of anticipating and undercutting typical excuses, for example, that embezzlement is "borrowing." Cressey (1956) once suggested such a strategy, although elsewhere he noted that countering such verbalizations would have little practical value (Cressey 1971). Most of us have seen similar efforts in department store dressing rooms ("Shoplifting Is a Crime."). There is little direct research on this strategy, but I suspect it has little effect. In the immediate context of a contemplated offense, if some excuses have been anticipated and countered, it is likely that other, more creative excuses could arise to take their place (Minor 1981, n. 6).

Although neutralization theory probably has little preventive potential, Matza's (1964) expansion of it may hold more promise. Recall Matza's concept of the "shared misunderstanding," in which each youth thinks the others are more delinquent than he is, and thus overestimates the prevalence of delinquent behavior. Following this logic, dissemination of accurate information on the prevalence of teenage drinking, smoking, and drug use (for example) may reduce the extent to which teens consider such behavior normative. This is precisely the logic of the "social norms" approach to prevention, and a variety of research shows that it does have some effect in reducing these behaviors (Perkins 2003).

Although neutralization theory probably has relatively little effect on prevention, it has had major effects on programs for *offender treatment*. For example, Braithwaite's (1999) re-integrative shaming conferences specifically counter neutralizing excuses, forcing the offender to take full responsibility for his actions. Yochelson and Samenow's (1976; Samenow 2004) psychiatric approach identifies a large number of "thinking errors" associated with offending. And a variety of cognitive-based therapies (e.g., Bush 1995) have become dominant in correctional treatment, many of which appear to have reasonable success (McGuire 1995). Indeed, Maruna and Copes (2004, 21) assert that "nearly every form of offender treatment—from the '12 steps' model of Alcoholics Anonymous to the confrontational techniques of therapeutic communities—involves strategies for 'overcoming denial' and challenging offender rationalizations."

Conclusion

Neutralization theory seems to make sense, at least as a partial explanation for developing delinquency among relatively minor offenders. It has great intuitive appeal and strong connections to a large number of other theoretical perspectives. Unfortunately, most of the research on neutralization is flawed, so we can't make strong assertions about how well the theory stands up empirically. My own view is that the theory does have some empirical merit, but the explanatory power is probably fairly low. With respect to practical implications of the theory, I'm not very sanguine about its potential for crime prevention, but it has found its way into various crime-reduction programs, with some apparent success.

References

Agnew, Robert. 1994. "The Techniques of Neutralization and Violence." *Criminology* 32: 555–580.

Akers, Ronald L. 1985. *Deviant Behavior: A Social Learning Approach*. 3d ed. Belmont, Calif.: Wadsworth.

Akers, Ronald L., and Christine S. Sellers. 2004. *Criminological Theories: Introduction, Evaluation, and Application*. 4th ed. Los Angeles: Roxbury.

Ball, Richard A. 1966. "An Empirical Exploration of the Neutralization Hypothesis." *Criminologica* 4: 22–32.

Benson, Michael L. 1985. "Denying the Guilty Mind: Accounting for Involvement in White-Collar Crime." *Criminology* 23: 583–608.

Bohner, Gerd, Marc-Andre Reinhardd, Stefanie Rutz, Sabine Sturm, Bernd Kerschbaum, and Dagmar Effler. 1998. "Rape Myths as Neutralizing Cognitions: Evidence for a Causal Impact of Anti-Victim Attitudes on Men's Self-Reported Likelihood of Raping." *European Journal of Social Psychology* 28: 257–268.

Braithwaite, John. 1999. "Restorative Justice: Assessing Optimistic and Pessimistic Accounts." In *Crime and Justice: A Review of Research*, edited by Michael Tonry. Vol. 25. Chicago: University of Chicago Press.

Bush, Jack. 1995. "Teaching Self-Risk Management to Violent Offenders." In *What Works: Reducing Reoffending*, edited by James McGuire. New York: Wiley.

Cohen, Albert K. 1955. *Delinquent Boys: The Culture of the Gang*. Glencoe, Ill.: Free Press.

Cressey, Donald R. 1971. *Other People's Money: A Study in the Social Psychology of Embezzlement*. Belmont, Calif.: Wadsworth.

______. 1956. "Prevention of Defalcations." In *Standard Handbook for Accountants*, edited by J. K. Lasser (pp. 4.30–4.45). New York: McGraw-Hill.

Cromwell, Paul, and Quint Thurman. 2003. "The Devil Made Me Do It: Use of Neutralizations by Shoplifters." *Deviant Behavior* 24: 535–550.

Dabney, Dean A. 1995. "Neutralization and Deviance in the Workplace: Theft of Supplies and Medicines by Hospital Nurses." *Deviant Behavior* 16: 313–331.

De Young, Mary. 1988. "The Indignant Page: Techniques of Neutralization in the Publications of Pedophile Organizations." *Child Abuse and Neglect* 12: 583–591.

Dunford, Franklyn W., and Phillip R. Kunz. 1977. "The Neutralization of Religious Dissonance." *Review of Religious Research* 15: 2–9.

Elliott, Delbert S., David Huizinga, and Suzanne S. Ageton. 1985. *Explaining Delinquency and Drug Use*. Beverly Hills, Calif.: Sage.

Festinger, Leon. 1957. *A Theory of Cognitive Dissonance*. Evanston, Ill.: Row, Peterson.

Heltsley, Martha, and Thomas C. Calhoun. 2003. "The Good Mother: Neutralization Techniques Used by Pageant Mothers." *Deviant Behavior* 24: 81–100.

Hirschi, Travis. 1969. *Causes of Delinquency*. Berkeley: University of California Press.

Lanier, Mark M., and Stuart Henry. 2004. *Essential Criminology*. 2d ed. Boulder: Westview Press.

Levi, Ken. 1981. "Becoming a Hit Man: Neutralization in a Very Deviant Career." *Urban Life* 10: 47–63.

Lilly, J. Robert, Francis T. Cullen, and Richard A. Ball. 1995. *Criminological Theory: Context and Consequences*. 2d ed. Thousand Oaks, Calif.: Sage.

Maruna, Shadd, and Heith Copes. 2004. "Excuses, Excuses: What Have We Learned from Five Decades of Neutralization Research?" In *Crime and Justice 2004–2005* (pp. 1–100). Chicago: University of Chicago Press.

Matza, David. 1964. *Delinquency and Drift*. New York: Wiley.

McGuire, James. 1995. *What Works: Reducing Reoffending*. New York: Wiley.

Minor, W. William. 1981. "Techniques of Neutralization: A Reconceptualization and Empirical Examination." *Journal of Research in Crime and Delinquency* 18: 295–318.

______. 1984. "Neutralization as a Hardening Process: Considerations in the Modeling of Change." *Social Forces* 62: 995–1019.

Perkins, H. Wesley, ed. 2003. *The Social Norms Approach to Preventing School and College Age Substance Abuse: A Handbook for Educators, Counselors, and Clinicians*. San Francisco: Jossey-Bass.

Priest, Thomas B., and John H. McGrath, III. 1970. "Techniques of Neutralization: Young Adult Marijuana Smokers." *Criminology* 8: 185–194.

Reckless, Walter C. 1967. *The Crime Problem*. 4th ed. New York: Meredith.

Redl, Fritz, and David Wineman. 1951. *Children Who Hate*. New York: Free Press.

Samenow, Stanton E. 2004. *Inside the Criminal Mind*. Rev. ed. New York: Crown.

Scott, Marvin B., and Stanford M. Lyman. 1968. "Accounts." *American Sociological Review* 33: 46–61.

Shields, Ian W., and Georgia C. Whitehall. 1994. "Neutralization and Delinquency Among Teenagers." *Criminal Justice and Behavior* 21: 223–235.

Sutherland, Edwin H. 1947. *Principles of Criminology*. 4th ed. Philadelphia: Lippincott.

Sykes, Gresham M., and David Matza. 1957. "Techniques of Neutralization: A Theory of Delinquency." *American Sociological Review* 22: 664–670.

Thompson, William E., Jack L. Harred, and Barbara E. Burks. 2003. "Managing the Stigma of Topless Dancing: A Decade Later." *Deviant Behavior* 24: 551–570.

Thurman, Quint C. 1984. "Deviance and the Neutralization of Moral Commitment: An Empirical Analysis." *Deviant Behavior* 5: 291–304.

Wolfgang, Marvin E., Robert M. Figlio, and Terence P. Thornberry. 1978. *Evaluating Criminology*. New York: Elsevier.

Yochelson, Samuel, and Stanton E. Samenow. 1976. *The Criminal Personality*. Vol. 1, *A Profile for Change*. New York: Jason Aronson.

5

Social Control Theories

Rather than assuming that offenders are different kinds of people, or people who have learned different antisocial behaviors, or people who have developed specific motives to offend, control theories seek to examine why everyone does not offend. In different ways they explore what prevents most people from committing crimes. Each of these kinds of theories then looks at mechanisms of control, parental control, self-control, and the social-psychological process of imposing external controls, in its explanation of crime. Social control theories are considered sociologically rooted because they look at the social processes and social organizational arrangements to help explain crime and deviance.

Most control theories assume that people are socialized into conventional behavior from an early age, but something breaks or weakens the bonds to convention and frees a person to deviate. This "broken bond" can occur through neutralization of the moral bind of law (as discussed in the previous chapter) or because social disorganization, isolation, and the breakdown of communities undermine a person's commitment to conform to the dominant or mainstream culture.

Another kind of control theory assumes that the very creation of a commitment to convention and to socially approved norms and values is difficult to achieve; it requires much investment of time and energy and considerable maintenance, and it can easily go wrong. If attachment, commitment, or stake in conformity does not form in the first place, humans are more likely to deviate and to break the law. This failure-to-bond theory has been attributed to a variety of factors, including parents' failure to provide a "secure attachment" that requires a responsible, lovingly responsive and sensitive parent who is empathetic and able to satisfy childhood needs for emotional and physical security. Others suggest the cause of a failure to bond is the inability to internalize personal self-control and the absence of direct external social controls such as the threat of punishment, the failure of indirect controls from parental monitoring and supervision, and a failure of internal or self-control, which for some depends on an internalized sense of guilt. Ties and bonds to conventional parents, school, friends, employers, and so on make crime too much of a risk for most people.

Yet another version of control theory explores the failure of some people to exercise sufficient self-control over situationally induced or opportunity-enhanced impulses to crime. This, too, is seen as the result of a failure by parents to train their children to resist the lure of sensation-seeking behavior for immediate gratification.

With control theories, it is a failure to bond, or a breaking of a bond, to conventional (i.e., law-abiding) society or the failure to develop the ability to resist impulses that allows people the freedom to commit crime. For some control theorists, this impulsivity is related to the failure to develop positive self-esteem.

Control theories advocate creating or strengthening ties to conventional society by strengthening involvement in conventional institutions and activities, by improving the quality of parenting, and by imposing direct and indirect controls and supervision.

5.1

Social Control and Self-Control Theory

TRAVIS HIRSCHI
University of Arizona
AND
MICHAEL R. GOTTFREDSON
University of California, Irvine

Authors of theories about the causes of crime and delinquency are likely to be uneasy about textbook accounts of their work. Textbooks are designed to appear to provide even-handed descriptions of the virtues and limitations of theories. The more theories they consider, the broader their appeal, and they consequently tend to describe a variety of perspectives. The more criticisms they provide of individual theories, the greater their apparent scholarship or coverage of the literature, and they consequently tend to emphasize problems and limitations. Commonly now in criminology, textbooks also list the public policy implications of each theory, apparently because they hope to provide students with another basis for choosing among them. Most textbooks judge the validity of criticisms by the frequency with which they are encountered. They often advocate putting theories together in a reasonable way, suggesting that the whole of the criminological enterprise is greater than the sum of its parts. Along the same lines, textbooks have a decided tendency to minimize the differences among theories.

Theorists, in contrast to all this, tend to advocate particular ideas and to stress the differences among them. If their logic and reading of the evidence led them to conclude that every idea enjoyed the same modest support in the data, and that all or most could be satisfactorily combined into one perspective about crime, there would be no point in going forward. If they believed that critiques of theories cannot be answered or taken into account, they would again abandon their efforts. So theorists believe that, at a minimum, textbooks should provide their responses to criticisms of their theories, should such responses be available. For us, such responses are easy to find. We have in various places dealt with all serious (not frivolous) criticisms of our theories (Gottfredson and Hirschi 1990; Hirschi and Gottfredson 1995; Hirschi and Gottfredson 2000).

One thing is clear: Systematic reviews of the best studies consistently report that control theories find broad empirical support in a variety of disciplines. For example: "A large number of empirical studies have attempted to test social control theory. Most of these studies conclude that social control theory is supported by the data"; "All . . . studies have found at least some support for Gottfredson and Hirschi's theory, and some have found fairly strong support"; "Control theories have more or less dominated criminology since Hirschi published his social control theory in 1969" (Vold et al. 2002, 187n, 192n, 194). A recent survey of empirical studies concludes that "[with some caveats] the meta-analysis reported here furnishes fairly impressive empirical support for Gottfredson and Hirschi's theory. . . . Taken together . . . these considerations suggest that future research that omits self-control from its empirical analyses risks being misspecified" (Pratt and Cullen 2000, 952). Lanier and Henry conclude that our social and self-control theory "has the highest level of [empirical] support of all theories of crime causation" (2004, 203). There is, in our judgment, no higher praise.

We could, if we wished, also claim relatively large numbers of supporters in the criminological community. By some counts, our supporters are a *plurality* of active scholars in the field. (More criminologists favor our theory over any other single theory.) In some ways, this is a mixed blessing. There are dozens of theories, and we cannot expect majority support. On the contrary, we can expect most textbooks to favor other theories, and to treat our theory as an important competitor. When they do so, two strategies are available to them: They can describe our theory as an inferior version of other theories; and/or they can be especially careful to list the faults and defects of our theory—that is, they can enumerate its logical difficulties, its distasteful implications, and facts it cannot explain. For their own purposes, textbooks tend to make full use of both of these strategies. In our view, both of these practices do more harm than good. The important elements of theories are concepts unique to them. If theory A says X, and theory B says Y, the interesting and important question is whether X or Y is more in accord with the facts. Saying that the theories are really the same theory makes one of them invalid or superfluous.

Our self-control theory may be deduced from and is an attempt to explain the following facts. (1) Differences between people in their tendency to commit criminal and deviant acts are observed at an early age and tend to persist over the life course. The difficult child is more likely to become an adolescent delinquent. The adolescent delinquent is more likely to commit criminal acts as an adult. The adult criminal is likely to continue to have marital, occupational, and drug problems later in life. (2) People who commit a given criminal or delinquent act are more likely to commit all other criminal or delinquent acts. Those who steal are more likely than others to use illegal drugs and to assault their spouses. Those who commit acts of fraud are more likely to be guilty of sex crimes such as rape. Indeed, (3) these tendencies extend to a wide array of acts that are not necessarily illegal, such as alcohol abuse and accidents. At the same time, (4) the tendency to commit most of the acts in question reaches a peak in the late teens and early twenties and then declines rapidly for the rest of life. These facts (early appearance, stability of differences, versatility of offending, and the age effect) are interrelated such that any one of them can be inferred from the others. Yet each tells something important about the nature of crime and criminality. The age effect is so strong that we cannot hope to explain it with the concepts and variables currently available to criminology. The appearance early in life (indeed, in childhood) of the acts in question tells us that they require minimal skill or learning. The variety of *acts* tells us that their common characteristic cannot be their criminality, their deviancy, their recklessness, or their sinfulness—because they are not all criminal, deviant, reckless, or sinful. The consistency of the *differences between people* over time tells us that something built into people is responsible for their continued involvement or lack of involvement in such acts. On inspection, it turns out that the common element in the acts themselves is that their benefits are immediate and their costs deferred. Put another way, crimes pay in the short run; in the long run, they do not. From this we infer the quality that prevents crime among some people more than it does among others. This quality we call "self-control," which we define as the tendency to consider the broader or long-term consequences of one's acts.

In our view, these facts require that the benefits and costs of criminal and delinquent acts must be to some extent inherent in the acts themselves—that is, they must be to some degree independent of legal, social, or religious definitions. Cigarette smoking produces an immediate, if mild, high; over months and years, it is dangerous to one's health. Theft produces immediate goods or money; over time, it puts one's job, career, or even freedom at risk. Driving at excessive speeds saves time; it also puts one's life (and the lives of others) in jeopardy. Shooting a convenience store clerk during a robbery eliminates a witness; it also invites massive, extended retaliation. Accounting that conceals a corporation's true financial worth sustains short-term confidence in the company; in the long-term, it can produce bankruptcy and convictions for fraud.

Some people, then, focus on immediate benefits, and tend therefore to engage in crime; others consider long-term costs, and tend therefore to avoid criminal acts. Our theory attempts to account for the origin of such differences in levels of self-control and to explain their consequences. Our theory does not assume that crime is learned. On the contrary, it assumes that the benefits of crimes and the means of committing them are obvious to everyone. ("Let's see. I could write a term paper on 'social control theory' or I could turn in the paper my roommate used last year. She got an A."). What must be acquired are concerns for the broader consequences of such acts—acquisitions best seen as inhibitions, factors potential offenders take into account in making decisions about whether to commit criminal or delinquent acts.

Efforts to integrate various theories should always be viewed with skepticism. Often, integration is made possible only by ignoring vital differences in the assumptions of the constituent theories. We are particularly sensitive to this issue. Because of their empirical support, our control theories are frequently adopted by one of their competitors (e.g., see Akers 2000).

A recent example illustrates this problem. In *Essential Criminology*, Lanier and Henry depict control theory as a version of social learning or differential association theory (2004, 180), and as an adjunct of labeling theory (2004, 187). According to them, differential association explains how criminal behavior is learned, while control theory explains how conventional behavior is learned. If, as they imply, the distinction between conventional and criminal behavior is arbitrary, these theories must overlap to a large degree. The choice between them should then hinge on which provides a better or more detailed description of the learning process. Unfortunately for this analysis, as noted, we reject the idea that "criminal activity" requires *learning* in any meaningful sense of the term; indeed, it is available the moment a person is able to recognize the possibility of quick and easy gratification of his or her desires. Nor do the "learning processes" described by Sutherland and Akers account for "conformity" as we define it. Our task is to explain the *generality* and *continuity* of conforming and deviant behavior. As a result, we could never say that "the principal part of the learning of [relevant] criminal behavior occurs in groups that make up the individual's major source of reinforcement" (Lanier and Henry, 2004, 166 citing Burger and Akers) because that would imply the likelihood of discontinuity (as individuals change groups) and specialization in one or another form of crime (as groups reward some criminal behaviors and punish others).

A central element of our self-control theory (and of all control theories) is the assumption that behavior is governed by its consequences. In social terms, this means that the control of deviant behavior requires that someone (1) monitor behavior, (2) recognize deviant behavior when it occurs, and (3) correct or punish it. *Essential Criminology* substitutes "labeling" for "recognition" in condition (2) (2004, 187) and thus calls into question a fundamental premise of control theory. Where we say that some acts are inherently deviant, *Essential Criminology* seemingly sides with the view that no act is inherently deviant, that "labels" are arbitrary and may well do more harm than good.

We do not wish to take issue with the idea that parents, teachers, and members of the criminal justice system sometimes overreact to minor forms of deviant behavior, or that such overreaction may cause lasting harm. But our theory assumes that reactions to behavior are necessarily governed by the natural consequences of the behavior—"Good boy!" tends to follow "good" behavior; "Bad girl!" tends to follow behavior having long-term negative consequences. At the same time, our theory does *not* assume that labels necessarily influence behavior—on the contrary, to be consistent with the facts listed above, it actually assumes that early in life labels lose their ability to affect one's level of self-control.

Control theory is not compatible with "social learning" or "labeling theory," and should not reap the benefits or bear the burdens of association with these illustrious perspectives.

As mentioned, we have elsewhere dealt at length with many criticisms of control theory (e.g., Hirschi and Gottfredson 2000). In the interest of space, we go directly to some common text criticisms of *self-control theory*, which, of course, tend to question the facts we take as its basis.

We call our theory "a general theory of crime" because it is designed to apply to a broad range of acts by a range of people unrestricted by race, sex, age, time, or culture. A common criticism of the theory is, of course, that it is not as general as it claims to be. For example, some assert that our theory does not apply to serious adult crime, to many white collar and organizational crimes, or even to the crimes of those "committed to conventional values" (Lanier and Henry 2004). Some say our theory is not applicable to whole groups of people: Lanier and Henry say that it "fails to explain gender differences in delinquency" (2004, 189). This is, of course, only a partial list of offenses and offenders at one time or another said by critics to lie outside the reach of the theory. As we read the research literature, however, claims of inapplicability have not fared well when put to the test in competent research. For example, Canadian researchers have shown that "an early and persistent general propensity to act in an antisocial manner" best explains sexual aggression (e.g., forcible rape) in a sample of adult males imprisoned for one of these offenses (Lussier et al. 2004). According to one of these researchers, their findings were "not well received" at a psychiatry-oriented conference (Lussier, personal communication). Psychiatrists, we can guess without fear of contradiction, would surely say that "self-control theory does not explain forcible rape." They, not we, would be wrong.

The fact is that the theory can deal with sex or gender differences in delinquency; indeed, one of our students wrote a first-class paper applying it to this topic well before the critics said it couldn't be done. We are at a loss as to how to deal with the use of particular acts by named individuals (e.g., Kenneth Lay or Richard Nixon) to call our theory into question. We could fall back on our belief, supported by experience, that everyone is capable of crime. Our theory allows this touch of reality. But there are costs in granting the provisional validity of this intellectual tactic. When we try to be serious about a subject, we are naturally drawn to abstract, simplified constructs, to logical systems that allow us to think rather than simply observe or report. The effort at seriousness frees us from the obligation to take into account the TV criminal of the day, however much he or she may offend our moral or political sensibilities.

Speaking of logical systems, many criminologists now join us in dismissing the charge that self-control theory is tautological (Pratt and Cullen 2000; Lanier and Henry 2004). In logic, tautologies are statements true by definition, as 2 x 2 = 4. We have more than once confessed to making such statements. In research, tautologies are statements that one variable predicts itself, as criminal behavior predicts criminal behavior. This particular "tautology" is true, but not necessarily so. You know that it is part of the foundation of our theory. Of course, what critics want to imply when they call our theory tautological is that it cannot be falsified, or that it tells us nothing they didn't already know. Fortunately for us, they often then go on to say that the theory is false because they know better!

As noted, textbooks routinely comment on the policy implications of our theory, that is, they say we pay little attention to such traditional "causes" of crime as peers, poor housing, inadequate employment, and criminal justice system bias. The fact is that we do deal in several places with these "factors," and, consistent with our theory, in all cases we conclude that they are at best of secondary importance. By the same token, we put little stock in efforts to control crime through enhancing or modifying the role of the criminal justice system. In our theory, the offender, please remember, does not consider the long range or broad implications of his acts; he or she is therefore relatively unaffected by increases in the certainty or severity of criminal penalties. This suggests to us that the responsibility for "crime control" should be returned to "ordinary citizens"—to families, friends, and teachers. Instilling self-control in children rather than building more prisons, and hiring more police and probation officers is what our theory seems to us to recommend as policy.

Over the years we have become increasingly wary of textbook treatments of theoretical work. For one thing, we no longer accept the idea of obvious and necessary links between theories and social policies. We have too often seen critics infer from our theory policies that we would reject. And we have too often seen them demean our theory by attacking its putative policy implications. Most contemporary theories, including control theories, are efforts to understand the origins of delinquency. They are not rooted in concerns about how to fix the problem or reduce its impact, and they do not require that we do anything we do not wish to do. As a result, they should not be judged by their alleged policy implications.

We are also increasingly impressed by how difficult it is to summarize the results of the large amount of complex high-quality empirical work in criminology as it applies to the adequacy of individual theories. Such difficulties are of course multiplied when one focuses on the "findings" of the field as a whole. The most sophisticated social and behavioral science methods are now routinely applied to crime data, and the number of excellent and challenging research projects is large and growing. Work such as this requires sustained and serious attention if anything but the most facile inferences are to be drawn from it.

Finally, we are more and more impressed by the long shadow disciplinary perspectives continue to cast over characterizations of theories and data about crime and delinquency. Evidence about the causes of crime and delinquency comes from many disciplines: from biology, psychology, economics, and sociology. But text authors tend to have been trained in one discipline only, and they aim their books at audiences within that discipline. As a result, they are perhaps too likely to allow the vision of their discipline to color their view and limit their understanding of criminological research, an interdisciplinary project that could well be characterized as among the most lively and exciting of all of the social and behavioral sciences.

References

Akers, Ronald L. 2000. *Criminological Theories*. 3d ed. Los Angeles: Roxbury.

Gottfredson, Michael, and Travis Hirschi. 1990. *A General Theory of Crime*. Stanford: Stanford University Press.

______. 1995. *The Generality of Deviance*. New Brunswick, N.J.: Transaction.

______. 2000. "In Defense of Self-Control." *Theoretical Criminology* 4: 55–69.

Lanier, Mark, and Stuart Henry. 2004. *Essential Criminology*. Boulder: Westview Press.

Lussier, Patrick, Jean Proulx, and Marc LeBlanc. 2004. "Criminal Propensity, Deviant Sexual Interests and Criminal Activity in Sexual Aggressors Against Women: A Comparison of Alternative Explanatory Models." Unpublished manuscript, School of Criminology, Simon Fraser University.

Pratt, Travis, and Francis Cullen. 2000. "The Empirical Status of Gottfredson and Hirschi's General Theory of Crime: A Meta-Analysis." *Criminology* 38: 931–965.

Vold, George, Thomas Bernard, and Jeffrey Snipes. 2002. *Theoretical Criminology*. 5th ed. New York: Oxford University Press.

5.2

Social Control Theory and Direct Parental Controls

Joseph H. Rankin
Wayne State University
AND
L. Edward Wells
Illinois State University

Social control theory arguably constitutes the most important theoretical framework in contemporary criminology for understanding the problems of crime and for developing new criminal justice policies. Indeed, calls for new programs to reduce crime invariably rely on the ideas of deterrence, restriction, discipline, and discouragement. What distinguishes social control theory as a distinct framework is (a) its focus on *restraints* rather than the conventional criminological focus on motivations as the key to explaining crime, and (b) its assumption that the motives or impulses for most criminal acts are relatively normal and universal (rather than aberrant or pathological). Thus, social control theory reverses the usual explanation of crime by viewing criminal behavior as less explainable in terms of the *presence* of something (deviant motivations) than in the *absence* of something (effective restraints).

Although the basic ideas of social control can be found in many theoretical models, several specific versions identify the kinds of controls that help to explain crime and delinquency. Undoubtedly, the most familiar is

Travis Hirschi's (1969) "social bonds" model, which views adolescents' behavior as controlled by emotional attachments to other persons and by behavioral commitments to law-abiding activities and memberships. In Hirschi's model, parents provide the major source of "attachment" to the conventional social order.

Nye (1958) provided an earlier version of social control theory that, although less detailed than Hirschi's, gives a more inclusive framework for conceptualizing the content of social controls. He identified four kinds of control through which society restrains individual impulses to socially prohibited behaviors:

1. *Direct control* relies on the coercive use of punishments and rewards to gain compliance with social rules—that is, the reliance on threats and bribes.
2. *Indirect control* relies on appeals to affective attachments and emotional investments in social relationships—that is, the reliance on loyalty, esteem, or embarrassment.
3. *Internalized control* relies on gradually changing people's beliefs or impulses through socialization, conditioning, persuasion, or brainwashing—that is, the reliance on education or "conversion."
4. *Opportunity control* relies on manipulating the behavioral alternatives from which people can choose in fulfilling their needs or in achieving their goals—that is, the reliance on situational or reality-perceiving manipulations.

With this typology, there is a fundamental issue in social control theory: Which of these forms of control is most effective in explaining and controlling crime and delinquency?

Initial research on social control theories focused largely on contrasting the effectiveness of direct versus indirect forms of control, particularly as these controls are embodied in the major social institutions of the family. Although popular opinion seemed to favor direct control as critically important (e.g., the universally quoted adage about "sparing the rod and spoiling the child"), the empirical research on juvenile delinquency generally disconfirmed the conventional wisdom. Both Nye (1958) and Hirschi (1969) argued that the utility of direct controls is limited among adolescents, especially older ones, because (a) adolescents become increasingly autonomous from their parents and more involved with peers, and (b) the effectiveness of direct control is limited by the difficulty of monitoring behaviors.

The premise that indirect controls are more effective than direct controls was generally supported in early empirical research. However, the certainty of this conclusion was partly a product of its ideological appeal (i.e., a liberal preference for social attachments to influence behaviors softly rather than use threats to coerce obedience), which undoubtedly limited empirical research on the effectiveness of direct controls through the mid-1980s. A few empirical studies during this period supported the argument that direct controls were less effective, although measurements of parental discipline were mostly indirect and weak. Correlations between delinquency and such variables as the amount of time spent in the company of parents, the amount of adolescent freedom from supervision (e.g., frequency of dating, availability of a car, freedom to dress as desired), the number of biological parents in the home, and the mother's employment status generally showed a negligible relationship with delinquency. Coupled with psychological research that showed spanking and physical discipline by parents correlated positively with children's delinquency and aggression (e.g., see Williams et al. 1992), these studies were regarded as solid empirical support for the ineffectiveness (even counterproductiveness) of direct controls.

Several related developments in the 1980s led researchers to reconsider the effectiveness of direct controls and to exhibit a renewed interest in better empirical research. Most fundamental was a generally conservative ideological shift toward more "classical" models of human nature and social justice and an emphasis on voluntaristic images of criminal behavior as chosen by rational actors who base their decisions on calculations of personal costs and gains. In this ideological context, coercive forms of control seem more natural, logical, and agreeable—certainly less objectionable philosophically and less readily dismissed by weak correlational research.

A second and related development was the revival of interest among criminologists in the "deterrence doctrine" as a scientifically credible theory and rational policy framework for reducing juvenile crime. Prompted by debates over correctional reform (including the waiver of juveniles to adult court to face tougher punishment) and the adoption of new policing strategies (including tougher enforcement of domestic violence laws), new studies found that direct coercive controls sometimes *could* have significant deterrent effects on crime and delinquency. These efforts moved the issue of direct control from the periphery to the center of social control research and also revealed the necessity of clarifying the basic terms by which direct controls are defined and measured.

A Reconceptualization of Direct Parental Controls

Renewed efforts to rigorously study the effectiveness of direct controls revealed the conceptual inadequacies of existing theory. Although the notion of direct control seems intuitively simple and readily understandable, it actually covers a broad and complicated set of issues. For example, to say that some parents are "strict" (i.e., exercise strong direct control) might mean several things. Parents may be strict in specifying an extensive list of rules and regulations for their children (including what they can wear, how much TV they can watch, and how much time they must spend on homework). They may be strict in keeping a close watch on their children's behavior (including frequent phone check-ins and restricted participation in unsupervised activities); alternatively, they may be harsh disciplinarians who administer tough, unconditional punishments for noncompliance with parental rules.

Any one of these examples constitutes "strict parenting," but the examples are not identical. Although parents might not actively monitor their children's activities, they may severely punish violations they do know about; or, maybe they punish severely but inconsistently and arbitrarily. Does close parental supervision constitute direct control (because parents are maintaining close surveillance of children's behaviors) or indirect control (because spending time with their children provides a form of attachment)? Indeed, much of the empirical uncertainty from earlier studies reflected ambiguity about what exactly was being measured and correlated.

Drawing upon research and theory by Patterson (1982) and Nye (1958), Wells and Rankin (1988) reconceived "direct parental controls" as having three components. *Normative regulation* is the process of "laying down the law" and making clear what children can and cannot do. Parents must specify explicitly what the rules and regulations are and the consequences for noncompliance. *Monitoring* children's behaviors for compliance or noncompliance entails supervision and surveillance—checking to make sure that parental rules and guidelines are followed.

Discipline and punishment of noncompliance comprises the application of unpleasant outcomes to sanction children's misbehaviors negatively. Although each component represents a distinct process, effective direct control requires the application of all three of these operations. Several landmark studies, for example, the comprehensive meta-analysis by Loeber and Stouthamer-Loeber (1986) and the forty-five-year longitudinal study by Sampson and Laub (1993), have clearly documented the importance of parental supervision as a major restraining factor on delinquency, but they do not clarify which components of the broad process of "supervision" are the most effective and how they specifically operate.

Beyond elaborating the components of direct control, an additional question asks how these variables may be causally related to behavioral control. The assumption of early research was an additive-linear model in which the various components of social control operate separately and independently (so that the total control exercised is simply the sum of all the component effects) and their influences on behavior are a linear outcome of their strengths (stronger control efforts invariably yield greater compliance). Although it is appealingly simple and has been universally adopted, this model is too simple. Research by Wells and Rankin (1988) and Seydlitz (1993) indicates that many forms of social control operate in a curvilinear fashion such that the greatest reduction in delinquent behavior is produced by a moderate amount of control; thus the researchers demonstrated that more control is not necessarily better. Indeed, increasing direct control beyond a medium amount can yield *negative* behavioral outcomes. Excessive control may generate more delinquency rather than more obedience because it can prompt anger, rebellion, and "acting out" behaviors. Such a pattern also explains that early studies may have shown low correlations for direct control variables because commonly used correlational measures assume a linear pattern of association between variables.

Another argument is that the different components of control may interact or mutually condition each other so that the effects of direct control are contingent on the levels of other (indirect) control variables. Perhaps the best known of these interactions is the combination of supervision (direct control) and attachment to parents (indirect control). The theoretical prediction is that the strongest effects of parental supervision occur when children are strongly attached to their parents affectively—what Baumrind (1966) calls "authori*tative* parenting." In contrast, strong disciplinary efforts combined with weak parent-child attachment (what Baumrind calls "authori*tarian* parenting") will be much less effective in restraining adolescent delinquent behaviors and may even produce the highest rates of delinquency. Although this interaction seems plausible and theoretically strong, empirical research has not confirmed it. Research by Rankin and Wells (1990) and Seydlitz (1993) both reported sizeable effects of direct controls (parental supervision and discipline) on delinquency, but these effects were not contingent upon the strength of parent-child attachment.

Beyond recognizing that control influences on delinquency may not be linear, recent research also indicates that the causal connection between parental control and delinquency may be bi-directional or reciprocal. Children are increasingly being viewed not only as a product of their parents but also as having an effect on their parents' behaviors (Gecas and Seff 1990). For example, children whose behavior is more delinquent may cause their parents to "get tough" and to adopt stronger forms of direct control (e.g., by keeping a closer watch over their children's activities or inflicting harsher penalties for rule violations) to make youth behavior conform with parental expectations. Alternatively, children whose behavior is persistently delinquent may lead their parents to give up on them (declare them a "lost cause") and to stop trying to control their behavior (as a waste of time). If the causal connection is in fact reciprocal, the correlations computed between parental control and youth behavior will be ambiguous because the correlations might represent either or both (in some unknown mixture) of these effects. To date, research on direct controls has yet to separate out whether parental control is more properly regarded as the cause or the effect of delinquency (Jang and Smith 1997; Simons et al. 2004). However, such research does indicate that the traditional view of parenting (in which parents mold their children through strong discipline) is overly simplistic and inadequate.

The Effects of Family Controls

Individual-Level Effects

Several current developmental theorists have argued that the impact of direct parental controls is *time-dependent*—that is, more important in particular age periods and less important in others. For example, Hirschi has dramatically modified his stance on effective sources of social control. In their *General Theory of Crime*, Gottfredson and Hirschi (1990) deemphasize the indirect controls of social bonds and parental attachments and strongly emphasize the internalized effects of self-control, a latent trait acquired early in childhood as a product of strong parental supervision and discipline (direct parental control). As children grow older, the internalized sense of self-control becomes the dominant restraint on their behavior, largely replacing direct parental control. Delinquents lack self-control because of ineffective child-rearing practices in the early years, when the trait of self-control is being developed. Strong direct controls exerted by parents later in adolescence cannot compensate for or correct weak self-control acquired in the early formative period. This enduring trait of self-control shapes children's risk-taking and rule-breaking behavior for the rest of their lives. A relatively large body of research has found much empirical support for the core propositions of this theory (e.g., see Pratt and Cullen 2000).

Contextual Effects

Because social control theories largely emerged as products of modern survey research, virtually all models of direct parental controls are *individual-level* analyses that seek to explain variations in delinquency by the differences in individual characteristics of adolescents. The family is viewed only through its direct influence on an individual child within that specific family. The weakness of this approach is its "atomism," that is, treating each family and child as a distinct, independent unit of analysis and viewing family-child dynamics as independent of their context or environmental setting. Anderson (2002) noted the limits of this view by arguing that the family as a control system is embedded in larger systems of control (economic, demographic, cultural, institutional, and ecological) that affect what the family does and how effectively it does it.

Arguably, the most important recent trend has been the development of multilevel models or explanations of social control. Actually, this trend is a rediscovery of ideas prevalent in the Chicago school, developed in the early twentieth-century, and aimed at explaining individual-level and community-level criminal patterns within the same theoretical framework. Recent updates in social disorganization theory have emphasized the importance of family structures and dynamics for shaping social control dynamics in the broader neighborhood and community.

Central to the idea of social disorganization as a precursor to increased crime is the loss of informal social control in the neighborhood; and central to the loss of neighborhood control is the weakening of family controls. According to Robert Sampson (1992), weaker family controls aggregate to the neighborhood level; there, they have an independent contextual effect on juveniles' behavior that is separate from their impact in their own family situations. "[Y]outh in stable family areas, regardless of their own family situation, have more controls placed on their leisure-time activities, particularly with peer groups" (Sampson 1992, 80). This prediction has been documented and confirmed in several recent studies (Hoffman 2002; Osgood and Anderson 2004; Wright and Cullen 2001). The research affirms that parents can have important direct control effects on delinquency beyond restraining their own children; they may also restrain the behavior of children in other families by adding to the neighborhood context of monitoring, supervision, and order maintenance.

Policy Considerations

The implications for policy and prevention lie in strengthening and developing more effective child-rearing practices (parental regulation, monitoring, and discipline). Early intervention programs should include parental disciplinary training such as when and how to discipline. Indeed, various recent delinquency prevention programs aimed at families in disadvantaged neighborhoods have focused not on altering the economic structure or physical conditions in the neighborhoods but on changing the supervision and discipline practices of parents in families with high-risk children.

Such behavior therapy techniques apply social learning and behavior modification principles to family prevention strategies in which parents themselves are an integral part of the program. Although this technique appears to have been successful in reducing noxious but not necessarily delinquent behaviors (e.g., whining, teasing, fighting), at least two questions remain in regard to its overall effectiveness: Can it effectively reduce more serious forms of delinquency usually committed outside the home environment? How long do the effects persist after treatment is terminated (Rankin and Wells 1987)? Certainly, ongoing theory and research is necessary to formulate the best methods for family interventions. A "shotgun approach" that treats all children and families alike is probably destined to fail.

There is some evidence to suggest that early intervention is more likely to succeed than that which occurs later in adolescence. Regoli and Hewitt (2003, 177) argue that "if the cause of delinquency is faulty parenting, there really is not much the juvenile justice system can do to overcome what was done to the child over many years." This statement is probably an accurate summary of opinion among many criminal justice professionals, but our position is not nearly so fatalistic. Indeed, there is reason to believe that behaviors can be changed among adolescents and young adults.

References

Anderson, Amy L. 2002. "Individual and Contextual Influences on Delinquency: The Role of the Single Parent Family." *Journal of Criminal Justice* 30: 575–587.

Baumrind, Diana. 1966. "Effects of Authoritative Parental Control on Child Behavior." *Child Development* 37: 887–907.

Gecas, Viktor, and Monica Seff. 1990. "Families and Adolescents: A Review of the 1980s." *Journal of Marriage and the Family* 52: 941–958.

Gottfredson, Michael, and Travis Hirschi. 1990. *A General Theory of Crime*. Stanford: Stanford University Press.

Hirschi, Travis. 1969. *Causes of Delinquency*. Berkeley: University of California Press.

Hoffman, John P. 2002. "A Contextual Analysis of Differential Association, Social Control, and Strain Theories of Delinquency." *Social Forces* 81: 753–785.

Jang, Sung Joon, and Carolyn A. Smith. 1997. "A Test of Reciprocal Causal Relationships Among Parental Supervision, Affective Ties, and Delinquency." *Journal of Research in Crime and Delinquency* 34: 307–336.

Loeber, Rolf, and Magda Stouthamer-Loeber. 1986. "Family Factors as Correlates and Predictors of Juvenile Conduct Problems and Delinquency." In *Crime and Justice: An Annual Review of Research*, edited by Michael Tonry and Norval Morris (pp. 29–149). Vol. 7. Chicago: University of Chicago Press.

Nye, F. Ivan. 1958. *Family Relationships and Delinquent Behavior*. New York: John Wiley.

Osgood, D. Wayne, and Amy L. Anderson. 2004. "Unstructured Socializing and Rates of Delinquency." *Criminology* 42: 519–549.

Patterson, Gerald R. 1982. *Coercive Family Process: A Social Learning Approach*. Vol. 3. Eugene, Oreg.: Castalia.

Pratt, Travis C., and Francis Cullen. 2000. "The Empirical Status of Gottfredson and Hirschi's General Theory of Crime: A Meta-Analysis." *Criminology* 38: 931–954.

Rankin, Joseph H., and L. Edward Wells. 1987. "The Preventive Effects of the Family on Delinquency." In *Handbook of Crime and Delinquency Prevention*, edited by Elmer Johnson (pp. 257–277). New York: Greenwood Press.

Rankin, Joseph H., and L. Edward Wells. 1990. "The Effect of Parental Attachments and Direct Controls on Delinquency." *Journal of Research in Crime and Delinquency* 27: 140–165.

Regoli, Robert, and John Hewitt. 2003. *Delinquency in Society*. 5th ed. Boston: McGraw Hill.

Sampson, Robert. 1992. "Family Management and Child Development: Insights from Social Disorganization Theory." In *Facts, Frameworks, and Forecasts* (pp. 63–93), edited by Joan McCord. New Brunswick, N.J.: Transaction.

Sampson, Robert, and John Laub. 1993. *Crime in the Making: Pathways and Turning Points Through Life*. Cambridge, Mass.: Harvard University Press.

Seydlitz, Ruth. 1993. "Complexity in the Relationships Among Direct and Indirect Parental Controls and Delinquency." *Youth and Society* 24: 243–275.

Simons, Ronald, Leslie Gordon Simons, and Lora Ebert Wallace. 2004. *Families, Delinquency, and Crime: Linking Society's Most Basic Institution to Antisocial Behavior*. Los Angeles: Roxbury.

Wells, L. Edward, and Joseph H. Rankin. 1988. "Direct Parental Controls and Delinquency." *Criminology* 26: 263–285.

Williams, Larry E., Lawrence Clinton, L. Thomas Winfree, and Robert Clark. 1992. "Family Ties, Parental Discipline, and Delinquency: A Study of Youthful Misbehavior by Parochial High School Students." *Sociological Spectrum* 12: 381–401.

Wright, John P., and Francis T. Cullen. 2001. "Parental Efficacy and Delinquent Behavior: Do Control and Support Matter?" *Criminology* 39: 677–705.

6

Social Ecology and Subcultural Theories

Theories described as social ecology and subcultural theories share the premise that the characteristics of specific places and/or cultural groups may make a person who inhabits those spaces, or who is engaged in the social networks formed in them, more or less prone to engage in crime. A person who enjoys supportive networks of people with close ties to organized communities is less likely to become an offender. Communities that are likely to produce crime are seen as fractured or broken. Crime occurs not because residents are forced into offending but because they make choices that are environmentally structured toward predatory actions—choices limited by the meaning of life in impoverished and disorganized settings. The shift from agrarian societies to urban societies involving the migration of dispersed populations into densely populated city neighborhoods has demonstrated that, relative to stable suburban environments, areas of transition tend to become rife with high rates of crime (at least of street crime). This was found particularly in London and Chicago, each city having been studied in fine detail by nineteenth- and early twentieth-century sociologists and social historians. Generally, the geographic area in question is a particular neighborhood, and the crime-promoting tendency is often related to the economic and social factors that shape and sustain these neighborhoods, such as poverty, high-density population, social disorganization, and conflicting cultures and subcultures. These economic factors are themselves tied to the politics of urban development, urban land use, and the alienation and abandonment experienced by those who inhabit these areas. Inhabitants of blighted neighborhoods feel excluded from the mainstream of society and, as a result, become hostile to all but those in, or closest to, their particular ethnic group. These problems are intensified when the most successful residents move out to the suburbs, leaving behind concentrations of those with the most problems. The accumulation of these problem-challenged residents serve as poor role models for children born into such environments, and this pattern further demoralizes the residents who remain; usually, they respond by withdrawing from society at large. This withdrawal makes people in such areas even more vulnerable to victimization as vital networks of informal social control are undermined. Sometimes entire cities fall victim to the same forces; indeed, the film producer Michael Moore has documented the economic blight and crime found in Flint, Michigan, conditions that are the result of decisions made by auto companies. In these settings, crime becomes an alternative, albeit risky, way to make a living.

There are also circumstances, such as migration and settlement, under which a person's indigenous cultural values may conflict with those of the dominant mainstream (law-creating) culture, resulting in crime. Sometimes, subgroups within a larger culture will harbor longstanding differences with the mainstream and with other subcultures; these differences can result in criminal acts, particularly when subcultural groups, such as gangs, provide young people with identity and support. In some cities, gangs, enjoying organizational features that span generations, have become permanent fixtures.

In these cities, the crime-creating environment is seen as a sociological problem requiring change, not so much to the individual—although training, skill development, and the inculcation of coping strategies have been suggested—but to the groups' values as well as to the geographic regions, and particularly to the economic and political forces that shape these areas. Not surprisingly, this type of intervention requires wider government policy because it is outside the domain of most criminal justice agencies. One exception is the movement in law enforcement policy towards problem-solving community policing, in which police officers work in partnership with community members to seek solutions to area problems that transcend arrest and incarceration.

Early social ecologists believed that the driving force of social change, bringing together different groups within the cities, would subside and that the dominant or mainstream culture would absorb the diversity of differences. The failure of assimilation and the permanence, rather than the transience, of criminal areas led to later revisions in the theory to account for this tendency, not least through the concept of "social capital," the dense social ties that produce supportive, nurturing, resource sponsoring, self-monitoring, and safe social environments.

6.1

Social Ecology and Collective Efficacy Theory

ROBERT J. SAMPSON
Harvard University

The idyllic notion of local communities as "urban villages" characterized by dense networks of personal ties is a seductive image, one that pervades traditional theoretical perspectives on neighborhoods and crime. The idea is that tight-knit neighborhoods are safe because of their rich supply of close social networks. Yet such ideal typical neighborhoods appear to bear little resemblance to those of contemporary cities, where weak ties prevail over strong ties and social interaction among residents is characterized more often by instrumentality than by altruism or affection. Moreover, the dark side of community is often neglected—social networks can, and often are, put to use for illegal or violent purposes.

The urban village model of cities is further compromised by the assumption that networks of personal ties map neatly onto the geographically defined boundaries of existing neighborhoods, such that neighborhoods can be conceptualized as independent social entities. In fact, social networks in the modern city frequently criss-cross traditional ecological boundaries, many of which are permeable and vaguely defined. Living in close proximity to high-crime neighborhoods, for example, may increase the risk of crime no matter what the density of social networks in one's home neighborhood. It follows that neighborhoods themselves need to be conceptualized as part of a larger network of spatial relations, thus motivating the idea of a "neighborhood's neighbors."

In this article I explore these issues by considering new theoretical developments in neighborhood social ecology that build on the important work of the past. Neighborhoods, after all, show remarkable continuities in patterns of criminal activity. For at least a hundred years, criminological research in the ecological tradition has confirmed the concentration of interpersonal violence in a small number of neighborhoods, especially those characterized by poverty, the racial segregation of minority groups, and the concentration of single-parent families (Sampson et al. 2002). The theoretical challenge is to explain these facts and account for why neighborhoods continue to matter in the modern city.

Social Disorganization Theory and Personal Networks

In the classic work of the Chicago School of urban sociology in the early twentieth century, it was thought that population density, low economic status, ethnic heterogeneity, and residential instability led to the rupture of local social ties, a form of social disorganization that in turn accounted for high rates of crime and disorder (Kornhauser 1978). Later in the century, the concept of social disorganization came to be defined as the inability of a community to maintain effective social order because it failed to realize the common values of its residents. This theoretical definition was formulated systemically—the allegedly disorganized community was viewed as suffering from a disrupted or weakened system of friendship, kinship, and acquaintanceship networks, and thus ultimately of socialization.

More recently, the intellectual tradition of community-level research has been revitalized by the increasingly popular idea of "social capital." Although there are conflicting definitions, social capital is typically conceptualized as embodied in the social ties among persons. In an influential version of this idea, Robert Putnam (2000) defines social capital as the networks, norms, and trust that facilitate coordination and cooperation for mutual benefit. The connection of social disorganization and social capital theory can be articulated as follows: Neighborhoods bereft of social capital, especially of dense social networks, are less able to realize common values and therefore cannot maintain the social controls that foster safety.

Although social disorganization theory has enjoyed considerable empirical support in the literature (Pratt and Cullen 2005), there are reasons to question the role of strong social ties in producing low crime rates. First, in some neighborhoods, strong ties may work to impede efforts to establish social control. William Julius Wilson (1978), for example, has argued that residents of very poor neighborhoods tend to be tightly interconnected through network ties but do not necessarily produce collective resources such as social control. He reasons that ties in the inner city are excessively personalistic and parochial in nature—socially isolated from public resources and more tied to familial needs.

Second, networks connect do-gooders as well as they connect drug dealers. In her study of a black middle-class community in Chicago, Pattillo (1999) specifically addresses the limits of tightly-knit social bonds in facilitating social control. She argues that dense local ties do promote social cohesion and hence inhibit crime, but at the same time they foster the growth of networks that impede efforts to rid the neighborhood of organized drug- and gang-related crime. In this way, dense social ties have positive and negative repercussions. In a consideration of networks, then, it is important to consider just what is being connected—networks are not inherently egalitarian or prosocial in nature.

Third, shared expectations for social control and strategic connections that yield social action can be fostered in the absence of thick ties among neighbors. As Granovetter (1973) argued in a seminal essay, "weak ties"—less intimate connections between people based on more infrequent social interaction—may be critical for establishing social resources, such as job referrals, because they integrate the community by way of bringing together otherwise disconnected subgroups. Consistent with this view, there is evidence that weak ties among neighbors, as manifested in middle-range rather than in either nonexistent or intensive social interaction, are predictive of lower crime rates (Bellair 1997).

Collective Efficacy Theory

Research on dense social ties reveals a paradox of sorts for thinking about crime. Many city dwellers have limited interaction with their neighbors and yet they appear to generate community-specific social capital. Moreover, urban areas where strong ties are tightly restricted geographically may actually produce a climate that discourages collective responses to local problems. To address these urban realities, Sampson et al. (1997) have proposed a focus on mechanisms of social control that may be facilitated by strong ties or associations, but do not necessarily require them. Rejecting the outmoded assumption that neighborhoods are characterized by dense, intimate, emotional bonds, they define neighborhoods in *ecological* terms and focus on variations in social cohesion and the shared expectations among residents for taking action to achieve social control. The theoretical concept of neighborhood *collective efficacy* captures the link between these two related but nonetheless distinct concepts—social cohesion of the collective (e.g., mutual support, trust) and shared expectations for control within that collective. Just as self-efficacy is situated rather than general (one has self-efficacy relative to a particular task), a neighborhood's efficacy exists relative to such specific tasks as maintaining public order and reducing crime.

To measure the social control aspect of collective efficacy, Sampson et al. (1997) asked residents whether their neighbors could be counted on to take action under various scenarios (for example, if children skip school and hang out on a street corner, or if the fire station closest to home is being threatened with budget cuts). The cohesion dimension was measured by items that capture the extent of local trust, willingness to help neighbors, a supportive fabric, a lack of conflict, and shared values. Published results show that after adjusting for a range of individual and neighborhood characteristics, including poverty and the density of friendship ties, collective efficacy is associated with substantially lower rates of violence. Neighborhoods high in collective efficacy predict significantly lower rates of violence, even where earlier experience of violence may have depressed collective efficacy because of fear.

Moving away from a focus on private ties, the use of the term "collective efficacy" is meant to signify an emphasis on shared beliefs in a neighborhood's capability in achieving an intended effect coupled with an active sense of engagement on the part of residents. Some density of social networks is essential, to be sure, especially networks rooted in social trust. But the key theoretical point is that networks have to be *activated* to be ultimately meaningful. In this way, collective efficacy helps to elevate the human agency aspect of social life over a perspective that restricts its attention mainly to the accumulation of stocks of social and economic resources. Distinguishing between the resource potential represented by personal ties and the shared expectations for action among neighbors represented by collective efficacy helps clarify the dense networks paradox. *Namely, social networks foster the conditions under which collective efficacy may flourish, but they are not sufficient for the exercise of control.* The theoretical framework of collective efficacy therefore recognizes the transformed landscape of modern urban life and holds that community efficacy may indeed depend on working trust and social interaction, yet it does not require that one's neighbor or the local police officer be thy friend.

Nonexclusive Social Networks and Building Collective Efficacy

It is important to recognize that social relationships are neutral in the sense that they can be drawn upon for negative as well as positive goals. Indeed, collective efficacy theory is open to criticism if resources and social ties are used for nefarious purposes rather than for collective benefits. We would not consider racial exclusion in the form of racially defended neighborhoods, for example, to be a desirable result of social networking. It appears that many neighborhood associations in U.S. cities in the 1960s and 1970s were, in fact, exploited by whites to keep blacks from moving into white working-class areas. In judging whether neighborhood structures serve collective needs, the theory of collective efficacy therefore applies the nonexclusivity requirement of a social good: Does its consumption by one member of a community diminish the sum available to the community as a whole? The concern of this article—safety from crime—is a quintessential social good that yields positive externalities of benefit to all residents of a community, especially its children.

As with other resources that produce positive externalities, collective efficacy is dependent on specific normative and structural contexts. The natural question that follows is this: What are the kinds of contexts that promote (or undermine) collective efficacy and nonexclusive social networks? The evidence is incomplete but suggests that the infrastructure of local organizations and voluntary associations help sustain capacity for social action in a way that transcends traditional personal ties. In other words, organizations are in principle able to foster collective efficacy, often through strategic networking of their own. Whether it be disorder removal, school improvements, or police responses, a continuous stream of challenges faces modern communities, challenges that no longer can be met by relying solely on individuals. Effective action depends on connections among organizations, connections that are not necessarily dense or reflective of the structure of personal ties in a neighborhood. Research supports this position by showing that the density of local organizations and the extent of voluntary associations among residents predict higher levels of collective efficacy, controlling for poverty, social composition, and the crime rate itself (Morenoff et al. 2001).

Inequality in other neighborhood resources also explains the production of collective efficacy. In particular, *concentrated disadvantage* and *residential instability* (especially lack of homeownership) predict lower levels of later collective efficacy, and the associations of disadvantage and housing instability with violence are reduced when collective efficacy is controlled. These patterns are consistent with the inference that neighborhood resources influence violence, in part, through the mediating role of neighborhood efficacy. Social resources and social networks thus create the capacity for collective efficacy, but it is the act of exercising control under conditions of trust that is the most proximate to explaining crime.

Networks of Neighborhoods

As I argued at the outset, networks need not be conceptualized only in personal terms. Neighborhoods are themselves nodes in a larger network of spatial relations. Contrary to the common assumption in criminology of independence among social units, neighborhoods are interdependent and characterized by a functional relationship between what happens at one point in space and what happens elsewhere—a neighborhood's neighbors matter.

Consider first the inexact correspondence between neighborhood boundaries and the ecological properties that shape social interaction. One of the biggest criticisms of neighborhood-level research concerns the artificiality of analytic boundaries; for example, two families living across the street from one another may be arbitrarily assigned to live in different neighborhoods even though they share social ties. Cross-neighborhood ties challenge the urban village and traditional theoretical model, which implicitly assume that neighborhoods represent intact social systems, functioning as islands unto themselves.

Second, spatial dependence is implicated because offenders are disproportionately involved in acts of crime and violence near their homes. From a routine activities perspective, it follows that a neighborhood's risk of violence is heightened by geographical proximity to places where known offenders live or to places characterized by ecological risk factors such as concentrated poverty or low collective efficacy.

A third motivation for studying spatial dependence relates to the notion that interpersonal crimes such as homicide are based on social interaction and thus subject to processes of spatial diffusion where effects may be felt far from the initial point of impact. Acts of violence may instigate a sequence of events that leads to further violence in a spatially channeled way. For example, many homicides are retaliatory in nature; a homicide in one neighborhood may provide the spark that eventually leads to a retaliatory killing in a nearby neighborhood. In addition, most homicides occur among persons known to one another and usually involve networks of association that follow a geographical logic.

There are good reasons, then, to believe that the characteristics of surrounding neighborhoods are crucial to understanding violence in any given neighborhood. Research supports this notion by establishing the salience of spatial proximity and the inequality of neighborhood resources that are played out in citywide dynamics. Racial segregation, manifested in these mechanisms of spatial inequality, explains how, despite similar income profiles, black middle-class neighborhoods are at greater risk for violence than white middle-class neighborhoods because of the former's greater proximity to poor, low collective efficacy areas. In short, crime is affected by the characteristics of spatially proximate neighborhoods, which in turn are affected by adjoining neighborhoods in a spatially linked process that ultimately characterizes the entire metropolitan system. Policies that focus solely on the internal characteristics of neighborhoods, as is typical, are simply insufficient.

Conclusion

The main point of this essay is that social ecology and collective efficacy are key factors in the explanation of why crime is so concentrated in certain neighborhoods. The density of social networks, however, is only one, and probably not the most important, characteristic of neighborhoods that contributes to collective efficacy in reducing crime. Concentrated disadvantage, residential stability, home ownership, voluntary associations, and organizational density appear to be equally important, if not more so, than interpersonal ties. Furthermore, neighborhoods themselves are part of a spatial network encompassing the entire city—not only are individuals embedded but so are neighborhoods.

The future of neighborhood research will probably be increasingly cross national and comparative in nature. Efforts are now underway seeking to examine the general role of spatial inequality and neighborhood efficacy in cities around the world. For example, Sampson and Wikström (2005) demonstrate that rates of violence are predicted by collective efficacy in Stockholm just as in Chicago, and that collective efficacy is promoted by housing stability and undermined by concentrated disadvantage—again similarly in both cities. These data are in accord with a cross-national theory of neighborhood social ecology and crime. Indeed, even though Chicago and Stockholm vary dramatically in their poverty levels and rates of violence, this does not necessarily imply, nor yield, a difference in the fundamental processes or mechanisms that link communities and crime. The emerging data are also consistent with a general approach to policy that emphasizes ameliorating neighborhood inequality in social resources, including metropolitan spatial inequality, and enhancing social conditions that foster the collective efficacy of residents and organizations.

References

Bellair, Paul E. 1997. "Social Interaction and Community Crime: Examining the Importance of Neighbor Networks." *Criminology* 35: 677–703.

Granovetter, Mark S. 1973. "The Strength of Weak Ties." *American Journal of Sociology* 78: 1360–1380.

Kornhauser, Ruth. 1978. *Social Sources of Delinquency*. Chicago: University of Chicago Press.

Morenoff, Jeffrey D., Robert J. Sampson, and Stephen W. Raudenbush. 2001. "Neighborhood Inequality, Collective Efficacy, and the Spatial Dynamics of Urban Violence." *Criminology* 39: 517–560.

Putnam, Robert. 2000. *Bowling Alone: The Collapse and Renewal of American Community*. New York: Simon & Schuster.

Pattillo, Mary E. 1999. *Black Picket Fences: Privilege and Peril Among the Black Middle Class*. Chicago: University of Chicago Press.

Pratt, Travis, and Frances Cullen. 2005. "Assessing the Relative Effects of Macro-Level Predictors of Crime: A Meta-Analysis." *Crime and Justice*, forthcoming.

Sampson, Robert J., Jeffrey D. Morenoff, and Thomas Gannon-Rowley. 2002. "Assessing Neighborhood Effects: Social Processes and New Directions in Research." *Annual Review of Sociology* 28: 443–478.

Sampson, Robert J., Stephen W. Raudenbush, and Earl S. Felton. 1997. "Neighborhoods and Violent Crime: A Multilevel Study of Collective Efficacy." *Science* 277: 918–924.

Sampson, Robert J., and Per-Olof Wikström. 2005. "The Social Order of Violence in Chicago and Stockholm Neighborhoods." In *Order, Conflict, and Violence*, edited by Stathis Kalyvas, Ian Shapiro, and Tarek Masoud. New York: Cambridge University Press, forthcoming.

Wilson, William J. 1978. *The Truly Disadvantaged: The Inner City, the Underclass, and Public Policy*. Chicago: University of Chicago Press.

6.2

Gangs as Social Actors

JOHN M. HAGEDORN
University of Illinois-Chicago

Today, with more than a billion people inhabiting slums in an increasingly urban world (UN-Habitat 2003), and with at least 1.3 billion people living on less than $1 per day (Castells 1996), gangs are more prevalent than ever. The concepts of classical criminology need reexamination to test their relevance in today's fast-changing world.

In the United States and Great Britain, subcultural explanations have always been among criminological theories possessing the most robust power to explain gangs. These explanations argue that within delinquent subcultures young boys (and a few studies include girls) rebel against the discipline of a dreary future in the factory by conforming to the law-violating norms of the group. Youth learned how to be a delinquent through contact with other delinquents as well as by identifying with and imitating media role models.

On the surface, it appears that subcultural and social learning theories may be well suited to describe the gangs of today. The mass media have much more influence globally than ever before and gangs are to be found in every part of the world: from Mumbai to Moscow; from Chicago to the Cape Flats; from Kono to Kingston. Young people have many more gang members to learn from, and a "gangsta" fashion statement consisting of chains, baggy pants, and "shades" exercises enormous influence over young people worldwide through the glitter of music videos.

This essay examines the industrial-era assumptions of subcultural theories and turns to the work of Manuel Castells and Alain Touraine to update and modify them. It finds contemporary gang subcultures are better understood by applying Castells's concept of "resistance identities" to ethnic gangs than by the strain version's of subcultural theory. Rather than defining subcultures as deviant or temporary subterranean versions of capitalist culture, this essay explores how the information age's dissociation of culture from social structure has transformed certain kinds of "identities" into a permanent source of meaning.

Industrial Era Subcultural and Social Learning Theory

The origins of subcultural theory lie in Edwin Suthlerland's (1934) differential association concepts as well as in earlier traditions of cultural anthropology. The apotheosis of United States subcultural theory was in the 1950s and 1960s when Walter Miller (1958) adapted an anthropological approach and Albert Cohen (1955) and Richard Cloward and Lloyd Ohlin (1960) developed aspects of Robert Merton's (1938) strain or anomie theory.[1] During the following decades, Akers's (1973) social learning theory more thoroughly examined how gang subcultures transmitted their values and criminal techniques to individual members.

There were several facets of these analyses, however, that either have not held up over time or have become outdated. Subcultural theorists were always hard pressed to explain why some individuals did *not* adhere to such reputedly powerful subcultural norms. But more important for this essay, the classic gang subcultures of Miller, Cohen, and Cloward, and Ohlin were *all ethnically neutral*. Miller's "lower-class culture" consisted of millions of Americans,[2] but he gave little consideration to ethnic variation. Nor does Cohen discuss possible ethnic differences in delinquent "reaction-formations." Cloward and Ohlin hint that Italians were their model for the criminal subculture, and African Americans living in housing projects their model for the violent subculture; but they emphasized neighborhood opportunity structures, not ethnicity.

Miller's non-ethnic definition of subculture strangely was based on a tradition of anthropological descriptions of primitive cultures. Cohen, Cloward, and Ohlin, and other epigones such as Irving Spergel (1964), in extending Merton's strain thesis, defined gang subcultures as fundamentally the result of delinquents' inability to conform to mainstream cultural norms because of their position in the social structure. None of these scholars examined specific ethnic or racial cultural reactions, apparently assuming that all such ethnic deviations, each being grounded in inequalities in capitalist society, were similar or inconsequential. Their focus also was mainly on males, and gender remained either unexamined or less important.

Although there were many differences between subcultural theorists, most held Enlightenment assumptions of the inevitability of progress and saw gangs as a "dysfunction" of modernizing society. Thus, in the 1960s, the Great Society adopted as its theoretical basis Cloward and Ohlin's "opportunity theory" stressing that increased opportunities would erode away gang subcultures. Like the Chicago School, subcultural theory generally assumed that race and ethnicity were not as important as space and class, and would "decline in significance" as society modernized.

Ron Akers expanded Sutherland's differential association theory by more clearly specifying the processes by which social structure influences the learning of criminal behavior, including an increased emphasis on "imitation" and symbolic learning from the mass media. However, for Akers too, race was treated mainly as a demographic or background variable.

The Work of Alain Touraine and Manuel Castells

While criminology debated the merits of control, strain, and subcultural theory (Short and Strodtbeck 1965; Kornhauser 1978), other disciplines were taking note of fundamental changes in society and their implications for alienated groups. Daniel Bell (1960) was among the first to argue that U.S. society was moving from a stage of industrial production to one of consumption and services.

The mass movements of the 1960s prompted sociologists such as Alain Touraine (1971) to question the assumptions of contemporary social theory, including its subcultural variants. Touraine reacted against subcultural theories for their constriction of the capacities of social action. His *Return of the Actor* (1988) was a call for sociology to escape stultifying social theories that trapped people in a conformist determinism (see also Taylor, Walton, and Young 1973; Bourdieu 1993).

Touraine's study of social movements moved beyond Marxist categories of class and Chicago School social ecology. The "programmed society," as he saw it, was marked by "demodernization" (2000, 76), the rupture between a market-dominated society and cultural identity: "As society comes increasingly to resemble a market in which there are no more ideological or even political issues at stake, all that remains is the struggle for money or the quest for an identity" (Touraine 1995, 181). Modernity itself, Touraine went on, was defined not only by rationalization but also by the "freedom of the actor," the capacity of humans to reflect on their own identities (1995, 274). The ravages of the market have created what both Touraine and Castells call a "Fourth World" of the socially excluded, which can be found mainly in the urban areas of rich and poor countries alike (see also Young 1999). Within ghettoes, barrios, and favelas, social organization with a racialized identity has become widespread:

> It has long been obvious in the United States that exclusion from the world of production and consumption encourages ethnicity, or in other words, an awareness of ethnic identity. The same thing is now becoming obvious in Europe. Those who are no longer defined by the work they do, largely because they are unemployed, define themselves in terms of what they are and, for many of them, this means their ethnic background. These counter-cultures are embodied in gangs, and often in forms of music with a high ethnic content. They become rallying points for a population which has been marginalized but which still wants to be part of the world that has rejected it. (Touraine 1995, 184)

Manuel Castells, Touraine's foremost disciple, called these countercultures "the exclusion of the excluders by the excluded" (1997, 9). Castells's three-volume, encyclopedic *Information Age* argued that the new "network society" was being torn, on the one hand, by unfettered global markets and, on the other, by the "power of identity." For Castells, "legitimizing," "resistance," and "project" identities were markers in a new age where culture has become "autonomous" to the material basis of our existence (1997, 478). When the world becomes too large to be controlled, Castells (1997, 66) says, "social actors aim at shrinking it back to their size and reach." Culture is thus strengthened across the globe *in opposition* to the unsettling speed of the new network society, and often takes the form of religious fundamentalism, nationalism, and communalism.

For Castells, this surge in identity includes the undermining of patriarchalism by women asserting their rights and identity as women. The crisis in the patriarchal family has meant "irreversible" gains for women of all classes and races. Similarly, the cultural response from the ghetto, Castells argues, is not a simple reaction to denied opportunity or industrial-era subcultures but a more permanent expression of outrage and a "culture of urgency" (1997, 64):

> End-of-millennium ghettoes develop a new culture, made out of affliction, rage, and individual reaction against collective exclusion, where blackness matters less than the situations of exclusion that create new sources of identity, for instance territorial gangs, started in the streets, and consolidated in and from the prison. Rap, not jazz, emerges from this culture. This new culture expresses identity, as well, and it is also rooted in black history, and in the venerable American tradition of racism and racial oppression, but it incorporates new elements: the police and penal system as central institutions, the criminal economy as a shop floor, the schools as contested terrain, churches as islands of conciliation, female-centered families, rundown environments, a gang-based social organization, violence as a way of life. There are the themes of new black art and literature emerging from the new ghetto experience. (1997, 57)

For both Touraine and Castells, a culture of outrage and organizations of the socially excluded are not temporary phenomena; they are the permanent and dangerous characteristics of those seeking to survive and hold on to an identity as a desperate solution to a world beyond their control.

A Brief Cultural History of U.S. Gangs in Late Modernity

In the U.S. industrial era, youth gangs were formed and eventually disappeared as their ethnic groups assimilated to American culture and the life-chances of their ethnic groups improved. Most criminological theory saw African Americans as just another ethnic group whose gangs and corresponding high rates of crime would disappear with their completion of the race relations cycle (for a review, see Hagedorn forthcoming).

By the late 1960s, however, it was becoming apparent that the classic notion of the assimilation of nonwhite groups was far from inevitable. As anticolonial movements swept the globe, ghettoes and barrios in the United States exploded with frustration over the failed promises of modernity. Fanon's (1963) notion that, in the first stage of resistance, the colonized inflict the most violence on themselves appeared to be borne out as "Black on Black" violence. Fanon's doctrines were reflected in the Black Panther Jonathon Jackson's nihilistic appeal to "revolutionary suicide."

Although many white gangs still existed in big cities, most were consciously racist, opposed as they were to the attention and dominance of the new black and Latino gangs. For their part, black gangs not only dabbled in revolutionary and nationalist politics but moved to succeed Italian and Sicilian control of vice in their neighborhoods. The repression of the late 1960s destroyed the black and Latino nationalist organizations such as the Black Panthers, the Brown Berets, and the Young Lords, but gangs emerged stronger than ever (Luis Rodriguez 2001).[3]

Within the prisons, nationalist, revolutionary, and Muslim identities were widely adopted by gang members in their attempts to mirror Malcolm X's transformation; for example, the narration of personal change by Monster Kody in Los Angeles (Shakur 1993). In Chicago, the Blackstone Rangers eventually morphed into the El Rukns, a quasireligious community organization (see also Barrios forthcoming). Although this was an extreme case, Black and Latino gangs and their members around the country adopted racialized, and often religious, identities and spouted procommunity rhetoric. Female gang members, and female gangs, apparently grew in number. As deindustrialization hit U.S. cities full force, gangs often became an economic organization dedicated to survival "by any means necessary," especially through the retailing of drugs to outcast ghetto dwellers and affluent whites.

As gangs in the early 1970s were entrenching in Chicago, Detroit, Los Angeles, and other cities, hip hop culture also began its ascent. The story is complex, but hip hop emerged in the South Bronx when Afrikaa Bambaata and others led youth away from gang banging to neighborhood-based hip hop groups. These rappers, MCs, breakers, and graffiti artists began a social movement that would transform youth culture around the world. Bambaata formed the Zulu Nation, which influenced some of the South Bronx's most famous rappers, including LL Cool J and Queen Latifah, and rap music began its drive toward its present cultural avant garde position (see Rose 1994).

Although Castells sees the culture of the ghetto as a nihilistic "culture of urgency," rap's original message was pro-community; rap upheld African heritage, was fun-loving and creative, and was deeply oppositional to white society. Hip hop has become a powerful cultural force that includes the values of community and self-indulgence, of violence and nonviolence, of communalism and a rampant love of money. By the late 1980s, "gangsta rap" had sprouted on the West Coast as a profane, hyperviolent, misogynist, and destructive voice within hip hop, a sardonic version of Cohen's malicious subculture. Los Angeles was the perfect home for gangsta rap, because, unlike New York, gangs there had not gone away but had *institutionalized* since the 1960s. They were also close to Hollywood, where the media corporations would quickly exploit this new genre.

But hip hop, like gangs, was not a fad. The outraged cry of "gangsta rap" had a certain legitimacy in broader circles as a tortured response to social exclusion and a raw, and sometimes poetic, description of survival in the ghetto. The popularity of rap in white suburbs and among youth around the world has given a black cultural shape to teenage rebellion, replacing earlier white icons such as Marlon Brando, Elvis Presley, and the Rolling Stones. Women receive conflicting messages of liberation and flagrant exploitation reflecting the conflicting gender roles in the ghetto as well as in the broader society.

Not only have gangs become permanent fixtures in the urban landscape, but the "gangsta" style has become the cultural cutting edge among youth worldwide.

Subcultures, Globalization, and Identity

Criminology needs to update and revise its subcultural analysis on gangs in at least two ways. First, subcultural and social learning theories, like other trends within criminology, have underestimated and misunderstood the importance of race. DuBois's (1902) notion that race was the fundamental dividing line of the twentieth century has proven to be more accurate than Robert Park's (1940) race relations cycle. Rather than declining in significance, race has become an essential part of the identity of the dispossessed, including their gangs. Classic subcultural and social learning theories have neglected to explore adequately the meaning of race and ethnicity as independent variables in explaining behavior, including that of gangs. Touraine's (2000, 195) point about French immigrant gangs is easily applied to gangs in the United States: "Their lack of involvement in the economy, unemployment and job insecurity lead some young immigrants to try to escape anomie by turning for support to gangs or local associations, the most active of which have a religious orientation."

Second, culture in the information age is stronger than even industrial era subcultural theorists imagined, and different in nature. Earlier notions of subcultures were derivative of a strong (U.S. or capitalist) culture of acquisition, and explored the meaning of the failure of delinquents to attain mainstream goals, at least temporarily. However, since the relative optimism of the earlier modern era, the promise of modernity has been all but extinguished among an increasing population of the "socially excluded," principally black and minority peoples. Subcultures cease to be "dysfunctional" and temporary, and become a permanent and meaningful way of life for the socially excluded, and diffused internationally by the mass media. Identity is no longer mainly what someone does, as was so in the victory of modern over traditional society, but has again become more of what one "is" as people define themselves ethnically and religiously as an anchor against the uncertain tides of globalization. Masculine roles are glorified as "warriors" for the faith or nation, and women are caught between freeing themselves from the bonds of traditional society and defending traditional beliefs in the face of Western cultural hegemony (see Moore forthcoming).

Castells, like other observers, decries the nihilism of "gangsta rap." But this "culture of urgency," destructively exploited by media conglomerates, is only one component of a broader, oppositional hip hop culture; indeed, the main arena for contesting the direction of young people, including gangs, may be hip hop itself. As Touraine (1995, 365) says: "Rather than turning their backs on this mass culture, intellectuals should be releasing its creativity and preventing it from being used for purely commercial purposes."

Gangs today are not "deviant subcultures," but many have become permanent organizations of the socially excluded with an oppositional cultural outlook that not only explains but also protests the conditions of their lives and provides an alternative identity. They must be seen as social actors whom we ignore at our peril. Castells (1998, 149), as usual, has the last word: "The making of a sizeable proportion of the underclass' young men into a dangerous class could well be the most striking expression of the new American dilemma in the information age."

Notes

1. In Great Britain, a similar flowering of subcultural theory took place describing the "mods and rockers" and other rebellious youth as subcultures providing a "delinquent solution" to alienation (Downes 1966). This essay will critique only American subcultural and social learning theories.

2. Miller claimed that lower-class culture influenced between 40 percent and 60 percent of all Americans and 15 percent, or 25 million, made up the "hard core" lower class.

3. This process appears to be not the result of a conspiracy, as some suggest, but a more universal process of globalization. For example, one Latin American journalist (COAV 2002) commented: "Until recently, a rebellious youth from Central America would go into the mountains and join the guerrillas. Today, he leaves the countryside for the city and joins one of the street gangs engaged in common crime without political objectives."

References

Akers, R. L. 1973. *Deviant Behavior: A Social Learning Approach*. Belmont, Calif.: Wadsworth.

Barrios, Rev. L. n.d.. "*A Spirituality of Liberation that Understands Our "Realidad Humana" Without Avoiding Our "Solidaridad Humana": An Experiment Identified as the Almighty Latin Kings/Queens Nation*." In *Gangs in the Global City: Reconsidering Criminology*, edited by J. M. Hagedorn. Champaign, Ill.: University of Illinois Press, forthcoming.

Bell, D. 1960. *The End of Ideology: On the Exhaustion of Political Ideas in the Fifties*. New York: Free Press.

Bourdieu, P. 1993. *The Field of Cultural Production*. New York: Columbia University Press.

Castells, M. 1996. *The Information Age: Economy, Society and Culture*. Vol. 1, *The Rise of the Network Society*. Malden, Mass: Blackwell.

______. 1997. *The Information Age: Economy, Society and Culture*. Vol. 2, *The Power of Identity*. Malden, Mass.: Blackwell.

Children in Organised Armed Violence. 2002. "From Guerrillas to Gangs." Originally 11/18/02 Paraná Online. http://www.paranaonline.org.br.

Cloward, R., and L. Ohlin. 1960. *Delinquency and Opportunity*. Glencoe, Ill: Free Press.

Cohen, A. 1955. *Delinquent Boys*. Glencoe, Ill.: Free Press.

Downes, D. M. 1966. *The Delinquent Solution: A Study in Subcultural Theory*. London: Routledge & Kegan Paul.

DuBois, W. E. B. [1902] 1989. *The Souls of Black Folk*. Reprint, New York: Penguin Books.

Fanon, F. 1963. *The Wretched of the Earth*. New York: Grove Press.

Hagedorn, J. M. n.d., a. "Gangs, Institutions, Race, and Space: The Chicago School Reconsidered." In *Gangs in the Global City: Reconsidering Criminology*, edited by J. M. Hagedorn. Champaign, Ill.: University of Illinois Press, forthcoming.

______. n.d., b. "Gangs in Late Modernity." In *Gangs in the Global City: Reconsidering Criminology*, edited by J. M. Hagedorn. Champaign, Ill.: University of Illinois Press, forthcoming.

Kornhauser, R. R. 1978. *Social Sources of Delinquency: An Appraisal of Analytic Models*. Chicago: University of Chicago Press.

Merton, R. K. 1938. "Social Structure and Anomie." *American Sociological Review* 3: 672–682.

Miller, W. 1958. "Lower Class Culture as a Generating Milieu of Gang Delinquency." *Journal of Social Issues* 14: 5–19.

Moore, J. W. n.d. "Female Gangs: Gender and Globalization." In *Gangs in the Global City: Reconsidering Criminology*, edited by J. H. Hagedorn. Champaign, Ill.: University of Illinois Press, forthcoming.

Park, R. 1940. *Race and Culture*. Chicago: University of Chicago Press.

Rodriguez, L. 2001. *Hearts and Hands: Creating Community in Violent Times*. New York: Seven Stories Press.

Rose, T. 1994. *Black Noise: Rap Music and Black Culture in Contemporary America*. Hanover, N.H.: Wesleyan University Press, published by University Press of New England.

Shakur, S. 1993. *Monster: The Autobiography of an L.A. Gang Member*. New York: Penguin.

Short, J. F., and F. L. Strodtbeck. 1965. *Group Process and Gang Delinquency*. Chicago: University of Chicago Press.

Spergel, I. A. 1964. *Racketville Slumtown Haulberg*. Chicago: University of Chicago Press.

Sutherland, E. H. 1934. *Principles of Criminology*. Chicago: J. B. Lippencott.

Taylor, I., P. Walton, and J. Young. 1973. *The New Criminology: For a Social Theory of Deviance*. New York: Harper and Row.

Touraine, A. 1971. *Post-Industrial Society*. New York: Random House.

______. 1988. *Return of the Actor*. Minneapolis: University of Minnesota Press.

______. 1995. *Critique of Modernity*. Oxford: Blackwell.

______. 2000. *Can We Live Together? Equality and Difference*. Stanford: Stanford University Press.

UN-Habitat. 2003. *Slums of the World: The Face of Urban Poverty in the New Millennium?* Nairobi, Kenya: United Nations Human Settlements Programme.

Young, J. 1999. *The Exclusive Society*. London: Sage.

7

Anomie and Strain Theories

These theories explore the way in which the organization of a society impacts the behavior of its members, and asserts that some forms of societal organization produce more crime than others. Anomie is the idea that during times of rapid change, particularly industrialization, the structural divisions created to maximize the production of goods and services can undermine the moral regulation of behavior. One example is a country that moves from an agricultural-based society to an industrialized society; another is an industrialized society that converts to a service-based or information-based economy. Where this structural change is accompanied by a culture that celebrates individual identity, achievement, and success, but at the same time neglects social responsibility, altruism, and mutual interdependence, the outcome is one of unlimited aspirations, some of which are pursued through criminal behavior. From the point of view of the recently developed institutional-anomie theory, the materiality of industrial society colors its social institutions, which, in turn, undermines their ability to provide adequate moral control; thus, higher rates of crime result.

Strain theory, a U.S. variation of this European concept of anomie, sees a clash between the inequality of the social structure and culturally uniform goals. This mismatch leads to strain and relative deprivation because those without the means cannot achieve their goals, but those who have the means succeed in achieving their goals. Adaptations to the strain of perceived relative deprivation include deviance from conformity and can include crime.

Strain theory assumes that humans are socialized to behave in predictable ways and are goal seeking; the specific goals pursued may vary between individuals, but most share the core societal goals of the American Dream: material success measured by money. Pursuing the American Dream is a driving force for much behavior; if the dream is blocked, the result can be frustration, depression, and anger, emotions that can convert to illegal behavior, either as an illicit means of achieving the desired goals or as a reaction to what is perceived as unjust treatment by the system.

This theory explicitly links macro-level variables (the type of society: capitalism, for example) with micro-level variables (such as frustration, anger, depression, suicide, and crime). From the point of view of strain theories, crime is a normal reaction to abnormal circumstances. Thus, the "health" of a society can be determined by the amount of crime present, or by the ineffectiveness of the society's social institutions to ameliorate these problems. Surprisingly, too little crime is just as pathological as too much crime. Too little crime would represent a rigid, over-controlling system. Too much crime would be found in societies undergoing rapid transformation. Other social factors may also come into play. For example, when the United States experienced tremendous social upheaval and change during the 1960s, crime skyrocketed; yet in the 1990s, crime levels consistently declined.

The policy implications of strain theories involve a variety of ways to change the society, including lowering aspirations, reducing inequalities, and enabling people who are suffering strain to better cope with it. By far the majority of policy suggestions and implementations from traditional strain theories have attempted to increase access to legitimate opportunities. Others have suggested intervening at the micro-level by stopping people from treating others badly and increasing their social supports and coping mechanisms. At the macro-level, global anomie theory suggests that governments should stop treating other nations badly and so reduce the unleashing of hostility against those with power from those without power.

7.1

General Strain Theory

ROBERT AGNEW
Emory University

General Strain Theory (GST) argues that certain stressors increase the likelihood of crime (Agnew 1992, 2006). These fall into three general categories: (1) the failure to achieve positively valued goals, such as money, status, and autonomy; (2) the loss of positively valued stimuli, such as property or a romantic partner; and (3) the presentation of negatively valued stimuli, such as verbal and physical abuse. Such stressors or strains make people feel bad and one of the ways they may cope is through crime. Crime may be a means to reduce strains or escape from them (steal the money one desires, run away from abusive parents); seek revenge against the source of the strain or related targets; or make oneself feel better (through illicit drug use). Not all strained individuals cope through engaging in crime, however. Strained individuals are most likely to engage in criminal coping when they are unable to engage in legal coping, when the costs of crime are low for them, and when they have a disposition toward crime.

This essay reviews the evidence on GST, describes recent developments in GST, and discusses directions for further research on GST. My discussion focuses on: (a) the types of strain most likely to lead to crime, (b) the reasons why strain leads to crime, (c) the factors that influence whether strained individuals cope with crime, and (d) the effects of the larger social environment on strain and the reaction to strain.

The Types of Strain Most Likely to Lead to Crime

Research suggests that a large number of strains or stressors increase the likelihood of crime (e.g., Agnew 2001, 2006; Agnew and White 1992; Aseltine et al. 2000; Baron 2004; Hoffmann and Cerbone 1999; Hoffmann and Miller 1998; Paternoster and Mazerolle 1994). Yet, many strains do not appear to increase crime. For example, the inability to achieve one's educational and occupational goals does not appear to lead to crime (Agnew 2001). This has raised a major question for GST: How can we explain why some strains are related to crime and others are not? I have argued (Agnew 2001) that strains are most likely to lead to crime when they are (1) seen as unjust, (2) high in magnitude, (3) associated with low social control, and (4) create some pressure or incentive for criminal coping.

Drawing on these criteria, I predicted that those strains *most* likely to increase crime include parental rejection; harsh or abusive discipline; negative school experiences, such as low grades and poor relations with teachers; abusive peer relations; chronic unemployment; work in poorly paid, unpleasant jobs; marital problems, including frequent conflicts and abuse; criminal victimization; homelessness; experiences with race/ethnic and gender discrimination; and the inability to achieve certain goals, such as autonomy, masculine status, and money. The strains *least* likely to increase crime include the burdens associated with the care of children and sick/disabled spouses; the excessive demands associated with prestigious, well-paid jobs; unpopularity with peers; and the inability to achieve educational and occupational success goals.

Data support most of these predictions (Agnew 2001, 2006), although certain of these predictions have not been well tested. Until recently, for example, there was little research on the effect of prejudice and discrimination, criminal victimization, and peer abuse on crime. However, a few recent studies suggest that these strains may increase the likelihood of crime (e.g., Agnew 2002; Agnew and Brezina 1997; Baron 2004; Eitle 2002; Eitle and Turner 2002; Simons et al. 2003). More research, however, is needed on the effect of these strains on crime. Also, researchers need to take better account of how strains work together to affect crime. GST predicts that strains are most likely to cause crime when they cluster together in time, thereby overwhelming the individual. Researchers, however, usually fail to investigate such clustering.

The Reasons Why Strains Lead to Crime: The Centrality of Anger

GST argues that the primary reason strains lead to crime is that they contribute to a range of negative emotions, such as anger and frustration. These emotions create pressure for corrective action, and they may also reduce the ability of individuals to cope in a legal manner, reduce concern for the costs of crime, and increase the individual's disposition for crime. Anger, for example, reduces the ability of people to reason with others; reduces awareness of, and concern for, the costs of crime (one is "consumed with rage"); fosters the belief that crime is justified (to "right a wrong"); and creates a desire for revenge. Given these arguments, it is perhaps not surprising that anger occupies a central place in GST and that most GST research has focused on this emotion.

Most studies show that strains increase anger and that anger, in turn, increases the likelihood of crime somewhat, especially violent crime (e.g., Agnew and White 1992; Aseltine et al. 2000; Baron 2004; Broidy 2001; Mazerolle and Piquero 1997). These studies, however, focus on what is known as "trait anger," or the individual's general tendency to experience anger (measured by asking people whether they agree with statements such as "I am a hot-headed person"). They do not examine what is known as "state anger," or the actual experience of anger. Two recent studies, however, have focused on state anger, and they found that individuals are likely to become angry after experiencing certain strains; this anger explains a substantial part of the effect of strains on crime (Jang and Johnson 2003; Mazerolle et al. 2003). Further research should devote more attention to state anger.

Researchers should also examine other negative emotions in addition to anger, including frustration, envy, jealousy, depression, and fear. A few recent studies suggest that strains increase certain of these emotions, which, in turn, increase crime (e.g., Jang and Johnson 2003; Simons et al. 2003). Researchers should also explore the possibility that different emotions lead to different types of crime. For example, anger may be especially conducive to violence; frustration and envy to property crimes such as theft; and fear to escape attempts such as running away and truancy. Related to this, research should examine the factors that influence the emotional reaction to strain; for example, why do some individuals respond to strains with anger, others with depression, and yet others with constructive, corrective, or protective action that may seek to prevent the negative strain from appearing again?

Finally, future research should also examine additional ways in which strains increase crime beyond their effect on negative emotions (see Agnew 2006). In this area, it has been argued that strains may reduce social control. For example, parental abuse may reduce one's bonds or ties to parents. It has also been argued that strains increase the likelihood of association with delinquent peers. For example, individuals who cannot gain money or status through legal channels may join gangs in an effort to enhance their status or to obtain money through illegal channels, such as selling drugs. Finally, strains may foster traits that are conducive to crime, such as low self-control. For example, individuals who are abused or harshly disciplined may develop an irritable disposition. A few studies provide tentative support for these arguments, but more research is needed (see Agnew et al. 2002; Hoffmann and Miller 1998; Paternoster and Mazerolle 1994).

Criminal Coping: Factors that Influence Whether People Cope with Strains Through Crime

Although certain strains increase the likelihood of crime, most people do not cope with strains through crime. GST, therefore, devotes much attention to factors that influence the likelihood of criminal coping. As indicated, people are more likely to engage in criminal coping when they lack the ability to cope in a legal or constructive manner, when they perceive the costs of crime as low, and when they are disposed to criminal behavior patterns. These factors, in turn, are said to be influenced by coping skills and resources (e.g., intelligence, social and problem-solving skills, levels of self-control); level of conventional social support (i.e., the extent to which others such as parents and teachers help them); level of social control (i.e., the extent to which others monitor their behavior and consistently sanction them for crime, their ties to conventional others, their education and job status, and their beliefs regarding crime); and their association with criminal others (who model criminal behavior, reinforce crime patterns, and teach beliefs favorable to crime).

Some research finds that these factors influence the likelihood of criminal coping, but other research does not (e.g., Agnew et al. 2002; Agnew and White 1992; Aseltine et al. 2000; Baron 2004; Hoffmann and Miller 1998; Jang and Johnson 2003; Mazerolle and Maahs 2000; Mazerolle and Piquero 1997; Paternoster and Mazerolle 1994). Although these mixed findings are troubling, there is reason to believe that they occur because the kind of survey data employed by criminologists makes it difficult to determine whether one factor influences the effect of another (see McClelland and Judd 1993 for an explanation of why this is so). For this reason, I have suggested that researchers examine the factors said to influence the effect of strain by using data from other sources, such as experiments (Agnew 2006; also see Mazerolle and Maahs 2000). Such research is starting to find more support for the predictions of GST. For example, many experimental studies examining rehabilitation and prevention programs provide support for GST. These studies usually focus on individuals who are experiencing strain, such as juveniles subject to a range of family and school-related strains. Successful programs typically reduce the likelihood of criminal coping by enhancing coping resources and skills (e.g., by teaching them problem-solving skills); providing increased social support (e.g., by assigning them mentors); increasing the level of control (e.g., by teaching their parents how better to monitor behavior and sanction misdeeds); and/or reducing association with criminal others (see Agnew 2005).

The Effect of the Larger Social Environment on Strain and the Reaction to Strain

GST was developed as a social-psychological theory; that is, it tries to explain individual differences in offending through individual characteristics and the immediate social environment of offenders (family, school, peer, and work environments). This is not, however, to discount the importance of the larger social environment. Indeed, recent work on GST has begun to take greater account of the larger environment by arguing that this affects the likelihood that certain categories of people will experience strains conducive to criminal behavior and that they will cope with these strains through crime. In particular, it has been argued that adolescent, lower-class males who are members of certain racial and ethnic groups and are resident in economically deprived communities are more likely to experience strains conducive to crime and are more likely to cope with them through crime (e.g., Agnew 1997; Brezina et al. 2001; Broidy and Agnew 1997; Hay 2003; Hoffmann and Johnson 2003; Kaufman et al. 2003; Mazerolle 1998; Piquero and Sealock 2004; Warner and Fowler 2003).

For example, it has been argued that males are more likely than females to experience strains such as harsh discipline, criminal victimization (except for sexual abuse), abusive peer relations, and trouble achieving goals such as masculine status (Agnew 2006; Broidy and Agnew 1997). Further, males are more likely to cope with such strains through crime because they are lower in self-control, lower in certain types of social control, and more likely to associate with criminal others—among other things. These differences between males and females stem in part from the larger social environment, including cultural beliefs regarding gender and differences in the social position of males and females.

Further work on GST needs to take greater account of the critical role of larger social forces in creating strain and influencing the reaction to strain. Such a task is beyond the scope of the present article, but I should note that it would be easy to link the insights of GST with those of macro-level theories focusing on the larger environment. Many macro-level theories argue that certain categories of people are more likely to experience particular strains and/or to react to strains through crime. Radical and Marxist theories, for example, argue that those in the lower classes are more subject to a range of strains (such theories sometimes argue that those in the upper classes are also subject to certain strains). Moreover, cultural theories argue that certain categories of people hold beliefs or values that increase the likelihood of their responding to strains through criminal behavior. GST, then, is compatible with many macro-level theories and future work should attempt to better integrate GST with these theories.

Summary

GST has much support, the data suggesting that the presence of a range of strains increases the likelihood of crime and that these strains affect crime partly through their impact on negative emotions. The research on those factors said to influence the effect of strains on crime has been mixed, but this will change as criminologists investigate such factors by using methods other than surveys.

GST, however, is far from a finished product. This essay has discussed several areas in which the theory might be further developed, including efforts to link GST with macro-level theories of crime. And still other areas can be listed (see Agnew 2006). For example, Walsh (2000) has recently discussed the ways in which GST might be better integrated with recent biological and psychological research (also see Agnew et al. 2002). GST, then, will likely experience further revision and development, although I am confident that the central idea of GST will remain unchanged: If you treat people badly, you increase the likelihood they will engage in crime.

References

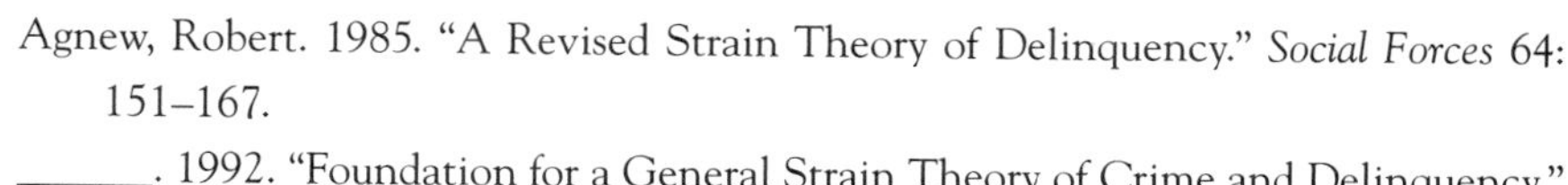

Agnew, Robert. 1985. "A Revised Strain Theory of Delinquency." *Social Forces* 64: 151–167.

______. 1992. "Foundation for a General Strain Theory of Crime and Delinquency." *Criminology* 30: 47–87.

______. 1997. "Stability and Change in Crime Over the Life Course: A Strain Theory Explanation." In vol. 7 of *Developmental Theories of Crime and Delinquency, Advances in Criminological Theory*, edited by Terence P. Thornberry. New Brunswick, N.J.: Transaction.

______. 2001. "Building on the Foundation of General Strain Theory: Specifying the Types of Strain Most Likely to Lead to Crime and Delinquency." *Journal of Research in Crime and Delinquency* 38: 319–361.

______. 2002. "Experienced, Vicarious, and Anticipated Strain: An Exploratory Study Focusing on Physical Victimization and Delinquency." *Justice Quarterly* 19: 603–632.

______. 2005. *Juvenile Delinquency: Causes and Control*. Los Angeles: Roxbury Press, forthcoming.

______. 2006. *Pressured Into Crime: An Overview of General Strain Theory*. Los Angeles: Roxbury Press, forthcoming.

Agnew, Robert, and Timothy Brezina. 1997. "Relational Problems with Peers, Gender, and Delinquency." *Youth and Society* 29: 84–111.

Agnew, Robert, Timothy Brezina, John Paul Wright, and Francis T. Cullen. 2002. "Strain, Personality Traits, and Delinquency: Extending General Strain Theory." *Criminology* 40: 43–72.

Agnew, Robert, and Helene Raskin White. 1992. "An Empirical Test of General Strain Theory." *Criminology* 30: 475–499.

Aseltine, Robert H., Jr., Susan Gore, and Jennifer Gordon. 2000. "Life Stress, Anger and Anxiety, and Delinquency: An Empirical Test of General Strain Theory." *Journal of Health and Social Behavior* 41: 256–275.

Baron, Stephen W. 2004. "General Strain, Street Youth and Crime: A Test of Agnew's Revised Theory." *Criminology* 42: 457–483.

Brezina, Timothy. 1998. "Adolescent Maltreatment and Delinquency: The Question of Intervening Processes." *Journal of Research in Crime and Delinquency* 35: 71–99.

Brezina, Timothy, Alex R. Piquero, and Paul Mazerolle. 2001. "Student Anger and Aggressive Behavior in School: An Initial Test of Agnew's Macro-Level Strain Theory." *Journal of Research in Crime and Delinquency* 38: 362–386.

Broidy, Lisa M. 2001. "A Test of General Strain Theory." *Criminology* 39: 9–33.

Broidy, Lisa, and Robert Agnew. 1997. "Gender and Crime: A General Strain Theory Perspective." *Journal of Research in Crime and Delinquency* 34: 275–306.

Capowich, George P., Paul Mazerolle, and Alex R. Piquero. 2001. "General Strain Theory, Situational Anger, and Social Networks: An Assessment of Conditional Influences." *Journal of Criminal Justice* 29: 445–461.

Colvin, Mark. 2000. *Crime and Coercion*. New York: St. Martin's Press.

Eitle, David J. 2002. "Exploring a Source of Deviance-Producing Strain for Females: Perceived Discrimination and General Strain Theory." *Journal of Criminal Justice* 30: 429–442.

Eitle, David, and R. Jay Turner. 2002. "Exposure to Community Violence and Young Adult Crime: The Effects of Witnessing Violence, Traumatic Victimization, and Other Stressful Life Events." *Journal of Research in Crime and Delinquency* 39: 214–237.

Hay, Carter. 2003. "Family Strain, Gender, and Delinquency." *Sociological Perspectives* 46: 107–136.

Hoffmann, John P., and Felicia G. Cerbone. 1999. "Stressful Life Events and Delinquency Escalation in Early Adolescence." *Criminology* 37: 343–374.

Hoffmann, John P., and Alan S. Miller. 1998. "A Latent Variable Analysis of General Strain Theory." *Journal of Quantitative Criminology* 14: 83–110.

Hoffmann, John P., and Robert A. Johnson. 2003. "A Contextual Analysis of Differential Association, Social Control, and Strain Theories of Delinquency." *Social Forces* 81: 753–785.

Jang, Sung Joon, and Byron R. Johnson. 2003. "Strain, Negative Emotions, and Deviant Coping Among African Americans: A Test of General Strain Theory." *Journal of Quantitative Criminology* 19: 79–105.

Kaufman, Joanne M., Cesar J. Rebellon, Sherod Thaxton, and Robert Agnew. 2003. "A General Strain Theory of the Race-Crime Relationship." Unpublished manuscript.

Mazerolle, Paul. 1998. "Gender, General Strain, and Delinquency: An Empirical Examination." *Justice Quarterly* 15: 65–91.

Mazerolle, Paul, and Jeff Maahs. 2000. "General Strain and Delinquency: An Alternative Examination of Conditioning Influences." *Justice Quarterly* 17: 323–43.

Mazerolle, Paul, and Alex Piquero. 1997. "Violent Responses to Strain: An Examination of Conditioning Influences." *Violence and Victims* 12: 323–343.

Mazerolle, Paul, Alex R. Piquero, and George E. Capowich. 2003. "Examining the Links Between Strain, Situational and Dispositional Anger, and Crime." *Youth & Society* 35: 131–157.

McClelland, Gary H., and Charles M. Judd. 1993. "Statistical Difficulties of Detecting Interactions and Moderator Effects." *Psychological Bulletin* 114: 376–390.

Paternoster, Raymond, and Paul Mazerolle. 1994. "General Strain Theory and Delinquency: A Replication and Extension." *Journal of Research in Crime and Delinquency* 31: 235–263.

Piquero, Nicole Leeper, and Miriam D. Sealock. 2004. "Gender and General Strain Theory: A Preliminary Test of Broidy and Agnew's Gender/GST Hypotheses." *Justice Quarterly* 21: 125–157.

Simons, Ronald L., Yi-Fu Chen, Eric A. Stewart, and Gene H. Brody. 2003. "Incidents of Discrimination and Risk for Delinquency: A Longitudinal Test of Strain Theory with an African American Sample." *Justice Quarterly* 20: 827–854.

Walsh, Anthony. 2000. "Behavior Genetics and Anomie/Strain Theory." *Criminology* 38: 1075–1108.

Warner, Barbara D., and Shannon K. Fowler. 2002. "Strain and Violence: Testing a General Strain Theory Model of Community Violence." *Journal of Criminal Justice* 31: 511–521.

7.2

The Origins, Nature, and Prospects of Institutional-Anomie Theory

RICHARD ROSENFELD
University of Missouri-St. Louis
AND
STEVEN F. MESSNER
University at Albany
State University of New York

A decade ago, we published the first edition of *Crime and the American Dream* (Messner and Rosenfeld 1994). At the time, "institutional-anomie theory" did not exist. That label for our thinking about the relationship between crime and social organization would come later, as empirical research based on our ideas began to emerge, and as we broadened the scope of our thinking beyond the particular cultural and social arrangements that characterize U.S. society (Chamlin and Cochran 1995; Messner and Rosenfeld 2001a). In this essay, we briefly summarize the main tenets of the theory and the empirical research it has stimulated. We then address criticisms of the theory and speculate about its probable future in the study of crime and its control.

The central idea underlying institutional-anomie theory (hereafter IAT) is that a society's level and types of crime are tied to how it is organized. All societies, no matter how small and simple or large and complex, can be characterized by a more or less distinctive *culture* and *social structure*. Culture refers to the values, goals, norms, and beliefs of a society's members, and social structure consists of the statuses and roles that link members to one another through mutual obligations and expectations. Culture defines the "rules of the game" in a particular society; social structure encodes those rules in interrelated social positions, providing "scripts" to guide the behavior of the players.

All societies, if they are to survive, must meet certain basic needs of their members. They must adapt to the environment, enable members to achieve collective goals, integrate members and their diverse activities around core values and beliefs, and maintain the fundamental cultural patterns over time. *Social institutions* are complexes of particular elements of culture and social structure that perform these basic functions of adaptation, goal attainment, integration, and pattern maintenance.[1]

Adaptation to the environment to meet the physical and material needs of a population is the chief function of the economy. Political institutions, or the "polity," enable a population to attain collective goals. Responsibility for social integration and the maintenance of cultural patterns falls to religion, education, and the family system. The interrelations among these institutions constitute a society as an ongoing concern and distinguish it from other societies. Although all institutions play a vital role in meeting basic material and social needs, rarely do they play equal roles. In most societies, one or another institution dominates the others by commanding greater allegiance and resources and by forcing other institutions to accommodate to its particular functions at the expense of their own. All societies, in other words, exhibit a distinctive *institutional balance of power* wherein some institutions are more equal than others.

We argue in *Crime and the American Dream* that the free market economy dominates the institutional structure of society in the United States. As a result, other institutions are more "market driven" than in other societies. Noneconomic institutions "bend" to the economy as plants to sunlight; their rewards and routines conform to economic requirements, and the very language used to describe them has economic overtones. Think of the accommodations families make to economic requirements: how work hours determine household meal and vacation schedules, how an employer's permission is needed if a mother needs to tend to a sick child; how raising a family above all requires having a job. Think of how the economy dominates political life in the United States, how much attention during elections is devoted to the candidates' "tax and spend" policies, how much more efficient government would be, we are told, if it were run like a business. Think of the enormous amount of money it takes to run for political office. Think of how competition for grades in school mimics the competition for income in the labor market.

Now consider how such an institutional arrangement affects the level and nature of crime. In his classic essay published in the 1930s, Robert Merton (1938) calls attention to the pervasive "anomie" in American culture. Anomie refers to a condition wherein the moral foundations of social norms have eroded. "Efficiency norms" that encourage people to achieve goals (primarily for monetary success) by any means necessary reign supreme in an anomic context. We maintain that the dominance of the free-market economy in the institutional structure reinforces "anomic" cultural tendencies that elevate the goal of material success above others and deemphasize the importance of using the legitimate means for attaining success. Under such cultural conditions people tend to cut corners, and they may disobey the law when it impedes the pursuit of economic gain. At the same time, the *social control* exerted by the polity, family, education, and religion is diminished when the institutional balance of power favors the economy. The *social support* institutions provide also weakens (cf. Cullen and Wright 1997). Diminished social control frees people from normative restraints; weakened social support pushes people to meet their material and other needs however they can. Both lead to high rates of criminality.

As Durkheim observed a century ago, all societies necessarily contain some level and type of crime. Although criminality increases when the economy dominates other institutions, alternative institutional configurations also can generate criminality, but of a different sort than that found in market societies. We have speculated that high levels of corruption result under conditions of political dominance and that the dominance of the so-called primordial institutions such as the family and religion leads to excessive social control and human rights abuses (Messner and Rosenfeld 2001a). No one to our knowledge has yet tested these implications of IAT. However, an accumulating body of research and theoretical commentary exists with respect to our portrait of crime under conditions of economic dominance, as typified in the United States.

Several studies offer support for the proposition that high levels of crime result when the economy dominates other social institutions. Our own research indicates that nations with broad and generous social welfare policies, designed to protect people from the unemployment and economic inequality resulting from market forces, have lower crime rates than those where such protections are lacking (Messner and Rosenfeld 1997). Additional studies have shown that noneconomic institutions *condition* the effect of market economies on crime such that the relationship between market outcomes and crime is weaker where these institutions are strong (Chamlin and Cochran 1995; Hannon and DeFronzo 1998; Pratt and Godsey 2003; Savolainen 2000; Stucky 2003). In a somewhat different interpretation of IAT, Maume and Lee (2003) hypothesize that noneconomic institutions *mediate* the effect of market outcomes on crime; they reason that certain conditions, such as economic inequality, undermine the strength of noneconomic institutions and, in turn, levels of crime rise. They find support for this hypothesis in an analysis of counties in the United States.

Even though promising, empirical support for IAT is far from uniform. In general, the theory's "structural" propositions relating crime to the institutional balance of power have fared better in the research literature than its "cultural" propositions linking crime to an anomic emphasis on the goal of material success (see Messner and Rosenfeld forthcoming). Studies of cross-national survey data show that Americans do not differ greatly from other populations in the importance they attach to financial success or their willingness to ignore the rules in the pursuit of goals (Cao 2004; Jensen 2002). However, we have criticized this research for misinterpreting the meaning of some of the survey items and neglecting to consider relevant items on which Americans do display the expected differences with other populations. We also question the exclusive reliance on sample surveys for measuring "culture." Culture to some degree stands apart from individual attitudes and beliefs, and survey responses may reflect uneasiness with, or opposition to, dominant cultural values as much as conformity to them (for an extended discussion, see Messner and Rosenfeld forthcoming). Nonetheless, we take seriously the criticisms of IAT from such studies, which, if nothing else, highlight the difficulties in measuring cultural differences between nations and of demonstrating the effects of culture on behavior.

Another important criticism of IAT is that it neglects the critical role of economic and social inequality in generating high rates of crime, as emphasized in Merton's anomie theory (Beeghley 2003; Bernburg 2002). Merton (1938, 1968) pointed to a contradiction in American society between the universal goal of monetary success and a class system that distributes economic opportunities unequally, thereby pressuring members of the lower classes to employ illegitimate means for achieving success. By extending Merton's theory to encompass the relations among the entire range of social institutions, we devote less attention to the direct criminogenic consequences of social stratification. Our intention is not to downplay inequality as a source of crime but to show how inequality and other market outcomes affect crime *in combination* with the operation of noneconomic institutions. The considerable research cited earlier on the moderating and mediating role of noneconomic institutions in the relationship between economic inequality and crime suggests that we have succeeded at least in interesting others in the interplay between economic and noneconomic institutions in the production of crime.

We depart from Merton in one critical respect. Whereas Merton highlights the disjuncture between the culture and social structure of American society, we emphasize their complementarity. Pronounced economic inequality is not incompatible with a cultural emphasis on competition, individual achievement, and monetary success that applies to all regardless of social position—the essence of the "American Dream." Indeed, if economic rewards were not unequal, if winners could not be distinguished from losers, it is difficult to see how people could be motivated to participate with any enthusiasm in the sometimes harsh and unforgiving competitive race to success. The promise of "making it" keeps the players in the game, and is it possible to "make it," to compete successfully, unless at least some other players are unsuccessful?

For this reason we would not use the term "sick society" to describe the United States or any other society that persists for very long (see Lanier and Henry 2004). In our view, such a characterization confounds a moral evaluation of the desirability of a particular form of social organization with an objective description of its intrinsic nature. There is nothing necessarily "sick," pathological, dysfunctional, or disorganized about a society organized to produce high rates of crime. On the contrary, IAT's central premise is that a particular level and type of crime are a normal outcome of a specified set of cultural and social arrangements. We are tempted to suggest, in fact, that a *low* level of predatory crime would be a sign of "something wrong" with a society that places a premium on the individual competitive pursuit of financial gain, encourages people to create ever more efficient means of besting others, and offers comparatively little protection or comfort to the unsuccessful. We would be on the lookout for something out of the ordinary, something abnormal, about unusually low or falling crime rates in a society organized for crime.

When we wrote the first edition of *Crime and the American Dream*, the United States was the leader of the developed industrial world in its rate of homicide and robbery. The burglary rates also placed it near the top of the list. Although the United States still retains the title as the "murder capital" among developed nations, we no longer lead in robbery, and our burglary rate places us in the middle of the pack. What has happened over the last decade that has depressed our crime rates relative to those of other advanced nations? To some degree, the relative position of the country has fallen as a result of rising crime rates elsewhere. In addition, the economic boom and the collapse of the urban crack markets and their attendant violence during the 1990s contributed to a marked decline in American crime rates, although how much of the crime drop can be attributed to such factors is difficult to say (Blumstein and Wallman 2000; Rosenfeld 2004). One factor that clearly does explain a sizeable portion of the crime drop and sharply distinguishes the United States from all other nations in the world is *mass incarceration*.

American imprisonment rates more than doubled between 1980 and 1990, and grew another 40 percent by 2003 (Beck and Gilliard 1995; Harrison and Beck 2004). The United States now incarcerates its population at a rate five to ten times those of other developed nations (Mauer 2003). The massive scale of incarceration in this country has almost surely depressed the recorded robbery rate and the rates of other serious offenses below what they would be in the absence of such policies. However, as Elliott Currie (1999) has argued, there is an ironic sense in which incarceration does not solve the "real crime problem" but merely drains the pool of criminals away from the public domain, where they can be counted, to institutional settings, where their criminality is hidden. Incarceration "hides" criminality in two important ways: Most obviously, many crimes committed in prisons never enter into the official crime records. In addition, incarceration limits the opportunity for the criminal propensities of prisoners to become manifested in criminal acts. This is, of course, a large part of the rationale for imprisonment—to incapacitate offenders—and it is a legitimate policy objective. Yet, to the extent that incapacitation is the operative goal of imprisonment, high levels of incarceration make the recorded crime rate a problematic indicator of the socially generated degree of *criminality*.

This is where the "sickness" analogy can be useful. As Currie (1999) has observed, if we were interested in assessing the extent to which social or environmental conditions produce physical illness, we would not systematically exclude from our count of diseased persons all those who have been admitted to hospitals. They are precisely the persons who have been most affected by disease. Yet, when we use the officially recorded level of crimes to reflect the criminality in society without adjusting for the size of the incarcerated population, this is essentially what we do. Consider how the rate of influenza in the population would change if a greater proportion of people with the flu were placed in hospitals, only to be dropped from the official influenza statistics. The official influenza rate would fall, but does it make sense to measure influenza without counting flu patients in hospitals? Does it make any more sense to measure "crime" without considering criminals in prisons? Perhaps it might, if persons released from prison were "cured" of criminality and no longer committed crimes. But most prisoners are eventually released from prison and they go on to commit new and often more serious crimes (Rosenfeld, Wallman, and Fornango 2005). Mass incarceration is, at best, a stopgap measure that temporarily suppresses the symptoms—crime—without curing the disease—criminality—the widespread motivation to commit crimes.

When used in this way, the sickness or disease metaphor draws attention to a question requiring greater theoretical and empirical development: How is the *social response* to crime rooted in the very same cultural and social conditions that give rise to criminality? This question poses intriguing research puzzles for a broad range of criminological perspectives, not simply IAT. But it has special relevance for theories that seek not only to explain crime but also to offer guidance for reducing it. IAT is such a theory. It has implications for *social policy* and for *social change*.

On the policy front, we have proposed initiatives, such as paid family leave and universal national service, which would protect families from the full brunt of market forces and socialize the young in the obligations and responsibilities of adulthood (Messner and Rosenfeld 2001b). Changes in sentencing policies that reduce imprisonment rates and more fully integrate convicted offenders in the social and moral life of their communities also are compatible with our thinking about crime and crime control in the

United States. But in the absence of more fundamental social change, only a moment's reflection is required to appreciate the obstacles in the way of such policy reforms.

Permanent reductions in criminality, as opposed to the stabilization of high crime rates, will require a tempering of the extreme materialism and competitive individualism of the American Dream. Those cultural changes, in turn, must be accompanied by a corresponding shift in the institutional balance of power that strengthens the social control and social support functions of noneconomic institutions. Until such changes occur, the crime reductions associated with this or that alteration in social policy will be limited; and unless they occur, significant policy reform is unlikely. Significant social change is not engineered by policymakers acting on their own but is created by *social movements*, organized groups of citizens dedicated to transforming conventional outlooks and institutional practices. We do not have to look far in our own history for examples. The twentieth-century civil rights and women's movements elevated the legal and social status of entire populations even as they exposed continuing inequities and left much unfinished business.

Social movements nearly always encounter stiff opposition and engender social conflict. Some criminological theories, the so-called conflict and critical perspectives (see Chapters 8 and 9), focus squarely on the entrenched social conflicts connected with class, racial, and gender inequalities. The anomie tradition has devoted far less attention to the role of social conflict in crime and its control, and in this respect Lanier and Henry (2004) are right to call it "reformist." Institutional-anomie theory departs from that heritage by emphasizing the necessity of social change for simultaneously achieving less crime and more justice. We suspect that some of its intellectual appeal lies in straddling diverse criminological traditions. Whether it is likely to have any lasting practical value as a guide for policy initiatives or a stimulant for twenty-first-century social movements is a question that must be answered by the reader.

Note

1. This description of the organization and survival requirements of societies comes from the sociologist Talcott Parsons (1951).

References

Beck, Allen J., and Darrell K. Gilliard. 1995. *Prisoners in 1994*. Washington, D.C.: U.S. Department of Justice.

Beeghley, Leonard. 2003. *Homicide: A Sociological Explanation*. Lanham, Md.: Roman & Littlefield.

Bernburg, Jon Gunar. 2002. "Anomie, Social Change, and Crime: A Theoretical Examination of Institutional-Anomie Theory." *British Journal of Criminology* 42: 729–742.

Blumstein, Alfred, and Joel Wallman, eds. 2000. *The Crime Drop in America*. New York: Cambridge University Press.

Cao, Liqun. 2004. "Is American Society More Anomic? A Test of Merton's Theory with Cross-National Data." *International Journal of Comparative and Applied Criminal Justice* 28: 17–31.

Chamlin, Mitchell B., and John K. Cochran. 1995. "Assessing Messner and Rosenfeld's Institutional Anomie Theory: A Partial Test." *Criminology* 33: 411–429.

Cullen, Francis T., and John Paul Wright. 1997. "Liberating the Anomie-Strain Paradigm: Implications from Social-Support Theory." In *The Future of Anomie Theory*, edited by Nikos Passas and Robert Agnew (pp. 187–206). Boston: Northeastern University Press.

Currie, Elliott. 1999. "Reflections on Crime and Criminology at the Millennium." *Western Criminology Review* 2, no. 1. http://www.wcr.sonoma.edu/v2n1/currie.html.

Hannon, Lance, and James DeFronzo. 1998. "The Truly Disadvantaged, Public Assistance, and Crime." *Social Problems* 45: 383–392.

Harrison, Paige M., and Allen J. Beck. 2004. *Prisoners in 2003*. Washington, D.C.: U.S. Department of Justice.

Jensen, Gary. 2002. "Institutional Anomie and Societal Variations in Crime: A Critical Appraisal." *International Journal of Sociology and Social Policy* 22: 45–74.

Lanier, Mark, and Stuart Henry. 2004. *Essential Criminology*. Boulder: Westview Press.

Mauer, Marc. 2003. *Comparative International Rates of Incarceration: An Examination of Causes and Trends*. Washington, D.C.: Sentencing Project.

Maume, Michael O., and Matthew R. Lee. 2003. "Social Institutions and Violence: A Sub-National Test of Institutional Anomie Theory." *Criminology* 41: 1137–1172.

Merton, Robert K. 1938. "Social Structure and Anomie." *American Sociological Review* 3: 672–682.

______. 1968. *Social Theory and Social Structure*. New York: Free Press.

Messner, Steven F., and Richard Rosenfeld. 1994. *Crime and the American Dream*. 1st ed. Belmont, Calif.: Wadsworth.

______. 1997. "Political Restraint of the Market and Levels of Criminal Homicide: A Cross-National Application of Institutional Anomie Theory." *Social Forces* 75: 1393–1416.

———. 2001a. "An Institutional-Anomie Theory of Crime." In *Explaining Criminals and Crime*, edited by R. Paternoster and R. Bachman (pp. 151–160). Los Angeles: Roxbury.

———. 2001b. *Crime and the American Dream*. 3d ed. Belmont, Calif.: Wadsworth.

———. n.d. "The Present and Future of Institutional-Anomie Theory." *Advances in Criminological Theory*. Forthcoming.

Parsons, Talcott. 1951. *The Social System*. New York: Free Press.

Pratt, Travis C., and Timothy W. Godsey. 2003. "Social Support, Inequality, and Homicide: A Cross-National Test of an Integrated Theoretical Model." *Criminology* 41: 611–643.

Rosenfeld, Richard. 2004. "The Case of the Unsolved Crime Decline." *Scientific American* (February): 82–89.

Rosenfeld, Richard, Joel Wallman, and Robert Fornango. 2005. "The Contribution of Ex-Prisoners to Crime Rates." In *Prisoner Reentry and Public Safety*, edited by J. Travis and C. Visher. New York: Cambridge University Press, forthcoming.

Savolainen, Jukka. 2000. "Inequality, Welfare State, and Homicide: Further Support for the Institutional Anomie Theory." *Criminology* 38: 1021–1042.

Stucky, Thomas D. 2003. "Local Politics and Violent Crime in U.S. Cities." *Criminology* 41: 1101–1135.

7.3

Global Anomie Theory and Crime

Nikos Passas
Northeastern University

My interest in the anomie tradition grew as I studied British cultural theories of deviance (e.g., Hall and Jefferson 1976) and left realism (Lea and Young 1984). These works made me realize that despite heavy criticism and an apparent abandonment of anomie theory by criminologists, some basic assumptions and logic had become ingrained in our thought. My first task was to make explicit this legacy and then to explore further the analytic potential of anomie by elaborating earlier statements of it as I was working on my dissertation at the University of Edinburgh.

When I started this work in the 1980s, there were three widely accepted interpretations of it that I took issue with. First, even though Merton stood "on the shoulders" of Durkheim, some argued that the theories and concepts of anomie put forward by the two sociologists were not the same. Second, Merton's version was accused of over-predicting lower-class crime and neglecting upper-class and organizational deviance. Third, Merton's frequent association with functionalist thought reinforced a view that his theory was inherently conservative and biased.

Many of my elaborations addressing the first two issues have been published (Passas 1990, 1997), but this is not so with the third. In my dissertation, I devoted a long chapter in an effort to show (a) that there are important differences between functionalism (a theoretical orientation) and functional analysis (a heuristic method of examining structural arrangements and problems); (b) that anomie theory is best linked to functional analysis rather than to functionalism; and (c) that functional analysis has been in effect guiding radical as well as conservative thinking about crime and its causes. As an illustration of how anomie theory can explain social change and progressive dynamic processes, I have employed this analytical framework to abortion and abortion law reform in Britain (Passas 2003).

Accumulating theoretical and empirical work has demonstrated that there is no class bias in anomie theory, which can explain lower-class street crime and upper-class organizational crime. I should reiterate here, however, my belief that the concept of anomie has not changed from Durkheim to Merton. They did present different arguments on what causes high aspirations and the goals-means disjunction; but for both of them, anomie denotes a loosened commitment to prevailing norms, a trend towards a legitimacy crisis (focused on particular rules). Anomie, then, refers to the weakened guiding power of normative standards, which can be caused by sudden social changes and disjunctions between culturally induced goals and available legitimate means, as well as other causes. It is around this concept that the "anomie tradition" evolves.

I am excited about two main directions of further theoretical elaborations, both of them stemming from, and parallel to, my "global anomie" argument (Passas 2000). The global anomie statement sought to connect criminology with the sociology of globalization and the economics of neoliberalism. As noted in that article, neoliberalism refers to "an economic and political school of thought on the relations between the state, on the one hand, and citizens and the world of trade and commerce, on the other. Because it espouses minimal or no state interference in the market and promotes the lifting of barriers to trade and business transactions across regional and national borders, it certainly becomes a motor of globalization" (Passas 2000, 21).

Neoliberal policies have been applied to rich and poor countries alike with the promise of economic growth, prosperity, freedom, democracy, self-sufficiency, and consumerism, even though the short-term could be characterized by painful austerity measures. In this process, safety nets and welfare state arrangements were reduced or abolished through waves of privatization and deregulation. Global anomie theory argued that economic misconduct and vulnerabilities to exploitation and victimization are expected outcomes of the systematic frustration of raised expectations and widening inequalities (economic, political, technological, power asymmetries). Some state protections were cut and others were allowed to wither at the time they were needed most. Simultaneously, international rules were undermined precisely when normative firmness and legitimacy became critical.

The process towards anomie and deviance without strain, as outlined in global anomie theory and described in Table 7.3.1 (Passas 2000), can be amended in global anomie as follows (Table 7.3.2).

TABLE 7.3.1 Social Processes Leading to Anomie and Deviance

The horizontal lines point to policy implications: this is where interventions can be attempted in order to block this process and prevent misbehavior.

Competitive forces, consumerism, Egalitarian discourse

↓ ←———

(Socially distant) comparative and normative reference groups

↓ ←———

Ends-legal means discrepancy (power/economic/legal asymmetries)

↓ ←———

Perception of injustice; Relative deprivation; Strain

↓ ←———

Anomie: rationalizations, deviant solutions (overemphasis on goals)

↓ ←———

Anomic: deviant subculture (normative referents)

↓ ←———

Deviance without strain

SOURCE: Nikos Passas (2000). "Global Anomie, Dysnomie, and Economic Crime: Hidden Consequences of Globalization and Neo-Liberalism in Russia and around the World." *Social Justice* 27, (2), p. 39.

TABLE 7.3.2 Global Anomie Theory

Neoliberal policies ("passe-partout" measures and forced regulatory symmetries)

↓ ←

Competitive forces and disadvantages (global north still subsidizes its industries)

↓ ←

Ends-legal means discrepancy (power/economic asymmetries), race to the bottom

↓ ←

Budget deficits, drop in welfare standards, social unrest, dependence on expatriates' remittances

↓ ←

Anomie: rationalizations, deviant solutions (e.g., blind eye to illegal immigration or dirty money, extremism/terrorism)

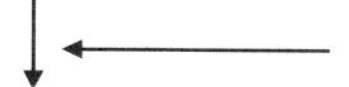

Anomic: deviant normative referents—institutionalization of extreme practices

↓ ←

Deviance without strain (adoption of similar practices by actors not yet in dire straits)

The next steps on the agenda are to seek compatibilities, or ways of "speaking" to other theories, while revising anomie theory to strengthen its relevance to the processes of globalization and transnational deviance, including terrorism. Let us briefly look at each in turn.

There are epistemological and other differences between the anomie tradition and control, labeling, or other perspectives. Yet many of these theories offer clues and hypotheses on the processes that may lead to anomie. How are localized or generalized crises of legitimacy in societal institutions or systems of governance created? Myriad research hypotheses and empirical tests can be inspired through this exercise. I have made some small beginnings in this project (Passas 1990, 1991, 1994, 1995, 1997, 2001), but much work lies ahead.

For example, Sellin's culture conflict theory can specify the conditions under which large numbers of people withdraw their allegiance to a normative framework. In the context of rising numbers of immigrants and ethnic, religious, or ideological polarizations, many sites manifest normative conflicts and unclear guidance to first- or even second-generation immigrants. In the light of global counterterrorism policies, the same withdrawal of allegiance applies to natives who see practices and rules, conceived in the global North, introduced at home. There are plenty of examples relative to financial controls, such as the requirements for the formal identification of clients in regions and cultures traditionally operating on the basis of trust; duties to create and keep records and to report "suspicious transactions" to authorities in places where predominantly informal economies have been the norm. Thanks to media globalism, tourism, and mobility in general, virtually all social groups are close to the "border" with another culture. Resistance and nationalism may be part of the "innovation" adjustment of anomie theory.

Sykes and Matza's techniques of neutralization are manifestations of the process whereby individual and collective actors withdraw their support from particular rules. The formation and perpetuation of such neutralizations into subcultures and the normalization of deviance process can constitute sources of anomie, which are generated by structural contradictions.

Further, the self-fulfilling prophecy of successfully attached labels and profiling practices against certain parts of a society (as we have seen in some cases in the aftermath of the September 11, 2001, attacks and the new powers introduced by the Patriot Act) may be the very sort of structural hurdle toward the attainment of legitimate goals that produces strain, stress, and deviance—leading again to the possible crystallization and normalization of deviance and deviance without strain. Clearly, connections with radical criminology are also possible and need no further elaboration here.

As we entered the new millennium, the world community found itself fractured, conflict laden, and seemingly unable to meet the challenges ahead. Unmet promises of economic development combined with grueling poverty and a lack of support for indigenous democracies frustrate the expectations of ordinary individuals and fuel resentment and fear in many corners of the globe. Indeed, outward support for totalitarian or dictatorial-style regimes, and the overt failure of many states to meet the basic needs of their citizens, feed global anomie. In this context, the option of martyrdom and insurgency becomes more likely and expectable.

Several current empirical areas exemplify the foregoing argument. One can take a look at the core Central Asian states, Kazakhstan, Kyrgyzstan,

Tajikistan, Turkmenistan, and Uzbekistan (the "Stans"), Iraq under coalition occupation, and Afghanistan, where the elected leader is unable to leave his residence without heavy protection provided by foreign guards.

Of course, each of these nations has its own history, politics, and economic situation based on diverse resources and demography. The Stans are five relatively new states, emerging from the Soviet Union and decades of communist rule. Communism may have provided little in the way of political or other freedoms, but little was expected and basic needs were, arguably, met. As leaders rose to take hold of the political reins, a new dialogue and fresh hopes emerged. In the new discourse, novel economic arrangements, free markets, and freedom of religion and democracy were common words. Reality, however, has failed to match the rhetoric for most Central Asians.

Economically, the people are largely impoverished; wealth from state resources is held in the hands of a few. Although some states have made marginal economic gains, relatively little trickled down to the populations at large in the way of social services or meaningful opportunities. The United Nations Children Emergency Fund (UNICEF) reported that child poverty has risen since independence (Sachs 2005; this is a UN report suggesting that we are far behind our goals of poverty reduction). In addition, drug use, particularly opiates, has risen.

Politically, democracy remains an unfilled promise because elections, when held, provide little opportunity for meaningful regime change. Security crackdowns on opposition groups, particularly Islamist parties, remain harsh. Citizens have "disappeared," and allegations of torture by the state apparatus are rife. The desire to practice peaceful Islam has been frustrated in some instances with brutality and torture, thereby contributing to escalation and radicalization. Terrorism and crime are growing. Islamic militancy is perceived as the great threat, and religious and physical repression by the state undoubtedly fuels recruitment drives. Meanwhile, powerful countries, including democracies, ally themselves with and support repressive regimes, such as that of Uzbekistan, as part of the "war on terror" as waged by the United States.

Meanwhile, in Iraq, a "coalition of the willing" led an unsanctioned war—called illegal by the UN Secretary General, and opposed by overwhelming majorities around the world—and removed a dictator by force with the promise of democracy, freedom, equality, prosperity, and security. Not many were sorry to see Saddam Hussein go. He was, after all, a ruler who tortured and killed his own citizens and eliminated political opposition. Not unlike the events in Central Asia, this "liberation" of the Iraqi people came with implicit and explicit hope of an indigenously developed democracy and a greater share in the economic wealth from the country's oil reserves. Not unlike those of Central Asia, Iraqi citizens have found their aspirations quashed by domestic instability and external alliances. Abu Ghraib, a prison once used by the Hussein government for torture and state murder, became a symbol of the inability of the United States to claim a high moral/normative ground. Reports of human rights abuses occurring in other locations in Iraq and Afghanistan by coalition forces have led to investigations, trials, and convictions, as well as arguments that we have only seen the tip of the iceberg.

Especially undermining are practices of what may be called "off-shore justice" in geographic as well as figurative senses. Detainees with virtually no rights (no formal charges, no published names, no contact with lawyer, family or the International Committee of the Red Cross) have gone missing. Others have been taken to Guantanamo Bay, where even FBI agents felt distaste about the harsh (and unproductive, incidentally) interrogations practiced by military and intelligence personnel (see original documents obtained by the ACLU at their Web site: http://www.aclu.org/International/International.cfm?ID=13962&c=3). It is significant that high-level memoranda in the U.S. administration sought to redefine torture and claim that long-standing international norms, such as the Geneva Conventions, did not apply to a class of unilaterally or arbitrarily defined "enemy combatants" and "terrorists." In such Orwellian or Kafkaesque conditions, global anomie theory would predict a further breakdown of national and international normative standards. The application of global anomie theory to this context would show how fact-free and culture-blind policies would not only be ineffective but would bring about counterproductive effects harmful to U.S. interests.

For instance, the theory would recommend careful planning of the peace in Iraq and Afghanistan and preparation of the population for the challenges ahead in a realistic way rather than through the promotion of lofty expectations and false promises. During the invasion, leaflets had called on Iraqi soldiers to lay down their arms, "not risk their life and the life of their comrades," but instead should "leave now, *go home, and learn, grow, prosper*" (Chandrasekaran and Ricks 2003; emphasis added). Instead of offering possibilities of growth and prosperity, one of the first actions of the coalition after the conquest of Baghdad was to lay off the entire army. This sudden unemployment, coupled with arbitrary arrests, home searches, and humiliations, would, according to anomie theory, have been expected to make for individual rage and subsequent insurgency.

The theory would have recommended either encouraging more reasonable expectations or matching the promises with clear and visible efforts to provide security, restore civilian infrastructure, offer employment, and bring various ethnic and religious groups together in an effort to create a new regime, thus paving the ground for a smoother transition. A prudent and informed policy would have involved active outreach or two-way communication with local elders and leaders from the beginning, instead of unilateral decisions that even British allies disagreed with. This would have supported the claim of liberation rather than create an environment where crime is rampant, parents are afraid to send their children to school (if they still stand and function), and where fighting the occupiers is considered an honorable activity, or even a duty. Creating the impression that one authoritarian regime was replaced by another, and thereby losing Iraqi hearts and minds, was critical to the widespread and increasingly sophisticated resistance and insurgency.

These are just some illustrations of how global anomie would have advised against a fight against terror with error. A lack of planning and theoretically or culturally informed policymaking has caused us to fight a war on terror while shooting ourselves in the foot. The consequences extend beyond the immediate areas of conflict. Authoritarian regimes elsewhere may refer to their own perceptions of terror risks and apply abusive measures aimed at political or religious repression. The moral authority to condemn sponsors of terror and oppressors around the world is thereby damaged. At the same time, citizens and organizations from the United States are at higher risk against their person, property, and ability to travel and conduct business profitably in several parts of the world.

What these examples show is that the systematic application of theory can illuminate a particular situation, which has its own inherent value, and also provide scholarly and practical applications for comparative purposes. Central Asia and Iraq are but two of many instances by which we can study and apply global anomie theory. However, by better understanding the process through a variety of case studies, the lessons of global anomie theory can assist policymakers in promoting local and global stability.

References

Chandrasekaran, Rajiv, and Thomas E. Ricks. "U.S. Opens War with Strikes on Baghdad Aimed at Hussein." *Washington Post*, March 20, 2003. http://www.jfkmontreal.com/cache/baghdad_strike/washingtonpost32003.htm.

Hall, Stuart, and Tony Jefferson. 1976. *Resistance Through Rituals: Youth Subcultures in Post-War Britain*. London: Hutchinson.

Lea, John, and Jock Young. 1984. *What Is to Be Done About Law and Order?* Harmondsworth, U.K.: Penguin.

Passas, Nikos. 1990. "Anomie and Corporate Deviance." *Contemporary Crises* 14: 157–178.

______. 1991. "Obediencia Moral Y Desobediencia Civil: El Caso De Los Berrigan." In *Ignacio De Loyola, Magister Artium En Paris 1528–1535*, edited by Julio Caro Baroja and Antonio Beristain (pp. 525–537). Donostia, Spain: Kutxa.

______. 1994. "The Market for Gods and Services: Religion, Commerce and Deviance." *Religion and Social Order* 4: 217–241.

______. 1995. "Continuities in the Anomie Tradition." *Advances in Criminological Theory* 6: 91–112.

______. 1997. "Anomie, Reference Groups, and Relative Deprivation." In *The Future of the Anomie Tradition*, edited by Nikos Passas and Robert Agnew (pp. 62–94). Boston: Northeastern University Press.

______. 2000. "Global Anomie, Dysnomie, and Economic Crime: Hidden Consequences of Globalization and Neo-Liberalism in Russia and Around the World." *Social Justice* 27: 16–44.

______. 2001. "False Accounts: Why Do Company Statements Often Offer a True and Fair View of Virtual Reality?" *European Journal on Criminal Policy and Research* 9: 117–135.

______. 2003. "Abortion and Abortion Law Reform in Britain: Anomie as a Theory of Deviance and Social Change." In *Criminological Studies: Festschift for Marangopoulos*, edited by A. Manganas (pp. 1083–1112). Athens, Greece: Sakkoulas Law Publisher.

Sachs, Jeffrey D. 2005. *Investing in Development: A Practical Plan to Achieve the Millenium Development Goals*. New York: United Nations.

8

Conflict and Radical Theories

Conflict and radical theories are each macro-level theories in that they assume that forces external to the individual, resulting from the organization of society as a whole, shape the nature of social institutions, and within these, channel the behavior of humans and their interactions. Thus they look to society's organizational structure, particularly its divisions or inequalities, as the cause, and as an indicator, of the type and level of crime that society will experience. These theories each view humans as potentially active creative entities who have the ability to shape their social world, but who also recognize that the world, in the form of hierarchical power structures, shapes them. Thus, although recognizing a degree of individual human agency, these theories ultimately see humans as repressed, co-opted, and manipulated for the benefit of dominant powerful interests.

According to these theories, crime stems from conflict between different segments of society fueled by a system of domination based on inequality, alienation, and injustice. Crime is harm that comes from differences in power, and it can be manifested in several ways. Crime can occur when dominant groups/segments define the behavior of subordinate segments as threatening their interests. Dominant groups use law as a weapon to criminalize others' behavior, and use the criminal justice system to enforce their own group's definitions of reality about what is unacceptable for the purpose of preserving their dominant positions in society. These theories also see crime occurring when dominant segments of society directly abuse subordinate segments, such as when corporations pollute the environment or violate health and safety regulations. Crime also is seen as a form of resistance by subordinate segments of society, both to their own domination and to perceived economic and social injustices. Finally, crime occurs when society promotes individual and egotistic interests at the expense of social, collective, altruistic, or humanistic interests.

Despite these similar views of the importance of inequalities as a cause of crime, there are pronounced differences between these theoretical perspectives. From the conflict perspective, inequalities can operate on several dimensions as individuals form groups that compete with other groups in a struggle for limited resources, power, status, and prestige. For example, students may compete for grades, faculty for tenure, police for higher arrest rates, and right-to-life groups for anti-abortion law reform. Thus conflict theorists recognize that crime may stem from differences in economic wealth, a clash of cultures, from the outcome of struggles over status, or from differences in ideology, morality, religion, race, and ethnicity. In this struggle for control, the law is seen a resource to be fought over and as a symbol and instrument of the group or groups who hold power. Through control over law, dominant groups are able to criminalize the behavior of those deviating from their own cultural standards and behavioral norms. Similarly, the criminal justice system is also a tool used to solidify power.

Radical theory, in contrast, drawing directly on Marxist theory, argues that crime is the consequence of a deeper *economic* conflict rooted in economic power and in the appropriation and concentration of wealth by a dominant minority in class-divided societies. They point to the structure of capitalism, based on the private ownership of property, which renders a society "criminogenic" by generating vast inequalities of wealth that provide the conditions for crime. In this view, either government and law are directly controlled by the economic elite or they play a mediating role that softens the worst excesses of exploitation and provides a semblance of legitimacy to the capitalist system.

Not surprisingly, each of these different versions of "conflict/radical" theory has variations in policy. Although radical theory advocates replacing the class inequalities of capitalism with a decentralized socialist society, conflict is more interested in minimizing the inequalities in the existing structure. Each, however, would agree that the existing system in which, as Jeffrey Reiman aptly said, "*The Rich Get Richer and the Poor Get Prison*" should fundamentally change.

8.1

Criminology and Conflict Theory

AUSTIN T. TURK
University of California, Riverside

In the 1960s, I began my effort to help reorient criminology from its ultimately futile quest to learn what is wrong with lawbreakers to the intriguing question of what is wrong with the societies that produce and reproduce criminals, and then discriminate in labeling and punishing them. I had learned to distrust political and religious ideologies that defined truth through allegiance to faith-based doctrines. I opted instead to use scientific research standards to establish what is probably true based on systematic empirical studies versus any notion of absolute truth (Turk 1982b).

From left and right, the reactions have been to me puzzling and provocative. (It is sometimes frustrating even to thick-skinned theorists to be misunderstood or misconstrued!) My earlier efforts to offer rigorous and testable propositions on conflict and criminality (Turk 1966, 1969) were in one assessment caricatured as providing a manual for oppressors aiming to maintain inegalitarian social orders (Taylor, Walton, and Young 1973, 266). Conversely, some textbook authors and panel discussants classified and criticized my work as appearing in some vague sense Marxist—apparently because I emphasized conflict instead of consensus as the fundamental reality and dynamic of politicized social life. Perhaps the basic concern has been that my theoretical work questions the assumptions of those who defend as well as those who attack social orders.

I had set out to identify the conditions that generate conflicts over norms (rules defining right and wrong), then to specify the factors that determine which people deviating from legalized norms are more and which less likely to be defined as criminals in such conflicts.

In an established legal order, most people have been conditioned to believe they are supposed to be either order-givers or order-takers. In my words, this means that some people learn *norms of domination* (that they are superiors, destined to command others), but that most people learn *norms of deference* (that they are inferiors and have to obey orders). The superiors are *authorities;* the inferiors are *subjects*. Criminality is a label imposed on subjects who resist the claims and impositions of authorities. Describing and explaining *criminalization*, the labeling of people as criminals, is the business of criminology. My approach is first to specify the conditions under which conflicts over legal norms are more or less likely, and then to specify the conditions under which the relative probability of criminalization is greater or lesser. At each stage, the key variable is whether the *cultural* (explicitly asserted) and *social* (actual behavioral) norms of subjects and authorities are congruent, that is, whether the stated norm (law or anti-law) and actual behavior agree. The probabilities of normative conflict, and then of criminalization, are predicted to be maximal in the "high-high" combination and minimal in the "low-low" combination. For example, if police enforce a law that forbids people from sleeping in parks but homeless people still insist on their right to use public space, then the congruence between cultural and social norms on both sides is high. Conflict is likely, and the risk of the criminalization of the homeless is greater than it would be if neither side had any real commitment to enforcing or defying the law. Whether considering the relative likelihood of conflict or the relative probability of criminalization, combinations of other variables determine the outcome. The probability of normative-legal conflict depends on whether subjects are organized and how sophisticated each side is in manipulating others. Given that a normative-legal conflict exists, the probability of criminalization varies with (1) whether first-level (police) and higher-level (prosecutors, judges) enforcers are committed to enforcing the law, (2) the relative power of enforcers and resisters, and (3) the realism of each party's actions in regard to their likely impact on the chances of success, defined as avoiding criminalization for resisters, and as stopping resistance for enforcers.

After formulating a theory of criminalization that predicts differences in criminality rates within an established legal order, I moved to the larger question of how legal orders generate or aggravate as well as resolve social conflicts (Turk 1976). Although not denying that law may help to prevent or resolve conflicts, I criticized the prevailing "moral functionalism" that assumes law is necessarily an effective institution promoting social peace and harmony. In defining law as a form of social power, I noted five dimensions of law power in the resources controlled and mobilized through legal mechanisms. These are (1) violence, or police or military power; (2) production, allocation, and the use of material resources, or economic power; (3) decisionmaking processes, or political power; (4) definitions of and access to knowledge, beliefs, and values, or ideological power; and (5) human attention and living time, or diversionary power. In various manifestations and combinations, these forms of power shape legal institutions and processes, often fostering or exacerbating conflicts instead of preventing or resolving them. For instance, gaining law power itself becomes a goal of conflict insofar as the law facilitates defending or advancing the interests or values of some parties against those of others. Law generates conflict by determining what kinds of activities are worth more, and what is the accepted range between the maximum and minimum rewards for different kinds of economic activity. Law defines the lines of social hierarchy, which may sharpen awareness and resentment of status differences, that is, differences in life chances. Law provides the opportunity and the means to deny the reality of conflicts by making it impossible or difficult for them to be articulated (not "justiciable"). And in many other ways law may preclude or hinder the informal resolution of disputes by explicitly pitting contending parties against one another, legitimating inequalities, and producing symbolic rather than acceptable decisions on issues in dispute. In sum, law is, at best, a mixed blessing in its impact on the formation and sustenance of social order.

The next step has been to show that the evidence supports conflict theory against traditional criminology's basic postulates, and that conflict criminology provides the essential cutting edge for the sociology of law (Turk 1984). The traditional postulates are (1) that harmfulness is synonymous with crime, as legally defined; (2) that objective standards for differentiating and measuring harmfulness exist in law; (3) that threats cannot or should not be countered by nongovernmental efforts (authorities alone have the means to deal with threats to society); (4) that the distinction between crime and not-crime is accurately made in the criminalization process, that is, the sequencing from police through prosecutorial to court decisions; and (5) that the law rests on consensus among enlightened (properly socialized) people on the meaning and definition of crime, the nature and degree of harmfulness and threat, the need for governmental rather than nongovernmental social control, and the characteristics and effectiveness of the criminal justice process. Because each of these postulates is refuted by the research evidence, I have concluded that traditional criminology cannot be intellectually defended; it persists only because it is politically useful and safe. The new criminology envisioned as replacing the old is seen as seeking to explain how socially defined deviance relates to *legalization*—the creation of substantive and procedural laws—and *criminalization*—the imposition of sanctions by agents of governmental control. Criminology viewed in this way offers a much needed integrating focus for "law and society" studies: law as a political instrument of social control that is specifically geared to coerce obedience as far as possible whenever authorities feel threatened.

From the outset, conflict theory has been challenged as having no relevance to crime control policymaking. The wrong assumption of the criticism is that crime control options must be "feasible" within the constraints of existing political-economic structures and regimes. In effect, this has left the debate to an either-or confrontation between those who assume that reformist tinkering will resolve conflicts (no major social changes needed) and those who assume that the only solution is to destroy the established social order and somehow construct one that is radically different. My view is that conflict criminology's postulates imply the radical transformation of our current system through specific policy initiatives (Turk 1995). Capital punishment, for example, is rejected by conflict theory, not on ethical or political grounds but because the inevitable biases in its administration exacerbate racial and class (economic) conflicts.

Not surprisingly, my focus has increasingly been on political criminality (Turk 1982a) and specifically on violence between those who defy and defend political authority structures (Turk 2003; 2004). The distinction between legal and illegal political violence is a political construction reflecting the usually greater power of authorities, not an objective product of legal reasoning. It follows that explaining political violence in specific cases requires analysis of the conditions under which the line is drawn.

Variations in the form and level of illegal political violence cannot be explained without also explaining legal political violence. Indeed, the two are linked in a reciprocal causal interaction constituting the key process in the social dynamics of political violence. The ultimate goal is to develop a predictive model of the process that accounts for the escalation and de-escalation of political violence as each side moves from coercive violence to injurious violence and then to destructive violence, or reverses direction. Briefly, *coercive violence* (e.g., authorities suspending civil liberties, resisters vandalizing symbols of authority) aims to persuade opponents to cease or reduce their political actions. *Injurious violence* (e.g., at the extreme, torture by either side) is intended to punish failure to respond to coercive persuasion. The goal of *destructive violence* (e.g., military "search and destroy" operations versus terrorist attacks on defenders and supporters of governmental authority) is to exterminate opponents and their supporters. In the final analysis, my position is that criminology necessarily becomes embedded in political sociology as we deal with the increasingly murky distinctions between legal and illegal, crime and not-crime, authority and power.

References

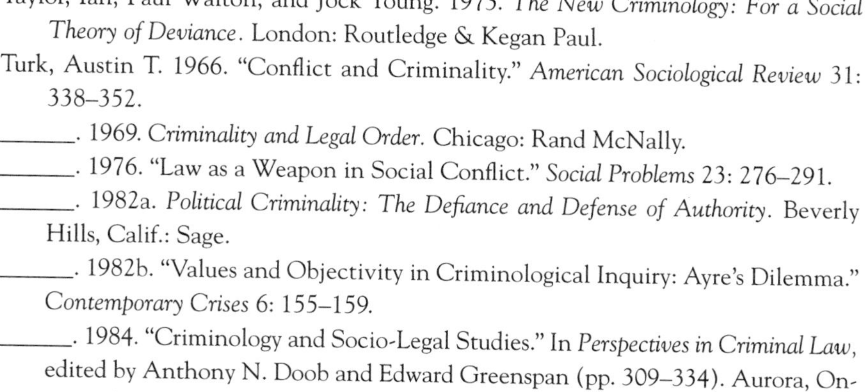

Taylor, Ian, Paul Walton, and Jock Young. 1973. *The New Criminology: For a Social Theory of Deviance*. London: Routledge & Kegan Paul.

Turk, Austin T. 1966. "Conflict and Criminality." *American Sociological Review* 31: 338–352.

______. 1969. *Criminality and Legal Order*. Chicago: Rand McNally.

______. 1976. "Law as a Weapon in Social Conflict." *Social Problems* 23: 276–291.

______. 1982a. *Political Criminality: The Defiance and Defense of Authority*. Beverly Hills, Calif.: Sage.

______. 1982b. "Values and Objectivity in Criminological Inquiry: Ayre's Dilemma." *Contemporary Crises* 6: 155–159.

______. 1984. "Criminology and Socio-Legal Studies." In *Perspectives in Criminal Law*, edited by Anthony N. Doob and Edward Greenspan (pp. 309–334). Aurora, Ontario: Canada Law Book.

______. 1995. "Transformation Versus Revolutionism and Reformism: Policy Implications of Conflict Theory." In *Crime and Public Policy: Putting Theory to Work*, edited by Hugh D. Barlow (pp. 15–27). Boulder: Westview Press.

______. 2003. "Political Violence: Patterns and Trends." In *Crime and Justice at the Millenium: Essays by and in Honor of Marvin E. Wolfgang*, edited by Robert A. Silverman, Terence P. Thornberry, Bernard Cohen, and Barry Krisberg (pp. 31–44). Norwell, Mass.: Kluwer Academic Publishers.

______. 2004. "The Sociology of Terrorism." *Annual Review of Sociology* (pp. 271–286). Palo Alto, Calif.: Annual Reviews.

8.2

The New Radical Criminology and the Same Old Criticisms

Michael J. Lynch
University of South Florida
AND
Paul B. Stretesky
Colorado State University

Radical criminology examines how forms of inequality, oppression, and conflict affect crime and law. In this essay, we will discuss three issues related to radical criminology. First, we examine the history of radical criminology as a school of criminological thought that came on the scene in the 1970s after having been largely abandoned fifty years earlier (Greenberg 1981). Second, we look at several popular criticisms directed at radical criminology. We argue that orthodox criminologists continue to critique radical criminology on the basis of a caricatured view about radical theories of crime and justice produced in the 1970s. In response to those criticisms, radical criminologists refined their approach to focus more intensely on empirical evidence. However, at the same time that radical criminologists became more focused on empirical evidence, other critical criminologies emerged and organized. One result of this organization was the formation of the Division of Critical Criminology within the American Society of Criminology in the 1980s. The creation of the Division helped to isolate radical criminology from other modern critical approaches. At the same time, orthodox criminology continued to reject radical criminology because of (1) its anchoring in political economic theory, (2) its outdated and inaccurate criticisms, and (3) its neglect of the empirical evidence radical criminologists had produced. As a result, radical criminology has tended to float between orthodox and critical criminological perspectives, and in a sense has been marginally acceptable to both approaches, though not integrated fully into either view.

Third, we provide a general critique of orthodox criminology, and conclude by pointing out ways that radical criminology can help direct research and policy. Specifically, we argue that orthodox criminology overemphasizes the causes of lower-class crime at the expense of explaining the crimes of the powerful. The latter crimes are important to consider because they cause more injury and death and cost society much more financially than lower-class crime.

Radical Criminology

The term "radical criminology" has been in existence for thirty years, though its definition has varied somewhat during this period. The roots of radical criminology can be traced to the early twentieth-century work of Willem Bonger ([1916] 1969), who published *Criminality and Economic Conditions*, a work that embraced an empirically informed Marxian view of society and crime. Bonger's main argument was that industrial capitalism produced societies where "egoism" rather than "altruism" dominates social life. Bonger's work suggests, then, that egoism (e.g., greed and selfishness) is the source of criminal thought and that crime in capitalist societies is acting out that thought.

It was not until the 1970s, however, that an identifiable position on crime and justice that could be defined as radical emerged (Beirne and Messerschmidt 2000). In the 1970s, radical criminology was associated with a wide variety of views influenced by the writings of Karl Marx (see Chambliss 1969; Platt 1978; Quinney 1974; Schwendinger and Schwendinger 1977; Spitzer 1975). These studies shared a common element that emphasized the association between class and crime, and class and justice; they also shared a commitment to social and economic change. As this "radical" view of crime and justice matured during the 1980s, the researchers who contributed to this perspective split off into separate specializations, a process that happens in most forms of scholarship as they mature. By the late 1980s, the Division on Critical Criminology (DCC) was formed to unite these specializations under one organization of researchers who shared a set of core concerns. The emergence of postmodern criminology, left realism, peacemaking, restorative justice, and feminist criminology, among other specialties, drew the attention of most members of the new DCC, leaving few researchers interested in traditional political economic views that form the basis of radical criminology (Lynch et al. 2000).

Radical criminology addresses crime and justice issues from the perspective of political economy. This view is highly influenced by radical economic theories that describe how economic structures influence the social organization of society. Of central concern in this view is how the political economy of class and race inequality impact crime and justice. In the late 1980s, and unlike other forms of critical criminology, radical criminological studies became more empirically oriented and offered a variety of tests of explanations of crime and justice. By accepting an approach that reflected the highly empirical work of radical economists (e.g., see the *Review of Radical Political Economy*), radical criminologists were attempting to provide a direct challenge to orthodox criminological explanations that, at least theoretically, were based on acceptance of the claims of positivism (e.g., the weight of empirical evidence should be used to test theory and to reject or accept claims as "true" or "false").

Over the past fifteen years, radical criminologists have produced numerous empirical studies, though the number of these studies cannot be considered large when compared to the number produced in other areas of criminological research. For radicals, the purpose of engaging in empirical research—using the same statistical methods that orthodox criminology has used to stake its knowledge claims—was to produce evidence concerning the explanatory value of radical explanations that would provide a direct challenge to orthodox criminology. By doing so, radicals hoped to produce the kind of evidence that would make it more difficult for orthodox criminologists to reject radical criminology as a theoretically abstract, empirically deficient pursuit. This effort has met with some success, and some orthodox criminologists have begun to appreciate and recognize the contribution that radical criminology can make to the study of crime and justice. We would be overly optimistic, however, if we led readers to believe that this tactic met with broad success. Today, orthodox criminologists tend to cling to a dated critique of radical criminology. We review some of these criticisms below.

Responding to the "Critics"

In our view, the criticisms offered of radical theories have remained unchanged for thirty years, despite the reorientation of radical criminological theory and research. Most of these criticisms were written in the 1970s and have been addressed by radical criminologists. But orthodox criminologists have not paid much attention to the reorientation of radical theories of crime and justice, nor have they revisited the criticisms of radical theory, nor offered legitimate empirical tests of radical propositions about crime and justice, nor attempted to incorporate the empirical regularities discovered by radical criminologists into mainstream theories of crime and justice. We will review four general criticisms of radical criminology:

1. Radical criminology lacks empirical support.
2. Concepts in radical criminology are too abstract and cannot be measured.
3. Radical criminology is a faulty theory of crime because socialism has failed.
4. Cross-national studies of crime and justice disprove the contentions of radical criminology.

Radical Criminology Lacks Empirical Support

There is now much empirical data supporting the contentions of radical criminologists. For instance, Herman and Julia Schwendinger (1997) have spent three decades collecting data and generating tests of their radically situated alternative to subcultural models of crime that demonstrate how class influences subculture formation and networks. Raymond Michalowski and Susan Carlson (1999) have produced empirically sophisticated tests of social structures of accumulation (SSA) theory and its uses for predicting trends in incarcerations and crime rates in the United States. These tests illustrate how SSAs condition the impact of unemployment on crime and imprisonment. In a series of articles, David Barlow, Melissa Barlow and Wes Johnson (1996), and Michael J. Lynch, Paul Stretesky, and Michael Hogan (1999) have tested long-cycle theories as explanations of criminal justice processes. These studies demonstrate how criminal justice cycles reflect economic cycles. SSA and long-cycle theory are both well-recognized components of modern radical economic models (Barlow, Barlow, and Chiricos 1995; Welch, Fenwick, and Roberts 1997).

In an effort to test the primary theoretical assumptions of radical criminology, Lynch (1988) has produced empirical tests assessing the effect of extracting surplus value on rates of crime, imprisonment, and policing. This research focuses attention on the key theoretical aspect of Marx's theory of capitalism: the ability of capitalists to extract surplus value from the production process, and its relationship to the process of economic marginalization.

Stretesky, Lynch, and Burns (2004) have published empirical studies relevant to radical criminology focusing on four areas: environmental justice hypotheses, the enforcement of corporate crime regulations, environmental contaminants that influence criminal behavior, and media reporting of corporate crime (see also Lynch, Stretesky, and Hammond 2000; Stretesky and Lynch 1999). David and Melissa Barlow and Ted Chiricos (1995) and David Altheide and Ray Michalowski (1999) have also made significant contributions to the study of crime in the media. The studies referred to above were produced during the last two decades and do not include important contributions to this literature by David Greenberg and Virginia West (2001), David Jacobs (1979), or John Hagan (1994). Nor does this brief summary refer to the empirical literature on dating violence by Walter DeKeseredy (1990), or the important crime survey work of the left realists (DeKeseredy and Schwartz 1991). Nor have we here alluded to the studies radical criminologists have produced examining racial biases in criminal justice processes. Our point is that the empirical literature associated with radical criminology is now relatively large, and it can no longer be claimed that this view has not been tested, or that empirical tests have resulted in the rejection of this view.

It is also important to note that the empirical studies generated by radical criminologists use a variety of advanced empirical applications and complicated methodologies. The Schwendingers (1997) have used sociometric analysis of relationships to produce three-dimensional representations of social relations between individuals and groups. Several studies have relied on time-series analysis and methods appropriate to the analysis of county-level data such as geographic information systems (GIS). Some of these studies involve the unification of data from criminal justice agencies as well as data from regulatory agencies, such as the Environmental Protection Agency (EPA), to address environmental justice, the meting out of penalties for corporate crime, and the ecological distribution of crime (Stretesky and Lynch 2004).

The continued neglect of these empirical findings by orthodox criminology challenges the claim that orthodox criminology is based on a value-neutral application of scientific principles to the study of crime and justice. Orthodox studies of crime never include the empirical measures central to radical explanations of crime and justice mentioned above. When orthodox criminologists attempt to measure radical propositions, they use weak measures, such as unemployment, that could represent a variety of theoretical positions (see, for example, Sutton 2000).

Critical criminologists also bear some responsibility for perpetuating this invalid criticism concerning the lack of empirical testing of radical theory. Many critical criminologists are hostile to empirical studies, and they reject empirical research as a valid means of understanding (for discussion, see Lynch, Michalowski, and Groves 2000). In their research, nonradical critical criminologists rarely refer to the empirical studies produced by radical criminologists. The consequence is that the empirical studies produced by radical criminologists—which support radical criminological views specifically and critical criminological views indirectly—are never incorporated into the broader literature on crime and justice.

You Can't Measure That: Radical Criminological Theory Is Too Abstract to Be Measured

This is a criticism that isn't directly presented in the literature, but one that we have received from reviewers responding to articles we have submitted to a variety of criminological journals. For example, Marx spent a good deal of time laying out the theory of surplus value and the various equations for its measurement. The equations for measuring surplus value have been repeated often and used in empirical studies produced by widely known and respected Marxian economists. However, reviewers of Lynch's work on surplus value have persistently argued that "surplus value can't be measured," or that the measure being used "is not what Marx meant." In such an environment it is difficult to publish studies that use one of the most important empirical measures of radical theories—one that describes the most basic operation of capitalist economies.

Likewise, our work on the association between levels of crime and the distribution of lead (Pb) in the environment was not well received by reviewers for criminological journals, even though research supporting this association had been reported in medical journals. Once again, reviewers noted that we could not measure lead levels in people or in the environment, even though this has been done by physicians and by the EPA. (Well-known criminologists have repeated these comments to us in person). To publish our findings, we turned to journals outside the field of criminology where this particular ideology was not an issue. Finally, to make our point, let us note that the editor of a leading criminological journal, summarizing reviews of one of our articles and the reason for its rejection, wrote: "Besides, radical criminology has pretty much had its day anyway."

The reviewer comments summarized above have been captured by the widely offered criticism that radical criminology is too abstract to be measured empirically. As noted above, numerous studies indicating that this criticism is invalid have been published. To be sure, some of the concepts used by early radicals were abstract, such as alienation (which, by the way, Marx claims can be measured by the rate of surplus value). These ideas, however, are no less abstract than anomie, or the social bond, or any number of other orthodox criminological concepts. Early radicals failed to develop precise empirical measures of their concepts. But just because they did not measure these concepts doesn't mean the concepts can't be measured; it just means that no one bothered to devise adequate measures, including mainstream critics who were too willing to reject radical explanations of crime and justice without empirical evidence.

Radical Criminology Is Inadequate Because of the Failure of Socialism

One direct criticism of radical criminology is that it is meaningless because socialism—which is widely assumed to be the ultimate agenda of radical criminologists as advocated in the early writings of Richard Quinney and Ian Taylor, Paul Walton and Jock Young—has failed. This is a purely ideological argument that misrepresents reality and lacks empirical support. To be sure, various nations have attempted to organize themselves as communist or socialist entities. What critics fail to acknowledge is that these nations incorrectly implemented the principles of communism as described by Marx and others, or at the very least became fixed in state bureaucracy rather than moving on to fully decentralized communism. For example, during the majority of its existence, the USSR was identified by economists as employing a form of *state-bureaucratic capitalism* (Cliff 1974), not socialism or communism. Further, no criminologist who has employed this criticism has bothered to note that no self-proclaimed communist societies developed on the industrial platform Marx identified as necessary to the success of communism, and that none developed the preferred form of democratic governance Marx favored. These nations are examples, not of the failure of radical criminology, but of the failure of the revolutionaries in these nations to accomplish their stated goals. Further, the nonexistence of fully communist nations is not a relevant criticism. For example, consider that the theory of democracy was invented several centuries before it was actually implemented.

Crime Rates in Socialist Nations Disprove the Contentions of Radical Criminology

The existence of crime in socialist nations has also been a powerful, yet misguided, criticism of radical criminology. Such a criticism misinterprets the premises of radical criminology. A number of nations with low crime rates have mixed political economies that include socialist principles that have helped to minimize the forms of social and economic inequality related to crime. Indeed, crime in these nations, such as Switzerland, Sweden, and Japan, is lower than in advanced, free-market capitalist societies such as the United States.

This criticism also has an interesting implication with respect to orthodox theories of crime. Although crime has not disappeared in the mixed socialist economies found in many other nations, it is certainly lower than in the model of capitalism represented by the U.S. economy. Does this mean, for example, that if crime results from deficient bonding, then mixed socialist economies provide conditions more conducive to forming effective social bonds? Could it mean that if life course influences crime, mixed socialist economies produce life courses that do a better job of promoting social harmony than capitalist life courses; that anomie is worse in capitalist than in mixed socialist economies?

Our Critique of Orthodox Criminology

In the 1930s, Sutherland (1939) sensitized criminologists to the widespread harms presented by corporate and white-collar crime. Since then, numerous studies have indicated that these crimes cause more injury and death and cost society much more in financial terms than ordinary criminal offenses. Orthodox criminology, however, has never shifted its focus, and it remains wedded to explaining the generally less harmful crimes of the lower classes. This has generated a preoccupation with lower-class crime, and policies to control lower-class crimes in the orthodox view. Yet we know that unnecessary surgery, which Reiman (1998) describes as a form of violence, kills more people than homicides. In addition, exposure to illegal acts of pollution kills several times as many people as homicides annually, and violations of workplace health and safety regulations also kill several times as many people as homicides each year. It is a rare exception when elite crimes, which harm many more people than street crimes, are the focus of orthodox criminology. Rather, the orthodox criminologists continue to focus on the individual delinquent or criminal, blaming, for example, families for the high rate of offending in the United States. But corporate offenders do not come from the kinds of families or social circumstances that impact the lower-class criminal. They do not suffer from weak bonds, nor are they the product of an irregular life course or disorganized communities. In the words of Sutherland (1949, 514): "The General Motors Corporation does not violate the law because of an Oedipus complex, the General Electric Company because it is emotionally unstable, the Anaconda Copper Company because of bad housing conditions, the Standard Oil Company because of a lack of recreational facilities, or any of them because of poverty as ordinarily understood."

By ignoring the crimes of the powerful, orthodox criminology has failed to address some of the major problems of our time. Consider two looming problems as examples: global warming and the impending oil crisis. If one pays attention to the scientific literature, global warming, the product of burning carbon releasing fuels (e.g., fossil fuels), is one of the two largest problems facing the modern world and its continued existence. Global warming issues are of interest to radical criminologists because they connect to political economic explanations, to regulation of the corporate environment and environmental laws, and to widespread victimization of the public by corporations operating a fossil fuel economy that have, until recently, promoted fossil fuel and avoided more environmentally conscious economic production alternatives.

Equally compelling is the impending oil crisis predicted by scientists. Geophysicists, although they don't agree on the exact date, agree that at current levels of consumption, the world will run out of oil around the middle of this century. Obviously, the end of oil has broad implications for the survival of humans. From a criminological perspective, the end of oil poses the possibility of devising interesting studies into state-corporate crime that would include examining the energy policy recommendations of the Bush administrations (see the Report of the National Energy Policy Development Group chaired by Vice President Dick Cheney, former CEO of Halliburton, one of the largest oil-product and service companies in the world). In addition, the end of the oil era poses severe limitations on energy use and would require the redesign of the entire criminal justice system, especially in nations such as the United States that operate massive fossil-fuel-reliant police and correctional systems.

Environmental issues are, in short, a major concern for the citizens of the world. Within the United States, for example, 100 million people are exposed to dangerous levels of smog every day. Meeting the challenge of devising and instituting policies, laws, and enforcement practices (as well as nonlegal responses) to address these issues will require the reorganization of society as well as the focus of academic research. Scientific evidence on various environmental issues suggests an increasing threat to the world presented by environmental pollution and the impending oil crisis. In contrast, in two thousand years, crime has not undermined society. The near future will tell whether orthodox criminology is up to the challenge of reorienting its approach away from its focus on ordinary crimes to produce research more responsive to the major harms that victimize the public.

References

Altheide, David, and Raymond Michalowski. 1999. "Fear in the News: A Discourse of Control." *Sociological Quarterly* 40: 475–503.

Barlow, David, Melissa Barlow, and Ted Chiricos. 1993. "Long Economic Cycles and the Criminal-Justice System in the United States." *Crime, Law and Social Change* 19: 143–169.

———. 1995. "Mobilizing Support for Social Control in a Declining Economy: Exploring Ideologies of Crime Within Crime News." *Crime and Delinquency* 41: 191–204.

Barlow, David, Melissa Barlow, and Wes Johnson. 1996. "The Political Economy of Criminal Justice Policy: A Time Series Analysis of Economic Conditions, Crime and Federal Criminal Justice Legislation, 1948–1987." *Justice Quarterly* 13: 223–242.

Bonger, Willem. [1916] 1969. *Criminality and Economic Conditions*. Reprint, Boston: Little, Brown.

Beirne, Piers, and James Messerschmidt. 2000. *Criminology*. Boulder: Westview Press.

Chambliss, William. 1969. *Crime and the Legal Process*. New York: McGraw-Hill.

Cliff, Tony. 1974. *State Capitalism in Russia*. London: Pluto Press.

DeKeseredy, Walter. 1990. "Male Peer Support and Woman Abuse: The Current State of Knowledge." *Sociological Focus* 23: 129–139.

DeKeseredy Walter, and Martin Schwartz. 1991. "British and United States Left Realism: A Critical Comparison." *International Journal of Offender Therapy and Comparative Criminology* 35: 248–262.

Greenberg, David. 1981. *Crime and Capitalism*. Palo Alto, Calif.: Mayfield.

Greenberg, David, and Virginia West. 2001. "State Prison Populations and their Growth, 1971–1991." *Criminology* 39: 615–653.

Hagan, John. 1994. *Crime and Disrepute*. Thousand Oakes, Calif.: Pine Forge Press.

Jacobs, David. 1979. "Inequality and Police Strength: Conflict Theory and Coercive Control in Metropolitan Areas." *American Sociological Review* 44: 913–925.

Lynch, Michael. 1988. "Surplus Value, Crime and Punishment." *Contemporary Crises* 12: 329–344.

Lynch, Michael, Michael Hogan, and Paul Stretesky. 1999. "A Further Look at Long Cycles and Criminal Justice Legislation." *Justice Quarterly* 18: 1101–1120.

Lynch, Michael, Raymond Michalowski, and Bryon Groves. 2000. *The New Primer in Radical Criminology*. Monsey, New York: Criminal Justice Press.

Lynch, Michael J., Paul Stretesky, and Paul Hammond. 2000. "Media Coverage of Chemical Crimes, Hillsborough County, Florida, 1987–1997." *British Journal of Criminology* 40: 111–125.

Lynch, Michael, Paul Stretesky, and Ronald Burns. 2004. "Determinants of Environmental Law Violation Fines Against Petroleum Refineries: Race, Ethnicity, Income, and Aggregation Effects." *Society and Natural Resources* 17: 343–357.

Michalowski, Raymond, and Susan Carlson. 1999. "Unemployment, Imprisonment, and Social Structures of Accumulation: Historical Contingency in the Rusche-Kirchheimer Hypothesis." *Criminology* 37: 217–249.

Platt, Tony. 1978. "Street Crime: A View from the Left." *Crime and Social Justice* 1: 2–10.

Quinney, Richard. 1974. *Critique of the Legal Order*. Boston: Little, Brown.

Reiman, Jeffrey. 1998. *The Rich Get Richer and the Poor Get Prison*. Boston: Allyn and Bacon.

Sampson, Robert, and Janet Lauritsen. 1997. "Racial and Ethnic Disparities in Crime and Criminal Justice in the United States." *Ethnicity, Crime, and Immigration Crime and Justice: A Review of Research* 21: 311–374.

Schwendinger, Herman, and Julia Schwendinger. 1977. "Social Class and the Definition of Crime." *Crime and Social Justice* 7: 4–13.

______.1997. "Charting Subcultures at a Frontier of Knowledge." *British Journal of Sociology* 48: 71–94.

Spitzer, Steven. 1975. "Toward a Marxian Theory of Deviance." *Social Problems* 22: 638–651.

Stretesky, Paul, and Michael Lynch. 1999. "Corporate Environmental Violence and Racism." *Crime, Law and Social Change* 30: 163–184.

______. 2004. "The Relationship Between Lead and Crime." *Journal of Health and Social Behavior* 45: 214–229.

Sutherland, Edwin. 1939. *Criminology*. Philadelphia: Lippincott.

______. 1949. "The White Collar Criminal." In *Encyclopedia of Criminology*, edited by Vernon C. Branham and Samuel B. Kutash (pp. 511–515). New York: Philosophical Library.

Sutton, John. 2000. "Imprisonment and Social Classification in Five Common-Law Democracies, 1955–1985." *American Journal of Sociology* 106: 350–386.

Welch Michael, Melissa Fenwick, and Meredith Roberts. 1997. "Primary Definitions of Crime and Moral Panic: A Content Analysis of Experts' Quotes in Feature Newspaper Articles on Crime." *Journal of Research in Crime and Delinquency* 34: 474–494.

9

Feminist and Gender Theories

Feminist theory in criminology challenges male power and the patriarchal social structure. Feminist criminologists see the major division around which conflict emerges as inequality built on either real or socially constructed differences between men and women. In either case, a patriarchal power structure results, which is harmful and oppressive to women. Patriarchy is the "law of the father" in which male activities and accomplishments are more valued than those of females, and in which societal institutions, from the family to the factory, are structured to privilege men. Feminists point out that within our patriarchal power structures men commit 80 percent of the serious crimes and that this overriding fact needs to be explained.

Those who have been called radical feminists tend to argue that the differences between men and women are real physiological differences that science and observation have clarified, and that these differences result in increased aggression and violence by men relative to women. Feminists who take more of a social constructionist perspective argue that the difference in male violence is a result of the gender-structured world and see crime as an outcome of the way males claim, build, and sustain their power. For them, crime stems from, and is an expression of, men's power, control, and domination over women. Crime is a manifestation of masculinity and is seen as one way of "doing gender." Overall, feminists claim that criminology, including radical criminology, has remained gender-blind and, as such, remains part of the "male stream"; it ignores activism, research, and theory drawn from women's experiences.

More recently, feminist thinking in criminology has moved beyond the simple division between men and women, recognizing that gender is not the central organizing theme but one of several divisions, including class, race, and ethnicity, that act together to oppress and channel women's lives. The intersection of these forces goes deeper in explaining the socially constructed nature of "femininity" and "sexuality" to incorporate the different cultural experiences, socialization patterns, labor market situations, and criminal justice experiences of women of color. This more integrative approach does not deny a gender analysis but requires that gender include sensitivity to racial and ethnic differences. It also builds on previous attempts by socialist and Marxist feminists to incorporate a class dimension into feminist theory. It goes beyond class and race distinctions and the simplistic black/white distinction within a gender analysis to incorporate different cultural experiences, such as those of Latino women, Asian women, Native American women, and women who are mentally or physically challenged, as part of a broadened feminist analysis.

From the feminist perspective, criminal justice policy needs to correct structural and institutionalized differences that expose women to victimization. For some, the reduction of crime is dependent upon the complete removal of patriarchy and its replacement with the values of matriarchy, that is, connectedness, nurturing, and creative difference. Other feminists question whether criminology and criminal justice are too restricted to analyze the harms that are labeled crimes; they argue that there is a richer and more liberating analysis available in feminist theory and social justice studies, one not confined by a perspective largely framed by men.

9.1

Feminist Thinking About Crime

Kathleen Daly
Griffith University

The central questions asked by feminist scholars concern the place of sex/gender relations in the shaping of crime, justice, and criminology. Until recently, feminist perspectives were absent from criminology and criminal justice textbooks. With the second wave of the women's movement in the 1970s, scholars who took feminist perspectives challenged the male-centeredness of the field. Initially, there was an attempt by those who came to be known as "liberal feminists" to describe the different roles of men and women in crime and criminal justice, and to point out that the differences in their involvement in crime and justice reflected differences in their opportunities. There was also a concern to make women visible as active subjects rather than as passive victims of male oppression. As a result of omitting women and gender, criminological theorizing about crime, both women's and men's, was seen as fundamentally flawed.

By the mid-1980s, feminists, drawing on critical social theory and a structural analysis of class and patriarchy, pointed out that women (and men) are subject to gendered power relations. In capturing the variety of approaches in the mid-1980s, Meda Chesney-Lind and I described differences between liberal feminism, radical feminism, Marxist feminism, and socialist feminism, showing how each differently conceptualized gender relations and strategies for social change (Daly and Chesney-Lind 1988).

Major shifts occurred in feminist thinking during the 1990s: Greater emphasis was placed on differences among women, representations of women and gender, and different epistemologies in knowledge production. This became particularly important for feminists influenced by poststructural, postcolonial, postmodern, and critical race theories, each of which drew attention to the discursive power of criminological and legal texts in representing sex/gender and women. This led to two developments: First, there emerged a proliferation of ways to relate sex/gender to crime and justice system practices, which have been collectively, though reluctantly, called "feminist criminologies" (Daly 2001). Second, there was recognition that criminology may be an unhelpful starting point from which to analyze how gender shapes crime and justice. For example, Carol Smart (1990a) rejected the idea of a "feminist criminology" because she saw that criminology could offer little to feminist scholarship, and she questioned the value of the criminological enterprise more generally. Other feminist scholars have seen the value in developing "gender aware criminologies" (Gelsthorpe 1997).

Feminist scholars are more likely to begin with theories of sex/gender, applying these to crime and criminal justice, than to begin with theories of crime from mainstream criminology. Among the central questions asked are how does sex/gender structure women's and men's identities and actions and how, as active agents, do men and women produce the structures that shape them? Approached in this way, feminist scholars are concerned with: (1) the intersections of class, race, and gender; (2) sex/gender as an accomplishment or a production—referred to as "doing gender"; and (3) sexual difference and the relation it has both to gender and the institutionalization of cultural and structural categories—referred to as "sexed bodies" (Daly 1997). Feminist scholars show relatively less interest in developing general theories of crime and greater interest in building theories about women's lawbreaking and victimization, the gendered qualities of crime and victimization, and the discursive power of dominant discourses (criminological and legal). Feminist modes of inquiry have become increasingly reflexive, and there are different epistemologies in producing feminist knowledge: empiricist, standpoint, and postmodern (Smart 1990a; Daly 1997).

Class-Race-Gender

This mode of feminist inquiry, which in the United States emerged from the struggles of black women in the civil rights movement, refers to the interrelationship of the multiple inequalities that structure identities and actions (Daly 1997; Simpson 1991; Daly and Maher 1998). The emphasis on multiple inequalities expands to include other hierarchies of power that are based on a variety of differences such as age and dis/ability. These inequalities are seen as an intersecting and interlocking matrix that excludes and subordinates some and includes and privileges others. Such exclusions are not deterministic; they are actively produced as men and women evoke the various dimensions of embodied structures through their relations and actions.

The production and reproduction of these multiple and intertwined dimensions of inequality take the form of a fluid social structure that is contingent rather than fixed. Using this kind of analysis, some feminist criminologists have examined crime from a variety of positions within the structural matrix. For example, in the late 1980s and early 1990s Lisa Maher (1997) studied female drug users in New York City drug markets to analyze their circumstances as offenders, mothers, wives, and victims, and to determine how these articulated with race and ethnicity. By moving within and between these structures of inequality, Maher showed the complex intermeshing of exclusions that structured women's life-worlds, identities, and courses of action at the height of the crack cocaine drug trade. She revealed how the enforcement of gender and racial divisions in the informal street drug economy limited women's economic opportunities, placed them at a disadvantage to men, and channeled them into sex work. Rather than viewing the women as pathologically addicted "crack mothers," Maher revealed them to be active agents working in the informal economy, although restricted by the combined effects of gender and the racialized power structure of the street. One of the ways women resisted their limited opportunities and the denigration of sex work was by "viccing" their clients, or robbing them. This illustrates the concept of "blurred boundaries," whereby women are at the same time victims of crime and offenders (Daly and Maher 1998). Indeed, for some feminist scholars, women's crime is viewed as resistance to victimization or as the criminalization of resistance (Campbell 1993; Chesney-Lind 1997). However, Maher's method of analysis offers a more complex reading of the interplay of victimization and volition. Although "viccing" gave women some degree of control and momentary power over the conditions of their work, it also rendered them even more vulnerable to further victimization.

Doing Gender

This feminist mode of inquiry focused on the situations, social practices, and interactions that socially construct gender and a gendered world. West and Zimmerman (1987, 129) described gender as a "situated accomplishment," which emerges as "an outcome of and rationale for . . . social arrangements" and "a means of legitimating [a] fundamental division . . . of society." They point out that the routine practices and recurring accomplishments create differences between men and women that "essentialize sexual natures" (1987, 138). This social constructionist argument was then extended to include the accomplishment of race and class, as in "doing race" and "doing class," and ultimately in the concept of "doing difference" (West and Fenstermaker 1995). From this perspective, interactive encounters become experiences that are raced, classed, and gendered, meaning that action is not engaged without being framed by these interactive dimensions, nor interpreted without being subjected to these lenses. Some critics have argued that a social constructionist mode of inquiry focuses too much on simple situated performances and ignores the significance and impact of power and oppression (Collins et al. 1995).

In applying the concept of "doing gender" to crime, James Messerschmidt (1993) draws on Giddens's (1984) structuration theory, which sees structure as enabling and constraining and as produced by interaction yet preceded by the interaction that continues to produce it as a mutually constitutive outcome. For Messerschmidt, crime is seen as one set of resources and embodied practices that enable men to accomplish masculinity, and it may be particularly invoked when other resources for this accomplishment are absent. From this perspective, crime is not only the outcome of its own social accomplishment but also the resource for it. As I have argued (Daly 1997, 37), the difficulty with this application is that it refocuses our attention on boys and men and differentiates them from all that is feminine. Its terms are specific to men and crime in that we would be unlikely to imagine that women's crime is a resource for doing femininity, a means of creating differences from boys and men. There is some value in this approach for explaining one kind of site for the production of masculinities, but not all crime could be explained in these terms. Other scholars have used a "doing gender" framework to examine gender in the criminal justice system (Martin and Jurik 1996).

Sexed Bodies

Drawing largely from Foucault's analysis of the male body as a site of disciplinary practices, this third mode of feminist inquiry focused on sexual difference and the relationship of sex and gender as corporeal and cultural categories. Moira Gatens (1996, reprint of a 1983 article) argues early on that we should view male and female bodies not as neutral but as "sexed" or embodied. She challenges the strong distinction typically drawn between "sex" (the biological categories of male and female) and "gender" (the social categories of masculinity and femininity). For Gatens, such a distinction assumes that the mind is a blank slate, ready to be re-socialized, and that there is no connection between the female body and femininity (or the male body and masculinity). This denies sex-specific corporeality, and the ability to see differences in how male and female bodies live out masculine and feminine behavior and experiences. Gatens aims to bring a materiality to the social and cultural construction of the body, and she proposed that gender is best viewed as "the way in which power takes hold of and constructs bodies in particular ways . . . both as their target and as their vehicle of expression" (Gatens 1996, 70).

Within this mode of inquiry, Elizabeth Grotz (1994) calls for a rethinking of our ideas about the body and rejects the ideas of those who see it as a real material natural entity with a pre-social existence; she also rejects the view that the body is socially, culturally, or otherwise constructed, without an intrinsic material existence. She argues that both are part of the constitution of bodies and help construct our view of bodies. Thus, she argues against sex as an essentialist category and gender as a constructionist category; rather, we should understand the interrelationship between these polarized positions.

Carol Smart, a pioneering feminist critic of criminological theory (Smart 1976), has more recently taken a "sexed bodies" approach in analyzing how law and legal practices construct "commonsense perceptions of difference" (Smart 1990b). By examining the crime of rape and rape trials, she shows how human subjects are constructed differently and can be transformed through differing discursive frames of reference. For example, the representation of the sexed woman, as the eternal victim in feminist discourse, is transformed into a deserving victim, a victimized sexed body, in legal discourse. Thus, Smart suggests that feminist discourse is unable to challenge the representation of women in rape law because it is forced to collude with the greater power of legal discourse in abstracting these differences (1990b). In a later work, Smart (1995) describes law as a gendering practice and a sexing practice; they work alongside each other, perpetuating the feminine woman and the biological woman.

As I have argued (Daly 1997), the sexed bodies mode of feminist inquiry has both value and problems. For example, it enables us to explore and understand how crime is differently experienced by male/female bodies, and by masculine/feminine subjects. It calls attention to the fact of sexual difference and sex-specific corporeality, with significant consequences for research, policy, and knowledge production itself. A problem with the sexed bodies perspective is that it may draw us back to viewing the world through the lens of sexual difference alone, and it may foreground sex and gender over other divisions such as race, ethnicity, and class.

Challenges and Prospects for Feminist Contributions to Criminology

Although some feminist scholars call for abandoning criminology as a starting point for analyses of crime and victimization, feminist inquiry will continue to make significant contributions to a criminological field that was once dominated by male concepts, theories, and assumptions. Feminist scholars' exposure of these limitations has brought about criticisms from some, who believe that feminist thinking is politically driven rather than neutral (Pinnick, Koertge, and Almeder 2003). Such critique is weakened with the realization that all theories, including mainstream criminological theories, are value-laden. Jody Miller (2003, 22) says, "The outright rejection of feminist criminology as 'too political' holds little ground as a legitimate critique." She points out that some of the most important critiques of feminist criminology have come from debates among feminists. Indeed, feminist thought has undergone major shifts over time, illustrated by the three modes of feminist inquiry discussed above: a shift from gender alone to a more inclusive consideration of class-race-gender; a shift from material structures alone to socially constructed forms of doing gender; and a shift from the mind-body dualism toward a more sophisticated understanding of the relationship between sexual and gender difference in sexed bodies. Where do feminist contributions to crime and criminal justice go from here?

In 1998, I outlined four ways in which criminology was building theories of gender and crime through feminist and nonfeminist perspectives (Daly 1998, 94–99):

1. *Gender Ratio of Crime:* What is the nature of, and what explains gender differences in lawbreaking and arrests for crime? This area is by far the most developed, as criminologists (largely, but not exclusively, nonfeminist) attempt to explain why boys and men are more involved in crime.
2. *Gendered Pathways:* What is the nature of, and what explains the character of girls'/women's and boys'/men's pathways to lawbreaking?
3. *Gendered Crime:* What are the contexts and qualities of boys'/men's and girls'/women's illegal acts? What is the social organization of particular offenses?
4. *Gendered Lives:* How does gender organize the ways in which men and women survive, take care of themselves and others, and find shelter and food? How does gender structure thinkable courses of action and identities?

Feminist researchers may address these areas with a focus on class, racial-ethnic, or other sources of variability; or they may take a "doing gender" or "sexed bodies" approach. However, field expansion comes from two sources: one that begins with theories of crime (mainstream); and the other, with theories of sex/gender (feminist). This expansion creates different types of knowledge about women, gender, and crime. For example, some wish to devise a "gender-neutral" theory of crime, which at the same time takes a "gendered" approach (Steffensmeier and Allan 1996). Gender-neutral theories of crime are, for me and other feminist scholars, unthinkable; and it is difficult to see the logic of a gender-neutral theory that purports also to be gendered (Daly 1998, 100). It is better to use feminist perspectives that explicitly address the profound significance of sex/gender (along with other social relations) in shaping human existence, human behavior, social institutions, and society. As feminist contributions to scholarship on crime and criminal justice continue to expand, we can look forward to significant contributions that critically engage and challenge the criminological imagination.

References

Campbell, Ann. 1993. *Men, Women and Aggression*. New York: Basic Books.

Chesney-Lind, Meda. 1997. *The Female Offender: Girls, Women and Crime*. Thousand Oaks, Calif.: Sage.

Collins, Patricia Hill, Lionel A. Maldonado, Dana Y. Takagi, Barrie Thorne, Lynn Weber, and Howard Winant. 1995. "Symposium: On West and Fenstermaker's 'Doing difference.'" *Gender & Society* 9: 491–506.

Daly, Kathleen. 1997. "Different Ways of Conceptualizing Sex/Gender in Feminist Theory and Their Implications for Criminology." *Theoretical Criminology* 1: 25–51.

______. 1998. "Gender, Crime and Criminology." In *The Handbook of Crime and Punishment*, edited by Michael Tonry (pp. 85–108). New York: Oxford University Press.

______. 2001. "Feminist Criminologies." In *The Sage Dictionary of Criminology*, edited by Eugene McLaughlin and John Muncie (pp. 119–121). London: Sage.

Daly, Kathleen, and Meda Chesney-Lind. 1988. "Feminism and Criminology." *Justice Quarterly* 5: 497–538.

Gatens, Moira. 1996. *Imaginary Bodies: Ethics, Power and Corporeality*. New York: Routledge.

Giddens, Anthony. 1984. *The Constitution of Society: Outline of the Theory of Structuration*. Oxford: Polity Press.

Grotz, Elizabeth. 1994. *Volatile Bodies: Toward a Corporeal Feminism*. St. Leonards, NSW: Allen and Unwin.

Gelsthorpe, Loraine. 1997. "Feminism and Criminology." In *The Oxford Handbook of Criminology*, edited by Mike Maguire, Rod Morgan, and Robert Reiner. Oxford: Oxford University Press.

Maher, Lisa. 1997. *Sexed Work: Gender, Race and Resistance in a Brooklyn Drug Market*. Oxford: Clarendon Press.

Martin, Susan E., and Nancy Jurik. 1996. *Doing Justice, Doing Gender*. Newbury Park, Calif.: Sage.

Messerschmidt, James, W. 1993. *Masculinities and Crime: Critique and Reconceptualization of Theory*. Lanham, Md.: Rowman and Littlefield.

Miller, Jody. 2003. "Feminist Criminology." In *Controversies in Critical Criminology*, edited by Martin D. Schwartz and Suzanne E. Hatty (pp. 15–27). Cincinnati, Ohio: Anderson.

Pinnick, Cassandra, Noretta Koertge, and Robert Almeder, eds. 2003. *Scrutinizing Feminist Epistemology: An Examination of Gender in Science*. New Brunswick, N.J.: Rutgers University Press.

Simpson, Sally. 1991. "Caste, Class and Violent Crime: Explaining Differences in Female Offending." *Criminology* 29: 115–135.

Smart, Carol. 1976. *Women, Crime and Criminology*. London: Routledge and Kegan Paul.

______. 1990a. "Feminist Approaches to Criminology, or Postmodern Woman Meets Atavistic Man." In *Feminist Perspectives in Criminology*, edited by Loraine Gelsthorpe and Allison Morris (pp. 70–84). Philadelphia: Open University Press.

______. 1990b. "Law's Power, the Sexed Body and Feminist Discourse." *Journal of Law and Society* 17: 194–210.

______. 1995. *Law, Crime and Sexuality: Essays in Feminism*. London: Sage.

Steffensmeier, Darrell, and Emilie Allan. 1996. "Gender and Crime: Toward a Gendered Theory of Female Offending." *Annual Review of Sociology* 22: 459–487.

West, Candice, and Sarah Fenstermaker. 1995. "Doing Difference." *Gender & Society* 9: 8–37.

West, Candice, and Don H. Zimmerman. 1987. "Doing Gender." *Gender & Society* 1: 125–151.

9.2

Masculinities and Theoretical Criminology

James W. Messerschmidt
University of Southern Maine

In the history of theoretical criminology, two luminaries are significant—Edwin Sutherland and Albert Cohen—because they placed masculinity on the criminological agenda. These two sociological criminologists were among the first to perceive the theoretical importance of the gendered nature of crime. Yet Sutherland and Cohen understood gender through a biologically based sex-role theory, the weaknesses of which are now well understood: It provides no grasp of gendered power, human agency, and the varieties of masculinities and femininities constructed historically, cross-culturally, in a given society, and throughout the life course (Connell 1987). Moreover, the social and historical context in which Sutherland and Cohen wrote embodied a relative absence of feminist theorizing and politics and a presumed natural difference between women and men (Messerschmidt 1993).

However, the rise of second-wave feminism—originating in the 1960s—challenged this masculinist nature of criminology by illuminating the patterns of gendered power that had been all but ignored. As a result of feminism, not only is the importance of gender to understanding crime more broadly acknowledged but also it has led to the critical study of masculinity and crime. Indeed, the gendered practices of men and boys raise significant questions about crime. Men and boys dominate crime.

Arrest, self-report, and victimization data reflect that men and boys perpetrate more of the conventional crimes, including the more serious of these crimes, than do women and girls. Moreover, men have a virtual monopoly on the commission of syndicated, corporate, and political crime. Thus, it is not surprising that criminologists have consistently advanced gender as the strongest predictor of criminal involvement. Consequently, studying masculinities provides insights into understanding the highly gendered ratio of crime in industrialized societies.

The three major contemporary theoretical perspectives conceptualizing the relationship between gender and crime are Hagan's (1989) power control theory; Agnew's (1992; 2001) strain theory; and Messerschmidt's (2004) structured action theory.

Hagan (1989) argues that in industrialized societies an instrument-object relationship exists between parents and children. Parents are the instruments of control and their objects are children, and this relationship shapes the social reproduction of gender. Hagan identifies two family structures based on women's participation in the paid labor market, "patriarchal" and "egalitarian." In patriarchal families, the husband/father works outside the home in an authority position and the wife/mother works at home. Patriarchal families, through sex-role socialization, "reproduce daughters who focus their futures around domestic labor and consumption, as contrasted with sons who are prepared for participation in direct production" (1989, 156). In egalitarian families, the husband/father and wife/mother both work in authority positions outside the home. These families "socially reproduce daughters who are prepared along with sons to join the production sphere" (1989, 157).

In both types of families, daughters are less criminal than sons because daughters are more controlled by their mothers. Hagan argues, however, that daughters in patriarchal families are more often taught by parents to avoid risk-taking endeavors; whereas in egalitarian families, daughters and sons are taught to be more open to taking risks. It is this combination of the instrument-object relationship and corresponding socialization of risk taking that affects delinquency. As a result, egalitarian families maintain smaller gender differences in delinquency: "Daughters become more like sons in their involvement in such forms of risk taking as delinquency" (1989, 158). Sons are, for the most part, ignored and gender differences in crime are explained by a concentration on the characteristics of mothers and daughters.

Agnew (1992) identifies three forms of "strain" that may lead to delinquency: the failure to achieve positively valued goals (such as disjunctions between expectations and actual achievements), the removal of positively valued stimuli from the individual (such as a loss of a girlfriend/boyfriend or death of a parent), and the presence of negative stimuli (such as child abuse/neglect or negative relations with parents). In examining strain in relation to gender and crime, Agnew (2001) concentrates on this question: Why do males have a higher crime rate than females? Answer: This is *not* because boys and men have higher levels of strain than girls and women. Instead, males experience different *types* of strain that are more likely to lead to crime. For example, Agnew (2001, 168) argues that because of sex-role socialization "males are more concerned with material success and extrinsic achievements, while females are more concerned with the establishment and maintenance of close relationships and with meaning and purpose in life." The resulting differences in strain, Agnew (2001, 169) argues, explain the greater rate of property crime among males. Moreover, there are important additional differences in social control and sex-role socialization. For example, for females, forms of strain involve a restriction of criminal opportunities and excessive social control: "It is difficult to engage in serious violent and property crime when one spends little time in public, feels responsible for children and others, is burdened with the demands of others, and is under much pressure to avoid behaving in an aggressive manner" (2001, 169). Because men are more likely to be in public, to experience conflict with others, and to suffer criminal victimization, they are more likely to be involved in violence. Thus, the different types of strain that men and women experience result in higher rates of crime by the former.

Agnew does not stop there, however, but adds that males and females also differ in their emotional responses to strain. Although males and females may both respond to strain with anger, they differ in their experience of anger; female anger is often accompanied by emotions such as fear and depression, whereas male anger is often characterized by moral outrage. In explaining these differences, Agnew (2001, 169), like Hagan, concentrates on sex-role theory, arguing that by reason of differences in "the socialization process," women learn to blame themselves for negative treatment by others and to view their anger as inappropriate and a failure of self-control; men blame others for their negative treatment and view their anger "as an affirmation of their masculinity." Consequently, men are more likely to commit violent and property crimes, whereas women are more likely to resort to self-destructive forms of deviance, such as drug use and eating disorders.

Power control and strain theories acknowledge gender inequality and conditionally focus on the social dimensions of behavior. In addition, the theoretical conceptualization of power control and strain do present interesting insights on gender differences in crime, and these insights present an opportunity for a politics of reform.

By concentrating on gender *differences* in crime, however, power control and strain theories ignore gender *similarities* in crime between men and women and disregard the differences *among* men and boys as well as *among* women and girls. Thus, these theories construct an essentialist criminology by collapsing gender into sex. They create an artificial polarization, thereby distorting variability in gender constructions and reducing all masculinities and femininities to one normative standard case for each: the "male sex role" and the "female sex role." Not only are there differences cross-culturally but also, within each particular society, masculine and feminine practices by men and by women are constructed according to class, race, age, sexuality, and particular social situation. These variations in the construction of masculinity and femininity are crucial to understanding the different types and amounts of crime. In addition, power control and strain theories require that we examine masculinity exclusively by men and boys and femininity by women and girls, thus ignoring masculinities and femininities by people: the way individuals construct gender differently. Consequently, power control and strain theories miss what must be acknowledged: Women and girls also construct masculine practices that are related to crime.

Because of the above problems with power control and strain theories, many sociologists of crime interested in masculinities have turned to structured action theory (Messerschmidt 1993, 1997, 2000, 2004). Following the work of feminist ethnomethodologists (West and Fenstermaker 1995), this perspective argues that gender is a situated social and interactional accomplishment that grows out of social practices in specific settings and serves to inform such practices in reciprocal relation—we coordinate our activities to "do" gender in situational ways. Crucial to this conceptualization of gender as situated accomplishment is West and Zimmerman's (1987) notion of "accountability." Because individuals realize that their behavior may be held accountable to others, they configure their actions in relation to how these might be interpreted by others in the particular social context in which they occur. Within social interaction, then, we facilitate the ongoing task of accountability by demonstrating that we are male or female through concocted behaviors that may be interpreted accordingly. Consequently, we do gender (and thereby crime) differently, depending upon the social situation and the social circumstances we encounter. "Doing gender" renders social action accountable through normative conceptions, attitudes, and activities appropriate to one's sex in the specific social situation in which one acts (West and Zimmerman 1987).

"Doing gender" does not occur in a vacuum but is influenced by the social structural constraints we experience. Social structures are regular and patterned forms of interaction over time that constrain and enable behavior in specific ways; therefore, social structures "exist as the reproduced conduct of situated actors" (Giddens 1976, 127). Following Connell (1987, 1995) and Giddens (1976), structured action theory argues that these social structures are neither external to social actors nor simply and solely constraining; on the contrary, structure is realized only through social action, and social action requires structure as its condition. Thus, as people "do" gender, they reproduce and sometimes change social structures. Not only are there many ways of "doing gender"—we must speak of masculinities and femininities—gender must be viewed as *structured action*, or what people do under specific social structural constraints.

In this way, gender relations link each of us to others in a common relationship: We share structural space. Consequently, shared blocks of gendered knowledge evolve through interaction in which specific gender ideals and activities play a part. Through this interaction, masculinity is institutionalized; it permits men (and sometimes women) to draw on such existing, but previously formed, masculine ways of thinking and behaving to construct masculinity for specific settings. The particular criteria of masculinity are embedded in the social situations and recurrent practices whereby social relations are structured (Giddens 1989).

Assuming that masculinities and femininities are not determined biologically, it makes sense to identify and examine possible masculinities by women and girls. Recent research has begun to move in this direction. For example, Jody Miller's (2001) important book, *One of the Guys*, shows that certain gang girls identify with the boys in their gangs and describe such gangs as "masculinist enterprises." Pointing out that unequal structured gender relations are rampant in the mixed-gender gangs of which these girls were members, certain girls differentiated themselves from other girls by embracing a "masculine identity." Similarly, recent life-history interviews of girls involved in assaultive violence suggests that some of these girls "do" masculinity by, in part, displaying themselves in a masculine way, by engaging primarily in what they and others in their milieu consider to be authentically masculine behavior, and by outright rejection of most aspects of femininity (Messerschmidt 2004). Nevertheless, like the girls in Miller's study, these girls found themselves embedded in unequal gender relations that disallowed them entrance into the same masculine place as the boys. Thus, their masculinity was constructed as different from, and subordinate to, that of the boys.

In short, structured action theory allows us to conceptualize masculinity and crime in new ways—ways that enable sociologists of crime to explore how, and in what respect, masculinity is constituted in certain settings at certain times, and how that construct relates to crime by men, women, boys, and girls.

References

Agnew, Robert. 1992. "Foundation for a General Strain Theory of Crime and Delinquency." *Criminology* 30: 47–87.

______. 2001. "An Overview of General Strain Theory." In *Explaining Criminals and Crime: Essays in Contemporary Criminological Theory*, edited by R. Paternoster and R. Bachman (pp. 161–174). Los Angeles: Roxbury.

Connell, R. W. 1987. *Gender and Power: Society, the Person, and Sexual Politics*. Stanford: Stanford University Press.

______. 1995. *Masculinities*. Berkeley: University of California Press.

Giddens, Anthony. 1976. *New Rules of Sociological Method: A Positive Critique of Interpretive Sociologies*. New York: Basic Books.

______. 1989. "A Reply to My Critics." In D. Held, and J. B. Thompson, eds., *Social Theories of Modern Societies: Anthony Giddens and His Critics* (pp. 249–301). New York: Cambridge University Press.

Hagan, John. 1989. *Structural Criminology*. New Brunswick, N.J.: Rutgers University Press.

Messerschmidt, James W. 1993. *Masculinities and Crime: Critique and Reconceptualization of Theory*. Lanham, Md.: Rowman and Littlefield.

______. 1997. *Crime as Structured Action: Gender, Race, Class, and Crime in the Making*. Thousand Oaks, Calif.: Sage.

______. 2000. *Nine Lives: Adolescent Masculinities, the Body, and Violence*. Boulder: Westview Press.

______. 2004. *Flesh & Blood: Adolescent Gender Diversity and Violence*. Lanham, Md.: Rowman and Littlefield.

Miller, Jody. 2001. *One of the Guys: Girls, Gangs, and Gender*. New York: Oxford University Press.

West, Candice, and Sarah Fenstermaker. 1995. "Doing Difference." *Gender and Society* 9: 8–37.

West, Candice, and Don H. Zimmerman. 1987. "Doing Gender." *Gender and Society* 1: 125–151.

10

Postmodernism and Critical Cultural Theory

Postmodernism is much larger than a criminological theory. It encompasses art, literature, architecture, and social movements, and is a subfield of many disciplines, including psychology, criminology, and sociology. Although considered by many mainstream (modernist) observers as abstract and difficult to understand, postmodernism draws attention to the socially constructed and tenuous nature of society's rules, values, and norms. Postmodernism is skeptical of science and scientific method and science's promise to deliver progress. It questions whether truth can ever be known and particularly questions the value of scientific methods as being any better at discovering truth than any other method of inquiry. Its advocates believe that rational thought is just one of several ways of thinking, and that it is not necessarily a superior way. It also believes (1) that rational thought is a form of power; (2) that knowledge is not cumulative, and (3) that there are pluralities of knowledge. It claims that all statements about knowledge are simply claims to truth rather than truth itself (in this there is a similarity to the radical social constructionism that has been a leading perspective in the analysis of social problems, including crime).

Postmodernism rejects the idea of hierarchies of knowledge and objects to "metanarratives," or unifying discourses of power that profess to provide answers to the fundamental questions of life. Ultimately, postmodernism is a reaction to the metanarrative of modernism and its reliance on reason and realism as central concepts in predicting and controlling the world. In contrast, postmodernism celebrates multiple perspectives and local knowledge as opposed to universal truth. It favors eclectism, pastiche, fragmented images, bits and bites, the collage of differences, random access, multiple views, and a resistance to privileged knowledges, believing that no one truth claim is superior to any other.

Given this approach, it is not surprising that the postmodernist study of crime differs from traditional social science methodologies such as survey research and analysis of statistical data that government and policymakers rely on. Postmodernism argues that knowledge is, at best, the result of an interpretative process, but more likely is the result of a political process, one enmeshed with the power of discourse. So, for example, although people may view what they take to be the same empirical "reality" differently, postmodernists not only question the different ways that knowledge about "reality" is produced but also investigate how the discourse itself constitutes the reality, which might not exist without it. For example, a police officer is seen in a physical struggle with a person. The acts that take place are prefaced on assumptions that persons dressed in certain ways (wearing a uniform) are accorded powers over others. Some may rush to the aid of the officer on the assumption that a crime is being perpetuated. Others may rush to the aid of the person being beaten on the assumption that police brutality is taking place. Yet another observer may have visions of a lucrative business opportunity and rush to grab a video camera. Meanwhile, a researcher may be taking notes. A postmodern interpretation would argue that the social context, a person's experiences, and other intangible factors constitute the whole, which is merely a pastiche of each voice as it represents one aspect of what is underway while simultaneously contributing to what appears to be real.

Thus, conventional scientific research methods are too narrow; they are but one voice. In 1974, in the best selling book on life, *Zen and the Art of Motorcycle Maintenance*, Robert Pirsig wrote: "What we have here is a conflict of *visions of reality*. The world as you see it right here, right now, is reality, regardless of what scientists say it might be. . . . But the world as revealed by its scientific discoveries is also reality, regardless of how it may appear" (1974, 49). For postmodernists, reality consists of the claims that different people make that it exists. All we have are representations claimed to be of something that doesn't exist outside the claims themselves.

Since the 1990s, a distinctive postmodernist criminology has emerged, the most elaborated version of which has been termed "constitutive criminology." This approach incorporates ideas of social constructionist theory, chaos theory, semiotics, and topology theory. Constitutive theory recognizes that the social structures of inequality are not only the source of the harm that is crime but are themselves crimes. Moreover, humans generate these inequalities through their use of discourse (talk), which create divisions and values. Once created, these socially constructed complex systems of inequality are self-perpetuating, and are sustained through the continued investment of energy into elaborating these inequalities. Applications of postmodernist constitutive theory appear in the form of edgework studies, in which crimes may be the outcome of thrills experienced as humans approach risks and test the limits of their control. Others have incorporated postmodernism into a new form of critical "cultural criminology" that explores the use and subversion of mass media images by those subject to the power of others' discursive practices. Here crime becomes a form of play and resistance, a means to escape the constraint of linear and orderly social structures.

The policy response of constitutive theory is to replace harm-producing discourse with discourse that is healthy and constructive and to invest energy into building institutional structures around this. Like anarchists, constitutive theorists believe in a decentralized system, one of restorative justice designed to reintegrate offenders, victims, and community. They also believe that "social judo" (turning the power of the offender back on itself) is preferable to a retributive system that adds new harms to those already present.

10.1

Postmodern Theory and Criminology

BRUCE A. ARRIGO
University of North Carolina, Charlotte

The application of postmodern theory to criminology emerged in the late 1980s and 1990s. As a relatively new theory about crime, it continues to evolve and undergo refinement. Since its inception, postmodern criminology has experienced considerable criticism because it challenges many of the taken-for-granted assumptions about science, knowledge, truth, and progress, and their respective relationships to crime, law, and justice. These criticisms generally fall into one of six categories.

Criticisms of Postmodernist Criminology

Too Skeptical in Orientation

Some critics (Hunt 1990; Matthews and Young 1992; Schwartz and Friedrichs 1994) argue that postmodern criminology does nothing more than "trash" criminal justice institutions (the penal, the psychiatric, the legal), the routine behavior of agents within these institutions (correctional workers, mental health professionals, police officers), and organizational decisions, practices, and policies that inform these activities. Those criminologists who adopt a postmodern influenced position (e.g., Henry and Milovanovic 1996) contend that their analysis emphasizes, through language, the social construction of reality and, thus, the arbitrary basis on which crime itself is defined. As such, there are no fundamental truths; no objective realities; no deep structures underscoring our existences. If this is correct, so goes the detractor's argument, why bother promoting reform? There are no agreed upon foundations or shared conditions from which to advance sustainable, meaningful social change.

Too Relativistic in Scope

Closely linked to the previous criticism is the conviction that postmodern criminology promotes an "anything goes" philosophy. As opponents of the theory assert, if definitions of crime are arbitrary (as mediated by language and what we say about harm), then any statement concerning the reality of crime and justice is as good as the next (Handler 1992). All views are equally worthwhile; no interpretation is more privileged than another. To substantiate this position, critics draw attention to how postmodern criminologists simply reveal the embedded contradictions and hidden inconsistencies lodged within various criminal justice texts (e.g., a court decision, an alternative criminological theory, the criminal law) without offering something more. These identified deficiencies become the basis for additional review and inspection followed by yet more probing inquiry into the essential incompleteness of the "text" in question. This interpretive process continues uninterrupted. In the final analysis, meaning itself exists without grounding.

Too Difficult to Define

Critics of postmodern criminology observe that the theory's orientation and scope make it cumbersome to define with precision (Hunt 1991). There are several strains of postmodern criminology (e.g., feminist, critical race, constitutive), and these versions mostly defy a unifying organization. Moreover, when analyzing notable variants of the theory, opponents charge that competing versions of postmodern criminology are put forth. This leads critics to wonder whether postmodern criminology represents a complete theory about crime or something else altogether.

Not a Theory

Some detractors claim that postmodern criminology is, at best, a collection of ideas about social reality (Arrigo and Friedrichs 1999). In short, by placing under a microscope society's assumptions about crime, criminals, and institutional responses to both, postmodern criminology does nothing more than raise several (interesting and novel) questions about the construction of certain crime and delinquency definitions over equally worthwhile others; how rules and laws are interpreted by decision brokers typically in support of the status quo; and why the criminal justice response to interpersonal, communal, and global violence restricts or thwarts wholesale structural change. However, because the claims of postmodern criminology cannot be tested in a traditional sense (i.e., they cannot be subjected to empirical verification or falsification), critics charge that this heretical and loosely configured assemblage of viewpoints is nothing more than a trendy, though thoroughly inadequate, approach to advancing criminological knowledge (Handler 1992; Hunt 1991).

Too Abstract and Elitist in Content and Terminology

One important dimension to postmodern criminology's limited potential to function as a bona fide theory is the complaint that it is difficult, if not impossible, to read, decipher, and comprehend (Michalowski 1993; Schwartz and Friedrichs 1994). Unfamiliar terminology borrowed from architecture, literary and communication studies, and the arts and humanities; complex formulae appropriated from the physical and natural sciences; and a narrative style that cuts across and incorporates various disciplinary perspectives result in a text that all too often is impenetrable. This criticism brings up a related concern; that is, the abstract writing is an exercise in elitism. As opponents contend, postmodern criminology's insistence on its own, idiosyncratic language benefits no one except those already well versed in its distinct and peculiar discourse. Moreover, because the writing can be abstract, technical, and obscure, critics allege that these efforts thinly disguise what is, after all, the absence of theoretical substance.

Too Removed from Policy Reform

Even if the concerns identified above could be hurdled, opponents of postmodern criminology assert that the theory is incapable of effectively altering social and public policy (Handler 1992). Because postmodern criminology stresses how language (discourse) shapes reality about crime and criminals, it advocates for replacement ways of talking about law, social control, deviance, punishment, and policing. However, detractors of the theory point out that an appeal to language alone cannot fundamentally change prevailing structural inequalities such as gender, race, and class disparities. As such, opponents insist that postmodern criminology is ill-equipped to contribute to the thorny policy debates in the field.

Addressing the Concerns

The preceding comments represent the misinterpretations and distortions of postmodern criminology (see Arrigo, Milovanovic, and Schehr 2000; and Henry and Milovanovic 1999, 2003 for a review and assessment of other related criticisms). Indeed, each of the criticisms enumerated above can be addressed through the insights of the theory. Several of the more noteworthy responses are succinctly presented below.

Affirmative Postmodern Theory

One orientation to postmodern criminology includes a healthy dose of skepticism and fatalism as identified by the critics. However, another orientation is more affirmative in its approach to crime and justice. Affirmative postmodern theory supports the need to trash or disassemble the texts about crime, criminals, and the criminal law. By carefully decoding the multiple meanings that lurk behind or through these texts, the student or researcher can uncover many of the veiled assumptions, implicit values, and hidden messages that inform criminal justice theory, research, and policy. In addition, though, affirmative postmodern theory supports the reconstitution of the text. For example, once a statute about sexually violent predators has been exposed for its internal contradictions and embedded inconsistencies, the question then is whether this text can be reassembled in a way that values alternative, different, or neglected viewpoints. As affirmative postmodern criminology reminds us, these replacement perspectives might be the bases on which greater prospects for citizen justice, social accord, and collective well-being could be achieved.

Positional, Relational, and Provisional Truths

The relativism associated with the skeptical form of postmodernism in general, and postmodern criminology in particular, is understandable. However, it is not applicable to the theory's more humanistic dimensions. In particular, affirmative postmodern criminology recognizes that truth and knowledge are always and already positional, relational, and provisional (Arrigo 2003). What this means is that definitions of crime, interpretations of criminals, and the meaning of the criminal law depend on several intervening and evolving factors. The position or standpoint from which we interpret events and people in the world, the intersubjective (shared) experiences we have with others regarding these events or people, and the contingent contexts (e.g., historical, political, cultural) in which both occur make absolute truth and objective knowledge a fiction. At best, there is partial comprehension, conditional truths, and fragmented knowing. As affirmative postmodern criminology reminds us, this is because the values of process, inclusivity, difference, and becoming are themselves an incomplete story about the social world humans make and inhabit.

Postmodern Theory Versus Postmodern Theories

Given the position that postmodernism adopts with respect to truth and knowledge, it is a mistake to speak of it as a unified theory. There are many strains of postmodern thought. In the realm of criminology, for example, some of these include critical race theory, feminist jurisprudence, constitutive theory, and psychoanalytic semiotics. Admittedly, each of these variants (and others) emphasizes certain aspects of the role that language plays in the construction of social reality. However, they all acknowledge that language is not neutral and that it functions to privilege certain ways of knowing, certain ways of being. Thus, the question that proponents of these respective postmodern criminologies pose is whether and to what extent the variables of race, gender, human agency, and the unconscious are meaningfully reflected in the prevailing narratives about crime, law, and justice. To the extent that they are not (identified through disassembling or deconstructing the text), postmodern criminology endeavors to reclaim more fully these distinct perspectives (undertaken by reassembling or reconstructing the text).

Modern Versus Postmodern Theory Construction

If one examines the theoretical contributions of postmodern criminology from within a modernist framework, it is reasonable to conclude that they are nothing more than a loose collection of curious ideas having limited utility. However, by applying the tools of modernist thinking (e.g., cause-effect logic, deductive reasoning, linear sense making) to postmodern theory is akin to fitting a square peg in a round hole. It simply does not work. Because postmodern theory rejects the scientific method (objective measurement) and rational thought (truth and knowledge as fundamentally discoverable), the modernist framework is not the mechanism by which to "test" the soundness of the theory or its potential insights. Indeed, for postmodernists, such an orientation fosters and perpetuates exclusivity. In the modernist approach, only a select few who share such privileged knowledge can make decisions for and about everyone else. This is why postmodern criminologists make local, temporary, and interpersonal claims about the reality of crime and criminals. Absolute knowledge and truth are artificial, built on uncertain, incomplete, and often harmful judgments about events and people.

Language as Value-Laden

Underscoring the postmodern orientation to science, truth, knowledge, and progress is the notion that language can function to invalidate or dismiss alternative (and useful) approaches to the knowledge process. As such, proponents incorporate insights from a wide array of disciplines and forge new, different, and more inclusive ways by which to speak about criminal justice institutions, actors, and practices. In the affirmative postmodern tradition, the intent is not to make the prose incomprehensible deliberately; rather, it is to demonstrate the subtleties or shadings of meaning (implicit assumptions and hidden values) that would otherwise go undetected in a conventional, taken-for-granted reading of a text.

For example, as I have argued (Arrigo 2002), when the legal and psychiatric systems refer to persons with mental illness as "diseased," "incompetent," "insane," "sick," and "in need of treatment," meaning is communicated. In short, the person is interpreted as out of control, as passive, and likely in need of help from others when making decisions. However, if the same person is described as a "psychiatric survivor," as "a mental health systems user," as "differently abled," and as a "consumer," meaning again is conveyed. This time, though, the message is that the person is in control, is active, and functions to make his or her own informed choices. The point is that when institutions (the courts, the hospitals, the prisons) principally rely on one approach to describe persons with mental illness, the possible interventions become that much narrower (e.g., civil commitment, criminal confinement, homelessness). This is because the language chosen conveys limited (and marginalizing) meanings, whether intended or not, which reduce how the person in question is understood and accepted by others. As such, affirmative postmodern criminology is an approach that seeks to avoid a semblance of elitist logic.

Social Change and Transformative Justice

To curtail the alienating effects of language (i.e., nonneutral), affirmative postmodern criminology argues for replacement discourses: ways of talking about crime, criminals, and the criminal law that more fully embody peoples' divergent expressions of self, others, and ongoing human social interaction (Henry and Milovanovic 1996; Milovanovic 1997). Proponents of the theory contend that this is a necessary step if the restrictive and oppressive assumptions, values, and messages communicated through the prevailing discourse on crime and justice are to be averted. Indeed, for advocates of affirmative postmodern criminology, meaningful policy reform *begins* by investing energy in the reconstruction of law, crime, and delinquency texts. These are deliberate attempts to locate, speak about, and legitimize with more completeness the humanity and dignity of us all. As adherents of the theory observe, this is the path to social change and transformative justice, critical components of any well-intended policy process (Arrigo, Milovanovic, and Schehr 2005).

Evaluation

Empirical findings linked to affirmative postmodern criminology are appreciable, especially those emphasizing a qualitative rather than quantitative approach to research. Among other topics, investigators have examined such critical issues and social problems as police communication, agency and resistance for women in prison, images of crime, courtroom decision-making, and the meaning of mental illness and criminal insanity (Henry and Milovanovic 1999). Overall, these and related studies demonstrate how the interpretations of reality that are spoken and enforced through customary criminal justice behavior and practice promote the interests of powerful groups (institutional authority) at the expense of alternative collectives (the poor, minorities, women). Perhaps more significant, however, is that postmodern crime and justice scholars often reveal why dramatic changes in how we think about, talk about, and make decisions within criminology are sorely needed. In short, state-sponsored agencies (e.g., jails, hospitals, courts) function to control, correct, or otherwise cleanse the differences that people embody and express.

Conclusion

Although the contributions of affirmative postmodern criminology are increasingly evident, the theory itself continues to evolve. Along these lines, three areas ripe for future research are noted. First, many of the concepts, terms, and formulae advocates of the theory appropriate warrant additional refinement. Making the insights of postmodernism more intelligible for a larger constituency of criminologists—especially those unfamiliar with it—will go a long way in advancing the theory's approach to knowledge. Second, one way to promote this agenda of accessibility is to focus on where and how aspects of affirmative postmodern criminology can be integrated with other criminological theories. To some extent, constitutive theory (Henry and Milovanovic 1996) has successfully moved in this direction. In addition, though, crime and justice researchers supportive of postmodernism must demonstrate where and how its assorted theoretical variants can be usefully synthesized (see Arrigo 1995; Milovanovic 2003; Williams and Arrigo 2004). This project would benefit students, instructors, policy analysts, and other interested groups, especially as they would then come to appreciate the connections among the different types of postmodern theories. Finally, attention to postmodern methodology is lacking. Social scientists sympathetic to postmodern inquiry who study crime, criminals, and criminal law must develop better models of theory testing. Admittedly, existing efforts typically focus on several approaches to critical discourse analysis (e.g., deconstruction, semiotics); however, this is inadequate. Researchers would do well to explain carefully those concepts linked to various postmodern methodologies and indicate how they then could be effectively used in the study of specific crime and justice phenomena.

In sum, several tangible and sensible future research directions are noted. If efforts of the sort proposed above were significantly undertaken, they could have an impact on the acceptance of affirmative postmodern criminology in the general academic community. This is a necessary first step in bringing meaningful reform to the policy agenda in law, crime, and justice.

References

Arrigo, Bruce A. 1995. "The Peripheral Core of Law and Criminology: On Postmodern Social Theory and Conceptual Integration." *Justice Quarterly* 12: 447–472.

______. 2002. *Punishing the Mentally Ill: A Critical Analysis of Law and Psychiatry*. Albany, N.Y.: State University of New York Press.

______. 2003. "Postmodern Justice and Critical Criminology: Positional, Relational, and Provisional Science." In *Controversies in Crime and Justice: Critical Criminology*, edited by M. D. Schwartz and S. Hatty (pp. 43–55). Cincinnati, Ohio: Anderson.

Arrigo, Bruce A., and David O. Friedrichs. 1999. "Can Students Benefit from an Intensive Engagement with Postmodern Criminology?" In *Controversial Issues in Criminology*, edited by J. R. Fuller and E. W. Hickey (pp. 149–166). Cincinnati, Ohio: Anderson.

Arrigo, Bruce A., Dragan Milovanovic, and Rob Schehr. 2005. *The French Connection in Criminology: Rediscovering Crime, Law, and Social Change*. Albany, N.Y.: State University of New York Press.

Handler, Joel 1992. "Postmodernism, Protest, and the New Social Movement." *Law and Society Review* 26: 697–731.

Henry, Stuart, and Dragan Milovanovic. 1996. *Constitutive Criminology: Beyond Postmodernism*. London: Sage.

______, eds. 1999. *Constitutive Criminology at Work: Applications to Crime and Justice*. Albany, N.Y.: State University of New York Press.

______. 2003. "Constitutive Criminology." In *Controversies in Critical Criminology*, edited by M. D. Schwartz and S. E. Hatty (pp. 57–69). Cincinnati, Ohio: Anderson.

Hunt, Alan. 1990. "The Big Fear: Law Confronts Postmodernism." *McGill Law Journal* 35: 507–540.

______. 1991. "Postmodernism and Critical Criminology." In *New Directions in Critical Criminology*, edited by Brian D. MacLean and Dragan Milovanovic (pp. 75–85). Vancouver, BC: Collective Press.

Matthews, Roger, and Jock Young. 1992. "Reflections on Realism." In *ReThinking Criminology: The Realist Debate*, edited by Jock Young and Roger Matthews. London: Sage.

Michalowski, Raymond J. 1993. "(De)construction, Postmodernism, and Social Problems: Facts, Fiction and Fantasies at the 'End of History.'" In *Reconsidering Social Constructionism: Debates in Social Problems Theory*, edited by James A. Holstein and Gale Miller. New York: Aldine de Gruyter.

Milovanovic, Dragan. 1997. *Postmodern Criminology*. New York: Garland.

______. 2003. *Critical Criminology at the Edge: Postmodern Perspectives, Integration, and Applications*. Westport, Conn.: Praeger.

Schwartz, Martin D., and David Friedrichs. 1994. "Postmodern Thought and Criminological Discontent: New Metaphors for Understanding Violence." *Criminology* 32: 221–246.

Williams, Christopher R., and Bruce A. Arrigo. 2004. *Theory, Justice, and Social Change: Theoretical Integrations and Critical Applications*. Norwell, Mass.: Kluwer Academic/Plenum Press.

10.2

Edgework: Negotiating Boundaries

Dragan Milovanovic
Northeastern Illinois University

Introduction

Voluntary risk-taking behavior, "edgework," is becoming an increasingly important focus of attention in various disciplines.[1] Understanding adrenaline rush experiences (be they by BASE-jumpers, motorcyclists, extreme downhill skiers, free-style rock climbers, stock traders, stick-up men, sneaky thrillers, hackers, high rollers, amusement park frequenters, etc.) necessarily implies an integrated micro- and macro-level of analysis.[2] Key studies have been by Stephen Lyng (1990), Katz (1988), O'Malley and Mugford (1994), and Ferrell et al. (2001). More recently, Stephen Lyng's edited book, *Edgework* (2005), provided the contours for much research to follow. Postmodernist analysis is especially well situated to provide the tools for critical inquiry.[3] In investigating and understanding edgework phenomena, scholars will develop clearer insights on the relation of the human subject to structure in historical conditions.

This essay will highlight several emerging and problematic theses in edgework studies: establishing a framework (state space) within which we can situate the minimal determinants for its activity; specifying the nature of boundaries or edges; reconciling paradoxical approaches in the study of risk taking; and specifying useful directions for its continued scholarly investigation.

Toward an Orientation in State Space

I have previously suggested a five-dimensional state space within which we may productively situate edgework (see Figure 10.2.1).[4] The first dimension consists of structural conditions and includes the explication of the political economic determinants in historical conditions (see, for example, O'Malley and Mugford 1994; Simon 2005). This dimension also includes gender, race, and class constructions and their intersections defining the availability of edgework experiences and their expressive possibilities (see Lois 2005). Recent work by risk theorists (Beck 1992;

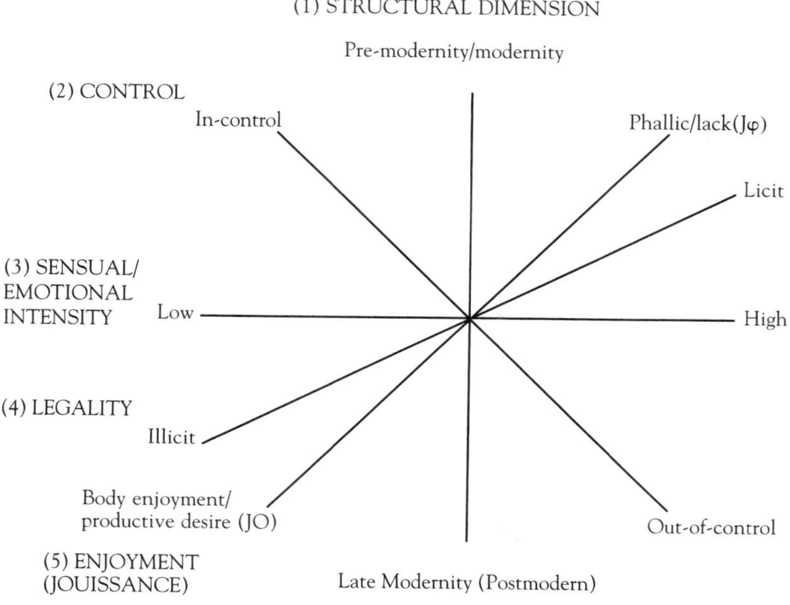

SOURCE: Adapted from Dragan Milovanovic (2003). *Critical Criminology at the Edge* (Monsey, NY: Criminal Justice Press and Greenwood Publishing), p. 248.

FIGURE 10.2.1 Dimensions of Edgework: State Space

Giddens 2000; Perrow 1999; Baker and Simon 2002; Simon 2005) suggests that we are in a historical period of "late modernity" (which others refer to as postmodern society). It is argued that since the mid- to late 1980s, capitalist society can be characterized by the prevalence of increasing risks as an integral component of its well-being.

The second dimension concerns being in control or out of control. In-control edgework experiences can be characterized by the exercise of self-control; out-of-control edgework experiences as a tendency to "let go." Reith's study (2005; see also Shewan et al. 2000) on drug usage is especially illuminating. Thus, on the in-control end of the continuum we have packaged edgework (e.g., video games, amusement parks, gaming, etc.). Traversing the continuum, we have workplace edgework, extreme sports, sneaky thrills, badass, righteous slaughter, and transcendental experiences.

The third dimension deals with sensual and emotional intensity (see Patton 2000, 72–76; Elias 1982; Campbell 1987). We see a range of intensities that appear with particular forms of edgework. At one extreme is a relatively mild intensity in packaged edgework. At the other, we see dramatic increases as one approaches the edge; approaching too close, or going over the edge, is an assured recipe for "brain lock" or sensory overload and leads to serious injury, unconsciousness, addiction, or death.

The fourth dimension concerns licit versus illicit activity. Many edgework experiences are legal activities. Some, however, cross the boundary of legality. This in itself seems to suggest certain adrenaline rush types of experience and modes of subjectification (see Katz 1988; Halleck 1967; Salecl 1992; Cohen 1955; Walter Miller 1955; William Miller 2005).

The fifth dimension includes the form and verbal expressibility of enjoyment (jouissance). It responds to O'Malley and Mugford's (1994, 209) call for a "phenomenology of pleasure." It concerns the "lived body" and what a body is capable of (see Deleuze 1983, on the forces of the body and will to power). At one end we note Jacques Lacan's notion of phallic jouissance (Jφ), at the other, jouissance of the body (JO). The former is constituted at the intersections of the symbolic and real order and is fundamentally based on a desire responding to lack (Lacan 1977); it deals with the limitations placed on articulating edgework experiences in conventional discourse. The latter, constituted at the intersections of the imaginary and real order, recognizes the inexpressible and ineffable nature of much of edgework experience. It is here, too, that we leave Lacan for Deleuze and posit a desire based on production (creative, life-fulfilling connections), not lack. But JO cannot be neatly placed within the confines of traditional discourse, even as various audiences insist that this be the case.

These five interacting dimensions provide the minimal determinants for a bona fide sociological investigation of the meaning of edgework experiences. Space limitations here prevent further explication, but we can envision these five dimensions interacting in such a way that certain "attractors" materialize in various structural locations and in changing historical conditions. A sociological approach would investigate the nature of these attractors, how they have arisen, how they dissipate, how new forms of attractors emerge. Take, for example, the newly emerging edgework of "parkours," described as "like skateboarding but without the skateboard" (George 2004). This extreme form of gymnastics (which has as its locus urban architectural spaces) emerged in the late 1980s in the suburbs of Paris and quickly spread to London. By the turn of the millennium it had emerged as an international movement. "Traceurs" have developed their own lingo, Web site,[5] meetings, training, chat lines, paraphernalia for sale, and remedies for injuries.

Boundaries or Edges

Edgework literature indicates that the critical component of doing adrenaline rush activity concerns negotiating some boundary, or "edge."[6] As Lyng (1990, 2005) tells us, these edges can be defined as the boundary between ordered and chaotic social reality, consciousness and unconsciousness, sanity and insanity, and the line between life and death. Lyng's (1990) early study indicated a certain absolute. Go over the edge and you die or suffer serious injury. Thus Lyng's skydivers approach the edge of being in or out of control and experience great satisfaction in overcoming extreme conditions. The "high" is in overcoming this extreme challenge. Go over the edge and the person undergoes "brain lock" or sensory overload; the jumper is then incapacitated with fatal results. Much of Katz's (1988) study also talks about various forms of edgework that approach boundaries. For the person doing "sneaky thrills" (i.e., a shoplifter) the buzz, the high is evading detection and the serious consequences that follow. Similarly, the "badass" and "street elite" attempt to conjure up an image of a person out of control, or clearly indicating a willingness to become out of control, assuring his victim's compliance. In our previously summarized five-dimensional sensitizing schema, we could see that various edges arise. These have a seductive appeal. People are attracted, are seduced by the boundaries themselves. The challenge is to explain this seductive quality.

More recently, however, some have disaggregated forms of edges and theorized a "normative edge." This edge is not absolute. The edgeworker can cross or transgress the boundary, but has the ability to return. This is especially so in criminal edgework (Lyng 2005, 28). It is the illegal act itself (our fourth element) that differentiates itself from the risk seekers mentioned above. Consider Martha Stewart and other recent high-profile corporate executives who went over the line. Thus, we could conceptualize risk takers negotiating two kinds of boundaries: in leisure and occupational activities, and in illicit forms of edgework (2005, 28).

We could also disaggregate a non-illicit from the normative edge approach, suggested by Lyng's (2005, 43) more recent examination. Following Foucault, Lyng suggests that the transgression of a limit, a "limit experience," "allow[s] the individual to put his or her powers to work in discovering new ways of being . . . a strategy for self creation" (2005, 43, 47). This would be an "ethics of the self," a position with which my suggestion below has affinities. But instead of drawing from Michel Foucault, I draw from the work of Gilles Deleuze. A Deleuzian approach would see transgressions as an occasion for activating an affirmative will to power and active forces (see Deleuze 1983; see also Patton's concise explanation of these ideas, 2000; see also Milovanovic 2003, 231–266; 2005a; 2005b).

Differentiating the third form of edges from the second, however, could be problematic. Consider Reith's (2005) study of drug consumption. Given the wide societal encouragement for the use of drugs as a corrective for various maladies, the line between licit and illicit becomes increasingly blurred and it is the juridico-medical control apparatus that draws the line and offers its disciplinary mechanisms for normalization.

Why Edgework?

Related to forms of edges is a question: To what, if anything, is the edgeworker responding? Can we begin to identify causal links? Lyng's early study suggests that the edgeworker was reacting to alienating conditions. Using a

Meadian-Marxian framework, he saw edgework as either a vehicle for escape or as a form of resistance to capitalist exploitation and alienation at the work place. More recent literature, however, has offered the suggestions that a societal-wide risk-taking ethic has emerged, especially since the mid-to late 1980s (Beck 1992). It is argued that late modernity demands edgework skills and encourages their development within the framework of legality. The floor bond trader is an exemplar *par excellence*. In this climate, some workers "embrace risk" (Lyng 2005, 9; Baker and Simon 2002). As Simon (2005, 206) informs us, "The opposition between institutional life and edgework collapses. Edgework is increasingly what institutions expect of many people." Thus edgework becomes integral to the normative order.

Consider, in the latter direction, Reith's (2005) analysis of drug usage. Reviewing Baudrillard's (1998) work on postmodernity and its stress on consumption, appearance, signs, images—the hyperreal—as opposed to the real bodily experiences, Reith argues that a new balance is demanded. She states (2005, 229) that first, understanding the meaning of drug usage must be placed in historical conditions defining acceptable and unacceptable behavior, where "normal" has acquired values of "rationality, moderation, and health"; "abnormal" values of "irrationality, excess, addiction, and risk." Given Baudrillard's point concerning the "culture of consumption," there now exists a boundary, an edge between being in control and out of control. The former is typified by the "recreational" or prescriptional drug users; the latter, by those who not only have crossed the boundary but have been unable to return because of their addiction: "Consumers are allowed to let go; to give in to excess; to dive into the action; to escape—but not *too* much" (2005, 234). In the culture of consumption, edgeworkers "also have to keep a bit back and exercise self-control. They are allowed to take risks, to go to the edge, but they have to be able to step back again. This is *regulated* excess, *controlled* risk" (2005, 234). The emerging risk-taking ethic, in short, encourages approaching the edge, exercising great self-control, and returning to the normative order.

While negotiating boundaries, the drug user enters the hyperreal where time and space are altered; he or she momentarily self-actualizes and experiences a transcendence from worldly affairs and limitations. But the drug user must use a high level of skill and control not only to transcend to reach a sufficient "high" but also to return to the "straight world" (Reith 2005; Shewan et al. 2000).

Paradox and Constitutive Theory

Lyng (2005) argues that the two approaches to edgework, resistance and escape on the one hand, a response to the emergent societal-wide risk-taking ethic in late modernity on the other, are diametrically opposed (the "edgework paradox"). Reith (2005, 242), too, recognizes the dilemma and shies away from reconciling the two by supporting a structural functionalist explanation. Constitutive theory (Henry and Milovanovic 1996) is a way of reconciling the apparent paradox.

Constitutive theory suggests that social reality is co-constructed: Historically contingent structural arrangements overdetermine the subject, while the subject, by way of everyday activity, advertently or inadvertently, co-produces or reifies its basic logic. This development is nonlinear, opening up the ubiquitous potential for disproportional effects through iteration (i.e., unintended consequences, latent effects, dialectics of struggle). Thus, we could support the "convergence" thesis and the escape/resistance thesis simultaneously. Escape and resistance that tests the boundaries, as well as those partaking of the risk-taking ethic who "push the envelope" in their respective fields, even crossing boundaries, could in fact be "functional" for further system-wide differentiation in late modernity, which in turn contributes to an overall autopoeitic normative system (i.e., autonomous and self-expanding), or ethical system, that supports risk taking, within limits. Where boundary crossers don't come back, now subjected to the bedeviling of control apparatuses (Matza 1969), they provide an assured population to be regulated, an ongoing invitation for "moral entrepreneurs," and bodies to be codified, regulated, and corrected by those patrolling the boundaries.

Constitutive theory, going beyond this linear model, also suggests that reification is not the only outcome; for some outcomes defy the proportionality assumed and lay the seeds for an entirely new order or subject. It is a small crack in the edifice of ubiquitous forms of control, even at the "capillaries" (Foucault 1977), that assures the possibility of ongoing transformative struggle.

Yet, we cannot hesitate in suggesting a possible third approach to edgework. The first, escape and resistance, is reactive in its approach and not only doesn't fully provide for the forms encouraged in risk society but also stands somewhat moot in explaining the edgeworker who is *not* escaping and resisting. In response to the second: is she/he merely responding only to the demands of a risk-taking ethic of late modernity? Perhaps some are partaking because it is an extension of their affirmative will to power.

Deleuzian Transpraxis

A Deleuzian perspective would begin with a Nietzschian-derived ontology ("realist," see Delanda 2002) in indicating that the cosmos is a plethora of unstable forces in movement with different speeds and different abilities to affect and be affected, chance bringing them into relation. *Active forces* lead to positive connections among forces and contribute to greater growth; they are transformative. *Reactive forces* are forces of "adaptation or conservation . . . and utilitarian accommodations" (Deleuze 1983, 41); they tend toward stasis, order, stability, rigidity, and reification. Forces tend to be "captured" in particular constellations in political economy with affects.[7] "Will to power"—not to be seen in the sense of domination of others, but in the sense of Eros, libido, and self-actualization—acts in the "piloting role" of forces. An *affirmative* will to power tends toward transcendence and transformation; a *negative* or *denying* will to power tends toward ressentiment, bad conscience, nihilism, and ascetic ideals (Deleuze 1983). Given the intersections of these two, we can identify the various "attractors" that may exist (Table 10.2.1).[8] We need to posit at least two coupled attractors, one being normativity (most of the time, edgeworkers, like others, live conformist lives) and at least one other.[9] Edgework in this framework, with the concomitant increased intensity, is what undermines a relatively stabilized configuration of forces; in the process, materializing novel affects and effects.[10]

TABLE 10.2.1 Will to Power and Forces

		Forces	
		Active	Reactive
Will to Power			
	Affirmative	affirmative-active	affirmative-reactive
	Negative	active-negation	negative-reactive

Edgework, of the escape and resistance form, can be situated in the upper right-hand corner as a reaction to alienation. In the Deleuzian perspective, this is an affirmative-reactive point attractor. It is, to follow Nietzsche, a slave morality. Boundaries and edges are still maintained, implicitly or explicitly. Similarly, the second form of edgework (embracing the emerging societal-wide risk-taking ethic), is connected to the affirmative-reactive attractor and thus is essentially accommodative and boundary maintaining, even as the edgeworker is engaged in adrenaline rush experiences. The negative-reactive attractor is what characterizes those who cross the edge and cannot come back or have a major impediment in coming back (i.e., addiction, loss of consciousness, death, major injury).[11] Without more, the former two types of edgework tend toward adrenaline rush experiences, but not necessarily to a concomitant realization of insights, epiphanies, turning points, or revelations. For the latter to occur, something more needs to take place. Deleuze's notion of "transmutation" is the key. We don't discount that adrenaline rush appears with some materialization of insights; but the balance is more toward the "high." The adrenaline rush produces intensities (Patton 2001, 71–72; Holland 1999, 34–35) that are "consumed" by the body (by way of enjoyment or suffering);[12] with more (e.g., activation of affirmative will to power), it becomes the basis of relatively better-formed revelations, insights, and epiphanies ("Oh, so that's what it was about!"; see also Deleuze and Guattari 1983, 18). Thus, intensity is a necessary but not sufficient condition.

For the greater materialization of revelations and relatively more stable transformations to occur, we suggest that a movement ("lines of flight") must take place following the logic developed by Deleuze (1983). This "line of flight" runs from the affirmative-reactive, to active-negation, and from there, by way of transmutation, to the affirmative-active attractor. An active negation (bottom left attractor) actively destroys the past or the given configuration of forces[13] and produces a transmutation to an affirmative-active attractor. Ultimately, it is genealogical analysis (Deleuze 1983; Patton 2000, 62–67) that studies how these lines of flight run their course and how to evaluate them.[14] (Take, for example, Malcolm X's autobiographical account of his transformation from petty thief to political activist.)

Epiphanies, insights, turning points, revelations, and momentary visions are generated while in this altered state of negotiating boundaries. We hypothesize that affirmative-reactive attractors differ in quantity and quality from the affirmative-active, the latter having greater and more stable symmetry between adrenaline rush and insights. During active-negation, ideas are more in flux, more ambiguous, less transformative, or only potentially transformative. For some, perhaps most, edgeworkers, these are momentary revelations and the edgeworker falls back to his or her everyday "real" world and awaits another day for edgework. Revelations, in other words, even where attaining a relatively more stable form, are too quick to be articulated in dominant symbolic form (Jφ); the ineffable nature (JO) often escapes more critical and genuine expression. For others, perhaps a small minority, the process is completed (Deleuze's and Nietzsche's "eternal return"): The previous configuration of forces producing accommodative practices to political economic realities is actively destroyed and replaced by an ethic of becoming-active, becoming-minor, becoming-revolutionary (Deleuze and Guattari 1987)—a permanent state of self-transformation (self-actualization) and the creation of metamorphic lines of flight toward what a body can do.

We could also posit that some dispositions of human beings can initially be located in the affirmative active quadrant. Here, no additional "push" needs explaining; edgework is but an extension of the lifestyle already attained; it already encompasses the attractor within which the possibility of doing edgework is situated. In sum, Deleuze's ethical mandate (see Hardt 1993), drawing respectively from Spinoza and Nietzsche, is this: "Become joyful, become active!"

Notes

1. See for example, studies on drugs (Reith 2005; Shewan et al. 2000); crime (Halleck 1967; Walter Miller 1955; William Miller 2005; Cohen 1955); leisure (Elias and Dunning 1986; Stanley 1996; Simon 2002; Holyfield and Fine 1997); and work (Simon 2005; Baker and Simon 2002). See the plethora of contemporary TV shows: *Fear Factor, Adrenaline Rush, The Extremists, Gravity Games, Fearless,* and even *Crocodile Hunter.*

2. Biopsychological approaches are reductionist, often minimizing the play of variability in phenotypical expression. These theories focus on neurotransmitters, dopamines, in the brain and argue that the risk taker is suffering from a "reward deficiency syndrome."

3. Note recent usage of Baudrillard, Lacan, Foucault, and Deleuze.

4. State spaces are always embedded in an n-dimensional space referred to as a manifold. In a previous essay (Milovanovic 2005a), I have shown how this manifold

takes the form of a Klein bottle, which is characterized by no boundaries (e.g., single surface), interactive effects, and no intersections.

5. See the Web site for "parkours": http://www.urbanfreeflow.com/UrbanFreeFlow/QuickLinks.htm; for BASE-jumpers, see http://www.bridgeday.info/.

6. See also Matza's (1969) "invitational edge" and Durkheimian-inspired boundary maintenance theory (Erikson 1966).

7. We (Henry and Milovanovic 1996) have referred to these as COREL sets. They are historically contingent and relatively stable coupled configurations of iterative loops. Deleuze would see these as "multiplicities."

8. An attractor is a region in state space towards which a dynamic system tends. Chaos theory has identified point, periodic, torus, and strange attractors.

9. Chaos theorists would call this a periodic attractor with a periodicity of two.

10. In a book in progress, *Deleuze and Justice*, I hypothesize that starting with a periodic attractor with periodicity of two (say normativity and affirmative-reactive), with perturbation (intensity being the key control parameter), a symmetry-breaking cascade (Delanda 2002) in the form of a Hopf transformation produces bifurcations: The periodic attractor dissipates into a possible torus (perhaps the normativity attractor becomes coupled with the affirmative-reactive and active-negative attractors), which, with even further perturbation (increase in intensity), may dissipate again into a chaos attractor (looks like butterfly wings) where one wing represents affirmative-active, the other active-negation (or other possible combinations). With more, this dissipates into an unpredictable realm of true chaos out of which dissipative structures (order out of disorder) or a point attractor may emerge in relatively more stable form (affirmative-active), but more likely a periodic attractor, normativity being coupled with it. In some cases, the negative-reactive attractor may attain prominence.

11. Some, however, do return—near death experiences, rehabilitation, turning points (active negation).

12. The subject is realized after the fact (Deleuze and Guattari 1983, 16–18).

13. A "deterritorialization," Deleuze and Guattari (1987).

14. Consider our (Henry and Milovanovic 1996) definition of crime identifying crimes of reduction and crimes or repression, and "excessive investors" in imposing differences.

References

Baker, Tom, and Jonathan Simon, eds. 2002. *Embracing Risk*. Chicago: University of Chicago Press.

Bataille, Georges. 1985. *Visions of Excess*. Oxford: Manchester University Press.

Baudrillard, Jean. 1998. *The Consumer Society*. London: Sage.

Beck, Ulrich. 1992. *Risk Society: Towards a New Modernity*. London: Sage.

Campbell, Colin. 1987. *The Romantic Ethic and the Spirit of Modern Consumerism*. Oxford: Basil Blackwell.

Cohen, Albert. 1956. *Delinquent Boys*. New York: Free Press.

Delanda, Manuel. 2000. *Intensive Science and Virtual Philosophy*. New York: Continuum.

Deleuze, Gilles. 1983. *Nietzsche and Philosophy*. New York: Columbia University Press.

Deleuze, Gilles, and Felix Guattari. 1983. *Anti-Oedipus*. Minneapolis: University of Minnesota Press.

______. 1987. *A Thousand Plateaus*. Minneapolis: University of Minnesota Press.

Duhigg, Charles. 2004. "Risk Addicts." *Chicago Tribune*, July 8, sec. 5, pp. 1, 10–11.

Elias, Norbert. 1982. *The Civilising Process*. Oxford: Basil Blackwell.

Elias, Norbert, and Eric Dunning. 1986. *Quest for Excitement*. Oxford: Basil Blackwell.

Erikson, Kai. 1966. *Wayward Puritans*. New York: Wiley.

Ferrell, Jeff, Dragan Milovanovic, and Stephen Lyng. 2001. "Edgework, Media Practices, and the Elongation of Meaning." *Theoretical Criminology* 5: 177–202.

______. 2005. "The Only Possible Adventure: Edgework and Anarchy." In *Edgework: The Sociology of Risk-Taking*, edited by Stephen Lyng. New York: Routledge.

Fine, G., and Lori Holyfield. 1996. "Secrecy, Trust, and the Dangerous Leisure." *Social Psychology Quarterly* 59: 22–38.

Foucault, Michel. 1977. *Discipline and Punish*. New York: Vintage Books.

George, Doug. 2004. "Flyboys." *Chicago Tribune*, August 27, sec. 5, pp. 1, 4.

Giddens, Anthony. 2000. *Runaway World*. New York: Routledge.

Goffman, Erving. 1967. "Where the Action Is." In *Interactional Ritual*, edited by Erving Goffman. Garden City, N.Y.: Doubleday.

Halleck, Seymour. 1967. *Psychiatry and the Dilemmas of Crime*. Berkeley: University of California Press.

Hardt, Michael. 1993. *Gilles Deleuze*. Minneapolis: University of Minnesota Press.

Henry, Stuart, and Dragan Milovanovic. 1996. *Constitutive Criminology*. London: Sage.

Holland, Eugene. 1999. *Deleuze and Guattari: Anti-Oedipus*. New York: Routledge.

Holyfield, Lori, and G. Fine. 1997. "Adventure as Character Work." *Symbolic Interaction* 20: 343–363.

Katz, Jack. 1988. *Seductions of Crime*. New York: Basic Books.

Lacan, Jacques. 1977. *Écrits*. New York: Norton.

Lois, Jennifer. 2005. "Gender and Emotion Management in the Stages of Edgework." In *Edgework: The Sociology of Risk-Taking*, edited by Stephen Lyng. New York: Routledge.

Lyng, Stephen. 1990. "Edgework: A Social Psychological Analysis of Voluntary Risk Taking." *American Journal of Sociology* 95: 851–886.

______, ed. 2005. *Edgework: The Sociology of Risk-Taking*. New York: Routledge.

Miller, William. 2005. "Adolescents on the Edge." In *Edgework: The Sociology of Risk-Taking,* edited by Stephen Lyng. New York: Routledge.

Milovanovic, Dragan. 2003. *Critical Criminology at the Edge*. Monsey, New York: Criminal Justice Press (and Praeger).

______. 2005a. "Edgework: A Subjective and Structural Model of Negotiating Boundaries. In *Edgework: The Sociology of Risk-Taking,* edited by Stephen Lyng. New York: Routledge.

______. 2005b. "Ethics of Edgework: Spinoza, Nietzsche, Deleuze." In *Philosophical Foundations of Crime,* edited by Bruce Arrigo and Christopher Williams. Chicago: University of Illinois Press.

O'Malley, Patrick, and Steve Mugford. 1994. "Crime, Excitement, and Modernity." In *Varieties of Criminal Behavior,* edited by Gregg Barak. Westport, Conn.: Praeger.

Patton, Paul. 2000. *Deleuze and the Political*. New York: Routledge.

Perrow, Charles. 1999. *Normal Accidents: Living with High Risk Technology*. Princeton: Princeton University Press.

Reith, Gerda. 2005. "On the Edge: Drugs and the Consumption of Risk in Late Modernity." In *Edgework: The Sociology of Risk-Taking,* edited by Stephen Lyng. New York: Routledge.

Salecl, Ranata. 1992. *The Spoils of Freedom*. London: Routledge & Kegan Paul.

Shewan, D., P. Dalgarno, and Gerda Reith. 2000. "Perceived Risk and Risk Reduction Among Ecstasy Users." *International Journal of Drug Policy* 10: 431–453.

Simon, Jonathan. 2002. "Taking Risks." In *Embracing Risk,* edited by Tom Baker and Jonathan Simon. Chicago: University of Chicago Press.

______. 2005. "Edgework and Insurance in Risk Societies." In *Edgework: The Sociology of Risk-Taking,* edited by Stephen Lyng. New York: Routledge.

Stanley, Christopher. 1996. *Urban Excess and the Law*. London: Cavendish.

10.3

Cultural Criminology

Jeff Ferrell
Texas Christian University

Building from a variety of theoretical trajectories in criminology and related disciplines, cultural criminology has emerged over the past decade or so as an orientation designed to engage specifically and directly with the cultural dimensions of crime and crime control. In its engagement with these various dimensions, cultural criminology emphasizes the essential role of meaning, image, and representation in shaping the reality of crime and the range of collective responses to it. As such, cultural criminology investigates the many ways in which the subcultural lives and activities of criminals, the symbolic operations of the mass media and popular culture, and the public practices of social and legal control intertwine.

Cultural criminology is meant to broaden the subject matter of criminology and to move criminological theory and research beyond narrow conceptions of crime and the cause of it. From the perspective of cultural criminology, the appropriate subject matter of criminology must include not simply "crime" but also the many images of crime and criminality that are produced and circulated by the mass media, and, likewise, the recurring campaigns of symbolic threat and moral panic that political and legal authorities orchestrate. At the same time, criminology must account for other sorts of situated cultural practices as well—for example, those by which criminals themselves create the emotions, meanings, and perceptions that drive and define their own criminality. Through this multifaceted cultural approach, criminology can better explain crime and crime control as the provisional products of meaningful human action; that is, as human endeavors shaped by purposeful activity on all sides and contested through perception and misperception. In the same way, a culturally informed criminology can develop more complex and humane critiques of crime and criminal justice and can expose the ways in which unfairness and injustice are constructed as part of an ongoing cultural process.

Cultural criminology blends the traditional substantive and analytic concerns of criminology with perspectives developed in the sociological, anthropological, and literary study of human culture. Cultural criminology has specifically developed from the symbolic interactionist tradition in criminology, especially as conceptualized in labeling theory and embodied in the naturalistic case study. From this view, the everyday reality of crime and criminal justice emerges from a web of human interactions that inevitably operate through the ongoing production and interpretation of symbolic meaning as encoded in language, image, and style. Given this, the reality of crime resides not in a particular action or event but in the flux of reactions and interactions through which the meaning of the action or event is negotiated and contested. A symbolic interactionist perspective suggests that phenomena such as crime and victimization, the fear of crime, and campaigns against crime are not static entities but complex and ongoing cultural processes. And these cultural processes—these ongoing cultural dynamics that define crime and crime control—cannot be captured in the statistical summaries of crime rates or other bureaucratic residues of criminality. They can be observed and understood only through the criminologist's immersion in the symbolic dynamics of criminal events and criminal subcultures, and through a criminological attentiveness to these dynamics in the media and culture of everyday life.

If this largely American symbolic interactionist perspective has formed one foundation for cultural criminology, the Birmingham School of Cultural Studies and the "new criminology" in Great Britain have formed the other. Beginning in the 1960s and 1970s, British scholars developed new, culturally informed perspectives on economic and political power, social inequality, and the role of criminal justice in underpinning power and inequality (Cohen 2002 [1972]; Hall and Jefferson 1976; Hall et al. 1978). These British scholars have increased their exploration of the cultural and ideological dimensions of social class through their investigation of leisure activities and illicit pleasures—such as drug use and joy riding as moments of stylized resistance to political and economic authority—and their examination of the stylistic and symbolic practices of youth subcultures that by turns reproduced and resisted dominant economic and legal structures. In addition, they have conceptualized political power and legal control as symbolic practices in their own right, exercised and enforced not only through handcuffs and jails but through high-profile public campaigns designed to promote particular fears and perceptions. Today, cultural criminology integrates the "symbolic" focus of symbolic interactionism with the "cultural turn" in British sociology and criminology in its attempt to account for the complex cultural dynamics that construct crime and crime control. In addition, cultural criminology draws on semiotic analysis, and the sensibilities of deconstruction and postmodernism, as it increasingly focuses on images that reference "real" events less than they emerge out of self-reverential media practices, and in turn loop endlessly through criminal subcultures and agencies of social control.

Significantly, cultural criminology proposes considerably more for criminology than a broader substantive focus attuned to media dynamics and the cultural practices of criminals; it also proposes new analytic orientations that in many ways directly confront the conventional methodological, theoretical, and philosophic foundations of criminology itself. To begin with, cultural criminologists argue that survey research methods and quantitative data analysis—the methodological and analytic underpinnings of much contemporary criminology—drain from crime the very experiential sensuality and cultural nuance that define it, leaving behind dry data sets and abstract cross-tabulations that are as uninteresting as they are uninformative. In fact, cultural criminologists suggest that it is perhaps the ability of these conventional approaches to produce culturally meaningless data sets that makes them valuable—valuable, that is, not for a deep understanding of crime and criminality but for the objectivist "value-free" mythology of social science and the efficient administration of the criminal justice system. In the same way, from the view of cultural criminology, rational choice theories and other currently popular instrumentalist models miss, and perhaps are designed to miss, the essential sensuality, excitement, and symbolic ambiguity of much everyday criminality (Ferrell 2004; Katz 1988; Young 2003, 2004).

A second philosophic and theoretical divergence is also suggested by the development of cultural criminology. Cultural criminologists argue that if symbolic discourse and stylized representation really matter, if they do indeed shape the reality of crime and justice, then they surely shape other worlds as well—including the practice of criminology itself. Put differently, cultural criminologists propose that particularities of symbolism and style reveal much about the worlds from which they emerge—about the values and practices of criminals, the contested politics of crime control, and thereby the practice and politics of criminology itself. Yet when they aim their cultural analysis at contemporary criminology, cultural criminologists find a disturbing criminological culture: a style of analysis so steeped in detached objectification and a style of communication so wanting in grace and elegance that together they manage to sanitize what would seem to be the most edgy and engaging of issues: crime, violence, transgression, and the pursuit of justice. Like other expressive products of human endeavor, statistical tables and turgidly written journal articles are cultural constructions in that they are forms of symbolic discourse and communication—but they are not particularly effective constructions, cultural criminologists argue, for communicating the lived reality of crime and crime control.

In their place, cultural criminologists propose analytic orientations more attuned to aesthetics, style, and meaning—that is, modes of research, analysis, and reporting better suited to capturing and communicating crime's cultural and experiential complexity (Ferrell 2005a). In this context, cultural criminologists, like the symbolic interactionists and labeling theorists before them, have increasingly turned to the construction of deep ethnographic accounts of criminality, and to the writing of evocative essays, first-person narratives, and autobiography. They have used documentary photography and "visual criminology" as a means of recording and analyzing crime's representational power. They have even begun experimenting with fiction, poetry, and visual art. "Criminology," cultural criminologists suggest, should denote the study of crime in all its cultural complexity—not just the traditional social science of crime.

Interpretations and Misinterpretations, Distortions and Critiques

Given that cultural criminology not only offers an alternative intellectual ethos for the practice of criminology but presents in many ways a direct confrontation with its present configuration, it is not surprising that a variety of critiques of cultural criminology, and perhaps some misinterpretations and distortions of its arguments, have emerged. The criticisms generally address cultural criminology's conceptualization of agency and power; its accounts of crime as meaningful situated experiences; and its preferred modes of research and reporting.

A first criticism suggests that by focusing only on surface phenomena as expressed in cultural vagaries of image and style, cultural criminology fails to engage with the actual structures of legal and economic power. Underlying such cultural phenomena, critics argue, are the real sources of power and control, and the real connections between crime and society: economic injustice, political manipulation, and structured inequality (for example, Hall and Winlow 2004). Such criticisms tend to resurrect the old dualisms that have long haunted sociological and criminological analysis: structure versus agency, form versus content, the "social" versus the "cultural." Cultural criminologists counter, though, that these dualisms falsely dichotomize the complex patterns through which power and control are constructed, and also miss the complex cultural process by which power, control, crime, and resistance are given meaning in everyday life. As historians have regularly recorded (for example, Aronowitz 1973; Marcus 1989), and as the British cultural theorists and "new criminologists" began to demonstrate decades ago, structures of power are at the same time cultures of power; power resides not only, perhaps not even primarily, in the ability to exert physical force or enforce economic harm but also in the ability to construct perceptions of such activities and define the meaning of everyday life. And if we can recognize this in looking back at the long sweep of history, we can see it even more clearly today in a world awash in twenty-four-hour media, in the symbolic politics of terror and fear, in high-profile wars on crime, and in the worldwide commerce in communication and style.

Critics sometimes accuse cultural criminologists of romanticizing crime and criminality, of discovering political resistance where there is none, and of celebrating too readily the subversive political potential of illicit meanings and styles; even theorists sympathetic to cultural criminology note that cultural criminology sometimes seems to veer toward a "romantic celebration of marginal subcultures" (Cohen 1996, 739). From this view, cultural criminologists' deep engagement with the cultural practices of criminals and other marginalized groups, and with the immediacy of criminal events, predisposes them to perhaps too great a sense of empathic understanding, or criminological *verstehen* (Ferrell 1997), of those they study. Although this failing is certainly a methodological possibility—the deep immersion that defines ethnographic field work carries with it the possibility of various perceptual and emotional distortions—the critique actually seems to reference two broader substantive and theoretical questions: First, against what standard can we judge cultural criminological accounts of crime and criminality to be romanticized? Accusations of "romanticizing" suggest a divergence from the "real" nature of crime and criminals—yet existing knowledge of crime and criminals hardly constitutes a useful benchmark in this regard. Statistical profiles produced by criminal justice agencies, secondhand criminological research derived from abstract survey methodologies, ideological residues of mediated anti-crime campaigns—all are certainly cultural constructions to be interrogated for their encoded meanings and agendas, but certainly none presents a baseline against which to judge the "real" nature of crime. In this context, alternative accounts produced by cultural criminologists may seem "romanticized" precisely because they produce more interpersonally attentive and culturally rich explanations of crime and criminality.

The second question: What constitutes politics and political resistance? As many studies have persuasively demonstrated, and as legal authorities' panicky reactions to marginal subcultures and their public displays of disobedience continue to confirm, illicit styles of expression can indeed carry significant political meaning, and the possibility of meaningful resistance to political authority. Moreover, although this political resistance may or may not overturn large-scale configurations of economic and political power, it may often produce significant changes in the practice of day-to-day living. And so, again, we arrive at the dynamics of power, politics, and control, and the methods through which criminologists might understand them. Conventional criminological approaches have tended to conceptualize power and control in terms of large-scale structures of patterned inequality, and so constructed their methodological procedures and their critiques of injustice in this domain. Cultural criminologists are more likely to conceptualize power and resistance in terms of carnivalesque rituals or the street politics of progressive social movements, for example, and so to investigate control, criminalization, and political resistance up close, that is, as played out in "the revolution of everyday life" (Presdee 2000; Ferrell 2002).

Finally, and perhaps most commonly, critics argue that cultural criminology has drifted away from the canons of social science and into the realm of tabloid reporting and front-page sensationalism. With its substantive focus on phenomena such as urban gangs, neo-Nazi violence, hip hop graffiti, sadomasochism, street toughs, and consumerism, they suggest, cultural criminology has resorted to pandering the worst of popular culture, and, along the way, has abandoned the rigorous objectivity of social scientific inquiry. Cultural criminologists tend to counter this dismissal of their work in three ways. First, they note that the substantive range of cultural criminology transcends these high-profile cases; in fact, newer work in cultural criminology engages with subjects ranging from phenomenology (Wender 2004) and the historical place of Lombroso (Morrison 2004a) to local cultures (Kane 2004), the administration of justice (Bovenkerk and Yesilgoz 2004), the Holocaust (Morrison 2004b), and the USA Patriot Act (Hamm 2004). Second, they suggest that critics perhaps confound cultural criminology's subject matter with its style of communication. After all, an account of skinheads or street toughs is not inherently engaging; it can be sensational, or it can be sleep-inducing—especially if presented in the conventional social science form of statistical tabulation and arid writing. Finally, cultural criminologists note that the "science" in "social science" has long operated more as anxious affectation than as accomplished reality—and that the greater the push for a social scientific criminology, the greater the harm that has been done, examples being the dehumanization of research subjects and the abstraction of human experience. In this sense, at least some cultural criminologists would welcome rather than worry over a wandering away from the canons of social science.

Developments and Directions

Among cultural criminology's more interesting and controversial trajectories is its continued engagement with issues of emotion and excitement as suggested by Jack Katz (1988), Stephen Lyng (1990), and others early in cultural criminology's emergence. Cultural criminologists continue to emphasize and explore the sensual "foreground" of crime, arguing that the vivid immediacy of criminal events offers important insights into crime's seductions and terrors. Caught up inside moments of criminality, cultural criminologists contend, participants construct meanings and emotions that can be neither predicted by abstract analytic models nor explained by simple notions of rational calculation. Instead, moments of crime and criminality spawn their own complex emotional politics and so generate situated displays of fear, pleasure, and excitement that in turn engage larger structures of power. Of course, the methodological implications of this model are themselves exciting, and to some critics, controversial: Criminologists must put themselves inside such situations, must engage with these situated meanings and emotions, if they are to understand the reality of crime. When this method has been undertaken, implications for writing and scholarship have followed as well; indeed, cultural criminologists are producing autobiographical or "autoethnographic" works that account for their own emotional involvement with their subjects of study (Ferrell 1996, 2002, 2005b; Presdee 2000).

A second trajectory has taken cultural criminology increasingly into the realms of urban life and the politics of urban space. From the view of cultural criminology, many of today's most visible crime controversies can be understood as conflicts over the meaning and symbolic control of urban space. In varying ways, youth gangs, graffiti crews, homeless folks, homeless activists, radical environmentalists, dumpster divers, street musicians, crime victims, and other urban residents all seek to remake the city in their image, to carve from the city cultural spaces appropriate to their politics and experiences. At the same time, legal and political institutions increasingly seek to remove such unauthorized images and activities from public view. Wrapping the city in a tightening web of legal and spatial controls—often in the interest of economic development and emerging economies of urban consumption—legal and political authorities undertake their own efforts at remaking the meaning of the city. Because of this, cultural criminologists argue, a sophisticated theorizing of urban life and attentiveness to the city's spatial and symbolic politics are essential to an understanding of contemporary crime (Ferrell 1996, 2002, 2005b; Hayward 2004).

These and other developments in cultural criminology increasingly involve international and cross-cultural research as well. From its founding in the interplay of U.S. and British research and theory, cultural criminology has continued to emerge as an orientation aimed at understanding the cultural and cross-cultural dynamics of crime. Of late, this aim has generated not only a widening range of cultural criminological scholarship from around the world but also theorizing and research designed specifically to explore the intersections of culture and crime that emerge from large-scale immigration, geographic and cultural dislocation, and global capitalism (Bovenkerk and Yesilgoz 2004; Ferrell et al. 2004; Kane 2004). Crossing borders real and imagined, cultural criminologists continue to explore new ways of conceptualizing and undertaking criminological scholarship, and to imagine new ways of confronting critically the intersection of culture, crime, and justice.

References

Aronowitz, Stanley. 1973. *False Promises: The Shaping of American Working Class Consciousness*. New York: McGraw-Hill.

Bovenkerk, Frank, and Yucel Yesilgoz. 2004. "Crime, Ethnicity and the Multicultural Administration of Justice." In *Cultural Criminology Unleashed*, edited by Jeff Ferrell, Keith Hayward, Wayne Morrison, and Mike Presdee (pp. 81–96). London: Cavendish/Glasshouse.

Cohen, Stanley. 2002 [1972]. *Folk Devils and Moral Panics*. 3d ed. London: Routledge.

______. 1996. "Review of *Cultural Criminology*." *Justice Quarterly* 13: 737–740.

Ferrell, Jeff. 1996. *Crimes of Style: Urban Graffiti and the Politics of Criminality*. Boston: Northeastern University Press.

______. 1997. "Criminological Verstehen: Inside the Immediacy of Crime." *Justice Quarterly* 14: 3–23.

______. 2002. *Tearing Down the Streets: Adventures in Urban Anarchy*. New York: Palgrave/Macmillan.

______. 2004. "Boredom, Crime, and Criminology." *Theoretical Criminology* 8: 287–302.

______. 2005a. "The Aesthetics of Cultural Criminology." In *Philosophy, Crime, and Criminology*, edited by Bruce Arrigo and Chris Williams. Champaign, Ill.: University of Illinois Press, forthcoming.

______. 2005b. *Empire of Scrounge*. New York: New York University Press.

Ferrell, Jeff, Keith Hayward, Wayne Morrison, and Mike Presdee, eds. 2004. *Cultural Criminology Unleashed*. London: Cavendish/Glasshouse.

Hall, Steve, and Simon Winlow. 2004. "'Barbarians at the Gate': Crime and Violence in the Breakdown of the Pseudo-pacification Process." In *Cultural Criminology Unleashed*, edited by Jeff Ferrell, Keith Hayward, Wayne Morrison, and Mike Presdee (pp. 289–300). London: Cavendish/Glasshouse.

Hall, Stuart, Chas Critcher, Tony Jefferson, John Clarke, and Brian Roberts. 1978. *Policing the Crisis*. London: Macmillan.

Hall, Stuart, and Tony Jefferson, eds. 1979. *Resistance Through Rituals*. London: Hutchinson.

Hamm, Mark S. 2004. "The USA Patriot Act and the Politics of Fear." In *Cultural Criminology Unleashed*, edited by Jeff Ferrell, Keith Hayward, Wayne Morrison, and Mike Presdee (pp. 287–299). London: Cavendish/Glasshouse.

Hayward, Keith. 2004. *City Limits: Crime, Consumerism, and the Urban Experience*. London: Cavendish.

Kane, Stephanie. 2004. "The Unconventional Methods of Cultural Criminology." *Theoretical Criminology* 8: 303–321.

Katz, Jack. 1988. *Seductions of Crime*. New York: Basic Books.

Lyng, Stephen. 1990. "Edgework: A Social Psychological Analysis of Voluntary Risk Taking." *American Journal of Sociology* 95: 851–886.

Marcus, Greil. 1989. *Lipstick Traces: A Secret History of the Twentieth Century*. Cambridge, Mass.: Harvard University Press.

Morrison, Wayne. 2004a. "Lombroso and the Birth of Criminological Positivism." In *Cultural Criminology Unleashed*, edited by Jeff Ferrell, Keith Hayward, Wayne Morrison, and Mike Presdee (pp. 67–80). London: Cavendish/Glasshouse.

Morrison, Wayne. 2004b. "'Reflections with Memories': Everyday Photography Capturing Genocide." *Theoretical Criminology* 8: 341–358.

Presdee, Mike. 2000. *Cultural Criminology and the Carnival of Crime*. London: Routledge.

Young, Jock. 2004. "Voodoo Criminology and the Numbers Game." In *Cultural Criminology Unleashed*, edited by Jeff Ferrell, Keith Hayward, Wayne Morrison, and Mike Presdee (pp. 13–27). London: Cavendish/Glasshouse.

______. 2003. "Merton with Energy, Katz with Structure." *Theoretical Criminology* 7: 389–414.

Wender, Jonathan. 2004. "Phenomenology, Cultural Criminology and the Return to Astonishment." In *Cultural Criminology Unleashed*, edited by Jeff Ferrell, Keith Hayward, Wayne Morrison, and Mike Presdee (pp. 49–60). London: Cavendish/Glasshouse.

11

Anarchism, Peacemaking, and Restorative Justice

These theoretical perspectives might seem unrelated until it is realized that each, in different ways, believes that government has been more of a problem than a solution for crime control. Each espouses a view of social order in which the power of government is removed or minimized; where rulers play no role, or only a limited role; and in which people resolve their own problems, deal with their own conflicts, and rebuild respect for each other. Anarchist criminology, which emerged in the late 1970s and reappeared in the 1990s, sees all hierarchical systems of power and authority, whatever their configuration, as flawed. It desires a more just world. Anarchy is a society without rulers, but this does not mean it is a society without order. Anarchists believe that without government intervention humans would be free to participate in organizing a world that best serves their communal interests. Peacemaking is also predicated on individual responsibility and a belief that consideration of the "other" is what binds society. Instead of making "war" on problems, peacemaking advocates believe that celebrating mutual respect and understanding are less likely to produce conflict, and when problems arise these should be approached in ways that diffuse them rather than solidify them. Generally, with each of these theories, hierarchical systems of power, control, and domination should be opposed, for these power structures create the divisions among humans that cause the conflicts that, ultimately, result in crime and other harms. Even in the more moderate restorative justice perspectives, government laws and punishment take a back seat in favor of reintegrative processes that emphasize the harmful nature of offenses, rather than offenders, and promote processes that are facilitative of reconciliation between victims and offenders.

Power, especially government power, but also corporate power, professional power, and agency power, may be the source of crime, and at minimum exacerbates the problems arising once harm has been committed. The state (government) makes war on crime and suppresses crime with violence or the threat of violence. This can be likened to a parent who spanks a child for hitting a sibling. State-sanctioned violence simply perpetuates a cycle that does not reduce crime but adds its own violence to that which has already occurred.

Anarchist criminologists believe that hierarchical systems of authority and domination should be opposed and that existing systems of justice should be replaced by a decentralized system of negotiated justice in which all members of society participate and share their decisions. Recent anarchist criminology is an "integration" of critical approaches, which seek to relate crime, as a meaningful activity of resistance, to its construction in social interaction and its larger construction through political and economic authority. Anarchists call for the replacement of the existing system of state-run criminal justice with a mutual aid system of decentralized face-to-face justice. This should be a system of "restorative justice" that incorporates 1980s "peacemaking" and "abolitionist" ideas rather than the mongering of war and fear that is typical of state control and punishment.

The concept of restorative justice mushroomed into a movement during the 1990s, and by 2005 had been the subject of more than one hundred books, its own journal *(Contemporary Justice Review)*, and numerous articles extolling its benefits to society, communities, families, offenders, and victims relative to its retributive government-based counterpart.

11.1

Needs-Based Anarchist Criminology

Larry Tifft
Central Michigan University
AND
Dennis Sullivan
Institute for Economic and Restorative Justice

Anarchist criminology is unique among the many criminologies because it grows out of a needs-based political economy of relationship and conception of justice. Its advocates are interested not only in pointing to those persons, groups, organizations, and nation-states that deny people their needs in everyday life but also in fostering social arrangements that alleviate pain and suffering by providing for everyone's needs. That is, advocates of an anarchist needs-based criminology are concerned with living in a way that brings about a just world and greatly reduces the harms done to people worldwide.[1]

Every day—in theory and practice—we find ourselves confronting power relations in all aspects of our lives. This calls attention to the need to transform all modes of human interaction based on claims of superiority, whether grounded in reasons of class, gender, race, age, sexual preference, intelligence, meritorious achievement, rights, or species. As advocates of needs-based justice for more than thirty years, we have, in our teaching, writing, and activism, been diligent and unfailing in providing a critique of all hierarchies, not only all institutional modes of oppression, domination, and harm (structural violence), but also all modes of interpersonal violence effected through the exercise of power and control (Mika 2001; Amster 2003, 2004).

We have assessed and condemned the harms and failures of the United States criminal justice system, calling it a "justice-industrial complex" (Sullivan 1980; Tifft and Sullivan 1980; Sullivan and Tifft 1998a, 2001). This critical assessment would not be possible without a contextual understanding of how institutional structures (e.g., patriarchy, economic inequality, political tyranny) and cultural constructs and beliefs (e.g., gender constructs and superiority beliefs) produce the criminal justice system and the ideological justifications for it. These institutional and cultural structures are also responsible for the unacceptable prevalence of the battering of women (Tifft 1993) and the neglect and abuse of children (Gil 1996), as well as the justifications for these acts of violence. These justifications also underlie the practices and policies of *Homo sapiens*' exploitation and denigration of other species for our survival (Singer 1973, 2003; Scruton 2003; Scully 2003; Godlovich, Godlovich, and Harris 1972; Bierne 1995). In *The Struggle to be Human* and *The Mask of Love*, published twenty-five years ago, and perhaps more vividly in our more recent work, *Restorative Justice: Healing the Foundations of Our Everyday Lives* (Sullivan and Tifft 2001), we have pointed out the direct connections between the larger structural and cultural contexts of our times and the personal realities of everyday life.

Our earliest collaborations were considered by many to be radically different, innovative, provocative, and unsettling. They were also sharply criticized and frequently categorized as polemical, utopian, and even "romantic." Many readers did not know how to respond to an anarchist critique, especially those academics steeped in reformist criminologies or the then-emerging, critical, Marxist criminologies. Indeed, although colleagues who have been part of the radical/critical criminological tradition have eventually said that our early work had a significant impact on their lives, it took nearly two decades before crimes by the state, a social harms definition of crime, and needs-based social justice concerns received formal recognition. This recognition today is in part a result of almost everyone's increased awareness of the tremendous effects that structural arrangements and structural violence have on our lives. These effects range from how adults interact as intimates and how we "take care of" our children and aging parents to how food is produced and distributed, which affects whether we have access to adequate nutrition and drinkable water. Hence, we have reached a common ground with a growing number of criminologists who have also dedicated their lives to expanding criminological inquiry beyond the discipline's traditional boundaries by explicating crimes by the state (e.g., Quinney 1998; Friedrichs 1998; Barak 1991, 1994) for reasons of profit (e.g., Michalowski 1985; Michalowski and Kramer 1987, 1998), and crimes for reasons of group survival and autonomy (e.g., Mika and McEvoy 2001) and for reasons of interpersonal power and control (e.g., Pepinsky 1991, 2000; Pepinsky and Quinney 1991; Ferrell 1994, 1995, 1998; Milovanovic and Henry 2001; Henry and Lanier 2001a; Henry and Milovanovic 1993, 1996).

Applying Anarchist Criminology

Our earliest work also drew the criticism that we had not adequately discussed the policy implications and specific applications of our theoretical perspective. Yet we had already begun to address these concerns in *The Mask of Love* (Sullivan 1980) by examining the nexus between the professional justice complex; the complexes of religion, medicine, education, psychoanalysis, and work; and the decisions and choices we make each day.[2] To more directly meet this criticism, we later provided a detailed literature review and analysis of the death penalty and the ideological messages this policy/practice served both in the United States and in the People's Republic of China (Tifft 1982, 1985). More recently, we have assessed in detail the numerous policies and interventions that have been implemented to respond to the battering of women. We concluded that these policies and practices have had little demonstrated effect and hold little potential for decreasing the prevalence of battering; this is principally because they leave the cultural and structural roots that produce this form of intimate violence intact (Tifft 1993; Tifft and Markham 1991). Similarly, in our recent writing and teaching, we have explored the current socially constructed conceptualizations of children and youth and the impact these constructs have had in producing schools in which teachers and administrators treat students as if they were suspected terrorists by monitoring and regulating their every movement; systematically dismiss their interests, voices, and talents; and respond to their needs and harms in such a way that it is surprising that so many children can regain their wits as adults (Tifft, Sullivan, and Sullivan 1998). Further, we have raised questions regarding how we as a species unreflectively assume that we are justified in exercising power and control over the environment (Bookchin 1971) and other species. Institutionally, and personally, many of us use other species to meet our needs without questioning the hypocrisy of calling for an end to violence for reasons of class, gender, race, and age, but not species. Perhaps the sweet taste of a ham sandwich is too much for many of us even to take into account how we treat these animals before they provide us sustenance.[3]

As our work together draws to a close, we have been exuberant in calling attention to the numerous programs that theorists, policymakers, and practitioners have called "restorative justice" (e.g., family conferencing, victim-offender reconciliation programs, and sentencing circles (Sullivan and Tifft 1998a, 1998b, 2000, 2001, 2004). We are advocates of many of these responses to interpersonal harms, especially when they meet the needs of those harmed and when the person who has chosen to harm others is young. However, we recognize that these responses, when not extended to confront and transform the cultural and social structural arrangements that underlie the needs of young people, their families, and their communities, are woefully inadequate in the task of decreasing the prevalence of such harms. Meeting the needs of those harmed and those who choose to harm might help these individuals, but there are so many similar others to be responded to that these individual-focused intervention measures not only become quickly scripted and ritualized, they become a state-organized charade. They are a charade because it is well understood that what we really need is a proactive, before-the-harm, needs-based, primary prevention, public health, social structural response to harm (Tifft 1993, 157; Sullivan and Tifft 2004). Yet such a response is not likely to be taken, for adopting a preventive approach would seriously undermine the arrangements of institutionalized power, inequality, and privilege in the society.

Again, when we talk about the necessity of structural change so that the needs of all are met, we inevitably return to point out the criminal nature of the state, its atrocities, and its violations of essential human needs through foreign and domestic social control policies (Tifft 1979, 1994–1995; Sullivan 1980; Tifft and Sullivan 1980; Tifft and Markham 1991). Most recently, we have applied our perspective to assess the tremendous rise in transboundary crimes, those committed, for example, by the World Bank, the International Monetary Fund, and other organizations that operate beyond the social control of the United Nations, any single nation-state, or any regulatory organization (Tifft 2003). These policies and projects have resulted in monumental human and environmental harm. They have economically colonized nations and undermined their sovereignty. They have created industrial and agricultural "free zones" expediting the exploitation of survival-driven labor by allowing global corporations to operate free of the necessity of paying living wages, free of constraining taxes, and free of substantial environmental, worker safety, or regulatory standards or enforcement. Starvation, malnutrition, impovertization, dislocation, intra-nation conflict, collective resource privatization, deforestation, biodiversity reduction, and "blowback"-generated terrorism are the results (Wonders and Danner 2002; Friedrichs and Friedrichs 2002). Such harms will not end with the wounding of those now directly affected, which is all of us. They will persist for generations and leave a scar on the human psyche, the despair from which our grandchildren and yours will have to struggle against to remedy.

We have complemented these inquiries with an examination of the social organization of our places of work and far too frequently found them to constitute a crime, not only against the physical body, but also against the human spirit and human dignity (Sullivan and Tifft 2001). Yet these crimes are but one component of the devastating corporate and corporate-state crimes to which we are subjected (Friedrichs 2002; Kauzlarich, Mullins, and Matthews 2003; Kramer, Michalowski, and Kauzlairch 2002). Not only do some decisionmakers in these organizations commit criminal acts for reasons of profit and market share, the very manner in which these entities are organized is criminal. Corporate organization dismisses needs, denies needs, and thwarts development; it is tyrannical because it disallows the people in a society meaningful participation in either the selection of decisionmakers or the development of policy and investment strategies (Chomsky 1996, 19).

Unless the people in our communities and society are major participants in decisions concerning what is produced, how it is produced (e.g., what the working conditions are; how the environment is affected), and how products and services are distributed, we will never have a way of life that we can call a democracy (Chomsky 1996). What we have now, and will have if we remain nonparticipants, is one or another mode of tyranny—a tyranny of the professional, the expert, or the executive officer who makes key decisions that critically affect our lives, the environment, and the future of humankind (Sullivan 2004b). So, like the political tyrannies (e.g., fascism, bolshevism) that have, in institutional form, passed into nonexistence, the prevailing global corporate mode of economic organizational tyranny must meet a similar fate. And not only will we have to create sustainable alternatives to this economic tyranny, but we will have to self-transform by bringing about a change in how we conceptualize ourselves and the ways we live. We will have to recognize once again the inherent human value of living an active, participatory life.

This is not an easy task because it requires that—in theory and practice—we examine the "true costs of things" (Sullivan 1993), for example, the true costs of buying into a way of life that packages a sense of self; the needs of this self are manufactured and marketed and must be purchased and consumed the way we purchase and consume commodities. The true, fully potentialed selves we could be are like walking and bicycling modes of transportation and the self-sustaining garden—all but dead—replaced by the car, the supermarket, the factory farm, and the market made-over self. Just as sad is that with these deaths come state-authorized executions, workplace deaths, and collective deaths through "grand area plans" and geopolitical wars, state-sponsored terrorism, and corporate environmental destruction. Is all this to obtain the resources necessary to keep ourselves commodified and our cars rolling us to our competency-disabling places of work (Tifft and Markham 1991; Tifft 1982, 1984–1985, 1985; Sullivan and Tifft 1998a, 1998b, 2001; Tifft and Sullivan, 2003)?

Extending Anarchist Criminology

Mark Lanier and Stuart Henry (2004, 28) have graciously acknowledged that we have in our years of collaborative writing continuously challenged other criminologists to expand the scope of criminology by extending the definition of crime substantively and processually (Tifft 1984–1985; Tifft and Sullivan 2001). Issues of power and needs are central to understanding the true extent and depth of crime and social harm, and the right place to start such an analysis is not with the law or the state but "with the wounds of people, with the wounded. From there [we] work [our] way out, but the story always starts beneath the bandages" (Sullivan 2004a, 150). It makes perfect sense that those who create the rules or laws, that is, those who exercise institutional power in a life sphere (e.g., political, economic, or family), attempt to define their exercise of power and harm as legitimate and therefore not harmful. It also makes sense that they try to convince you/us that their declarations of superiority are beyond reproach regardless of the severity of the wounds they inflict (Kennedy 1970). But this does not mean that it makes sense for any one of us to accede to these power exercises or to pretend that the wounds they inflict personally and institutionally do not exist.

The acts of power brokers and the law attempt to separate those "victims" they define as worthy of our attention from those they define as unworthy. In the instance of law, the relationships between law and power and between power and harm are masked. Law legitimates, and penal law attempts to reinstate a variety of structurally violent patterns of social inequality by, for example, legalizing highly exploitative modes of production and distribution, institutionalizing participatory injustice, and sanctifying human degradation and indignity. It also prescribes a variety of retributive, penal responses that are indisputably violent. We tried to bring these truth assertions to everyone's attention years ago in *The Struggle to Be Human* and *The Mask of Love*. If such legal arrangements constitute grave social harms against our individual and collective well-being, it follows then that we should consider these social arrangements, at a minimum, a principal subject of criminological inquiry. What does it say about the American Society of Criminology and the Academy of Criminal Justice Sciences? The vast majority of their members still do not touch on these matters in their work. What are we to say of the publishing industry? Its products, especially introductory criminology and criminal justice texts, reflect a version of inquiry that does not dare its readers to examine the basic assumptions and definitions upon which the criminological enterprise is founded (Pfohl 1981, 118). Past these issues, we doubt that next month you will be prancing along easy street feeling assured that the tentacles of the national security state and the fear-based penal society exist only for limiting the freedoms and grasping the bodies of radically different others.

Regardless of your responses to these matters, it does not make sense that any one of us should accede to accept narrow legal boundaries of what constitutes harm, crime, and human well-being. Contrary to what we think Mark Lanier and Stuart Henry (2004, 28) infer to be our position regarding actually having the state criminalize harmful acts for reasons of state or those for profit and market share, we do not advocate criminalizing these acts, which would be an additional act of state violence. We do not advocate any mode of violence, whether intrapersonal, interpersonal, or structural. What we do advocate is that these harmful modes of production/distribution, political exclusion, and human degradation be not only examined as crimes, but be dissolved, replaced. Here is where the other dimension of our work comes in. Our work is focused on transforming structurally violent, needs-denying social arrangements into democratic, participatory decisionmaking, needs-affirming, and needs-meeting ways of organizing social life—at work, in the family, in school, in our communities, and in the society.

In this sense we are, as Mark Lanier and Stuart Henry (2004, 329), Richard Quinney (1991, 12), and John Wozniak (2002), among others, have correctly stated, peacemaking criminologists (Sullivan and Tifft 1998a) and advocates of restorative justice (Sullivan and Tifft 1998b, 2001, 2004). Our interest is not in responding to personal, market, and nation-state violence with personal, state, or supra-state violence. As Daniel Berrigan pointed out to his long-time friend Ernesto Cardinal, who had embraced violence as a response to violence done him and his people, "We look around at our culture: an uneasy mix of gunmen, gun makers, gun hucksters, gun researchers, gun runners, guards with guns, property owners with guns. A culture in which the guns put out contracts on the people, the guns own the people, the guns buy and sell the people, the guns practice target on the people, the guns kill the people. The guns are our second nature, and the first nature is all but obliterated; it is gunned down" (Berrigan 1988, 169–170). We seek to keep alive the mutual aid and cooperative spirit of our first nature; therefore we disavow all violence by responding to perceived harms, injustices, violence, and power exercises with interactive processes that promote an airing of differences in reality claims and foster reconciliation, responsibility-taking, and need-meeting. And, to be true to the spirit of restorative justice (Zehr and Mika 1998) these processes must be as inclusive as possible such that each agreement reached is a symbolic commitment to meeting everyone's needs and a practical plan for moving in this direction.

However, peacemaking and restorative justice efforts need to move past interpersonal encounters and address the social structural roots of violence and the structurally violent forms of organization that include far too many of us in their managerial patterns as objects and as doers of harms. In these matters, we are persuaded that human difference and conflict are positive forces in continuously altering social life in the direction of sustainability, freedom, and well-being. They can be the source of the kinds of personal initiative that Kropotkin saw as so essential to the continuation of the species. But we are equally convinced that interpersonal violence and, more deeply, the structurally violent arrangements that encourage people to undertake intrapersonal and interpersonal violent responses to these conditions or arrangements, are not a positive force in human survival and well-being.

Beyond Criminology: Living Our Lives

The journey that we have taken to develop and present an anarchist, needs-based criminology has not been without fellow travelers. Hal Pepinsky (1978, 1991, 1999, 2000), David Gil (1989, 1990, 1996, 1998, 1999, 2000), Jeff Ferrell (1994, 1995, 1999), Richard Quinney (1991, 1995, 1998; Tifft 2002a), and Randall Amster (2001, 2003, 2004) have offered similar critiques of structural violence and the hierarchical political economies of workplace, family life, and culture. They, too, have been engaged in providing a roadmap for living our lives in a needs-meeting manner and fostering "equality of well-being" for all.

As should be evident by now for a multitude of reasons, an anarchist needs-based criminology extends far beyond the scope of the discipline's usual array of criminologies, though we are pleased to see some of this perspective included in the new integrated criminologies (Barak 1998; Barak and Henry 1998; Henry and Lanier 2001a; Lanier and Henry 2004; Milovanovic and Henry 2001). However, we are essentially talking about more profound changes, changes in our daily lives: interacting with your intimate partner differently; living with your children differently; collaborating with coworkers differently; helping children develop their talents differently; making collective investment decisions differently; and making self-development decisions differently. Perhaps the characterizations of our early work, that we were polemical, utopian, romantic, and unsettling, contain some truth. Offering a vision of a more just world is necessary and unsettling. We have all along intended to challenge everyone who reads our work to join us in organizing all the spheres of our being, all the spheres of our lives differently—cooperatively, collaboratively, consensually (Sullivan and Tifft 2004). It has been and is no surprise that our work, and that of others who have chosen a similar path, is so commonly dismissed, excluded. A critique of power and hierarchy is not marketable, as is the work published in *Criminology*; it offends and leads to discomfort. For all its life-producing, life-enhancing, and, perhaps, life-saving elements, it could destroy one's career. We challenge you to get out of power and bring democracy and equality to life! Dream, think about life, act, organize.

We appreciate those who have taken our ideas to heart, who believe that we, like our predecessors and contemporaries, are on to something essential for creating a world in which, as Peter Maurin said, "it is easier for people to be good." We desire a world where it is easier to be kind and to extend ourselves to others. We desire a world in which we are more aware of the possible effects and the actual effects of our actions on others, and therefore knowingly we become less frequently harmful and unresponsive to others.

We remain aware that our version of an anarchist, needs-based criminology has been an eye-opener and a heart-opener for some of our colleagues and readers. We present an uncertain, ever-changing vista on how we might engage life personally and collectively. We offer a dynamic and innovative challenge for how we might organize individual and cooperative work that will make us more human while not jeopardizing our sustenance. And we are pleased with the conclusion that the essence of needs-based criminology is "100 per cent what the study of crime should be: an explicitly moral, sometimes painfully personal exploration of harm in all its forms" (Maruna 2003, 253). An anarchist, needs-based criminology should transcend criminology. Attentive to the needs of our critics and reflective of our own development, we have, in our most recent writing, tried to provide numerous specific, down-to-earth illustrations of how people today are struggling to create family life, workplace life, learning-place life, and societal arrangements that are needs-based (Sullivan and Tifft, 2004).

Ethics

As a first principle for creating such arrangements, we encourage you neither to exercise power over another nor to allow yourself to become subjected to the power exercise of another (Wieck 1975, 146). Turned around, this becomes a needs-based version of the golden rule, one that shifts the basis of interaction from a self-based, projected version of well-being to an other-based and self-based version. It entails finding out from the other and those who have that person's best interests (needs) at heart what the other person's real needs are. It entails, as well, making every effort to meet those needs. Thus, the "rule shift" moves from the dictum "interact with another in a way that you would like to be interacted with were you in that person's circumstance" to "interact with another in the way that this other person wishes you to interact with him or her, unless this request (to help that person meet expressed needs) violates your personal ethics or appears to request that you enter the relational world of power and control." This dictum requires that we let others know what our needs are; it is interactive. There is a difference between choosing to serve others and being their slave.

A second principle for organizing our lives with each other entails movement away from hierarchical patterns, from power, from a life of singular self-interest to a continuous commitment to others and to shared core values; one that initiates continuous change in these patterns. To illustrate briefly, many couples are continuously engaged in ways to organize their lives together so they can live as intimate equals. Schwartz (1994), among other researchers, presents us with a clear vision of how these couples organize their lives as peers (Sullivan and Tifft 2001). Trying to live as equals, they make decisions about family life together; they have equal access to the family's resources, funds, and discretionary monies; they act on the belief that each person's life path, no matter its direction or fiscal contribution, is of equal consideration; and they establish no greater than perhaps a 60/40 split in dividing the tasks that constitute the adult component of the family's homework. In these families, being with the children is neither a self-sacrificing task nor a burdensome chore (Sullivan and Tifft 2001, 2004).

Human Nature

But this kind of change will not occur without changes in one's self and this requires an understanding of what or who that self is. Our criminology has been criticized for positing a primordial self that has needs and desires outside of social interaction (Marshall 2002), or that we offer an untenable, naturalistic assumption about the peaceable nature of humanity (Woolford 2003). We hope we have shown in the preceding paragraphs that neither of these assertions is correct. Our sociological conceptualization of self and identity insists that different conceptualizations of the self, as well as our needs and individual desires, are differentially developed and fostered or thwarted in differing cultural, interactional, and structural contexts. Social contexts, ideas, and feelings feed back into one another to create a socially constructed self—a self that is differently imagined and actualized in differently organized and historically situated political economies (e.g., rights-based, deserts-based, and needs-based) (Miller 1976). Far from holding a substantively primordial view of human nature or a naive one about the goodness of humankind, we, following Kropotkin, see human nature as dualistic—as composed of two sets of contrasting feelings. In the first set are feelings that respond to the human need for solidarity, for feeling a oneness with others—a certain essential humanness or commonality. These feelings induce us to care for one another, to help one another, and to cooperate to meet our common needs. They also lead us to respond in a participatory and peaceful way, as equals, to the conflicts and disputes that inevitably arise.

In the second set are feelings that respond to the human need to assert one's individuality—one's different-ness or uniqueness. These feelings induce us to break the social and cultural constraints that collectivities (e.g., groups, communities, organizations, states) press upon us. They stimulate creativity, risk taking, and social change—what Kropotkin called initiative—while impeding social stagnation, group tyranny, and suppression. However, these feelings may also induce us to assert individual, categorical, cultural, or group superiority and lead us to objectify, demonize, and control others for our own individual/group ends. The search and struggle for us all in our self-expression, interaction with others, work, and activism—indeed, in all areas of our daily lives—is to imagine and attempt to create ways of organizing social life that might produce collective well-being and solidarity, and, as well, meet individual needs. In this way we might simultaneously stimulate the creative and diverse energies of each individual and thwart all assertions and institutionalizations of superiority.

Conclusion

In conclusion, needs-based, anarchist criminology offers a view of a nonhierarchical, dynamic, egalitarian society; a substantive critique of existing social relationships; a set of specific assertions about human nature and needs; a theory concerning the generation of harms and nonviolent, needs-meeting responses to harm; a set of value-guided ethics, principles, policies, and programs; and a needs-based vision of just relations between us and our environment.

Notes

1. It should be pointed out that *The Struggle to Be Human* and *The Mask of Love* were the first thorough examinations of crime and punishment from an anarchist, needs-based perspective. However, Alex Comfort, the British novelist, poet, and medical doctor, wrote a book on delinquency with anarchist underpinnings in 1950 titled *Authority and Delinquency in the Modern State: A Criminological Approach to the Problem of Power*. Paul Goodman's 1956 book, *Growing Up Absurd: Problems of Youth in the Organized System*, examined delinquency from an anarchist perspective.

2. *The Struggle to Be Human* was completed in 1976. With great persistence we attempted for nearly three years to have this manuscript published in the United States and actually had two different signed contracts for its publication, both of which were rescinded. Our first publisher decided to void his contract with us, concluding that the publication of this book would ruin his reputation and detract from the sales of his other offerings. The second publisher voided our contract by threatening to cancel the book series within which *The Struggle* had been accepted if the series editor insisted on its publication. It appeared to us that no publisher wanted to be associated with an anarchist treatise on crime and punishment. A decision was then made to write a saleable corrections textbook, the proceeds from which would be used to self-publish *The Struggle*. The result, it turned out, was not a saleable textbook but an anarchist, needs-based treatise on the justice-industrial complex called *The Mask of Love*. Ironically, while the "textbook" was being written, Stuart Christie, a British anarchist who lived in the Orkney Islands, after being shown *The Struggle* in late 1979, wanted to publish it immediately. When Kennikat decided to publish *The Mask of Love* right away, somewhat serendipitously, the two books appeared in 1980 within months of each other. If *The Struggle* had a hard time finding an audience right away, so did *The Mask*, for, among other reasons, the "correctional world" had been inundated with the theory of "just deserts." In 1976, Andrew Von Hirsch's *Doing Justice: The Choice of Punishments* had appeared and academics and practitioners alike embraced its merits-based ideology with fervor. Clearly, "the times" were not receptive to a corrections book based on anarchist, needs-based thinking and practice.

3. In a basic introductory criminology course, Dennis Sullivan uses texts that raise the fundamental issues of species-ism, the enforcement by *Homo sapiens* of its asserted superiority over animals. Perhaps the next sharply contested frontier for defining acts as crimes will be the killing of animals for the sustenance of *Homo sapiens*. In most

instances, students today find such questioning to be close to insanity, as if eating animals were part of some preordained human prerogative. See De Grazia (1996); Scully (2003); Scruton (2003); Singer (1973, 2003); Beirne (1995); and Godlovitch, Godlovitch, and Harris (1972) for the main issues raised over species-ism from conservative, liberal, and radical political perspectives.

References

Amster, Randall. 2001. "Changing Rainbows: Utopian Pragmatics and the Search for Anarchist Communities." *Anarchist Studies* 9: 229–252.

______. 2003. "Restoring (Dis)order: Sanctions, Resolutions, and Social Control in Anarchist Communities." *Contemporary Justice Review* 6: 9–24.

______. 2004. "Breaking the Law: Anti-Authoritarian Visions of Crime and Justice." *The New Formulation* 2: 12–16.

Arrigo, Bruce. 1999. *Social Justice/Criminal Justice: The Maturation of Critical Theory in Law, Crime and Deviance*. Belmont, Calif.: West/Wadsworth.

______. 2000. "Social Justice and Critical Criminology: On Integrating Knowledge." *Contemporary Justice Review* 3: 7–37.

Barak, Gregg. 1994. "Crime, Criminology, and Human Rights: Toward an Understanding of State Criminality." In *Varieties of Criminology: Readings from a Dynamic Discipline*, edited by Gregg Barak (pp. 253–268). Westport, Conn.: Praeger.

______. 1998. *Integrative Criminologies*. Boston: Allyn and Bacon.

______. 2003. "Revisionist History, Visionary Criminology, and Needs-Based Justice." *Contemporary Justice Review* 6: 217–226.

______, ed. 1991. *Crimes of the Capitalist State: An Introduction to State Criminality*. Albany, N.Y.: State University of New York Press.

Barak, Gregg, and Stuart Henry. 1999. "An Integrative-Constitutive Theory of Crime, Law, and Social Justice." In *Social Justice/Criminal Justice: The Maturation of Critical Theory in Law, Crime, and Deviance*, edited by Bruce A. Arrigo (pp. 152–175). Belmont, Calif.: West/Wadsworth.

Beirne, Piers. 1995. "The Use and Abuse of Animals in Criminology: A Brief History and Current Review." *Social Justice* 22: 5–31.

Berrigan, Daniel. 1988. "Letter to Ernesto Cardenal: Guns Don't Work." In *Daniel Berrigan: Poetry, Drama, Prose*, edited by Michael True (pp. 169–179). Maryknoll, N.Y.: Orbis Books.

Bookchin, Murray. 1971. *Post-Scarcity Anarchism*. Berkeley: Ramparts Press.

Cavalieri, Paola. 2001. *The Animal Question: Why Non-Human Animals Deserve Human Rights*. Translated from the Italian by Catherine Woollard. Oxford: Oxford University Press.

Chomsky, Noam. 1996. "You Say You Want a Devolution?" *Progressive* (March): 18–19.
Comfort, Alex. 1950. *Authority and Delinquency in the Modern State: A Criminological Approach to the Problem of Power*. London: Routledge & Keegan Paul.
De Grazia. 1996. *Taking Animals Seriously: Mental Life and Moral Status*. Cambridge: Cambridge University Press.
Friedrichs, David O., ed. 1998. *State Crime*. Vols. 1 and 2. Aldershot, U.K.: Ashgate/Dartmouth.
______. 2002. State-Corporate Crime in a Globalized World: Myth or Major Challenge? In *Controversies in White-Collar Crime*, edited by Gary W. Potter (pp. 53–71). Cincinnati, Ohio: Anderson.
Friedrichs, David O., and Jessica Friedrichs. 2002. "The World Bank and Crimes of Globalization: A Case Study." *Social Justice* 29: 13–36.
Ferrell, Jeff. 1993. *Crimes of Style: Urban Graffiti and the Politics of Criminality*. New York: Garland.
______. 1994. "Confronting the Agenda of Authority: Critical Criminology, Anarchism, and Urban Graffiti." In *Varieties of Criminology*, edited by Gregg Barak (pp. 161–178). Westport, Conn.: Praeger.
______. 1995. "Anarchy Against the Discipline." *Journal of Criminal Justice and Popular Culture* 3: 86–91.
______. 1999. "Anarchist Criminology and Social Justice." In *Social Justice/Criminal Justice: The Maturation of Critical Theory in Law, Crime, and Deviance*, edited by Bruce A. Arrigo (pp. 91–108). Belmont, Calif.: West/Wadsworth.
Gil, David G. 1989. "Work, Violence, Injustice, and War." *Journal of Sociology and Social Welfare* 16: 39–53.
______. 1990. *Unraveling Social Policy*. 4th ed. Rochester, Vt.: Schenkman Books.
______. 1996. "Preventing Violence in a Structurally Violent Society: Mission Impossible." *American Journal of Orthopsychiatry* 66: 77–84.
______. 1998. *Confronting Injustice and Oppression*. New York: Columbia University Press.
______. 1999. "Understanding and Overcoming Social-Structural Violence." *Contemporary Justice Review* 2: 23–35.
______. 2000. "Rethinking the Goals, Organization, Designs, and Quality of Work in Relation to Individual and Social Development." *Contemporary Justice Review* 3: 73–88.
Godlovitch, Stanley, Roslind Godlovitch, and John Harris. 1972. *Animals, Men and Morals: An Enquiry into the Maltreatment of Non-Humans*. New York: Taplinger.
Goodman, Paul. 1956. *Growing Up Absurd: Problems of Youth in the Organized System*. New York: Vintage.
Henry, Stuart, and Mark M. Lanier. 2001a. "The Prism of Crime: Toward an Integrated Definition of Crime." In *What Is Crime? Controversies Over the Nature of*

Crime and What to Do About It, edited by Stuart Henry and Mark M. Lanier (pp. 227–243). Lanham, Md.: Rowman and Littlefield.

______. eds. 2001b. *What Is Crime? Controversies Over the Nature of Crime and What to Do About It*. Lanham, Md.: Rowman and Littlefield.

Henry, Stuart, and Dragan Milovanovic. 1993. "Back to Basics: A Post-Modern Definition of Crime." *Critical Criminologist* 5: 1–2, 12.

______. 1996. *Constitutive Criminology: Beyond Postmodernism*. Thousand Oaks, Calif.: Sage.

Kauzlarich, David, Christopher W. Mullins, and Rick A. Matthews. 2003. "A Complicity Continuum of State Crime." *Contemporary Justice Review* 6: 241–254.

Kramer, Ronald, Raymond Michalowski, and David Kauzlarich. 2002. "The Origins and Development of the Concept and Theory of State-Corporate Crime." *Crime & Delinquency* 48: 263–282.

Kropotkin, Peter. 1924. *Ethics: Origin and Development*. New York: Mother Earth Publications.

______. 1968. *The Conquest of Bread*. New York: Benjamin Blom.

Kennedy, Mark. 1970. "Beyond Incrimination: Some Neglected Facts of the History of Punishment." *Catalyst* 5: 1–16.

Lanier, Mark M., and Stuart Henry. 2004. *Essential Criminology*. 2d ed. Boulder: Westview Press.

Marshall, Anna-Maria. 2002. Review of *Restorative Justice: Healing the Foundations of Our Everyday Lives*, by Dennis Sullivan and Larry Tifft. *The Law and Politics Book Review* 1: 38–41.

Maruna, Shadd. 2003. Review of *Restorative Justice: Healing the Foundations of Our Everyday Lives*, by Dennis Sullivan and Larry Tifft. *British Journal of Criminology* 43: 252–254.

Michalowski, Raymond. 1985. *Order, Law, and Crime: An Introduction to Criminology*. New York: Random House.

Michalowski, Raymond, and Ronald Kramer. 1987. "The Space Between Laws: The Problem of Corporate Crime in the Transnational Context." *Social Problems* 34: 34–53.

______. 1998. "Globalization and Shifting Legal Spaces: An Inquiry into Transnational Corporate Crime Under the New World Order." Paper presented at the American Society of Criminology Meeting, Washington, D.C.

Mika, Harry. 1992. "Mediation Interventions and Restorative Justice: Responding to the Astructural Bias." In *Restorative Justice on Trial: Pitfalls and Potentials of Victim-Offender Mediation International Research Perspectives*, edited by Heinz Messmer and Hans-Uwe Otto (pp. 559–567). Dordrecht, Netherlands: Kluwer.

______. 2001. Foreword to *Restorative Justice: Healing the Foundations of Our Everyday Lives*, by Dennis Sullivan and Larry Tifft (pp. xv–xxvii). Monsey, N.Y.: Willow Tree Press.

Mika, Harry, and Kieran McEvoy. 2001. "Restorative Justice in Conflict: Paramilitarism, Community, and the Construction of Legitimacy in Northern Ireland." *Contemporary Justice Review* 4: 291–319.

Miller, David. 1976. *Social Justice*. Oxford: Oxford University Press.

Milovanovic, Dragan, and Stuart Henry. 2001. "Constitutive Definition of Crime: Power as Harm." In *What Is Crime? Controversies over the Nature of Crime and What to Do About It*, edited by Stuart Henry and Mark M. Lanier (pp. 165–178). Lanham, Md.: Rowman and Littlefield.

Pepinsky, Harold E. 1978. "Communist Anarchism as an Alternative to the Rule of Law." *Contemporary Crisis* 2: 315–327.

______. 1991. *The Geometry of Violence and Democracy*. Bloomington, Ind.: Indiana University Press.

______. 1999. "Peacemaking Primer." In *Social Justice/Criminal Justice: The Maturation of Critical Theory in Law, Crime, and Deviance*, edited by Bruce A. Arrigo (pp. 52–70). Belmont, Calif.: West/Wadsworth.

______. 2000. "Living Criminologically with Naked Emperors." *Criminal Justice Policy Review* 11: 6–15.

______. 2003. Review of *What Is Crime? Controversies over the Nature of Crime and What to Do About It*, edited by Stuart Henry and Mark M. Lanier. *Contemporary Sociology* 31: 84–85.

Pepinsky, Harold E., and Richard Quinney, eds. 1991. *Criminology as Peacemaking*. Bloomington, Ind.: Indiana University Press.

Pfohl, Steven. 1994. *Images of Deviance and Social Control: A Sociological History*. New York: McGraw-Hill.

Quinney, Richard. 1991. "The Way of Peace: On Crime, Suffering and Service." In *Criminology as Peacemaking*, edited by Harold E. Pepinsky and Richard Quinney (pp. 3–13). Bloomington, Ind.: Indiana University Press.

______. 1995. "Socialist Humanism and the Problem of Crime: Thinking About Erich Fromm in the Development of Critical/Peacemaking Criminology." *Crime, Law, and Social Change* 23: 147–156.

______. 1998. "Criminology as Moral Philosophy: Criminologist as Witness." *Contemporary Justice Review* 1: 347–364.

Schwartz, Pepper. 1994. "Modernizing Marriage." *Psychology Today* (September/October): 54, 56, 58–59, 86.

Scully, Matthew. 2003. *Dominion: The Power of Man, the Suffering of Animals, and the Call to Mercy*. New York: St. Martin's Press.

Scruton, Roger. 2000. *Animal Rights and Wrongs*. London: Metro Publishing.

Singer, Peter. 1973. "Animal Liberation." *New York Review of Books* (April 5). http://www.nybooks.com/articles/article-preview?article_id=9900.

______. 2003. "Animal Liberation at 30." *New York Review of Books* (May 15). http://www.nybooks.com/articles/16276.

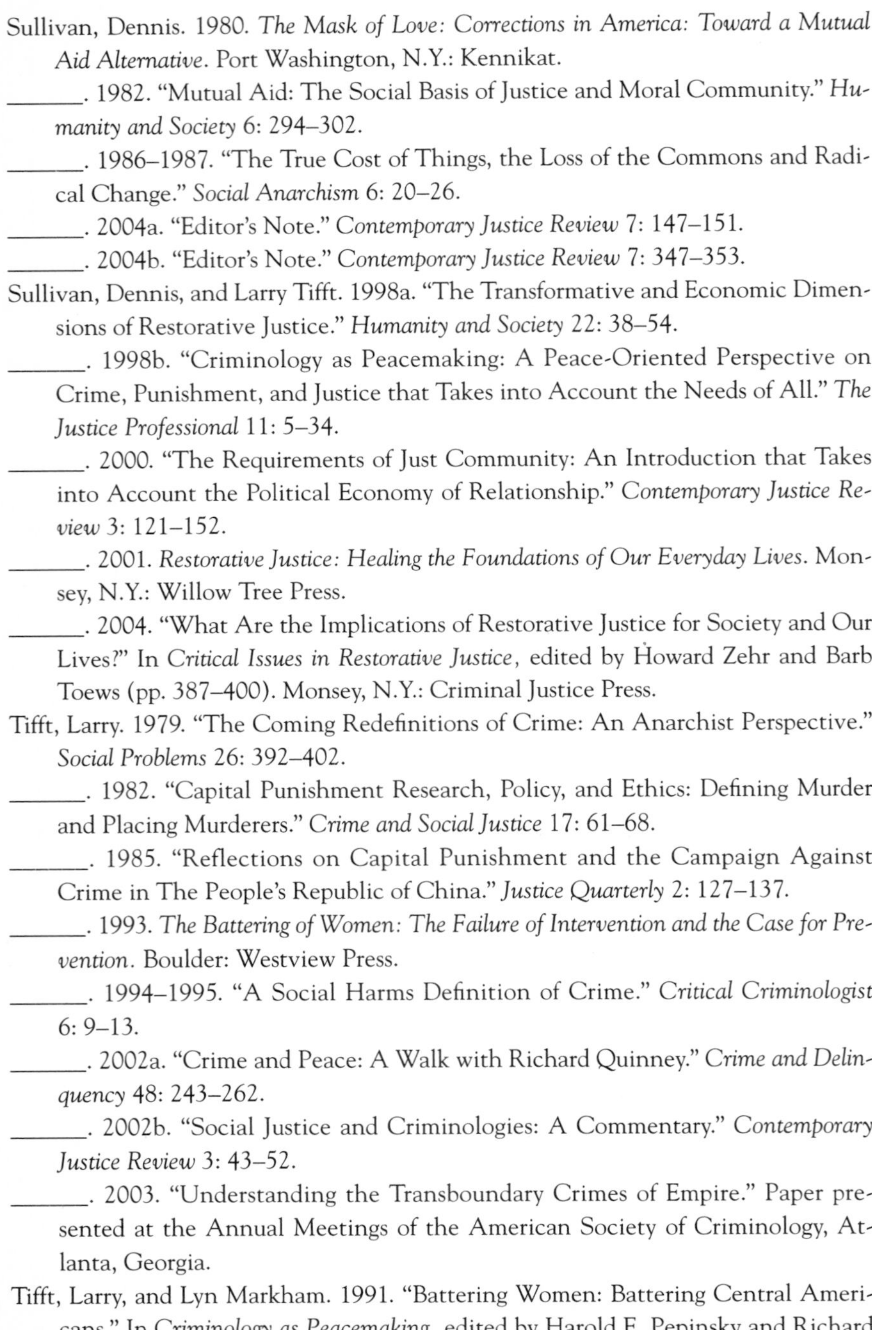

Sullivan, Dennis. 1980. *The Mask of Love: Corrections in America: Toward a Mutual Aid Alternative*. Port Washington, N.Y.: Kennikat.

______. 1982. "Mutual Aid: The Social Basis of Justice and Moral Community." *Humanity and Society* 6: 294–302.

______. 1986–1987. "The True Cost of Things, the Loss of the Commons and Radical Change." *Social Anarchism* 6: 20–26.

______. 2004a. "Editor's Note." *Contemporary Justice Review* 7: 147–151.

______. 2004b. "Editor's Note." *Contemporary Justice Review* 7: 347–353.

Sullivan, Dennis, and Larry Tifft. 1998a. "The Transformative and Economic Dimensions of Restorative Justice." *Humanity and Society* 22: 38–54.

______. 1998b. "Criminology as Peacemaking: A Peace-Oriented Perspective on Crime, Punishment, and Justice that Takes into Account the Needs of All." *The Justice Professional* 11: 5–34.

______. 2000. "The Requirements of Just Community: An Introduction that Takes into Account the Political Economy of Relationship." *Contemporary Justice Review* 3: 121–152.

______. 2001. *Restorative Justice: Healing the Foundations of Our Everyday Lives*. Monsey, N.Y.: Willow Tree Press.

______. 2004. "What Are the Implications of Restorative Justice for Society and Our Lives?" In *Critical Issues in Restorative Justice*, edited by Howard Zehr and Barb Toews (pp. 387–400). Monsey, N.Y.: Criminal Justice Press.

Tifft, Larry. 1979. "The Coming Redefinitions of Crime: An Anarchist Perspective." *Social Problems* 26: 392–402.

______. 1982. "Capital Punishment Research, Policy, and Ethics: Defining Murder and Placing Murderers." *Crime and Social Justice* 17: 61–68.

______. 1985. "Reflections on Capital Punishment and the Campaign Against Crime in The People's Republic of China." *Justice Quarterly* 2: 127–137.

______. 1993. *The Battering of Women: The Failure of Intervention and the Case for Prevention*. Boulder: Westview Press.

______. 1994–1995. "A Social Harms Definition of Crime." *Critical Criminologist* 6: 9–13.

______. 2002a. "Crime and Peace: A Walk with Richard Quinney." *Crime and Delinquency* 48: 243–262.

______. 2002b. "Social Justice and Criminologies: A Commentary." *Contemporary Justice Review* 3: 43–52.

______. 2003. "Understanding the Transboundary Crimes of Empire." Paper presented at the Annual Meetings of the American Society of Criminology, Atlanta, Georgia.

Tifft, Larry, and Lyn Markham. 1991. "Battering Women: Battering Central Americans." In *Criminology as Peacemaking*, edited by Harold E. Pepinsky and Richard Quinney (pp. 114–153). Bloomington, Ind.: Indiana University Press.

Tifft, Larry, and Dennis Sullivan. 1980. *The Struggle to Be Human: Crime, Criminology, and Anarchism*. Sanday, Orkney, U.K.: Cienfuegos Press.

______. "A Needs-Based Social Harms Approach to Defining Crime." In *What Is Crime? Controversies Over the Nature of Crime and What We Should Do About It*, edited by Stuart Henry and Mark M. Lanier (pp. 179–203). New York: Rowman and Littlefield.

Tifft, Larry, John Sullivan, and Dennis Sullivan. 1998. "Discipline as Enthusiasm: An Entry into the Recent Discussion on the Moral Development of Children." Paper presented at the Annual Meeting of the Association for Humanist Sociology, Pittsburgh, Pennsylvania.

Von Hirsch, Andrew. 1976. *Doing Justice: The Choice of Punishments*. New York: Hill & Wang.

Wieck, David. 1975. "The Negativity of Anarchism." *Interrogations: Revue Internationale de Recherche Anarchiste* 5: 25–55.

Wonders, Nancy A., and Mona Danner. 2002. "Globalization, State-Corporate Crime, and Women: The Strategic Role of Women's NGO's in the New World Order." In *Controversies in White-Collar Crime*, edited by Gary W. Potter (pp. 165–184). Cincinnati, Ohio: Anderson.

Woolford, Andrew. 2003. Review of *Restorative Justice: Healing the Foundations of Our Everyday Lives*, by Dennis Sullivan and Larry Tifft. *Canadian Journal of Criminology and Criminal Justice* 45, no. 1. http://www.ccja-acjp.ca/en/cjcr33.html.

Wozniak, John F. 2002a. "The Voices of Peacemaking Criminology: Insights into a Perspective with an Eye Toward Teaching." *Contemporary Justice Review* 3: 267–291.

______. 2002b. "Toward a Theoretical Model of Peacemaking Criminology: An Essay in Honor of Richard Quinney." *Crime & Delinquency* 48: 204–231.

______. 2003. "On Behalf of but Far Beyond Restorative Justice." *Contemporary Justice Review* 6: 187–191.

11.2

Peacemaking

HAL PEPINSKY
Indiana University, Bloomington

Peacemaking is the art and science of transforming violent relations into safe, trustworthy, mutually respectful, balanced relations. By "violent relations" I mean those in which some persons or groups "get over" on others, that is, "power plays" inflicted by some people on others. At the level of relations between individuals, we know many of these violent relations as "crime"; for instance, when one person kills another, or invades another's body as in assault and rape, or takes or uses another's belongings without the victim's consent. At the level of relations among groups, we know violent relations in many forms, as in enslavement, oppression, and discrimination. At the level of organizations, violent relations appear in the form of corporate malfeasance, environmental pollution, and unsafe labor conditions. At the level of societies and nation-states, we know violent relations as the exploitation of resources, genocide, and war. Criminologists have generally tried to explain why some people make power plays on others in ways that happen to be defined by governments as unlawful, and to propose how to get individual actors to stop that violence. Criminologists have only relatively recently tried to explain why organizations and governments themselves engage in such violence.

Peacemaking, as I see it, is different from conventional criminology in two respects: First, peacemaking postulates that violence, even violence committed to stop other violence—as in policing, criminal justice, and wars on crime—breeds more violence. Violence in one form, as in economic exploitation, can breed counterviolence in other forms, as in embezzlement or sabotage. And so violence in all its forms, whether legal or not, is a problem for a would-be peacemaker.

Second, criminology and criminal justice are focused on what *not* to do and how to stop people from relating to others in certain ways. Yet measures used to stop violence often channel and focus it rather than replace it. At the extreme, all crime and human violence can be stopped by human extinction; and there is a sense in which this deluded sense of removing violence by violence accompanies the notions of retribution and just deserts in which additional harm is inflicted by the state, and by incapacitation, under the guise of "protecting the public." What occurs here is that violence is concentrated on some (prison guards, other prisoners, prisoners' families) rather than on members of the wider society (see Milovanovic and Henry 2005). Peacemaking, by contrast, focuses on identifying forms of human relations that are satisfying and fulfilling to all participants, and on seeking ways to transform violent relations into good, constructive, and beautiful human relations. At the individual level, would-be peacemakers consider alternative options to criminal prosecution and the punishment of offenders, for example, victim-offender mediation: organizing conferences or circles involving victims and offenders, and other community support, in order to repair relations damaged by violence. They also develop agreements for giving redress and recognition to victims' losses while giving offenders ways to habilitate themselves—an approach to "crime" now generally known as "restorative" or "transformative justice" (Sullivan and Tifft 2001). At the group and organizational level, would-be peacemakers seek to democratize human relations, as in converting corporations into worker/client owned-and-operated enterprises using "intermediate" or "appropriate" technology (Schumacher 1999), or, as in my own case, democratizing college classes so that students' beliefs and feelings weigh as heavily as instructors' in evaluating criminal justice issues (Pepinsky 2005), in democratizing relations between parents and children (see again Sullivan and Tifft 2001), or between teachers and schoolchildren (Kohn 1996), or in negotiating settlements among warring parties (Fisher et al. 1991).

Peacemaking Criminology and Its Criticisms

In the spring of 1986, I returned to a country I consider a second home, Norway, on a research Fulbright to study "peaceful societies." My studies there led me to my broad definition of violence and of its peacemaking antithesis, which I called "unresponsiveness" (Pepinsky 1988). I had for some years been in touch with Richard Quinney, who at the time was fleshing out his own ideas of introducing the Buddhist "way of peace." Richard suggested that we call for contributions to an edited book on "criminology as peace." I suggested that we focus on making peace instead of characterizing "peace" as a state to achieve. Following a series of conference sessions on peacemaking criminology in 1987 we compiled the first statement: *Criminology as Peacemaking* (Pepinsky and Quinney 1991). The book was divided into religious, feminist, and critical approaches to peacemaking in criminology. Soon, in textbooks, "peacemaking criminology" was being cited as a new school of criminological thought and research. John Fuller (1998) even published a criminal justice text subtitled *A Peacemaking Perspective*.

Critics were quick to assess the significance of this "school," "approach," "perspective," or "paradigm." As I have argued elsewhere (Pepinsky 2001a, 204), the three main criticisms of peacemaking criminology are that (1) it is not a theory; (2) it is impractical; and (3) it is privileged.

Essentially, the first criticism states that peacemaking criminology is a conglomeration of goodhearted works that has no unifying theory or frame of analysis. However, although peacemaking criminology is not a theory in a conventional sense of explaining crime, it does embody theories about how peace is made and it hypothesizes that reconnecting broken social relations will produce less future violence rather than add more violence and deprivation. From this perspective, peacemaking is in the same "theoretical" category as retribution, incapacitation, and deterrence; although not theories, each embodies, albeit fundamentally, different assumptions about what prevents future violence.

A second criticism, that peacemaking is impractical, suggests that people will not behave in ways that make them safer because they prefer to react to crimes with force. This is clearly an empirical question. Peacemaking is not dreamt up in a vacuum; it relies on a rich body of empirical evidence and tested propositions about what separates people and what brings them together. However, predicting that people will be safer or more at risk does not mean that people will actually adopt behaviors that make them safer; so from that point of view, the "practicality" criticism suggests that people will choose to continue to create risk in spite of, and perhaps because of, their fear of peace. The failure to adopt peace as a method of justice is a reflection of society's self-defeating behavior, but it is not a valid criticism of the process of how to create peace.

Finally, realist criminologists have criticized peacemaking for failing to understand the victim's pain of oppression, and how those subjected to oppression have a need to violently overthrow their oppressors. Historically, this need has met with some success. That peacemaking criminologists, as theorists, are often privileged can be said of most theorists. The critical question is do we have to experience the pain of oppression to see how to escape its clutches? To paraphrase Mimi Silbert, founder of the "peacemaking" Delancey Street Foundation for ex-offenders in San Francisco: "You don't have to experience drugs to see how bad drug abuse can be. I don't have to shoot dope to see the pain. Drug users are here to learn how to become nonusers and how to build their lives, and pick themselves up when they fall, without the use of drugs as a crutch." The same could be said for violent offenders, whether individuals or corporations.

My Theory of Peacemaking

If one takes all work labeled peacemaking criminology as a whole, it becomes quite diverse, even in defining what "peacemaking" means. Peacemaking is a little like democracy: It sounds nice, and is an attractive label to put on one's criminological efforts, but it can also mean virtually anything to anyone who claims to be doing it or studying it. Such are the perils of popularity that a term becomes so widely and broadly used as to end up meaning essentially nothing. Although one of its founding authors in criminology, I am not entitled to claim ownership of the use of "peacemaking" in criminological research and practice. I cannot say that others who adopt the label are misusing it. At the same time, I am not accountable for the scholarly rigor of any peacemaking criminology but my own. The most recent synthesis of my theory of peacemaking can be found in Pepinsky (2001b). Here I will summarize the basic elements and recent directions of that theory.

My biggest stumbling block was figuring out a way to define the difference between violence and peacemaking. Years of studying the measurement of crime and criminality led me to conclude that there was no theoretically adequate way to do so. For one thing, what is labeled a crime and who is labeled a criminal is politically and economically arbitrary. For another, the more heinous the crime of personal violence (as in ritual human sacrifice and the parental rape of children), the more hidden the criminality. I postulate that for all measures of crime and criminality will ever tell us, an underlying, hidden reality is that rich and powerful people are as likely as poor young men of color—the prototypic criminal class—to commit the most serious crimes, that is, those of personal violence, including murder, and to indulge in theft, fraud, and corruption, especially if the concept of crime is expanded to include the socially injurious crimes of the structurally powerful. I see no foundation for treating one group of people as more criminal than another. As I wrote in Pepinsky (1988), the greatest violence of all is the violence of silence—that suffered by victims too weak and isolated to have their victimization noticed, let alone responded to. And so even within the realm of violence that is legally defined as criminal, peacemaking requires that the voices of the weakest among us especially need to be strengthened and validated. I find that children are the ultimate underclass. Should the day ever come when racial and class discrimination end, I suspect that children will still be regarded as less competent, less qualified to shape their own agendas, than adults.

My epiphany in Norway was to recognize that the difference between social relations that promoted anxiety, fear, and loss, and those that felt safe, honest, and trustworthy, lies in whether the members of a relationship hang on to fixed, substantive goals or agendas (e.g., getting someone to "behave," or maximizing profit), or change what they are after or attending to repeatedly as they continually learn where other people in the relationship are coming from, and where their interests lie. I find it ironic that so many of us celebrate a dedication (one might say "an addiction") to reaching high goals efficiently and effectively, which is literally, by definition, as I see it, a violent approach to interaction. It is only as people keep shifting their priorities and objects of attention to accommodate the ever-changing situation of those with whom they interact that power plays turn into the give-and-take of power sharing, which I originally called "responsiveness" and "democratization" and now call "peacemaking" as well.

Peacemaking, then, is a matter of how we orchestrate our responses to one another, including our responses to violence. It is a matter of the process by which we respond to one another rather than a matter of achieving prescribed outcomes. I have a favorite saying that captures each actor's role in peacemaking: "Show up. Pay attention. Tell the truth, and don't be attached to outcome."

I have seen this called a Navajo saying. Navajo have told me that they don't know whether the saying is Navajo, but that they could imagine a Navajo's saying it. It conforms well to how the Navajo peacemaking tradition is described (as by Yazzie and Zion 1996): "Showing up" means participating in interaction. "Paying attention" means listening to others empathically; that is, noticing what other participants are feeling and working to understand their concerns and interests. "Telling the truth" means being honest about expressing one's own feelings, concerns, and interests. And "not being attached to outcome" means being prepared, upon reflection, to shift one's own concerns and objectives to accommodate those of others.

Notice that although peacemaking has much in common with concern for due process, peacemaking rejects the premise of the substantive rule of law—that consequences of actions be defined before cases arise; that legislators, for example, prescribe sentences for crimes without hearing the parties' concerns in cases at hand. So, for instance, in the victim-offender mediation sessions that I facilitate, it is my job to empower the parties in conflict to decide what is most important to them, to design their own agreement to repair the damage to their relationship as they, not I or a penal statute, define the needs and interests at hand. To me, some of the most gratifying agreements are those the terms of which no one could foresee before the parties met. Ideally, too, mediation agreements are concrete and limited in time so that thereafter the parties can continue reorienting and restructuring their own social lives. This is the process by which conflict can move from being a source of division to becoming a source of cooperation.

The same happens when I succeed in democratizing my college classes: The issues we address and the views we exchange emerge through the progress of our oral and written conversations rather than through my laying out in a syllabus a schedule of issues and materials that we will consider throughout the semester, or through my testing whether students know what I consider in advance to be the right answers in what they write for their grades (Pepinsky 2005, forthcoming). As I tell my students, my primary criterion of how successful a class has been is how much I learn from them about how to frame issues as we address and learn from our differences of experience and perspective.

Empathy fuels and in turn is fed by the peacemaking process. At the level of each individual's participation, I find that people need to experience others' empathy for their own concerns and interests, that is, to have assurance that their own feelings and opinions matter to others and hence to themselves before they can hear and show empathy to others. For instance, in the classroom, to get others to hear my views and take them seriously, I find it vital that I show appreciation and respect, especially to students who openly express fundamental disagreement with me. When someone disagrees with me, I try to do what mediators call "active listening." Before I state my own response, I try to restate what I have heard, and then seek reassurance that I have heard what the other person really meant to tell me. Peacemaking entails learning to be comfortable with open disagreement. Contrary to a stereotype I often encounter, that peacemaking means just being nice and agreeable, peacemaking requires that conflicts be brought into the open and embraced so that each participant reaches his or her own conclusions as the conversation progresses. From this perspective, personal responsibility means being open about, and accountable for, what you really feel and think, rather than glossing over differences just to get along. When, in that process, people manage to let go of attachment to outcome, they find that they can work out ways to get along as they become more tolerant of difference among themselves and as they allow themselves to retain their own individuality.

I find that in violent relations people tend to focus on what others should do to solve their problems, but in peacemaking each participant continuously reflects on the question, "What should I do next to respond to the issue at hand?" Is it my turn to express what I think and feel? Is it my turn to listen to others, or to seek out the feelings and views of those who least express themselves? As the Navajo and others conceive it, violent relations are essentially social conversations that are out of balance; in effect, some people are doing most of the talking or getting and others are doing most of the listening or giving. The task of the would-be peacemaker, then, is to try to introduce balance (*hozho* in Navajo) into the conversation. One of the things I tell parties when I introduce a victim-offender mediation session is that I am committed to our continuing the conversation until everything has been said that every party thinks needs saying. Notice, too, that this runs counter to strict rules of evidence, of what can and cannot be said, in courts of law.

These, then, are some of the basic elements I have found that enable people to build trust and responsibility among themselves, to be able to let down their guard with one another, to move beyond the point at which people depend on their capacity for commanding obedience from others, to trust power sharing among those whose sensibilities and interests, inevitably, diverge substantially. I have only begun to flesh out elements of the peacemaking process. There is a world of study and experimentation to be done in refining and applying peacemaking processes. That has become my calling as a criminologist.

References

Fisher, Roger, William Ury, and Bruce Patton. 1991. *Getting to Yes: Negotiating Agreement Without Giving In*. 2d ed. New York: Penguin.

Fuller, John R. 1998. *Criminal Justice: A Peacemaking Perspective*. Boston: Allyn and Bacon.

Kohn, Alfie. 1996. *Beyond Discipline: From Compliance to Community*. Alexandria, Va.: Association for Supervision and Curriculum Development.

Milovanovic, Dragan, and Stuart Henry. 2005. "Constitutive Penology." In *Encyclopedia of Prisons and Correctional Facilities*, edited by Mary Bosworth (pp. 154–157). Thousand Oaks, Calif.: Sage.

Pepinsky, Harold E. 1988. "Violence as Unresponsiveness: Toward a New Conception of Crime." *Justice Quarterly* 5: 539–563.

______. 2001a. "Peacemaking Criminology." In *The Sage Dictionary of Criminology*, edited by E. McLaughlin and J. Muncie (pp. 203–204). London: Sage.

______. 2001b. *A Criminologist's Quest for Peace*. http://www.critcrim.org/critpapers/pepinsky-book.htm.

______. 2005. "Peacemaking in the Classroom." *Criminal Justice Review*. Forthcoming.

Pepinsky, Harold E., and Richard Quinney, eds. 1991. *Criminology as Peacemaking*. Bloomington, Ind.: Indiana University Press.

Schumacher, E. F. 1999. *Small Is Beautiful: Economics as If People Mattered: Twenty-Five Years Later with Commentaries*. Vancouver: Hartley & Marks.

Sullivan, Dennis, and Larry Tifft. 2001. *Restorative Justice: Healing the Foundations of Our Everyday Lives*. Monsey, N.Y.: Criminal Justice Press.

Yazzie, Robert, and James Zion. 1996. "Navajo Restorative Justice: The Law of Equality and Justice." In *Restorative Justice: International Perspectives*, edited by Burton Galaway and Joe Hudson (pp. 157–173). Monsey, N.Y.: Criminal Justice Press.

11.3

Reintegrative Shaming[1]

John Braithwaite, Valerie Braithwaite, and Eliza Ahmed
RegNet, Australian National University

Beyond the Shaming Penalties Debate

In the legal academy there has been a growing debate on "shaming penalties"—such as requiring drunk drivers to put signs on their cars saying they were convicted of drunk driving (Kahan 1996). Reintegrative shaming theory gives an account of why this should make crime worse (Braithwaite 1989). The popularizing of shaming penalties in the American law review literature and some recent court decisions was one motivation of Martha Nussbaum (2004) in writing *Hiding from Humanity: Disgust, Shame and the Law*. Nussbaum argues, persuasively, that it is an unconscionable threat to our liberty and an assault on our humanity to humiliate, to consciously set out to induce shame. She finds Braithwaite's theory mostly innocent of seeking to do this:

> Braithwaite's ideas are not only very far removed from those of Kahan and Etzioni—as he himself stresses—but also quite unconnected to traditional notions of shaming punishment, and rather part of the universe of guilt punishments. Braithwaite himself acknowledges this point, when, in recent writings, he uses the term "Shame-Guilt" in place of the simple "shame" for the emotion that (within limits) he favors, and when he describes the spectatorial emotion he seeks as a "just and loving gaze." (Nussbaum 2004, 241)

Restorative justice theorists are actually not preoccupied with either shame or guilt punishments, but with de-centering punishment in regulatory institutions while acknowledging the significant place that punishment will always have within them. The biggest implications of *Crime, Shame and Reintegration* are macro-sociological in a Durkheimian sense. They are that societies failing to communicate the idea that rape is shameful (without creating widespread defiance among rapists) will see a lot of rape. Societies that fail to communicate the notion that environmental crime is shameful (without creating business subcultures of resistance to environmental regulation) will destroy the planet. Societies that manifest no shame in defying and manipulating international law will create more catastrophes like Iraq and the unlawful treatment of prisoners that is characteristic of such conflicts.

Cultural Variation in Stigmatization, Reintegration, and Repair of the Self

In Japanese culture, apology can amount to a dissociation of that evil part of the self that committed a wrong (Wagatsuma and Rossett 1986). Japanese idiom sometimes accounts for wrongdoing with possession by a *mushi* (bug or worm). Criminals are hence not acting according to their true selves; they are under attack by a mushi, which can be "sealed off" and so enable reintegration without enduring shame (Wagatsuma and Rossett 1986, 476).

Navajo culture is another with especially rich restorative accomplishment through its peacemaking traditions. The Navajo concept of *nayéé* is an interesting part of this accomplishment (Coker 1999, 55). Farella (1993) explains that *nayéé*, or monsters, are things that spoil a person's enjoyment of life, such as depression, obsession, and jealousy. "The benefit of naming something a *nayéé* is that the source of one's 'illness'—one's unhappiness or dysfunctionality—once named can be cured." (Coker 1999, 55). And healing ceremonies are about helping people to rid themselves of *nayéé*.

There seems a major difference between stigmatizing cultures and cultures such as these, where the vague and subjective threat to a person's integrity of self is named to make it concrete and able to be excised. Naming to excise a bad part of self creates different action imperatives for a society from naming to label a whole self as bad (such as naming a person a junkie, criminal, or schizophrenic). The former kind of shame can be discharged with the expulsion of the *mushi* or *nayéé*. The latter kind of stigma entrenches a master status trait, such as schizophrenic, that dominates all other identities. We can learn from other cultures the possibility of healing a damaged part of a self that is mostly good.

Shadd Maruna's (2001) powerful study, *Making Good: How Ex-Convicts Reform and Rebuild Their Lives*, showed that serious offenders who went straight had to find a new way of making sense of their lives. They defined a new ethical identity for themselves that meant they were able to say, on looking back at their former criminal selves, that they were "not like that anymore" (Maruna 2001, 7). Those in his persistent recidivist sample, in contrast, were locked into "condemnation scripts" whereby they saw themselves as irrevocably condemned to their criminal self-story.

This suggests a restorative justice that is about "rebiographing," restorative storytelling that redefines an ethical conception of the self. Garfinkel (1956, 421–422) saw what was at issue in "making good": "The former identity stands as accidental; the new identity is the basic reality. What he is now is what, after all, he was all along." So, Maruna found systematically that desisters from crime reverted to an unspoiled identity. As with the *mushi* and *nayéé*, the desisters had "restoried" themselves to believe that their formerly criminal self "wasn't me." Howard Zehr (2000, 10) makes the point that whether we have victimized or been victimized, we need social support in the journey "to re-narrate our stories so that they are no longer just about shame and humiliation but ultimately about dignity and triumph."

Shame Acknowledgment

Eliza Ahmed (2001) finds that different ways of managing shame as an emotion can make crime or bullying worse. She argues that the empirical literatures of child development and criminology are consistent with the prediction that stigmatizing shaming (stigmatization) makes crime worse, but that reintegrative shaming reduces crime. Stigmatization means shaming whereby the wrongdoer is treated disrespectfully as an outcast and as a bad person. Reintegrative shaming means treating the wrongdoer respectfully and empathically as a good person who has committed a bad act and making special efforts to show the wrongdoer how valued he or she is after the wrongful act has been confronted.

Among restorative justice practitioners there has been a raging debate over whether shame and shaming are useful concepts in their work. Restorative justice is about the notion that because crime hurts, justice should heal. This is an alternative to the view that justice must be punitive—responding to hurt with hurt that is the wrongdoer's "just deserts." Some restorative justice advocates, therefore, argue that shame and shaming have no place in restorative justice because shaming is a kind of hurting and shame is a destructive kind of hurt that can make crime and injustice worse.

Ahmed (2001) argues that these critics are right when shaming is stigmatizing and shame is unacknowledged. However, to acknowledge shame and discharge it and to shame acts of injustice reintegratively are both important for preventing injustice and enabling restoration. So shame and pride are indispensable conceptual tools for understanding the effects of restorative justice. This does not mean that social movement advocates should actually use the word "shame" as part of their reform rhetoric; with restorative justice, as Braithwaite and Mugford (1994, 165) have suggested, responsibility and healing are likely to supply a more politically resonant, more prudent discourse than shame.

Still, the point is that no progressive social movement is likely to be effective without shaming and promoting the just acknowledgment of shame. Restorative justice cannot be effective without shaming needlessly punitive practices such as the death penalty and skyrocketing imprisonment. The social movement against apartheid could not have been effective without shaming racism and urging its architects to acknowledge their shame for the evils they had perpetrated. Although social movements can never change the world for the better by sweeping shameful truths under the carpet, a restorative justice argument is that they can be more effective through truth and reconciliation (shaming that is reintegrative) than through truth and stigmatization, retribution that replaces one outcast group with another.

No actor can be effective through denying shame and eschewing the challenge of understanding its dynamics. This is especially so in debates around crime—from juvenile justice to genocide and apartheid—where shame is so acute. Ahmed (2001) shows that failure to acknowledge shame and discharge it is, in different ways, a characteristic of school bullies and the victims of bullying. Healthy shame management is important in preventing bullying on both the offender side and the victim side.

Ahmed (2001) distinguished between "Shame Acknowledgment" and "Shame Displacement." Shame Acknowledgment involves the discharging of shame through accepting responsibility and trying to put things right. Shame Displacement means the displacement of shame into blame and/or anger toward others. The combination of acknowledgment without displacement is a shame management style associated with children who avoid becoming either perpetrators or victims of bullying. But other children adopt counterproductive practices, displacing shame onto others and refusing to acknowledge that harm was done. Until they learn to turn these practices around, they are less likely to move out of bullying.

The shame problems that Ahmed found victims have, and that restorative justice might address, are the internalization of the idea that I am being bullied because there is something wrong with me as a person—the internalization of shame. The shame problem of bullies is a failure to acknowledge shame when they have done something wrong and a tendency to externalize their shame as anger. Restorative justice needs to help them be more like non-bully/non-victims, who acknowledge shame when they do something wrong, who resist externalizing or internalizing their shame, and who thereby manage to discharge shame.

Testing the Theory of Reintegrative Shaming

Four forms of testing and elaboration of the theory of reintegrative shaming were advocated by Braithwaite (1989, 108–123)—ethnographic, historical, survey research, and experimental. The most impressive experimental research has been Lawrence Sherman, Heather Strang, and Daniel Woods's (2000) Re-Integrative Shaming Experiments (RISE) on 1,285 Canberra criminal offenders. To date, this program has produced mixed results, with a reduction of recidivism in the violence experiment and an increase in the property experiments (Sherman 2003). Reintegrative shaming theory has been a motivating framework only for some restorative justice programs. However, the theory does specifically predict that this kind of intervention will reduce crime regardless of whether those implementing it have any discursive consciousness of the theory of reintegrative shaming. The theoretically relevant features of restorative justice are the confrontation of the offender in a respectful way with the consequences of the crime (shaming without degradation), explicit efforts to avert stigmatization (e.g., opportunities to counter accusations that the offender is a bad person with testimonials from loved ones that she is a good person), and explicit commitment to ritual reintegration (e.g., maximizing opportunities for repair, restoring relationships, and promoting apology and forgiveness that are viewed as sincere).

Hence, reintegrative shaming theorists (controversially) interpret the success of experiments such as McGarrell et al.'s (2000) Indianapolis Juvenile Restorative Justice Experiment in substantially reducing recidivism as support for the theory. And they so interpret Latimer et al.'s (2001) meta-analysis of thirty-two mostly nonexperimental studies with control groups that found a statistically significant effect of restorative justice on recidivism. Braithwaite's (2002) own review of the literature concludes that restorative justice practice is slowly improving in theoretically important ways, and that the most recent evaluations are increasingly encouraging about the efficacy of the intervention.

But RISE analyses of the impact of reintegrative shaming on outcomes have not been completed, so cynics are justified in reserving judgment on whether shaming has anything to do with productive and counterproductive outcomes. Restorative antibullying programs in schools, often referred to as whole school antibullying programs, are another area where Braithwaite (2002, 59–61) concludes that bullying reduction has been substantial. Ahmed's (2001; Braithwaite, Ahmed, and Braithwaite forthcoming) has been the only work that has explored whether reintegrative shaming effects might be crucial here.

The other kind of theoretically relevant body of largely experimental research that has continued to accumulate since 1989 has been in the tradition of Baumrind's (1967) distinction between authoritarian parenting (which Braithwaite [1989] conceptualized as parenting heavy in stigmatizing shaming), permissive parenting (reintegration without disapproval of wrongdoing), and authoritative parenting (reintegration with firm disapproval of wrongdoing—reintegrative shaming). Braithwaite, Ahmed, and Braithwaite (forthcoming) have reviewed the substantial evidence that has continued to accumulate that authoritarian parenting reduces children's self-control as well as social skills, peer acceptance, social competence, self-esteem, and school achievement. Not surprisingly, children of authoritarian parents often externalize problems, have difficulty in controlling emotions, and display traits of narcissism and depression. Permissive parenting (sometimes described as overindulgence, or reintegration without shaming) has continued to be associated with school dropout, substance use, narcissism, and peer victimization. Authoritative parenting has continued to be associated with positive outcomes, including lower delinquency, substance use, and internalizing and externalizing behavior. Authoritative parenting assists the internalization of behavioral standards followed by action in accordance with them. It is related to peer acceptance, social competence and school adjustment, empathy, altruism, school achievement, self-confidence and self-esteem, concern for right and wrong, taking responsibility for one's own actions, and reduced truancy and alcohol abuse (Braithwaite, Ahmed, and Braithwaite forthcoming).

A multitude of qualitative observational studies of restorative justice conferences have also been important for theory elaboration (Braithwaite 2002) as well as qualitative and historical research on business regulatory enforcement. Various researchers have posited reintegrative shaming, post hoc, as a variable that makes sense of their results (Chamlin and Cochrane 1997; Hagan and McCarthy 1997; Sampson and Laub 1993; Sherman 1992).

There has been much less empirical research in the survey research tradition of theory testing than one might have expected in the sixteen years since *Crime, Shame and Reintegration* was published. The first published study by Makkai and Braithwaite (1994) found that Australian nursing home inspectors with a reintegrative shaming philosophy were successful in substantially improving compliance with regulatory laws in the two years after inspections, but compliance substantially worsened when inspectors adopted a stigmatizing philosophy. Subsequent studies by Lu (1999), Deng and Jou (2000), Hay (2001), Tittle, Bratton, and Gertz (2003), and Zhang and Zhang (2004) provide a much more mixed picture that Braithwaite, Ahmed, and Braithwaite (forthcoming) have sought to reconcile and interpret by modifying the conditions under which different versions of the theory apply.

Conclusion

The debate about reintegrative shaming has been individualistic. Commentary that warns of real dangers of shame with offenders who have already experienced too much shame in their lives often falls into the trap of implying that there is no need for institutions of criminal justice that communicate the shamefulness of predatory crime. Without institutionalized processes, rituals of significant cultural salience that confront assaults on our persons and property, how are the young to learn the ancient curriculum of crimes? How are victims' demands for retribution to be managed if they are not vindicated through rituals that confront the reason the crime was wrong? Without shaming, how can an Edwin Sutherland, or social movements against specific forms of white-collar crime such as environmental or cyber crime, constitute shamefulness in new criminal curricula? Comparative historical research on how the shamefulness of crime is constituted, sustained, and compromised in cultures and subcultures remains understudied. This is especially true at the level of macrosociological studies of whole societies as opposed to studies of Chicago slums, and is even more true at the level of transnational epistemic communities that constitute new knowledges of transnational crimes such as terrorist financing and people smuggling.

Note

1. This is a much shortened and revised version of Braithwaite, Ahmed, and Braithwaite (forthcoming).

References

Ahmed, Eliza. 2001. "Shame Management: Regulating Bullying." In *Shame Management Through Reintegration*, by E. Ahmed, N. Harris, J. Braithwaite, and V. Braithwaite (pp. 211–314). Cambridge: Cambridge University Press.

Baumrind, Diana. 1967. "Child Care Practices Anteceding Three Patterns of Preschool Behavior." *Genetic Psychology Monographs* 75: 43–88.

Braithwaite, John. 1989. *Crime, Shame and Reintegration*. Cambridge: Cambridge University Press.

______. 2002. *Restorative Justice and Responsive Regulation*. Melbourne: Cambridge University Press.

Braithwaite, J., E. Ahmed, and V. Braithwaite. n.d. "Shame, Restorative Justice and Crime." In *Advances in Criminological Theory*, edited by F. Adler, F. Cullen, J. Wright, and K. Blevins. New York: Transaction, forthcoming.

Braithwaite, John, and Stephen Mugford. 1994. "Conditions of Successful Reintegration Ceremonies: Dealing with Juvenile Offenders." *British Journal of Criminology* 34: 139–171.

Chamlin, Mitchell, and John Cochrane. 1997. "Social Altruism and Crime." *Criminology* 35: 203–228.

Coker, Donna. 1999. "Enhancing Autonomy for Battered Women: Lessons from Navajo Peacemaking." *UCLA Law Review* 47: 1–111.

Deng, X., and S. Jou. 2000. "Shame and the Moral Educative Effects on Deviant Behavior in Cross-Cultural Context." *Proceedings of Criminology Theory and Its Applications in the Year 2000*. Taipei, Taiwan: National Taipei University.

Farella, John. 1993. *The Wind in a Jar*. Albuquerque, N.M.: University of New Mexico Press.

Garfinkel, Harold. 1956. "Conditions of Successful Degradation Ceremonies." *American Journal of Sociology* 61: 420–424.

Hagan, John, and Bill McCarthy. 1997. *Mean Streets: Youth Crime and Homelessness*. Cambridge: Cambridge University Press.

Hay, Carter. 2001. "An Exploratory Test of Braithwaite's Reintegrative Shaming Theory." *Journal of Research in Crime and Delinquency* 38: 132–153.

Kahan, Dan. 1996. "What Do Alternative Sanctions Mean?" *University of Chicago Law Review* 63: 591–653.

Latimer, Jeff, Craig Dowden, and Danielle Muise. 2001. *The Effectiveness of Restorative Justice Practices: A Meta-Analysis*. Ottawa, Canada: Department of Justice.

Lu, Hong. 1999. "Bang Jiao and Reintegrative Shaming in China's Urban Neighborhoods." *International Journal of Comparative and Applied Criminal Justice* 23: 115–125.

Makkai, Toni, and John Braithwaite. 1994. "Reintegrative Shaming and Regulatory Compliance." *Criminology* 32: 61–385.

Maruna, Shadd. 2001. *Making Good: How Ex-Convicts Reform and Rebuild Their Lives*. Washington, D.C.: American Psychological Association.

McGarrell, Edmund, Kathleen Olivares, Kay Crawford, and Natalie Kroovand. 2000. *Returning Justice to the Community: The Indianapolis Juvenile Restorative Justice Experiment*. Indianapolis, Ind.: Hudson Institute.

Nussbaum, Martha. 2004. *Hiding from Humanity: Disgust, Shame and the Law*. Princeton: Princeton University Press.

Sampson, Robert, and John Laub. 1993. *Crime in the Making: Pathways and Turning Points Through Life*. Cambridge, Mass.: Harvard University Press.

Sherman, Lawrence. 1992. *Policing Domestic Violence*. New York: Free Press.

______. 2003. "Reason for Emotion: Reinventing Justice with Theories, Innovations, and Research." 2002 Presidential Address, The American Society of Criminology. *Criminology* 41: 1–38.

Sherman, Lawrence, Heather Strang, and Daniel Woods. 2000. *Recidivism Patterns in the Canberra Reintegrative Shaming Experiments (RISE)*. Canberra, Australia: Centre for Restorative Justice, Australian National University.

Tittle, Charles, Jason Bratton, and Marc Gertz. 2003. "A Test of a Micro-Level Application of Shaming Theory." *Social Problems* 50: 92–617.

Wagatsuma, Hiroshi, and Arthur Rosett. 1986. "The Implications of Apology: Law and Culture in Japan and the United States." *Law and Society Review* 20: 461–498.

Zehr, Howard. 2000. "Journey of Belonging." Paper presented to the Fourth International Conference on Restorative Justice, Tuebingen, Germany.

Zhang, Lening, and S. Zhang. 2004. "Reintegrative Shaming and Predatory Delinquency." *Journal of Research in Crime and Delinquency* 41: 433–453.

12

Left Realist Theories

Left realism emerged in opposition to radical theory's left idealism that celebrated the offender as a primitive revolutionary. Left realists found left idealism to be an overly romanticized version of the predatory offender who creates so much real fear among the relatively poor populations in many urban environments. Instead, left realists focus on the reality and seriousness of harmful "street" crime that is created by impoverished working-class neighbors upon their own kind. Left realism emphasizes the relationship between offenders, victims, the public, and the criminal justice system. Advocates believe that the polarizing effects of capitalism divide societies into the "haves" and "have nots" while simultaneously promoting competitive individualism and greed. This "exclusive society," as Jock Young has called it, marginalizes and abandons its poor; they suffer relative deprivation, frustration, and anger, which they express through disrespect and violence inflicted on each other. Added to their misery and self-destruction is a class-biased criminal justice system that targets primarily lower-class and minority males, the most vulnerable of the excluded, who are then also punished by the criminal justice system. More recently, left realists have also added another element of oppression, that inflicted by powerful corporations, although left realists prioritize street offenders in much of their research.

In some ways, left realism is similar to strain theory in its emphasis on the polarizing effects of capitalist inequality and the resulting problems of relative deprivation and exclusion. It is similar too in stressing how, in reaction to exclusion, some of those most affected resort to self-interested acts of crime. Yet, left realism differs from strain theory in that it is more critical of capitalism as a system of inequality and that it advocates socialism as a long-term objective. In other ways left realism is similar to radical theory, and in recent years it has shared a feminist critique, criticizing patriarchy as another form of inequality and exclusion. Yet left realism differs from radical versions of radical and feminist theory in that it pushes for the immediate democratization of social institutions through the existing political structure, and it advocates for support programs designed to mitigate the harsh inequalities in the present system rather than waiting for revolutionary change. For example, left realists want to reintegrate the "excluded" segments of the population through job training and education-for-work programs, strengthen and democratically control the criminal justice system of capitalist society, and work to reduce the disparities in the capitalist system through progressive reforms.

12.1

Inequality, Community, and Crime

Elliott Currie
University of California, Irvine

Much of the work I've done in recent years can be seen as an attempt to reaffirm—but also to expand and to deepen—what I take to be some core, essential truths in criminology. One of the most central of those truths is that a high level of violent crime is a *cost* of certain kinds of social arrangements: It is not primarily or even significantly explainable as a reflection of innate biological proclivities, the weakness of the criminal justice system, or any of the other views that became fashionable, in the United States and other countries, from the 1970s onward. It is part of the price we pay for maintaining societies that are wracked by a constellation of larger social ills—including extremes of inequality, economic deprivation and insecurity, and a pervasive culture of predatory competition.

I began developing these ideas in a serious way in response to the rapid, and in many ways unexpected, drift of theory and social policy toward the right from the 1970s onward—a development that brought an increasing reliance, in the United States and, to a lesser degree, in some other countries, on mass incarceration as the dominant response to crime. To me, as to many other criminologists, this seemed to stand much of what we knew about crime and punishment on its head. Oddly, we were throwing out much of what we knew just as its truth and relevance were increasingly being confirmed—both by formal research and by developments in the outside world.

When I was studying crime and justice for the first time as a graduate student in the late 1960s, it was widely accepted, for example, that we knew something about where violence on the American level *came* from. Our most prominent theories, along with an already abundant body of empirical research, made a convincing argument that it came from certain fundamental fault lines in our society—especially the effects of economic and racial inequality and, in particular, the absence of hope and opportunity in the inner cities. A second, and closely related, consensus flowed from this recognition: that we could not punish our way out of the problem. Because violence was a symptom of these deeper structural ills, the criminal justice system would necessarily be a limited (though certainly important) tool in dealing with it. We were, in fact, already overusing the justice system as a means of crime control, and too often we were using it in the wrong ways as well: We warehoused offenders in prison, where they languished and often became worse, while doing remarkably little either to keep them out of trouble in the first place or to reintegrate them into society once they were back in it. (For a classic statement of this consensus, see President's Commission 1967.)

At the time, all this seemed so self-evident to me that after I finished graduate school I moved away from studying crime for some years and concentrated on exploring some of those larger structural problems that seemed so obviously to breed crime, especially poverty, economic inequality, and the destruction of stable work. So it was more than a little perplexing that by the mid-1970s and into the 1980s it was being widely said that none of these problems had much to do with crime—even that it was foolish and misleading to talk about "root causes" of crime at all—and that the main reason we had so much crime was that we had grown too lenient with people who broke the law. The corollary was clear: We could, after all, punish our way out of the crime problem: "prison works" (see Wilson 1973). The older consensus had been effectively displaced by a new and distinctly harsher vision, and that vision helped, along with broader political and cultural shifts, to usher in an era of mass incarceration that remains a defining feature of life in the United States and that was unprecedented in our own history or that of any other industrial nation.

These developments propelled me back into writing about crime. It seemed clear to me that the more "structural" approach to understanding and dealing with crime that I'd grown up with had been pushed aside, not because it had been seriously challenged intellectually but because it had been overwhelmed politically. The arguments used to justify the troubling combination of criminal justice expansion and social retreat in the 1970s and early 1980s seemed weak and unconvincing, and I thought it was important to say so. Yet it was also true that the older consensus had its limitations as well—limitations that had helped open it to attack and doom it to political marginality. My book *Confronting Crime: An American Challenge* was an effort to reassess both visions in the light of the best research available (Currie 1985).

The subtitle—*An American Challenge*—reflected the book's central assertion that, contrary to what were increasingly popular views, serious violent crime was not simply a function of individual proclivity or, as some writers argued, of the universal effects of prosperity and democracy: It varied according to what kind of society you lived in. And, by looking at why we in the United States suffered this affliction more than nearly every other country in the world, we could understand something not only about how to deal more effectively with our own problem but about how to understand the roots of violence generally.

The aim was to create a synthesis of existing research that would underpin an analysis of why the United States was so exceptional when it came to violent crime. The objective was to demonstrate that the currently favored explanation, the leniency of our justice system, couldn't be the real explanation, and simultaneously affirming, with important qualifications, the truth of the pre-1970s "structural" consensus.

The qualifications grew out of my sense that the earlier tradition had not taken its own conclusions seriously enough. If violent crime, on the scale we experienced it in the United States, was really a symptom of deep-rooted social inequalities and dislocations, then combating it over the long term would have to mean tackling those deeper conditions much more seriously than we had in the past. We had never, for example, launched a full-bore attack on mass poverty or the effects of deindustrialization, even at the height of the liberal consensus of the 1960s, and that helped explain why violent crime was still so much with us—as well as the growing appeal of more repressive approaches to controlling it. The older "liberal" view had failed to deliver the goods—not primarily because its analysis was faulty, but because its implications weren't put into practice in social policy on the scale that was required. Indeed, there was a tendency in this kind of thinking—one that grew more pronounced as liberals increasingly abandoned more sweeping visions of social change in the 1970s and 1980s—to hope that minor tinkering with the justice system, or a smattering of funds for small-scale prevention or rehabilitation efforts, would add up to a strategy against the violence that increasingly consumed the cities.

This did not mean that smaller-scale efforts at prevention and rehabilitation had no place in an anticrime strategy—far from it. Indeed, the book argued for greater investment in a range of interventions from preschool programs to rehabilitation in youth prisons. But it did suggest that even the best such efforts would be swimming upstream if we did not also do something about deepening poverty, blasted opportunities, and pervasive economic insecurity.

This line of thought was extended in *Reckoning* (Currie 1993), a similar effort at synthesis of what we knew about the roots of America's almost equally exceptional drug problem. Again, the strategy was to look exhaustively at what the evidence told us about the roots of drug abuse: to argue, in effect, that variations in drug-abuse levels did indeed *have social roots*, and that efforts to wage "war" on drugs without confronting these roots were doomed to failure, and would also distort the criminal justice system in ways that were both inhumane and counterproductive—ways that would be difficult to undo in the future. But this analysis also suggested that some popular alternatives to the conventional drug war were considerably less promising than many believed them to be—in good part because they ignored the corrosive effects of inequality and community disintegration on people's willingness to use drugs to excess. Many people believed that we could reduce the U.S. drug problem dramatically simply by expanding treatment for addicts; but the evidence suggested that, although good treatment was indeed desperately needed, the high rates of treatment failure pointed to the inability of treatment, alone, to dent a problem rooted in stubborn and predictable social conditions. Similarly, although we certainly needed to rein in the "war" on drugs that had helped to cram the prisons without doing anything to reduce drug abuse, decriminalizing drug use would not be a panacea, either. The U.S. drug problem was not, as some suggested, solely a creation of the drug war itself: It was also a cost, once again, of the enduring structures of inequality and deprivation that distinguished the United States from many other advanced societies.

I tried to put some of these thoughts into more systematic form in the article "Market, Crime, and Community" (Currie 1997), which, as its subtitle suggested, was an attempt to develop a "mid-range theory of post-industrial violence." The article called for a "holistic" approach to understanding criminal violence in contemporary societies—one that could encompass a range of effects on the social, economic, political, and cultural levels, and thereby move beyond the fragmentation of theory that, I thought, too often characterized the way we thought about the roots of crime. I wasn't aiming for a "general" theory of criminal violence, which seemed too broad to be of much use in explaining how violence manifested itself across the contemporary world, but for an analysis of the ways in which violent crime was generated by the specific set of social, economic, and cultural arrangements that I termed "market society." The United States was distinctive among the advanced nations in the extent to which its social life was shaped by the imperatives of private gain—my definition of "market society"—and it was not accidental that it was also the nation plagued with by far the highest levels of serious violent crime, for market society created a "toxic brew" of overlapping social effects. It simultaneously created deep poverty and a widened inequality, destroyed livelihoods, stressed families, and fragmented communities. It chipped away at public and private sources of social support and promoted a corrosive ethos of predatory individualism that pits people against each other in the scramble for personal gain.

This view is sometimes described as a version of the "conflict" theory of crime, but I don't think that is quite accurate. It might better be described as a variety of "social democratic" theory, one that has considerable similarity to what in the United Kingdom especially has been called "left realism" (Lea and Young 1984; Young 1991; Taylor 1999). It is an approach that links variations in serious crime to variations in key social structural conditions and policies, and that is distinguished by its activist and ameliorative implications: If crime is heavily rooted in social structures and social policies that are created by human agency, then on its present level it is not an inevitable fact of modern life but is alterable through social action.

My own sense, perhaps self-serving, is that the central arguments of this line of thinking have never been successfully challenged intellectually. The empirical research of the last several years—some of which I've summarized in a later book, *Crime and Punishment in America* (Currie 1998)—confirms the importance of inequality and insecurity as potent breeding grounds for violent crime; so does the evidence of experience, as the spread of these problems under the impact of "globalization" has brought increased social disintegration and violence across the world in its wake.

Though the approach is most critical of conservative theorists, they have rarely responded directly to it, preferring in general to avoid having to grapple with uncongenial evidence (but see Currie and Wilson 1991). More critiques have come from the left than the right, and they fall into several categories. Some argue, for example, that this approach is naively reformist in its implications—that it fails to acknowledge the barriers to change inherent in the structure of modern capitalism. This criticism does not dispute that "market" societies create powerful pressures toward violence, but it does doubt that much can be done about those pressures short of dismantling the system altogether. I have some sympathy for that position, but the problem with it is that violence has been reduced in many other advanced capitalist societies, without resorting to correspondingly high levels of incarceration, to levels that seem stunningly low by U.S. standards. The variation among those societies in street violence remains extraordinary, and I'd argue that it is largely due to the systematic differences in social policy that can coexist within the generic frame of modern capitalism. It is true that some of these differences in levels of crime (and in the response to crime) are narrowing, especially to the degree that other countries have adopted parts of the U.S. social model. But it also remains true that the United States isn't Sweden, or even France or Germany, when it comes to violent crime, or to rates of imprisonment. And this difference isn't merely academic: It translates into tangible differences in the risks of victimization and the overall quality of life.

A second criticism, for which I have considerably less sympathy, is that this view takes street crime too seriously; it overstates the threat posed by street violence and fails to emphasize that other forms of crime, especially white-collar crime, have a more damaging social impact. As a result, it is complicit in the misleading construction of the crime problem that has dominated anticrime policy in the United States and elsewhere. I think this critique reflects what the British criminologist Jock Young has called "The Great Denial"—the refusal to acknowledge the very real destructiveness of the "ordinary" crime that is routinely generated by adverse social conditions. That view—which Young and others have called "left idealism" and which I've sometimes described as "liberal minimalism" (Young 1991; Currie 1991)—seems to me to take an obvious point too far; it is surely true that governments have underemphasized the crimes of the rich and powerful, but it does not therefore follow that the violence of the poor and powerless is a minor issue or a problem of little human or moral significance in its own right. The reluctance to take street violence seriously helped to define progressives as people who had nothing credible to say about an issue that was profoundly affecting the lives of ordinary people in the United States and, increasingly, throughout much of the world. And it accordingly helped usher in the dominance of more repressive views and strategies, that, though wrongheaded, at least had the political virtue of responding to people's very real fears.

How have these views fared in the real world? The bad news is that they have had relatively little impact on social policy, which continues to move in directions that are antithetical to what these ideas implied or to what some of us advocated. There are important exceptions to this rather bleak assessment; in particular, the reaffirmation of the value of preventive and rehabilitative efforts and the corollary critique of reliance on incarceration as a crime-control strategy find happy echoes in the spread of treatment-oriented drug courts and in significant efforts in some states to remove minor offenders from prison. There is also growing acknowledgment that we need to do a much better job of preparing offenders for return to the community on release; indeed, serious plans to address "reentry" issues have been put on the political agenda in some states. The importance of early intervention and family support programs likewise finds considerable support in the world of policymakers and practitioners; although, as with rehabilitation, the necessary resources have rarely followed.

But in other ways, social policy in the United States, and in many other countries as well, has, if anything, gone backwards on many of the issues raised by this line of thinking about crime. We continue to chip way at our already minimal system of social supports for the vulnerable; at the same time, we press forward with economic policies that, by keeping wages low and intensifying job insecurity, foster ever-widening inequality and deepen the stresses on families and communities that many of us have singled out as being crucial sources of violence. We continue to rely on mass incarceration as our primary bulwark against crime despite an abundance of evidence that doing so is not only ineffective but also self-defeating. When I reviewed these trends a few years ago, I wrote that "it is difficult to think of another area of social policy, with the possible exception of welfare, where there has been such a startling divergence between understanding and action"(Currie 1998, 6). I'm afraid the statement still holds today.

These tendencies are especially troubling because they are increasingly taking place on a worldwide scale. What we somewhat misleadingly call "globalization"—really the spread of "market" principles to virtually every corner of the world—threatens to increase inequality, instability, and violence wherever it touches while simultaneously diminishing the political capacity for meaningful social change. Formerly stable and prosperous countries in the developed world are busily dismantling the social protections that traditionally helped to keep their rates of violent crime low: Parts of the developing world that were once relatively tranquil are becoming breeding grounds for gang violence, official repression, and a growing illicit traffic in drugs and people. The world will not be able to build enough prisons to contain this volatility. The future under this model of social and economic development does not look pretty. Fortunately, it is not the only future we can envision.

References

Currie, Elliott. 1985. *Confronting Crime: An American Challenge*. New York: Pantheon Books.

______. 1991. "Crime and Drugs: Reclaiming a Liberal Issue." In *Franklin D. Roosevelt and the Future of Liberalism*, edited by John F. Sears (pp. 71–88). Westport, Conn.: Meckler.

______. 1993. *Reckoning: Drugs, the Cities, and the American Future*. New York: Hill and Wang.

______. 1997. "Market, Crime, and Community: Toward a Mid-Range Theory of Post-Industrial Violence." *Theoretical Criminology* 1: 147–172.

______. 1998. *Crime and Punishment in America*. New York: Metropolitan Books.

Currie, Elliott, and James Q. Wilson. 1991. "The Politics of Crime: The American Experience." In *The Politics of Crime Control*, edited by Kevin Stenson and David Cowell (pp. 33–61). London: Sage.

Lea, John, and Jock Young. 1984. *What Is to Be Done About Law and Order?* Harmondsworth, U.K.: Penguin.

President's Commission on Law Enforcement and Administration of Justice. 1967. *The Challenge of Crime in a Free Society*. Washington, D.C.: U.S. Government Printing Office.

Wilson, James Q. 1973. *Thinking About Crime*. New York: Basic Books.

Young, Jock. 1991. "Left Realism and the Politics of Crime Control." In *The Politics of Crime Control*, edited by Kevin Stenson and David Cowell (pp. 146–160). London: Sage Publications.

12.2

Left Realist Theory

Walter S. DeKeseredy
University of Ontario Institute of Technology
and
Martin D. Schwartz
Ohio University

There are many aspects of left realist theory, but perhaps the most important contribution made by this progressive school of thought is the focus on street crimes. As noted below, this emphasis led to a relative shortage of left realist work on crimes of the powerful (e.g., state-sponsored terrorism), which is arguably a shortcoming but definitely not a fatal flaw. Yet, an original impetus for the entire field was the tendency of the left to focus mainly on corporate and state crimes. Some theorists spent much time explaining away concern with street crime as moral panics created by sensationalist media or by fear-mongering politicians. On the left, many theorists still downplay the seriousness and extent of violence by underclass members for fear of pathologizing the poor, helping to gain support for conservative draconian punishment policies, or being accused of racism for arguing that people of color commit many of these crimes. Certainly one cannot deny that a great deal of crime fear throughout the Western world comes from this combination of a lurid and melodramatic media and politicians who discovered that one can win a deluge of votes by painting all minority youth as drug-using criminals out to harm honest folk (Mann and Zatz 1998).

Left realists, however, contend that some portion of the portrayal is real. Street crime is essentially intraracial and intraclass: Inner-city youth are responsible for a great deal of robbery, burglary, and physical and sexual assault, and their victims are also inner-city residents. To some extent, many of these crimes are committed by minority youth, but the victims who suffer the most from street crimes are also minority youths, adults, and families. For example, African American men aged from eighteen to twenty-four had homicide victimization rates that were more than thirty-four times higher than the rate for white females (Fox and Zawitz 2000). No matter how important crimes of the powerful might be, and left realism does not dispute that working-class people are massively oppressed by the crimes of corporations and the state, these crime victimization rates make it clear that it is inner-city residents who bear the brunt of crime in the United States.

Starting in the late 1970s, Jock Young and some of his British colleagues argued that it was essential for people on the left to recognize that when it came to street crime, the problem is men located at the bottom of the socioeconomic ladder. Further, these men are responsible for most of the harassment of women and various minority groups. Recognizing this, they asserted, was "realism." Unfortunately, there are many realists, but most are conservative theorists (e.g., James Q. Wilson) and politicians. Many have been responsible for the vote pandering that created the U.S. policies of radical incarceration and increased death penalty use that have devastated minority communities while providing little change in a crime rate already dropping drastically. The contribution of left realists was to argue that it was possible to be a realist while also pushing for left-oriented progressive solutions to crime.

A central assertion of left realist theory is that chronic urban poverty and an exclusionary labor market are major symptoms of "turbo-charged capitalism" (Luttwak 1995), which, in turn, spawn predatory street crimes and acts of intimate violence committed in socially and economically marginalized communities. Left realists, however, argue that absolute poverty (a state of being very poor) cannot explain such behavior because most very poor people are not criminals, either in North America or around the world. Rather, left realists are concerned with relative poverty, which suggests that income (poverty) experienced as being unfairly low compared to that of the rest of society creates a feeling of economic disenfranchisement. This latter feeling is more helpful in understanding crime in inner-city communities than absolute poverty (DeKeseredy, Alvi, Schwartz, and Tomaszewski 2003).

Thus, left realists argue that people do not commit armed robberies just because they cannot afford North Slope jackets or LeBron James athletic shoes. It is the relative deprivation experienced as being at or near the economic bottom of society that provides a definition of injustice. Although this can occur in many sectors of society, the structural changes in North American society in recent decades that have left many youths without jobs or hope have removed most of the barriers to interpersonal violence and economic crime. This "solution" by these youths to the problem of relative deprivation is often the result of the rampant individualism promoted by a modern capitalist society (Young 1999).

Left realists also argue that people who lack a legitimate means of solving the problem of relative deprivation may come into contact with other frustrated disenfranchised people and form subcultures, which, in turn, encourage and legitimate criminal behaviors. For example, receiving respect from peers is highly valued among ghetto adolescents who are denied status in mainstream, middle-class society. A problem is that, too often, respect and status are granted by inner-city subcultures to those who are violent in certain situations (DeKeseredy and Schwartz 2005).

Still, it is essential to note that, unlike culture of poverty theorists (Lewis 1966; Banfield 1974), such subcultures are not seen by left realists as "somehow alien to the wider culture" (Young 1999, 86). The truth is that they, like most North Americans, want to achieve the American Dream and its related status but lack the legitimate means to do so (Messner and Rosenfeld 2000). Much youth violence, for example, is based not on random violence but on obtaining the very expensive objects of mass culture that are being promoted as most desirable in any given year, such as MP3 players. Except for their willingness to use individualistic violent solutions to obtain such items, criminal youths share the same values as other youths. In fact, the most serious criminal subcultures are "based on all-American notions of work as an area of rugged individualism and competition which is sanctioned by a film industry that carries the message of didactic violence" (Young 1999, 87).

The above only touches on a piece of the complex theoretical background of left realism. Yet left realism is not just a theoretical enterprise.

Rather, left realists use local victimization surveys to challenge mainstream interpretations of crime and official conservative statistics. Perhaps the best known of these surveys are the Islington Crime Surveys done in London. A more recent example is the Quality of Neighborhood Life Survey (QNLS) conducted in a Canadian public housing community (DeKeseredy et al. 2003). This survey focused heavily on woman abuse, sexual harassment, and the verbal harassment of gays, lesbians, and people of color in public places—topics that are not found in mainstream victimization surveys.

An important part of left realism is that it offers short-term policy proposals aimed at what Messerschmidt (1986) terms "chipping away" at the capitalist patriarchal order. Traditionally, left realists have devoted extensive investigation to democratic control of policing and community participation in crime prevention, although such areas as corporate crime have also been objects of policy proposals (DeKeseredy and Goff 1992; Michalowski 1983). More recently, Walter DeKeseredy, Martin Schwartz, and Shahid Alvi (2000) put gender at the forefront of policy proposals and focused on short-term profeminist men's strategies aimed at curbing woman abuse. North American left realists such as Elliott Currie (1985, 1993) and DeKeseredy and his colleagues (2003) routinely call for measures such as affordable and decent housing, meaningful jobs, and state-sponsored daycare to help curb woman abuse, the sale and use of "hard drugs" (e.g., crack), and predatory street crime.

Problems with Left Realist Theory

Perhaps the strongest attack on left realism is that it does not mirror the theories for which it was designed to provide an alternative. For example, it is a theoretical model that calls upon the left and provides role models for the left to become heavily involved in short-term progressive solutions and to attempt to improve the lives of working-class people, women, and ethnic and cultural minorities. Left realism is committed to a transition from a capitalist patriarchal social order to one that is socialist and feminist in nature, but it does not explicitly call for the overthrow of the current state, or even the legal system, which some left-wing scholars deem to be a serious flaw. Generally, this is best seen as a question of energy. Throughout Europe and North America, many sociological and criminological theorists talk mainly to each other, usually in difficult prose, and have little, if any, communication with the working-class people they write about. Their record of success in overthrowing legal systems is weak, and even where socialism has thus far been successful, it is difficult to argue that the state socialist countries of the Eastern bloc provided a better legal system than those of the flawed West. Left realists have thus limited their attention to short-term progressive solutions to concrete problems. As suggested above, the origins of left realism lie in the feeling that leftist theory was unconcerned with the victimization from below of working-class people.

Although left realism embraces elements of radical and socialist feminism, as evident in some of the original work on violence against women (e.g., Jones, MacLean, and Young 1986), no attempt has been made within left realism to theorize women's experiences of crime as suspects, offenders, defendants, and inmates (Carlen 1992). The issues of why women's offenses are distinct from men's and the sexist nature of the criminal justice system have been given short shrift. Thus, an important agenda item for left realism is to develop a theory of women's offending, one that is integrated and heavily informed by feminist work done by scholars such as Meda Chesney-Lind and Jody Miller. Women, too, suffer from relative deprivation, belong to the same subculture as men, and are exposed to the same mass media and cultural influences promoting capitalist and individualist materialist acquisition, all of which should give them the motivation needed to commit street crimes for the purpose of obtaining desired objects. Yet, compared to men and boys, they do not do this. Left realist theory is still weak on why this is so.

Left realists began to examine women's issues by looking at violence against women. Most of this work, however, was based on a single factor analysis—that such violence can ultimately be placed on the doorstep of the patriarchy. In a society that empowers males at the expense of females, many males feel that it is their right to treat women in any way they wish. Others feel that violence is an acceptable way to "keep in line" women they define as "theirs." The starting point of a feminist realist perspective on violence against women came with Jayne Mooney's book *Gender Violence and the Social Order* (2000). Others expanded on her work. For example, DeKeseredy and Schwartz (2002) integrated an economic exclusion/left realist argument with a feminist/male peer support model to explain woman abuse in public housing. Certainly, there is no question that the field is in need of more multifactor left realist theories concerning woman abuse; at the same time, more work is needed to explore the experiences of women from different ethnic and cultural backgrounds.

One of the sharpest attacks on left realism is that it ignores state and corporate crime. This criticism is inaccurate and accurate at the same time. An important tenet from the beginning of left realist theory is that working-class people are victimized from above and below at the same time—harmed by corporations and the state from above and by street criminals from below. Although the central impetus and focus of the theory was to correct an imbalance of theorists who looked to victimization only from above, the field began to produce important works in the area of corporate crime, such as the work of Pearce and Tombs (1992) and DeKeseredy and Goff (1992). Further, Basran, Gill, and MacLean's (1995) work on Punjabi farm workers documents how short-term struggles can benefit working-class ethnic minority groups. Yet there is no question that an important focus of left realists has been to correct the imbalance created where left theorists have not fully examined street crimes, this focus being to the detriment of looking at state and corporate crime, particularly in light of economic disasters such as Enron and U.S. "security concerns." Attempts to rekindle left realist efforts in these areas would be useful.

Left realists have documented many cases of racist attacks on the streets, but there has not been rich theoretical investigation of hate crimes. Of course, we don't know what left realists would say about terrorist attacks such as the one that killed several thousand people on September 11, 2001. Still, it is important to emphasize that one theoretical perspective cannot, and perhaps should not, be expected to explain every crime and every societal reaction to it.

Conclusion

It is often said at academic conferences and elsewhere that left realism is no longer a major subdiscipline of critical criminology. If this is true, why, then, do so many people continue to review this school of thought in popular undergraduate texts and in scholarly books and journals? Note, too, that left realism is still the subject of sharp attacks from both left- and right-wing criminologists. Indeed, left realism is not dead, and we contend that this perspective is just as important now as it was during the Reagan and Thatcher years when it was born. For example, given that the United States is currently run by a government decidedly committed to cutting even more social services, further weakening environmental and occupational health and safety legislation, and widening the gap between the rich and poor over the next four years, the question "What is to be done now?" is hardly a trivial one because these and other right-wing strategies are likely to help increase the predatory crime rate. Consider, too, that an immediate progressive response to the new right-wing assault on women's rights, civil liberties, same-sex relationships, and other progressive elements of our society is much needed. Left realism offers a progressive complex theory and a set of "best practices" that are given selective inattention by those seeking to preserve the status quo and by left-wing scholars who inaccurately portray this perspective as little more than "an exercise in dubious politics and the cult of personality" (O'Reilly-Fleming 1996, 5).

This is not to say that improvements are not necessary. Here, we briefly outlined some of the major limitations of left realism and we fully expect that they and others will be effectively addressed in the near future. Indeed, we are already beginning to see major revisions of left realist theory as exemplified in Jock Young's (1999) *Exclusive Society*. For example, as Yar and Penna (2004, 538) correctly point out in their critique of this book, Young's recent theoretical work integrates left realism with "more recent trends in social and cultural theory." Further, our own theoretical work on woman abuse in public housing attempts to link left realism with issues of central concern to Marxist political economists, social exclusion theorists, and feminist scholars. Regardless of what directions left realism takes, in this current political economic context it is absolutely necessary to advance new ways of thinking realistically about crime and social order from a progressive standpoint.

References

Banfield, E. C. 1974. *The Unheavenly City Revisited*. Boston: Little, Brown.

Basran, Gurcharn S., Charan Gill, and Brian D. MacLean. 1995. *Farmworkers and Their Children*. Vancouver: Collective Press.

Carlen, Pat. 1992. "Women, Crime, Feminism, and Realism." In *Realist Criminology: Crime Control and Policing in the 1990s*, edited by John Lowman and Brian D. MacLean. Toronto: University of Toronto Press.

Currie, Elliott. 1985. *Confronting Crime: An American Challenge*. New York: Vintage.

______. 1993. *Reckoning: Drugs, the Cities and the American Future*. New York: Hill and Wang.

DeKeseredy, Walter S., Shahid Alvi, Martin D. Schwartz, and E. Andreas Tomaszewski. 2003. *Under Siege: Poverty and Crime in a Public Housing Community*. Lanham, Md.: Lexington.

DeKeseredy, Walter S., and Colin Goff. 1992. "Corporate Violence Against Canadian Women: Assessing Left Realist Research and Policy." *Journal of Human Justice* 4: 55–70.

DeKeseredy, Walter S., and Martin D. Schwartz. 2002. "Theorizing Public Housing Woman Abuse as a Function of Economic Exclusion and Male Peer Support." *Women's Health and Urban Life* 1: 26–45.

DeKeseredy, Walter S., and Martin D. Schwartz. 2005. "Masculinities and Interpersonal Violence." In *Handbook of Studies on Men & Masculinities*, edited by Michael S. Kimmel, Jeff Hearn, and R. W. Connell. Thousand Oaks, Calif.: Sage.

DeKeseredy, Walter S., Martin D. Schwartz, and Shahid Alvi. 2000. "The Role of Profeminist Men in Dealing with Woman Abuse on the Canadian College Campus." *Violence Against Women* 6: 918–935.

Fox, James A., and M. W. Zavitz. 2000. *Homicide Trends in the United States: 1998 Update*. Washington, D.C.: U.S. Department of Justice.

Jones, Trevor, Brian D. MacLean, and Jock Young. 1986. *The Islington Crime Survey*. London: Gower.

Lewis, Oscar. 1966. "The Culture of Poverty." *Scientific American* (November): 19–25.

Luttwak, E. 1995. "Turbo-Charged Capitalism and Its Consequences." *London Review of Books* (November): 6–7.

Mann, Coramae Richey, and Marjorie S. Zatz. 1998. "Before and Beyond the Millenium: Possible Solutions." In *Images of Color, Images of Crime*, edited by Coramae Richey Mann and Marjorie S. Zatz. Los Angeles: Roxbury.

Messerschmidt, James W. 1986. *Capitalism, Patriarchy, and Crime: Toward a Socialist Feminist Criminology*. Totowa, N.J.: Roman & Littlefield.

Messner, Steven F., and Richard Rosenfeld. 2000. *Crime and the American Dream*. 3d ed. Belmont, Calif.: Wadsworth.

Michalowski, Raymond J. 1983. "Crime Control in the 1980s: A Progressive Agenda." *Crime and Social Justice* (Summer): 13–23.

Mooney, Jayne. 2000. *Gender, Violence and the Social Order*. New York: St. Martin's Press.

O'Reilly-Fleming, Thomas. 1996. "Left Realism as Theoretical Retreatism or Paradigm Shift: Toward Post-Critical Criminology." In *Post-Critical Criminology*, edited by Thomas O'Reilly-Fleming. Toronto: Prentice-Hall.

Pearce, Frank, and Steve Tombs. 1992. "Realism and Corporate Crime." In *Issues in Realist Criminology*, edited by Roger Matthews and Jock Young. London: Sage.

Yar, Majid, and Sue Penna. 2004. "Between Positivism and Post-Modernity? Critical Reflections on Jock Young's *The Exclusive Society*." *The British Journal of Criminology* 44: 533–549.

Young, Jock. 1999. *The Exclusive Society*. London: Sage.

13

Integrated Theories and Pause for Reflection

Many criminologists, and even more of our students, have noted that all theories are adequate for explaining some events, activities, or motivations, but that they fall short of explaining every type of crime and every form of criminality. Although total exploration may not be achievable, regardless of how many theories are developed or how much more sophisticated each new theory may claim it is over those that have gone before, one group of theories does attempt a more comprehensive explanation. Integrative theories emerged in the late 1970s as a new direction in the causal explanation of crime.

Theoretical integration involves combining two or more existing theories into a new theory. This new movement in theory development was towards combining aspects of different theories, and even incorporating entire theories, into a comprehensive meta-theory that would have greater explanatory power. So, for example, one component of integrated theory might focus on the biological conditions that predispose persons toward antisocial behavior, another might focus on psychological development, a third on the social learning process, a fourth on the impact of social control, and a fifth on the effects on both the broad class structure and social ecology in which these different processes are located. Some theorists, whose contributions we have included in earlier chapters, consider their own work to be integrative; for example, Diana Fishbein's article in our chapter on biological theories could just as easily have been included in the integrative section.

Those engaging in integration do so for a variety of reasons, not least because of a desire to arrive at central anchoring notions in theory, to provide coherence to a bewildering array of fragmented theories, to achieve explanatory completeness, to advance scientific progress, and to synthesize related aspects of causation and their implications for social control to further the development of more comprehensive policy.

Unfortunately, creating a combination of theories is much more difficult than it would seem. Different theories have different underlying assumptions that are often irreconcilable; for example, is human nature inherently good or bad, and, if it embodies some combination of self-interest and cooperation, how do we establish the balance of each? Does that balance vary? Do we have free will to make rational decisions or is this so limited by other factors, such as biology and situational environment, that determinism is a more accurate description? Do some have more freedom than others, yet both commit crimes for other reasons? Do we focus on a micro- or a macro-level of analysis, and if both, in what combination? Do we reject or embrace the scientific method, or do we combine aspects of qualitative or quantitative methods? But what about those, such as postmodernists, who reject scientific methods entirely; how are they incorporated? Is government the cure for crime or, as anarchist criminologists believe, the cause of it? If some of each, how do we assess the appropriate level to which harm should be reduced? Despite these inherent problems, criminologists have made remarkable strides with theoretical integration. Part of their success is due to acceptance of some of these seemingly contradictory positions.

After reviewing essays by leading integrationists, we conclude this book with a unique essay by Richard Quinney. Quinney's essay documents his personal journey, which in many ways has been an intellectual synthesis of a wide range of theoretical positions. Quinney's path, in many respects, parallels the course taken by criminological theory over the second half of the twentieth century, and into the twenty-first century. Quinney raises the fundamental ethical question of our own role as criminologists, and he asks us to think about what we do; he leaves the question of criminological theory incomplete, available for future analysis, exactly where a theory text should end.

13.1

The Integrated Systems Theory of Antisocial Behavior

MATTHEW ROBINSON
Appalachian State University

There have been dozens of attempts to create thorough and logically complete integrated theories of delinquency, criminality, and other forms of antisocial behavior. Although, like all theories, the Integrated Systems Theory (IST) has limits, it may be the "most ambitious, comprehensive interdisciplinary attempt so far to move integration of criminological theory to new heights" (Lanier and Henry 2004, 351). In this article I will first briefly review previous attempts to develop an integrated theory before discussing my own development of Integrated Systems Theory and stating how it is different from what went before.

Integrated Theory

As this book shows, there are many other theoretical perspectives, including several integrated theories. Most criminological theories are rooted in one or two academic disciplines, making them disciplinary, or at best, multidisciplinary. Genuinely integrated theories are interdisciplinary, which means that they attempt to integrate contributions from all empirical academic disciplines. An interdisciplinary approach makes criminological theory much more effective at explaining antisocial behavior and criminality because the theory is based on the empirical research of a wide range of academic disciplines.

However, most integrated theories, being selective, do not seek to incorporate the whole range of disciplines. Many combine two or three previous theories (typically from the same academic discipline, usually sociology). For example, Elliott's integrated theory (Elliott 1994; Elliott, Huizinga, and Ageton 1996; Elliott et al. 1996) combines the perspectives of social disorganization, strain, social bonding, and social learning. Farrington's integrated theory (Farrington 1989, 1993, 1994, 1996) combines an economic perspective with the perspectives of social bonding and social learning. Thornberry's integrated theory (Thornberry 1987, 1997; Thornberry et al. 1994, 1998) combines the perspectives of social disorganization, social bonding, and social learning.

These theories are examples of conceptual integration (e.g., see Liska, Krohn, and Messner 1989). Conceptual integration takes concepts from different academic theories and puts them together into a single theory. These theories tend to add concepts only from theories within the same academic discipline, an approach that is myopic and incomplete.

An exception is Shoemaker's (1996) integrated theory, which is more comprehensive because it combines economic conditions, political conditions, biological predispositions, and personality traits with the perspectives of anomie, social disorganization, and social learning. Shoemaker's approach is an example of propositional integration (Liska, Krohn, and Messner 1989), and includes end-to-end integration (in which one proposition is used to predict another) and up-and-down integration (in which one proposition subsumes other related propositions). This approach does not synthesize knowledge from multiple theories; instead, it represents a new specification of older theories where factors from single- or multiple-factor theories have either been added or subtracted. Genuine integration requires specification of interactive effects between key concepts and behavior.

Vila's (1994) general evolutionary ecological paradigm overcomes some of these problems. It suggests that ecological-level factors, macro-level factors, and micro-level factors interact to produce an individual's strategic style, which then increases or decreases a person's likelihood of criminality. According to Vila, ecological-level factors are "interactions between individuals, their activities in a physical environment, and their interactions with the physical environment, macro-level factors are systematic interactions between social groups, and micro-level factors are how an individual becomes motivated to commit a crime" (1994, 326). A person's strategic style can be best understood as how the person regularly behaves, which would include his or her preferred way of dealing with problems, of adapting to stress, and of pursuing goals.

Vila posits the following view of human nature and behavior: "Humans are complex, dynamic, and self-reinforcing systems. Very small differences between individuals, combined with early random events and systematic processes, tend to 'push' development toward different styles of behavior. Eventually, we 'lock into' a particular style. Once a strategic style dominated by antisocial and criminal behavior is locked in, it is very difficult to change" (1994, 338). Vila argues that various criminogenic factors come together and interact to affect the probability of criminality for any given person. Vila's integrated ecological paradigm "treats human behavior as the outcome of systematic processes that are dynamic, complex, and self-reinforcing; that is, they involve ongoing interactions between many interconnected components, and the action of one component in the system affects subsequent actions of other components" (1994, 312). Whether a person does or does not become motivated to commit criminal acts, then, results from "interactions over the life course between biological, sociocultural, and developmental factors" (1994, 315).

Vila combines the biological, psychological, and sociological perspectives of social bonding, social learning, and strain, but he does not give us a theory that has specific testable propositions; however, these can be derived from this paradigm.

Finally, Barak's (1998) integrative-constitutive theory is genuinely interdisciplinary and includes criminogenic factors from a wide range of disciplines that makes it arguably the most general theoretical approach developed to date. Yet, this is problematic because several of the variables in Barak's approach are not testable, including factors from psychoanalysis and humanistic/psychological approaches such as the psyche, censored desires, imagery, style, and symbolic meaning. Barak explicitly argues for including factors that are neither testable nor falsifiable, and for a postmodern approach rather than a positivistic one.

Barak also covers the contributions of radical, critical, Marxist, and feminist criminology, attempting to integrate them into one model. Barak's approach is not a theory in the strict definition of that term because it does not put forth testable propositions. Instead, Barak offers literature reviews of different approaches to explaining crime organized around the academic disciplines from which the theories arose. Paradoxically, rather than integrate knowledge, this method serves to reinforce artificial boundaries in knowledge that make integration more difficult.

The first genuinely integrated systems theory was developed by C. Ray Jeffery and was based on the systems perspectives of Whitehead (1925), Lewin (1935), Murray (1938), and especially Miller (1978). Miller (1978) characterized human behavior as a product of factors interacting among seven different living systems. This systems approach was first applied to criminological theory by C. Ray Jeffery (1990) in his book, *Criminology: An Interdisciplinary Approach*, and called the "integrated systems perspective" (ISP). Jeffery's ISP was interdisciplinary, which means that it combines the contributions of numerous academic disciplines for the purpose of better understanding human behavior. It asserts that various criminogenic factors interact among all levels of analysis—cell, organ, organism, group, community/organization, and society—to produce antisocial and criminal behavior.

Figure 13.1.1, derived from Jeffery's work, shows these levels of analysis. Each level of analysis represents a living system that survives on its own and can be studied independently of the others (e.g., biologists study cells, neurologists study organs, psychologists study individual organisms, sociologists study groups). Jeffery's ISP, like general systems theory, assumes that there are factors, concepts, or variables at each of these levels of analysis that influence the likelihood of antisocial behavior.

The levels are connected, which means that each system above is part of the systems below it and each system below is made up of all the systems above it (e.g., cells make up organs, which make up organisms, which make up groups, etc.). Thus a change in one level or system leads to a change in all levels or systems. Take, for example, the influence of genes on all levels. Genetic flaws can produce chemical imbalances of the brain (organ level), which can lead to mental illnesses such as depression and schizophrenia (organism level), which can lead to antisocial behavior that is likely to strain families (group level), impact neighborhoods and hospitals (community/organization level), and ultimately affect the entire country in which individuals afflicted with mental illnesses live (society level).

After C. Ray Jeffery and his colleague Frederic Faust, both of Florida State University, developed, wrote, and taught about this perspective, it was further refined, developed, and expanded by several graduate students over the years (see Fishbein, for example, in this volume). Yet, a book-

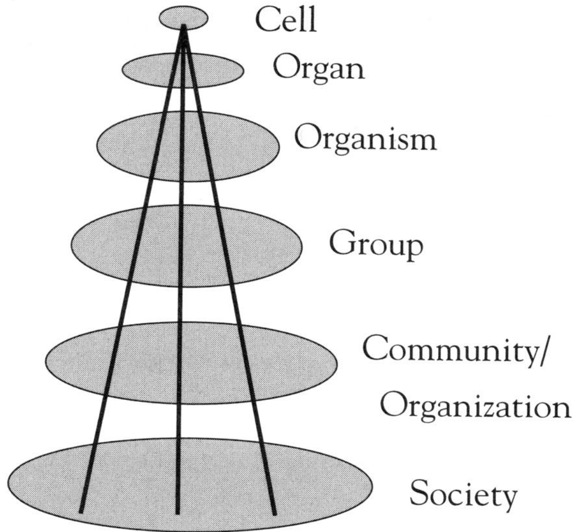

SOURCE: Matthew B. Robinson (2004) *Why Crime? An Integrated Systems Theory of Antisocial Behavior*. Upper Saddle River, NJ: Pearson Educational Inc, p. 39.

FIGURE 13.1.1 Levels of Analysis in the Integrated Systems Perspective

length treatment based on this perspective did not emerge until the publication of *Why Crime? An Integrated Systems Theory of Antisocial Behavior* (Robinson 2004). In this work, I take a positivistic scientific approach, draw together only factors that can be observed and measured/falsified, and specify testable propositions and specific interactive and intervening effects between variables.

Known Facts of Crime and a Summary of Criminogenic Factors

The Integrated Systems Theory (IST) is based on a list of facts about crime—relationships that have been verified through multiple tests of various theories of crime. Box 13.1.1 lists these facts of crime. Some of the facts apply only to street crime, whereas others apply to street crime and to other forms of criminality (such as white-collar and corporate crimes). Also, some relate more to antisocial behavior (behavior that violates societal

BOX 13.1.1 Facts of Crime

1. Antisocial behavior is normal (everybody does it) and it starts early in life.
2. Most people start committing illegal acts as juveniles.
3. Most people will grow out of illegal behavior if left alone (maturation).
4. The earlier a person starts committing antisocial behavior (early starters), the more likely he or she will continue to commit it and the more serious his or her antisocial behavior will likely be.
5. Offenders who do not stop committing antisocial behavior (life-course persistent offenders) are different than those who do stop (adolescent-limited offenders).
6. Even serious, repeat criminals can stop committing crime in conjunction with meaningful marriages and fulfilling careers (turning points).
7. Crime of most types is committed disproportionately by males.
8. Crime of most types is committed disproportionately by people living in large cities.
9. People who have friendships with criminals are more likely to engage in all types of crime.
10. People who do not believe strongly in the importance of complying with the law are more likely to violate the law.
11. Street crime is committed disproportionately by 15- to 25-year-olds.
12. Street crime is committed disproportionately by unmarried people.
13. Street crime is committed disproportionately by people who have experienced high residential mobility and who live in areas characterized by high levels of residential mobility.
14. Young people who are weakly attached to their schools are more likely to engage in street crime.
15. Young people who have low educational and occupational aspirations are more likely to engage in street crime.
16. Young people who do poorly at school are more likely to engage in street crime.
17. Young people who are weakly attached to their parents are more likely to engage in street crime.
18. Being at the bottom of the class structure, whether measured by socioeconomic status, socioeconomic status of the area in which the person lives, being unemployed, being a member of an oppressed racial minority (e.g., blacks in the US), increases rates of offending for street crime.

SOURCE: Adapted from John Braithwaite (1995) *Crime, Shame and Reintegration*. Cambridge: Cambridge University Press (chapter 3).

norms and may be maladaptive and/or harmful to others). The IST is not meant to explain any particular type of crime, but instead is aimed at explaining the general likelihood that a person will indulge in antisocial behavior, particularly someone who is maladaptive in nature and especially who harms others (e.g., someone who commits violent street crime, corporate crime).

The IST is consistent with these facts and can also explain why they are true. The IST is also built around known risk factors that have been identified by scholars in numerous academic disciplines (e.g., sociology, psychology, biology, behavioral genetics, neurology, anthropology, economics). Risk factors are things in the real world that increase one's risk of indulging in antisocial behavior upon exposure, especially when exposure is frequent (frequency), regular (regularity), intense (intensity), and occurs early in life (priority). In developing the theory, the first step was to list the propositions that have already been verified through the empirical tests of scores of crime theories across many disciplines. True to the interdisciplinary approach of the integrated systems perspective, these propositions dealt with topics such as genetics, brain structure (parts of the brain), brain function (levels of neurotransmitters and enzymes in the brain and hormone levels in the blood), brain dysfunction (head injury, exposure to environmental toxins, maternal drug use during pregnancy), personality traits, intelligence levels, mental illness, diet and nutrition, drug consumption, family influences, peer influences, social disorganization, routine activities and victim lifestyles, deterrence, labeling, anomie, strain, culture conflict and subcultures, race, class, and gender.

The IST is similar to what Bernard (2001, 337) calls the risk factor approach whereby "risk factors associated with an increased or decreased likelihood of crime" are identified. Because there are "many such risk factors," every academic discipline can potentially add something to our understanding of the etiology of human behavior, including criminality. This approach assumes that "some people are more likely than others to engage in crime, regardless of the situation they are in; and some situations are more likely to have higher crime rates regardless of the characteristics of the people who are in them" (Bernard 2001, 341).

After careful study and thorough review of various risk factors, the goal was to focus on those propositions that had been regularly verified and to omit those that were not testable, that had not been consistently supported, or that were not shown to increase crime risk, such as educational and religious factors. Building the IST required specifying how and in what ways the various risk factors would likely interact to produce antisocial behavior in individuals (Bernard 2001), including interactive and intervening effects between the numerous risk factors at different levels of analysis, and also examining Vila's question: "What relationships and processes tend to be fundamentally important for understanding changes over time in the . . . behaviors of any social organism?" (1994, 313). Miller (1978, 1) predicted that a systems explanation of behavior would "select, from among different and sometimes opposing viewpoints, fundamental ideas already worked out by others, and fit them into a mosaic, an organized picture of previously unrelated areas." This was one of the goals of the IST.

The Integrated Systems Theory of Antisocial Behavior: Risk Factors and Relationships with Antisocial Behavior

The following are the philosophical assumptions underlying the Integrated Systems Theory:

- People choose whether or not to commit crime.
- People's choices are influenced by factors beyond their control.
- The factors that influence people's choices (and hence their behaviors) are risk factors and protective factors.
- These risk and protective factors exist among six levels of analysis, including cells, organs, organisms, groups, communities/organizations, and society.
- Exposure to risk factors generally increases the risk of antisocial and criminal behavior, especially when exposure is frequent, regular, intense, and occurs early in life.
- Exposure to protective factors generally decreases the risk of antisocial and criminal behavior, especially when exposure is frequent, regular, intense, and occurs early in life.

Figure 13.1.2 visually illustrates the IST. Each numbered arrow depicts relationships between risk factors and antisocial behavior. The figure explains why people start committing antisocial behavior (early) and why they continue committing it.

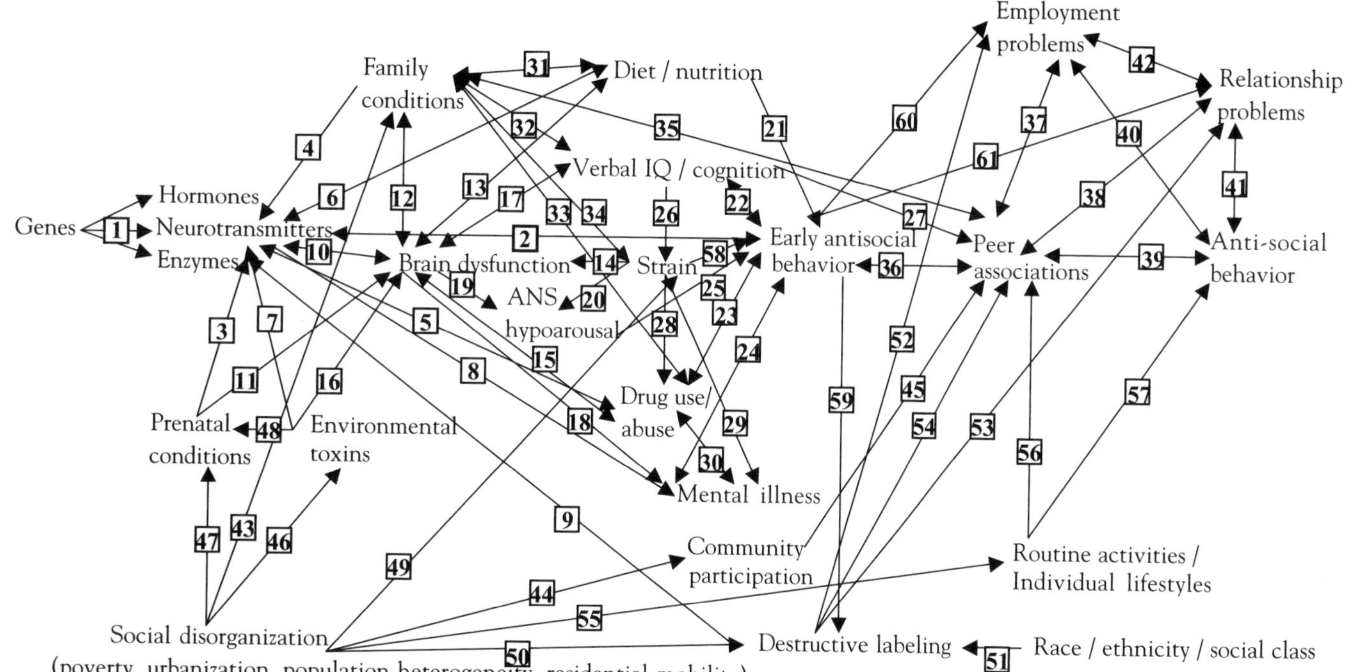

SOURCE: Matthew B. Robinson (2004) *Why Crime? An Integrated Systems Theory of Antisocial Behavior.* Upper Saddle River, NJ: Pearson Educational Inc, p. 267.

FIGURE 13.1.2 Relationships in the Integrated Systems Theory (IST)

Propensities for antisocial behavior begin at the moment of conception, when genes are passed from parents to their offspring. Genes influence levels of brain chemistry (neurotransmitters and enzymes) and influence levels of hormones in the body (arrow 1). High levels of the neurotransmitters dopamine and low levels of serotonin and norepinephrine increase the risk of antisocial behavior. Furthermore, low levels of the enzyme MAO increase the risk of antisocial behavior, as does high levels of the hormone testosterone and low levels of the stress hormone cortisol (arrow 2). Levels of these substances are also affected by prenatal conditions, including drug use/abuse during pregnancy, unhealthy diet/nutrition during pregnancy, and stress during pregnancy (arrow 3). Some forms of aggression will also increase testosterone levels and likely affect brain chemistry as well, which suggests the relationships will be reciprocal.

Once a child is born, these chemicals are affected by family conditions such as inconsistent discipline, harsh discipline, and unaffectionate parenting (arrow 4), as well as by consumption of drugs (arrow 5), level of nutrition (arrow 6), and exposure to environmental toxins (arrow 7). Relationships between brain chemistry and drugs and nutrition are likely reciprocal: Once brain chemistry is changed, cravings for certain drugs and foods increase. Abnormal levels of neurotransmitters produce severe mental illnesses (arrow 8).

Whether or not early antisocial behavior results from abnormal levels of neurotransmitters, the effects of destructive labeling can also affect levels of these substances (arrow 9). Levels of neurotransmitters, enzymes, and hormones can increase the risk of early antisocial behavior, but it is likely that they will not precede antisocial behavior without the influence of other factors.

Brain dysfunction suggests abnormal brain activity; therefore logic suggests that forms of it, such as head trauma, also affect levels of these substances (arrow 10). In the figure, six sources of brain dysfunction are identified, including harmful prenatal conditions (arrow 11), harmful family conditions (arrow 12), abnormal diet/nutrition (arrow 13), perceptions of strain (arrow 14), drug abuse (arrow 15), and exposure to environmental toxins (arrow 16). Relationships between brain dysfunction and the following factors are reciprocal: harmful family conditions, abnormal diet/nutrition, and drug abuse. This means that once brain dysfunction is experienced, it is likely that family conditions will worsen as parents struggle to deal with the outcomes, and individuals suffering from forms of brain dysfunction will be more susceptible to making themselves feel better through abnormal diets and drug abuse (self-medication).

As shown in the figure, individual outcomes of brain dysfunction include increased risks of family disruption (arrow 12), abnormal diet (arrow 13), drug abuse (arrow 15), lower verbal IQ, cognitive deficits (arrow 17), mental illness (arrow 18), and autonomic system (ANS) hypoarousal (arrow 19), which is also produced by stress or perceptions of strain (arrow 20). Several of these organism-level risk factors increase the likelihood of early antisocial behavior, including abnormal diet/nutrition (arrow 21), low verbal IQ/cognitive dysfunction (arrow 22), drug use/abuse (arrow 23), mental illness under certain circumstances, such as in the presence of delusions and drug abuse (arrow 24), and ANS hypoarousal (arrow 25). It is likely that the relationships between antisocial behavior and verbal IQ/cognitive dysfunction, drug use/abuse, and mental illness are reciprocal, because once antisocial behavior begins, individuals are at greater risk for experiences that will impair cognition, for situations where drug use and abuse are prevalent, and of being diagnosed with minor if not serious mental illnesses. Low verbal IQ/cognitive problems also lead to perceptions of strain (arrow 26) and likely increase the risk of associating with others with similar problems (arrow 27).

Drug use/abuse (arrow 28) and mental illness (arrow 29) can result from experiences of general strain; each can be considered a means of coping with negative or noxious stimuli. There is also a reciprocal relationship between drug use/abuse and mental illness (arrow 30). Drug use often serves as a trigger for major brain disorders, such as manic depression, and people suffering from major mental illnesses may use/abuse drugs as a form of self-medication.

At the group level, family conditions and peer associations are both important factors for antisocial behavior. Family conditions affect the diet/nutrition of children because parents largely determine what children eat (arrow 31), IQ level/cognition (arrow 32), the likelihood of drug use/abuse in adolescents (arrow 33), and experiences of general strain (arrow 34). Each of these relationships can be reciprocal given that what affects a child affects all the groups he or she is part of, including the family. Finally, family conditions also affect peer associations (arrow 35), and peer associations affect family conditions; thus the relationship is reciprocal. Specifically, failure to supervise children and monitor their behavior increases the likelihood that children will associate with deviant peers; in turn, associations with deviant peers interfere with the ability of families to correct the behavior of their children.

Peer associations are often preceded by early antisocial behavior (arrow 36), so that people sharing similar outlooks on life and certain characteristics band together. Yet, reciprocally, peer associations are also reinforced by antisocial behavior. Associations with deviant peers often interfere with employment opportunities and experiences (arrow 37) and with other relationships (arrow 38) and vice versa because problems in employment and other interpersonal relationships can increase the importance of deviant peer associations. As associations with deviant peers typically follow early antisocial behavior, reciprocal reinforcement of antisocial behavior occurs in the group context, making continued antisocial behavior more likely (arrow 39). Employment problems (arrow 40) and relationship problems (arrow 41) both increase the risk of antisocial behavior, and antisocial behavior likely will increase these problems. Employment problems and relationship problems also reciprocally feed off each other (arrow 42).

Group-level factors are also affected by community- and organization-level factors. For example, conditions of social disorganization such as poverty, population heterogeneity, and residential mobility make it harder for families to regulate the behavior of their children and peers (arrow 43). These conditions also make it more difficult for residents to participate in community organizations (arrow 44). Low levels of community participation increase the ability of deviant peers to congregate without adequate supervision (arrow 45). Conditions of social disorganization, such as poverty and urbanization, increase the likelihood of exposure to environmental toxins (arrow 46). Poverty also is detrimental to healthy pregnancies (arrow 47), as is exposure to environmental toxins (arrow 48). Living in poverty (especially in the United States, a rich society) increases perceptions of relative deprivation and thus strain (arrow 49).

Living in conditions of social disorganization increases the risk that an individual will be labeled in a destructive manner by agencies of social control, largely because such areas are the most heavily policed (arrow 50). Being a member of a racial or ethnic minority (e.g., African American or Hispanic) and/or being a member of the lower class also increases the risk of destructive labeling (arrow 51). Being labeled a delinquent, criminal, or deviant increases the likelihood of employment problems (arrow 52), of relationship problems (arrow 53), and of forming associations with deviant peers (arrow 54). Such problems with employment, relationships, and associating with other antisocial people will increase the risk of continued antisocial behavior.

Social disorganization also is related to patterns of routine activities in a community as a result of the lifestyles of residents and space users (arrow 55), which thus affect peer associations (arrow 56) and the likelihood that one will engage in antisocial behavior. The effects of lifestyle patterns on antisocial behavior are through the creation of suitable opportunities for antisocial behavior (arrow 57).

Strain, historically treated as a society-level factor because of its relationship with anomie theory, is important in this model. It is general strain (really an individual level factor) that increases the risk of early antisocial behavior (arrow 58). Early antisocial behavior increases the risk of being labeled in a harmful way (arrow 59), and when antisocial behavior appears in adolescence or later, it will likely lead to employment problems (arrow 60) and relationship problems (arrow 61).

The Integrated Systems Theory of Antisocial Behavior: Developmental Aspects

The IST incorporates the risk factors into a developmental timeline, suggesting greater or lesser import for some factors at different times over the life-course. Figure 13.1.3 shows this timeline. Although research shows there may be more than one path to antisocial behavior, the figure depicts when risk factors from the IST are first likely to influence a person's behavior. The information in this figure is based on the growing literature of developmental criminology (e.g., see Benson 2002; Huizinga et al. 1998; Kelley et al. 1997; Kumpfer and Alvarado 1998; Piquero and Mazerolle 2001).

Several of the risk factors begin before birth, such as inheriting genetic propensities, maternal drug use/abuse during pregnancy, maternal diet/nutrition during pregnancy, stress during pregnancy, and exposure to environmental toxins during pregnancy. The effects of diet/nutrition, family influences, chemical imbalances in neurotransmitter and enzyme levels, brain dysfunction, environmental toxins, hypoarousal of the ANS, and low verbal IQ/cognitive problems are likely to begin in early childhood. Given the unique demands of adolescence, the risk factors of hormones, drug

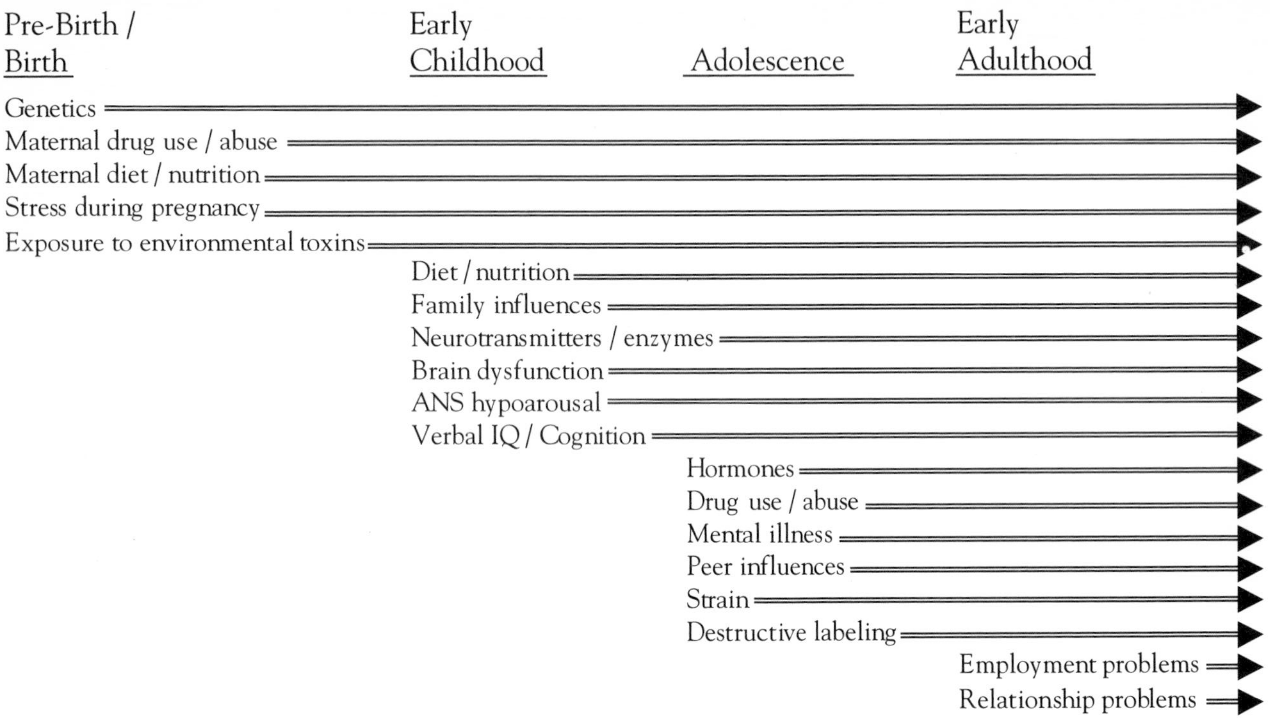

Pre-Birth / Birth

Early Childhood

Adolescence

Early Adulthood

Genetics
Maternal drug use / abuse
Maternal diet / nutrition
Stress during pregnancy
Exposure to environmental toxins
Diet / nutrition
Family influences
Neurotransmitters / enzymes
Brain dysfunction
ANS hypoarousal
Verbal IQ / Cognition
Hormones
Drug use / abuse
Mental illness
Peer influences
Strain
Destructive labeling
Employment problems
Relationship problems

SOURCE: Matthew B. Robinson (2004) *Why Crime? An Integrated Systems Theory of Antisocial Behavior.* Upper Saddle River, NJ: Pearson Educational Inc, p. 270.

FIGURE 13.1.3 Development of Antisocial Behavior in the Integrated Systems Theory (IST)

use/abuse, mental illness, peer influences, general strain, and destructive labeling are most likely to occur during this time. Finally, employment problems and relationship problems are most likely to occur in early adulthood.

This developmental timeline is not meant as an absolute; it is simply a way of visualizing when certain risk factors are most likely to begin to have deleterious effects on individuals. Generally, the earlier risk factors begin to influence people (priority), the greater the likelihood that individuals will commit acts of antisocial behavior. Also, the more risk factors a person is exposed to during any stage of life, the more likely antisocial behavior will occur.

Conclusions and Policy Implications

The IST has not yet been subject to testing as a whole, but because it is consistent with empirical evidence and built around previous tests of the risk factors presented, the main premises should be supported in future tests. Tests of the IST should be conducted using longitudinal data that are sensitive to the trajectory laid out. Scholars must test for reciprocal relationships, or two-way causality and interactive effects. The theory does not require that all the risk factors in the model be present for antisocial behavior to occur; rather, the greater the number of factors present, the greater the likelihood that antisocial behavior will occur. The theory is probabilistic, which means that the presence of these risk factors increases the likelihood of antisocial behavior.

The effects of the risk factors on behavior will depend on the frequency, regularity, intensity, and priority of a person's exposure, so that the more often a person is exposed (frequency), the more consistently one is exposed (regularity), the earlier a person is exposed (priority), and the stronger the factor (intensity), the more likely antisocial behavior will occur. Finally, the presence of protective factors will counteract the effects of risk factors.

Given that the theory is built on a solid foundation of empirical research pertaining to risk factors and antisocial behavior, it is possible to derive policy implications from it to prevent the onset of antisocial behavior. Logical policies would entail reducing a population's frequency, regularity, intensity, and priority of exposure to antisocial risk factors and/or increasing one's exposure to protective factors. Of most importance is reducing the clustering of disadvantages, for the cumulative effects of exposure to numerous risk factors is likely far worse than the periodic exposure to one or two risk factors.

The policy implications of the IST call for a broader and more sustained effort at crime prevention through risk reduction, as opposed to the reactive and largely failing criminal justice policies that we currently pursue (Robinson 2005).

References

Barak, G. 1998. *Integrating Criminologies*. Needham Heights, Mass.: Allyn and Bacon.

Benson, M. 2002. *Crime and the Life Course: An Introduction*. Los Angeles: Roxbury.

Bernard, T. 2001. "Integrating Theories in Criminology." In *Explaining Crime and Criminals*, edited by R. Paternoster and R. Bachman. Los Angeles: Roxbury.

Braithwaite, J. 1995. *Crime, Shame and Reintegration*. New York: Cambridge University Press

Elliott, D. 1994. "Serious Violent Offenders: Onset, Developmental Course and Termination." *Criminology* 34: 1–22.

Elliott, D., D. Huizinga, and S. Ageton. 1985. *Explaining Delinquency and Drug Use*. Beverly Hills, Calif.: Sage.

Elliott, D., W. Wilson, D. Huizinga, R. Sampson, A. Elliott, and B. Rankin. 1996. "The Effects of Neighborhood Disadvantage on Adolescent Development." *Journal of Research in Crime and Delinquency* 33: 389–426.

Farrington, D. 1989. "Early Predictors of Adolescent Aggression and Adult Violence." *Victims Violence* 4: 79–100.

______. 1993. "Childhood Origins of Teenage Antisocial Behaviour and Adult Social Dysfunction." *Journal of the Royal Society of Medicine* 86: 13–17.

______. 1994. "Early Developmental Prevention of Juvenile Delinquency." *Criminal Behaviour and Mental Health* 4: 209–227.

______. 1996. "The Explanation and Prevention of Youthful Offending." In *Delinquency and Crime: Current Theories*, edited by J. Hawkins. New York: Cambridge University Press.

Huizinga, D., A. Weiher, S. Menard, R. Espiritu, and F. Esbensen. 1998. "Some Not So Boring Findings from the Denver Youth Survey." Paper presented to the annual meeting of the American Society of Criminology, Washington, D.C., November 11–14.

Kelley, B., R. Loeber, K. Keenan, and M. DeLamatre. 1997. "Developmental Pathways in Boys' Disruptive and Delinquent Behavior." *OJJDP: Juvenile Justice Bulletin*. Washington, D.C.: U.S. Department of Justice.

Kumpfer, K., and R. Alvarado. 1998. "Effective Family Strengthening Interventions." *OJJDP: Juvenile Justice Bulletin*. Washington, D.C.: U.S. Department of Justice.

Jeffery, C. 1990. *Criminology: An Interdisciplinary Approach*. Englewood Cliffs, Calif.: Prentice-Hall.

Lanier, M. M., and S. Henry. 2004. *Essential Criminology*. Boulder: Westview Press.

Lewin, K. 1935. *A Dynamic Theory of Personality*. New York: McGraw-Hill.

Liska, A., M. Krohn, and S. Messner. 1989. "Strategies and Requisites for Theoretical Integration." In *The Study of Crime and Deviance: Theoretical Integration in the Study of Deviance and Crime, Problems and Prospects*, edited by A. Liska, M. Krohn, and S. Messner. Albany, N.Y.: State University of New York Press.

Miller, J. 1978. *Living Systems*. New York: McGraw-Hill.

Murray, H. 1938. *Explorations in Personality*. New York: Oxford University Press.

Piquero, A., and P. Mazerolle. 2001. *Life-Course Criminology: Contemporary and Classic Readings*. Belmont, Calif.: Wadsworth.

Robinson, M. 2004. *Why Crime? An Integrated Systems Theory of Antisocial Behavior*. Upper Saddle River, N.J.: Prentice-Hall.

———. 2005. *Justice Blind? Ideals and Realities of American Criminal Justice*. Upper Saddle River, N.J.: Prentice-Hall.

Shoemaker, D. 1996. *Theories of Delinquency*. 3d ed. New York: Oxford University Press.

Thornberry. T. 1987. "Toward an Interactional Theory of Delinquency." *Criminology* 25: 863–891.

———. 1997. "Some Advantages of Developmental and Life-Course Perspectives for the Study of Crime and Delinquency." Introduction to *Developmental Theories of Crime and Delinquency*, edited by T. Thornberry. New Brunswick, N.J.: Transaction.

Thornberry, T., A. Lizotte, M. Krohn, M. Farnworth, and S. Jang. 1994. "Delinquent Peers, Beliefs, and Delinquent Behavior: A Longitudinal Test of Interactional Theory." *Criminology* 32: 47–83.

Thornberry, T., M. Krohn, A. Lizotte, C. Smith, and P. Perter. 1998. "Taking Stock: An Overview of the Findings from The Rochester Youth Development Study." Paper presented to the annual meeting of the American Society of Criminology.

Vila, B. 1994. "A General Paradigm for Understanding Criminal Behavior: Extending Evolutionary Ecological Theory." *Criminology* 32: 311–360.

Whitehead, A. 1925. *Science and the Modern World*. New York: Macmillan.

13.2

Applying Integrated Theory

A Reciprocal Theory of Violence and Nonviolence[1]

GREGG BARAK
Eastern Michigan University

Since the publication of my work on integrative theory (Barak 1998), I have sought to develop an integrative theoretical approach to explain violence. Most general theorizing on violence is one-dimensional. It is usually focused on the individual and interpersonal nature of violence to the relative exclusion of the institutional and structural natures of violence and nonviolence, and much less to the interplay between these three spheres of violence. Either by failing to take into account the multiple and changing variables of nonviolent and violent behavior at the individual level or by taking into account these dynamic elements or processes at the interpersonal level without simultaneously doing so at the institutional and structural levels is to fall short of a comprehensive explanation of nonviolence that is capable of accounting for the reciprocal and cumulative effects that lead to or sustain violent or nonviolent outcomes. Problems associated with one-dimensional, overly deterministic, single—or even multivariable—and interpersonal explanations of prosocial and antisocial behavior typically ignore more relevant variables than they explore. These have fortunately been supplemented by the emergence and development of integrative modeling and life-course perspectives in the fields of child development, criminology, deviance, and violence (Barak 1998; Caspi et al. 1987; Catalano and Hawkins 1996; Colvin 2000; Elde 2001; Huang et al. 2001; Laub and Sampson 1993; Moffitt 2001; Piquero and Mazerolle 2001; Robinson 2004; Sampson and Laub 1993; Tittle 1995).

These newer epistemological approaches, when applied to violence and nonviolence, assume a complexity of human interacting variables that cut across the behavioral motivations and the cultural constraints. However, virtually all these theories fail to take into account the social histories of the institutional and structural patterns of violence in relationship to the individual life histories (Barak 2003). As argued below, the interactive spheres or patterns of interpersonal, institutional, and structural violence and nonviolence have reciprocal and accumulating influences that are relevant to the production and reproduction of individual-adversarial and collective-mutualistic behaviors. Derived from an extension of the same logic used by the more traditional integrative, pathway, and multidimensional theories, the reciprocal theory of violence and nonviolence adds to the interpersonal relations by incorporating the institutional and structural relations that can reinforce or diminish violence and nonviolence. Each of the three integrative and overlapping domains of violence and nonviolence interact within the dialectics between adversarialism and mutualism that universally intersects virtually all individuals, groups, and nation-states alike. At its core, my reciprocal theory argues that the struggle between violence and nonviolence is a struggle about the contradictory relations or tensions between adversarialism and mutualism because these express themselves as competing properties. There are also pathways for culturally organizing personal and societal identities that, ultimately, navigate and guide individual, institutional, and structural behavior with respect to violent and nonviolent outcomes.

On Adversarialism and Mutualism as Key to Understanding the Dialectics of Violence and Nonviolence

Adversarial models of social intercourse assume that one engages in antagonistic behavior to overcome another, to achieve revenge, and/or to arouse envy. Adversarialism also assumes that parties oppose each other's interests more than they share anything in common. Similarly, adversarial paradigms assume that conflicts are the essence of life, and that living consists of enduring them, winning as many as possible, and learning how, when necessary, to live with losing them. Adversarialism normally excludes all other opportunities but antagonism and battle. At the same time, the identities of the self and the other, and the relationship between them, are defined in terms of conquering and submitting. Adversarialism, especially the more compulsive forms (i.e., competition for the sake of competition), represents a cultural defense mechanism or system that promotes the denial or circumvention of the necessary work to overcome the unnecessary and destructive tensions in the self and in the larger society (Kohn 1992). In the process, adversarialism encourages alienation and estrangement while it supports extreme individualism and isolationism.

In contrast, mutualistic models of social intercourse assume that we engage in cooperative behavior because of the experience of deep fulfillment in social connections. Mutualism also assumes that pleasures are to be derived from sharing common interests and that individuals and societies can reside in peaceful relationship with themselves and others. Some years ago, Erik Erikson (1964) emphasized that reciprocal relations, for example, between the infant and the mother, epitomize the potential for reciprocal relations between the self and others as well as the self and society. Similarly, when Erikson used the term "mutuality," he was referring to the processes by which two or more persons support and nourish each other for the enhancement of all.

In spite of the contradictions between adversarialism and mutualism, Gordon Fellman (1998, 25–26) captures the reciprocal relations between the two:

> Adversarialism culminates, individually, in feelings of rage that can escalate into total hatred and violence. Mutuality culminates in love. . . . Whereas hatred wants to destroy, love wants to celebrate, to embrace, and finally, to merge. Adversarialism expresses Thanatos, the death force, the determination to separate, to distance, to define the self in terms of what one is not. Mutuality is Eros; it flowers in the subtle, caring, loving recognition of parent and child delighting in each other. Mutuality, like love that is its essence, expresses the yearning to merge with something.

In true dialectical style, the two paradigms of adversarialism and mutualism are not mutually exclusive; within each model there are features of the other. For example, in times of warfare and during other times of intense competition, people take great pleasure in cooperating against those whom they oppose. In business, sports, or politics, people coordinate actions with their allies against their competitors, opponents, or enemies. Alone and together, they enjoy the thrill of victory; alone and together, they also endure the agony of defeat.

Whether adversarial or mutualistic, the pleasures of cooperation or competition need not be organized; they could be spontaneous actions or reactions, individual or collective. For illustration, group hatred, such as racism or sexism that can potentially escalate into genocide or mass rape, is a stylized way of *opposing* the other as well as of enjoying *solidarity* with similarly inclined people. By contrast, group love, such as holism or environmentalism that may potentially spawn healthier communities or more balanced ecosystems, is a stylized way of *connecting* with the other as well as of enjoying *solidarity* with all human beings and other species, including one's "enemies." At the same time, within the spirit of holism and environmentalism there is also a component of adversarialism: Not only are the participants in these social movements working against their individual and organizational adversaries, at least initially or superficially, but also they are doing so in opposition to some aspects of nature such as diseases involving animals (including human beings) and vegetation.

According to the adversarial paradigm, people are defined as dangerous, as potential competitors, and as inevitable combatants. By contrast, according to the mutualistic paradigm, people are defined as others who can be known partly through knowing oneself, as allies who can be trusted to respect feelings and vulnerabilities alike, and as potential friends. Adversarialism sees human interactions as primarily a series of "zero-sum" games with only winners and losers; mutualism sees these interactions as potentially a series of "win-win" exchanges, or negotiations and compromises, in which all parties to a conflict can become benefactors.

Adversarial values tend to give greater importance to battle, fighting, and tough-mindedness than to bending, friendship, and serenity. They tend to support conflict, combatants, and litigants rather than cooperation, negotiation, and restoration. Nonadversarial or mutualistic values, such as enjoying good health, feeling secure and comfortable in one's environment, exploring sensuality, caring for others, and finding pleasure in a great range of people and experiences, gives greater importance to peacemaking and social justice and to more equitable treatment for all. It also gives greater emphasis to the flexibility and diversity of the mind rather than to structured conformity, vilification, and revenge; in short, a situation of making love rather than war, a situation where the pleasures of nonviolence depend on adjusting needs and desires to those of others. Adjustment such as this is possible by virtue of the capacity to take the role of the other, a central form of which is empathy.

The problem, however, is that such empathy with the feelings of the other is anathema to the adversarial paradigm because of its associated exclusionary practices of dehumanizing, humiliating, and/or denigrating the other, as well as its selective discourses of demonization and vilification. Empathy and identification with the other is not only an inclusive merging act; it may also be thought of as the dialectical opposite of competition. In other words, the mutualism of empathy reveals the necessary projections of adversarialism, which at their base stem from two constituents—anger and rage—that are essential properties of the social psychology of oppression. At the same time, part and parcel of the dynamics of winning is the undermining as much as possible of all respect for, and trust in, someone or something else. In short, desires for justice, safety, and non-exploitation are sacrificed for "victories" of accumulated money and power. In its most virulent forms, of course, adversarialism is violence, murder, war, and environmental destruction.

At its core, mutualism rejects the idea of an adversarial impulse or imperative to seek advantage over others as either natural or ethical. To enhance the human condition, mutualism assumes that people need to draw from their own subjective histories as well as from objective history and compassion. Specifically, in the context of violence, recovering from violence, and nonviolence, mutualism understands how important it is that people identify with the hurts of others by recognizing their own hurts and the energies of resentment and rage, and it advocates that they do so. Adversarialism, by contrast, especially the compulsive forms indulged in by "competition addicts," or the pathological forms expressed by "habitual perpetrators," assumes material and emotional scarcity, whether one is referring to money, medals, honor, promotions, acceptance, love, or some other icon. Mutualism rejects the adversarial belief in the necessity of competition and the addiction to winning.

Underlying the dynamics of adversarialism are, often, the transferences of unresolved personal problems. For example, anger, if not rage as well, is problematic for just about everyone, even though most people do not succumb to its influences. At the same time, rather than confront these repressed feelings, and rather than deal in a spirit of mutualism with the anger found in families, at work, and in public life, a spirit of adversarialism redirects this anger at opponents. Hence, anyone or anything may be a legitimate enemy, including ideas, social structures, subcultures, and selected individuals and groups that are viewed negatively and/or associated with evil.

By projecting anger onto others, such as minorities, police, the media, and pedophiles, people are able to preserve images of themselves not as angry but as reasonable and moral. This kind of dualistic thinking about "good" or "bad" and "loving" or "hating" denies the fuller and more complex realities of self, other, and society. In short, because individuals and groups are typically not all loving, or all hating, but rather some combination of the two, it becomes essential that both of these expressions of the individual and collective body are addressed. This is needed if social and political reconciliation between these contradictory feelings is to emerge and develop.

On the Reciprocity of Violent and Nonviolent Properties and Pathways

There is a diversity of violent and nonviolent expressions found throughout families, neighborhoods, classrooms, boardrooms, workplaces, country clubs, and in a variety of settings involving other groups of people as well as institutions such as the military, law enforcement, judiciary, mass media, and the church. There are also common or established "properties" and "pathways" that operate across a two-sided continuum of interpersonal, institutional, and structural relations of social and cultural organization that simultaneously promote violence (adversarialism) and nonviolence (mutualism). The interconnections between the interpersonal, institutional, and structural spheres constitute a reciprocal playing field where the constellations of pathways to violence and nonviolence are mutually reinforced, resisted, or negotiated.

Properties of Violence and Nonviolence

The properties of violence are the essential attributes, characteristics, elements, factors, situations, routines, hot spots, and conditions identified by the ad hoc, life-course, developmental, and integrative theories of antisocial behavior. These properties of violence, unsanctioned and sanctioned, may include negative emotional states involving feelings of alienation, shame, humiliation, mortification, rejection, abandonment, denial, depression, anger, hostility, projection, and displacement. They may also include a lack of emotional states associated with the properties of nonviolence such as empathy and compassion stemming from the positive experiences of love, security, attachment, bonding, identification, altruism, and mutualism.

When the properties of violence, or "emotional pathogens," as James Gilligan (1997) refers to them, form in the familiar, subcultural, and cultural interactions between individuals and their social environments, and these states of being are not checked or countered by the states of being associated with the properties of nonviolence, then the potential persists for violent interactions involving the battered psyches of persons, groups, and nation-states alike. That is, feelings of shame and humiliation, or of self-esteem and well-being, may be experienced by individuals, families, communities, tribes, nations, and other social groupings or subcultural stratifications based on age, gender, class, religion, ethnicity, sexual orientation, and so on. In summary, to the extent that individuals and groups feel abandoned by or bonded with their parents, peers, schools, communities, and nation-states, or to the extent that people experience connection or disconnection, they will be likely to relate or not relate, to identify or not to identify, to empathize or not to empathize, to take or not to take responsibility, to project or not to project hostility and aggression, to make war or love, to make violence or nonviolence, to be anxious and uptight, or to be contented and calm.

Pathways to Violence and Nonviolence

Over time and space, the transitions or trajectories toward or away from violence and nonviolence accumulate and form an array of divergent pathways that may facilitate or impede one state of being over the other. It makes sense, therefore, to view adversarialism, violence, and abuse, or mutualism, nonviolence, and empathy, as occurring along a two-sided continuum where the actions of individuals, groups, and nation-states are capable of stimulating, accommodating, or resisting pathways to one or the other. In time and place, these pathways refer to the spatial webs of violence and nonviolence expressed at the familiar, subcultural, and cultural levels of social, political, and economic organization.

All combined, there are nine possible pathways to violence and nine possible pathways to nonviolence. In the structural spheres of violence and nonviolence alone, for example, there are the same informational, financial, and media networks that form an underside of global capitalism, global terrorism, and global peacemaking. Whether operating for prosocial, antisocial, or no particular purposes, these expanding infrastructures have created virtual realities in which once-secure societies now find themselves becoming "permeable webs that both allow and require new communication systems, circulation patterns and organizational structures" (Taylor 2001, B14). As societies and people adapt, as we find ourselves moving from industrial to network organization, and as the new technologies interact both with isolated individuals and with collective villages of globalized culture, pathways to violence and nonviolence are reproduced.

A Reciprocal Theory of Violence and Nonviolence

The "reciprocal theory of violence and nonviolence" assumes that as the interpersonal, institutional, and structural levels of violence and nonviolence and as the number of pathways to violence and nonviolence converge in time and space, then at least three things occur: First, the severity or intensity of violence and nonviolence swells in magnitude. Second, the incidents of violence and nonviolence become more or less prevalent. Third, the distinguishing factors of the spheres of interpersonal, institutional, and structural violence and nonviolence become less distinct.

Moreover, the reciprocal theory argues that cases involving extreme pathways to nonviolence may be best represented by straight lines. In the majority of instances that involve moderate or mild expressions of violence or nonviolence, these may be better represented by curving lines. These social interactions do not exactly correspond to the ideals of positivist science and linear development, nor are these interactions as predictable as social scientists might like, yet patterns of violence or nonviolence emerge in between the properties and pathways that correspond to aggregate life histories and sociocultural experiences (see Figure 13.2.1).

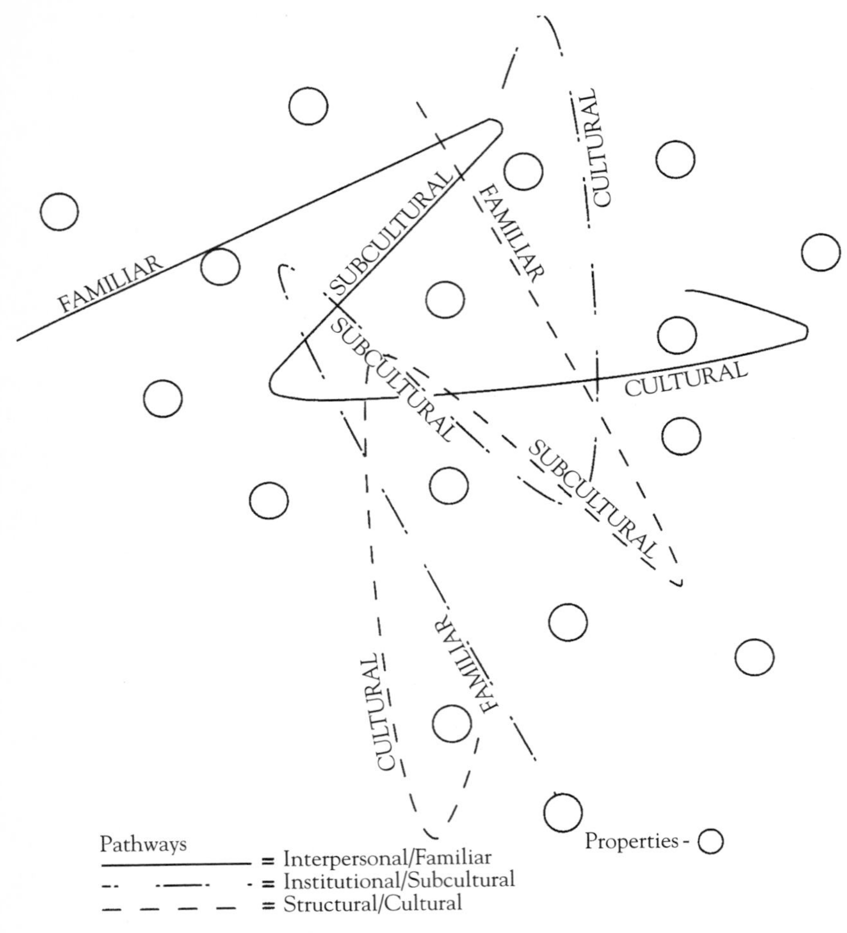

SOURCE: Gregg Barak (2003) *Violence and Nonviolence: Pathways to Understanding*. Thousand Oaks, CA: Sage, p. 159.

FIGURE 13.2.1 Pathways to Violence/Nonviolence

With respect to the two-sided continuum of violence and nonviolence, the properties and pathways are viewed as dialectical. With respect to these relations, any person is capable, more or less, of acquiring the properties both for prosocial and antisocial behavior or for developing pathways to violence and nonviolence. In the life of the individual, group, organization, nation-state, or larger global order, the countervailing forces of these dialectical relations of violence and nonviolence reveal individual and collective histories that may be linear and/or nonlinear in evolution, or they may zigzag. At times, for instance, the interpersonal, institutional, and structural properties conducive for violence and nonviolence are moving in parallel or synchronic fashion. At other times, they may be in opposition or in perpendicularity.

On the interpersonal level, these dialectical situations are understandable because from birth people are exposed to interactions and conditions that reflect varying opportunities and risks for developing prosocial and antisocial behavior. Similarly, on the institutional and structural levels, involving policymaking and implementation, for example, dialectical relations may prevail: There are also starts and stops, zigzagging, forward and backward movement, privatizing and publicizing, regulating and deregulating, and so on. Finally, in the relative scheme of cross-cultural and multination relations, most individuals, institutions, and structures have been less likely to have engaged in the extremes of the two-sided continuum of violence and nonviolence than in the milder forms of each.

In sum, at the interpersonal, institutional, and structural levels of interaction, the reciprocal theory of violence and nonviolence hypothesizes three things. First, that the properties of violence and nonviolence are cumulative. The more (or fewer) properties characteristic of violence or nonviolence that are present, the more or less likely it is that violence or nonviolence will occur. Second, as the familiar, subcultural, and cultural pathways to violence and nonviolence combine, overlap, and interconnect, expressions of violence and nonviolence will become more or less intense and, conversely, more or less common. Third, the properties of and pathways to violence and nonviolence are mutually and inversely related. In other words, social relationships exist within and between the levels of interpersonal, institutional, and structural violence, and when those properties and pathways common to individuals, organizations, and nation-states converge in everyday reality, they work to reinforce and support the reproduction of violence or nonviolence.

Note

1. I would like to thank the editors of this volume for their very constructive input on an earlier version of this paper presented at the American Society of Criminology Meetings held in Nashville, Tenn., November 2004.

References

Barak, G. 1998. *Integrating Criminologies*. Boston: Allyn and Bacon.

______. 2003. *Violence and Nonviolence: Pathways to Understanding*. Thousand Oaks, Calif.: Sage.

Caspi, A., G. H. Elder, and D. J. Bem. 1987. "Moving Against the World: Life-Course Patterns of Explosive Children." *Developmental Psychology* 23: 308–313.

Catalano, R. F., and J. D. Hawkins. 1996. "The Social Development Model: A Theory of Antisocial Behavior. In *Delinquency and Crime: Current Theories*, edited by J. D. Hawkins (pp. 29–43). New York: Cambridge University Press.

Colvin, M. 2000. *Crime and Coercion: An Integrated Theory of Chronic Criminality*. New York: St. Martin's Press.

Elder, G. 2001. "Time, Human Agency, and Social Change." In *Life-course Criminology: Contemporary and Classic Readings*, edited by A. Piquero and P. Mazerolle (pp. 3–30). Belmont, Calif.: Wadsworth.

Erikson, E. 1964. *Insight and Responsibility*. New York: Norton.

Fellman, G. 1998. *Rambo and the Dalai Lama: The Compulsion to Win and Its Threat to Human Survival*. Albany, N.Y.: State University of New York Press.

Gilligan, J. 1997. *Violence: Reflections on a National Epidemic*. New York: Vintage.

Huang, B., R. Kosterman, R. F. Catalano, J. D. Hawkins, and R. Abbott. 2001. "Modeling Mediation in the Etiology of Violent Behavior in Adolescence: A Test of the Social Development Model." *Criminology* 39: 75–108.

Kohn, A. 1992. *No Contest: The Case Against Competition*. Boston: Houghton Mifflin.

Laub, J., and R. Sampson. 1993. "Turning Points in the Life Course: Why Change Matters to the Study of Crime." *Criminology* 31: 301–325.

Moffitt, T. 2001. Adolescence-Limited and Life-Course Persistent Antisocial Behavior: A Developmental Taxonomy. In *Life-Course Criminology: Contemporary and Classic Readings*, edited by A. Piquero and P. Mazerolle (pp. 91–145). Belmont, Calif.: Wadsworth.

Piquero, A., and P. Mazerolle, eds. 2001. *Life-Course Criminology: Contemporary and Classic Readings*. Belmont, Calif.: Wadsworth.

Robinson, M. 2004. *Why Crime? An Integrated Systems Theory of Antisocial Behavior*. Upper Saddle River, N.J.: Pearson/Prentice Hall.

Sampson, R., and J. Laub, 1993. *Crime in the Making: Pathways and Turning Points Through Life*. Cambridge, Mass.: Harvard University Press.

Taylor, M. C. 2001. "Unplanned Obsolescence and the New Network Culture." *Chronicle of Higher Education* (December 14): B14-B16.

Tittle, C. 1995. *Control Balance: Toward a General Theory of Deviance*. Boulder: Westview Press.

13.3

Criminologist as Witness

Richard Quinney
Northern Illinois University

We are all witnesses to the life of our times. Witnesses in one way or another to the joys and the sorrows of being human in a particular time and place. We are witnesses to the sufferings around us and within us. And at times we are moved by conscience to observe and report these sufferings. "This thing I'm telling you about, I saw with my own eyes," reports a woman who witnessed a mass killing a century ago. Witnessing comes out of awareness, and it is an act of conscience. If physical actions follow, they do so because there has been awareness and there has been witnessing.

As criminologists, especially, we are in a position to observe the human conditions and sufferings of our times. We have devoted much of our lives to observing these conditions and sufferings. The subject of our attention, crime, is by definition that of suffering. Crime is the window through which we understand the world that produces crime. We soon realize that there can be no decrease in crime without the ending of suffering. The primary object of our attention is thus suffering rather than crime. We are students of suffering, and we bear witness to suffering.

One's biography as a criminologist can be traced as a journey in witnessing. As part of the movement for a critical criminology, my life has been a gradual development in understanding crime and the emergence of the criminal justice system. Along the way, I have thought critically about crime and about being a criminologist.

My own development as a critical criminologist—in a collective effort with other criminologists—can be seen as a progression in the life course. In other words, my thoughts and my actions have developed and changed as I have experienced the world—as I have aged. There is no separation between the life of the mind and the life of the one who is doing the thinking. I have attempted to make sense of the world while living in that world.

When I began graduate school in 1956, the dominant stance in the social sciences—in sociology in particular—was the acceptance of existing social conditions. Perhaps because of my background, at the edge of two worlds, town and country, I became an observer and critic of the status quo. Some of this background I would later allude to in articles, and I would discuss more fully in my autobiographical books *Journey to a Far Place*, *For the Time Being*, and *Borderland*. As I studied sociology, I became greatly interested in the social problems endemic to the country. Asking, of course, why? And, how could things be different? The United States, in the midst of the cold war, seemed to be driven more by class, conflict, and inequality than by the consensus suggested in the prevailing social theory and national ideology. I thus pursued a class and conflict theory as I began to write and to teach in a series of colleges and universities.

Clearly, what was defined as crime was a product of the economic and political life of the country. Criminal laws were constructed to protect special interests and to maintain a specific social and moral order. This understanding of law and order was evident in the events of the time: the civil rights movement for racial equality, the protests against the war in Vietnam, and the revolts within universities. At the same time, a legal apparatus, called the "criminal justice system," was emerging to control threatening behavior and to preserve the established order. Critical criminology developed with an awareness of these events and conditions. By many names—radical, Marxist, progressive—a critical criminology was created to understand and to change the direction of the country.

My travels through the 1960s, the 1970s, the 1980s, and the 1990s were marked by a progression of ways of thinking and acting. From the social constructionist perspective to phenomenology, from phenomenology to Marxist and critical philosophy, from Marxist and critical philosophy to liberation theology, from liberation theology to Buddhism and existentialism. And then to a more ethnographic and personal mode of thinking and being. It is necessary to note that in all these travels nothing was rejected or deleted from the previous stages. Rather, each new stage of development incorporated what had preceded it. Each change was motivated by the need to understand crime in another or more complex way, in a way excluded from a former understanding. Each stage incorporated the changes that were taking place in my personal life. There was to be no division between life and theory, between witnessing and writing.

In the preface to my book *The Social Reality of Crime*, published in 1970, I stated that my purpose was to provide a reorientation to the study of crime. It was my intention to create a new theoretical perspective for criminology: I would draw from past criminology but inform the new perspective with the sensibility that was forming at the end of the 1960s.

I left New York for a long sabbatical in North Carolina at the beginning of the 1970s. I resigned my tenured professorship at New York University to live and to write away from the confines of the university. I needed time for reflection and time to write about what was happening in the United States—as reflected in the criminal law and the emerging criminal justice system. I began my book *Critique of Legal Order* with a call for a critical understanding of crime and the legal system. With a critical Marxian philosophy, I suggested, we could demystify the existing social order and, at the same time, create a mode of life that would move us beyond the exploitation and oppression of capitalism. I offered a critical theory of crime control in American society, and observed that only with the making of a socialist society will there be a world without crime.

During the mid-seventies, I moved again, this time to the New England city of Providence, Rhode Island. I began working on a book about Providence and about my life there, and about the reconstruction of social and moral order. I turned my attention to the study of theology, especially the theology of Paul Tillich, and brought my current thinking into criminology. I pursued the thesis that we are all at the same time the products of our culture and the creators of it. I quoted Marx, who stated concisely that people make their own history "but they do not make it just as they please; they do not make it under circumstances chosen by themselves, but under circumstances directly encountered, given and transmitted from the past." My argument was, as it continues to be, that criminology is a cultural production that shares the character of such other productions as philosophy, religion, and art. The criminologist is engaged in a cultural practice that interprets and gives meaning to the existing society. Our productions are located in the class relations of the existing society, and our critical understandings are part of the struggle for a better society. The objective in knowing the world critically is to change it. Criminology is to be more than a reflection of the world; it is part of the process through which the world is transformed.

At the end of the 1970s, I published my book *Class, State, and Crime*. My purpose was to provide a structural interpretation of the current developments in crime and criminal justice. When I revised the book for a second edition, published in 1980, I incorporated my thoughts on a socialist theology. I argued that our whole being, personal and collective, is defined by the historically specific goals and demands of advanced capitalism. The social and moral problems of contemporary society are the result of capitalist development. The solution to crime and social injustice is ultimately a transformation that is fundamentally socialist.

In 1983, the time had come for me to return to my homeland in the Midwest. I would teach sociology for the next fifteen years at Northern Illinois University. Upon being given the Edwin H. Sutherland award for contributions to criminological theory, I presented my thoughts on being a criminologist—a criminologist who is also living a daily life that includes keeping a journal and carrying a camera to photograph the landscape. My song was "On the Road Again" by Willie Nelson. Along the way, I was beginning to see criminology as the making of myths that necessarily have consequences in the social worlds we create. Criminology—as part of the making of myths—is as much art as it is science. We are the makers of myths, and because of this, we must take great care in what we think and what we do. And there was the awareness of the passing of time: "Gee, ain't it funny how time just slips away?"

One's personal life cannot be separated from mental productions—at least I have found this to be true in my life and work. Life is a spiritual journey. Add to this a sense that absolute reality is beyond human conception, that all that exists is transient, and that human existence is characterized by suffering. With all this, you have the makings of a special kind of criminology. By the end of the 1980s, I placed these thoughts and experiences into my own criminology. The essay titled "The Way of Peace: On Crime, Suffering, and Service" presents this criminology; it assumes that crime is suffering and that crime will end only with the end of suffering, only when there is peace. This is a peacemaking criminology, a nonviolent criminology of compassion and service that seeks to eliminate crime by lessening the suffering in us and in the world.

Finally came the realization that whatever we may be doing as criminologists, we are engaged in a moral enterprise. Our underlying questions are always: How are we human beings to live? Who are we, and of what are we capable? How could things be different? Whether or not we are educated as moral philosophers, and whatever the nature of our criminology, we operate with an implicit moral philosophy and we are constantly engaged in the construction of moral philosophy. And, most important, we are witnessing to our times. We are witnesses to suffering, to violence in its many forms, to hatred and greed, to inequality and injustice, and to the possibilities of peace and social justice. Witnessing is an active vocation that is grounded in a particular moral stance toward human existence.

As criminologists, we are witnesses to the various forms of violence, to the atrocities, and to the sufferings of many people. As with journalists, photographers, peace workers, and fellow social scientists, we witness and report the suffering throughout the world. Observations and reports are made of the Holocaust, the ethnic wars, illness and starvation, sexual abuse, and the many other sufferings of being human in the modern world.

The witness obviously is not a neutral observer that a simplistic dichotomy of active agent and passive observer might suggest. The witness is certain to be in the right place at the right time. And once there, the witness is moved by conscience to observe and report what is being witnessed. If physical actions follow, they follow because first there has been the witnessing. Without witnessing, no subsequent action is wise and appropriate. Witnesses act with clarity and purpose because they have the awareness and conscience to do so. Ready and with open mind, the witness truly sees what is happening, and knows what further action should be taken. Without witnessing, an action is unfocused, confused, and little more than a chasing of the wind.

There is plenty for the criminologist to witness. Make your own list of what we, as criminologists, should be witnessing. My own current witnessing is to the kinds of suffering and violence that are a systematic and structured part of contemporary existence. In fact, the largest portion of violence is structured and is generated or committed by governments, corporations, the military, and agents of the law.

The war at home is against the poor. It is a war that is waged to maintain inequality so that the rich can maintain their wealth. Entire populations are being held hostage in poverty, sickness, addiction, and brutality against one another—remaining unemployed, underemployed, and uneducated. Prisons are overflowing, and prison construction and operation are growing industries. The rich not only create the war, to secure their position, but also profit from the war. In our own nonviolent actions and protests, founded on witnessing, we take our stand. "Which side are you on?" is still the relevant question.

Directly associated with the war on the poor, the war to keep a minority of the population rich, is capital punishment. The death penalty—state-sponsored murder—is the final resort of a violent and greedy minority. That the practice of capital punishment is supported by so many is all the more reason for criminologists as witnesses to expose, to analyze, and to protest. Someday, I am certain, historians will note that the United States was one of the last nations to continue to violate the most basic of human rights: the right to life. It was one of the last nations to systematically violate the rights of its own citizens.

Everything we do as criminologists is grounded in a moral philosophy. Whatever we think and do, our criminology is the advancement of one moral philosophy or another. And each moral philosophy generates its own kind of witnessing—in the events to be witnessed and in the forms of witnessing. The work in criminology that is historically important is the work that is informed by a moral philosophy. As witnesses, we are on the side of life; we have reverence for all life. Such is the way of peace.

References (Selected Chronology)

Quinney, Richard. 1970. *The Social Reality of Crime*. Boston: Little, Brown.

______. 1971, "Dialogue with Richard Quinney." *Issues in Criminology* 6 (Spring): 41–54.

______. 1973. "There's a Lot of Folks Grateful to the Lone Ranger: With Some Notes on the Rise and Fall of American Criminology." *The Insurgent Sociologist* 4 (Fall): 56–64.

______. 1974. *Critique of Legal Order: Crime Control in Capitalist Society*. Boston: Little, Brown.

______. 1978. "The Production of a Marxist Criminology." *Contemporary Crises* 2 (July): 277–292.

______. 1980. *Class, State, and Crime*. 2d ed. New York: Longman.

______. 1985. "Myth and the Art of Criminology." *Legal Studies Forum* 9: 291–299.

______. 1988. "Crime, Suffering, Service: Toward a Criminology of Peacemaking." *The Quest* 1 (Winter): 66–75.

______. 1991. *Journey to a Far Place: Autobiographical Reflections*. Philadelphia: Temple University Press.

______. 1995. "Socialist Humanism and the Problem of Crime: Thinking About Erich Fromm in the Development of Critical/Peacemaking Sociology. *Crime, Law and Society* 23: 147–156.

______. 1998. *For the Time Being: Ethnography of Everyday Life*. Albany: State University of New York Press.

______. 1998. "Criminology as Moral Philosophy, Criminologist as Witness." *Contemporary Justice Review* 1: 347–364.

______. 2000. *Bearing Witness to Crime and Social Justice*. New York: State University of New York Press.

______. 2001. *Borderland: A Midwest Journal*. Madison: University of Wisconsin Press.

Contributors

Robert Agnew is professor of sociology and violence studies at Emory University in Atlanta, Georgia. His research focuses on the causes of crime and delinquency, especially strain theories of delinquency. Recent books include the second edition of *Juvenile Delinquency: Causes and Control* (2005) and *Why Do Criminals Offend? A General Theory of Crime and Delinquency* (2005). He is currently completing a book on his general strain theory titled *Pressured into Crime: An Overview of General Strain Theory*.

Ronald L. Akers is professor of criminology and sociology (formerly department chair, center director, and associate dean) at the University of Florida. He has conducted extensive research in criminological theory, alcohol and drug behavior, sociology of law, juvenile delinquency, and corrections. He is author of *Criminological Theories: Introduction, Evaluation, and Application* (2004); *Drugs, Alcohol and Society* (1992); *Deviant Behavior: A Social Learning Approach* (1997); and *Social Learning and Social Structure: A General Theory of Crime and Deviance* (1998) and numerous articles in criminological and sociological journals. He is former president of the American Society of Criminology and of the Southern Sociological Society and former chair of the criminology section of the American Sociological Association. He is a recipient of the Edwin H. Sutherland Award from the American Society of Criminology and has been inducted onto the Roll of Honor of the Southern Sociological Society.

Bruce A. Arrigo is a professor in the Department of Criminal Justice at the University of North Carolina at Charlotte. He holds additional appointments in the psychology department and the public policy program. He is author of numerous books and articles exploring critical and applied themes in criminological and social theory, law and psychology, and justice studies. He serves as editor for the book series Critical Perspectives in Criminology and Criminal Justice and Psychology. He is a fellow of the American Psychological Association (2002) and the Academy of Criminal Justice Sciences (2005).

Gregg Barak is professor of criminology and criminal justice at Eastern Michigan University. He is author and/or editor of eleven books, including *Violence and Nonviolence: Pathways to Understanding* (2003), and numerous book chapters and articles, including "A Reciprocal Approach to Peacemaking Criminology: Between Adversarialism and Mutualism" in *Theoretical Criminology* 9 (2) 2005. Barak is also a fellow of the Academy of Criminal Justice Sciences and recipient of the Critical Criminologist of the Year Award in 1999.

Piers Beirne is professor of criminology and legal studies at the University of Southern Maine. He has also taught sociology and criminology in England, at the University of Wisconsin-Madison, and at the University of Connecticut-Storrs. His recent books include *Inventing Criminology* (1993), *Issues in Comparative Criminology* (1997, edited with David Nelken) and *Criminology* (2005, with Jim Messerschmidt). He was the founding coeditor (with Colin Sumner) of the journal *Theoretical Criminology*. His current research is in the area of green criminology, especially nonhuman animal abuse.

John Braithwaite, Eliza Ahmed, and Valerie Braithwaite are researchers in the Regulatory Institutions Network, Australian National University. In 2001, they published (with Nathan Harris) *Shame Management Through Reintegration*. They continue to work together on school and workplace bullying, tax compliance, and on developing shame management theory.

Ronald V. Clarke is professor at Rutgers University and visiting professor at the Jill Dando Institute of Crime Science, University College, London.

He was employed for fifteen years in the British government's criminological research department, where he had a significant role in the development of situational crime prevention and the British Crime Survey. He is founding editor of *Crime Prevention Studies* and author or joint author of nearly two hundred books, monographs, and papers, including *The Reasoning Criminal* (1986), *Situational Crime Prevention: Successful Case Studies* (1997), *Superhighway Robbery* (2003), and *Become a Problem Solving Crime Analyst* (2003).

Derek B. Cornish. After working at the British Home Office's Research Unit, Derek Cornish joined the Department of Social Science and Administration at the London School of Economics. He now lives in the United States, where he is visiting professor at Wichita State University's School of Community Affairs, and is an associate of the Gill Dando Institute at University College, London. He recently co-edited (with Martha Smith) *Theory for Practice in Situational Crime Prevention* (2003), and they are currently editing another book on preventing public transport crime.

Elliott Currie is professor of criminology, law and society in the School of Social Ecology, University of California-Irvine. His research includes the study of criminal justice policy in the United States and other countries, causes of violent crime, social context of delinquency and youth violence, etiology of drug abuse and the assessment of drug policy, race, and criminal justice. He is author of several books including *Confronting Crime* (1985), *Reckoning: Drugs, the Cities, and the American Future* (1993), *Crime and Punishment in America* (1998), and the recently published *The Road to Whatever: Middle Class Culture and the Crisis of Adolescence* (2004). He is co-author of *Whitewashing Race: The Myth of a Color-Blind Society* (2003).

Kathleen Daly is professor of criminology and criminal justice, Griffith University, Brisbane. She writes on gender, race, crime and justice, and on restorative justice and Indigenous justice. Her book, *Gender, Crime, and Punishment* (1994), received the Michael Hindelang award from the American Society of Criminology. From 1998 to 2004, she received three major Australian Research Council grants to direct a program of research on restorative justice and the race and gender polices of new justice practices in Australia, New Zealand, and Canada. She is vice president of the Australian and New Zealand Society of Criminology.

William S. Davidson II is University Distinguished Professor in the Department of Psychology at Michigan State University, where he also serves as chair of the Ecological/Community Psychology Graduate Training Program, director of the Adolescent Diversion Project, and senior scientist of the Michigan Public Health Institute. He is author of numerous articles and co-author of six books, including *Alternative Treatments for Troubled Youth* (with R. Redner, C. M. Mitchell, and R. Amdur, 1990). He is editor of the *American Journal of Community Psychology*.

Walter S. DeKeseredy is professor of criminology and justice studies at the University of Ontario Institute of Technology. DeKeseredy has published more than fifty refereed journal articles and ten books on topics such as woman abuse, crime in public housing, and other contemporary social problems. In 2004, he and Martin D. Schwartz received the Distinguished Scholar Award from the American Society of Criminology's (ASC) Division on Women and Crime. In 1995, DeKeseredy received the Critical Criminologist of the Year Award from the ASC's Division on Critical Criminology.

Jeff Ferrell is professor of criminal justice at Texas Christian University. He is author of *Crimes of Style* (1996), *Tearing Down the Streets* (2001/2002), and *Empire of Scrounge* (2005), and lead co-editor of four books, most recently *Cultural Criminology Unleashed* (2004). He is founding and current editor of the NYU Press book series Alternative Criminology, and one of the founding and current editors of the journal *Crime, Media, Culture: An International Journal* (Sage, London). In 1998 he received the Critical Criminologist of the Year Award from the American Society of Criminology.

Diana H. Fishbein has a joint Ph.D. in criminology and psychobiology from Florida State University. She is currently director of the Transdisciplinary Behavioral Science Program for RTI International. Previously, she was prevention director at the HIDTA Research Program at the University of Maryland. Fishbein began as professor of criminology at the University of Baltimore and scientific investigator at the University of Maryland, School of Medicine and the National Institute on Drug Abuse. She then became senior researcher with the U.S. Department of Justice. Her publications include four books and numerous chapters, monographs, scientific articles, and policy papers.

Michael R. Gottfredson is professor of criminology, law, and society and of sociology, as well as executive vice chancellor at the University of California, Irvine. He received his A.B. from the University of California, Davis and Ph.D. from the State University of New York-Albany. He is co-author and/or editor of *Control Theories of Crime and Delinquency* (2003), *The Generality of Deviance* (1994), *A General Theory of Crime* (1990), *Decisionmaking in Criminal Justice* (1988), and *Victims of Personal Crime* (1978), as well as numerous articles in criminology.

John M. Hagedorn is senior research fellow at the Great Cities Institute at the University of Illinois-Chicago and associate professor of criminal justice. He is principally engaged in a long-term study of the history of gangs in Chicago. He has studied children in gangs for a ten-nation study of children in organized armed violence and is participating in the Social Science Research Council Working Group on children in armed conflict. He is editor of the forthcoming *Gangs in the Global City: Exploring Alternatives to Traditional Criminology*. Previous books include *People and Folks: Gangs, Crime and the Underclass in a Rustbelt City* (1998). He and his partner, Mary Devitt, have six kids, two grandchildren, and a dog.

Stuart Henry is professor of social science and chair of the Department of Interdisciplinary Studies in the College of Urban, Labor and Metropolitan Affairs at Wayne State University. Henry's research focuses on issues of crime, deviance, and social control. He has published twenty-one books, including *Criminological Theory* (with Werner Einstadter, 1995) and *Constitutive Criminology* (with Dragan Milovanovic, 1996). His most recent books include: *What Is Crime?* (with Mark Lanier, 2001) and *Essential*

Criminology, second edition (with Mark Lanier, 2004). He serves on the editorial boards of *Theoretical Criminology* and *Critical Criminology*.

Travis Hirschi is Regents Professor Emeritus at the University of Arizona. He is author of *Causes of Delinquency* (1969) and co-author (with Michael Gottfredson) of *A General Theory of Crime* (1990).

Mark M. Lanier is associate professor of criminal justice at the University of Central Florida. He holds an interdisciplinary doctoral degree from Michigan State University. He has published numerous articles in a variety of disciplinary journals including those dealing with public health, criminal justice, criminology, law, and psychology. His funded research is on youth and HIV/AIDS and community policing. He co-authored (with Stuart Henry) *Essential Criminology* (1998; 2004) and co-edited (with Stuart Henry) *What Is Crime?* (2001).

Sarah Livsey is a doctoral student in the Ecological/Community Psychology Graduate Training Program at Michigan State University.

Michael J. Lynch is professor in the Department of Criminology at the University of South Florida. His recent publications have appeared in journals in several different disciplines, including sociology, medicine, anthropology, Black studies, environmental studies, criminology, and criminal justice. He is co-author of *The New Primer in Radical Criminology* (2000).

James W. Messerschmidt is professor of sociology in the criminology department at the University of Southern Maine. He is the author of numerous books and papers on masculinities and crime, including *Masculinities and Crime* (1993), *Crime as Structured Action* (1997), *Nine Lives* (2000), and *Flesh and Blood* (2004).

Steven F. Messner is Distinguished Teaching Professor of Sociology at the State University of New York-Albany. His research focuses on the relationship between social organization and crime, the spatial patterning of crime, crime in China, and the situational dynamics of violence. In addition to his publications in professional journals, he is co-author of *Crime and the American Dream* (1994; 2001), *Perspectives on Crime and Deviance* (1998), *Criminology: An Introduction Using ExplorIt* (2003), and co-editor of *Theoretical Integration in the Study of Deviance and Crime* (1989) and *Crime and Social Control in a Changing China* (2001).

Dragan Milovanovic is professor of justice studies at Northeastern Illinois University. He received his Ph.D. from the State University of New York-Albany. He has authored numerous books and journal articles in the area of postmodern criminology, law, and social justice. His most recent books are *Critical Criminology at the Edge* (2004) and *An Introduction to the Sociology of Law,* third edition (2003). He is editor of the *International Journal for the Semiotics of Law.*

W. William Minor received his Ph.D. from Florida State University in 1975. He has taught criminology and sociology at the University of Maryland and Northern Illinois University. Formerly chair of the department of sociology, he currently serves as associate dean of the College of Liberal Arts and Sciences at Northern Illinois University. Earlier in his career most of his research focused on control theory, neutralization, and deterrence of crime. More recently, he has also pursued interdisciplinary work, publishing (with geographer Fahui Wang) research on the relationship between employment accessibility and crime rates. Currently his scholarly interests also include environmental sociology.

Nikos Passas is professor of criminal justice at Northeastern University. He specializes in the study of terrorism, white-collar crime, corruption, organized crime, and international crime. He has published more than seventy articles, book chapters, reports, and books in eleven languages including *Legislative Guide for the Implementation of the UN Convention Against Transnational Organized Crime* (2003), *Informal Value Transfer Systems and Criminal Organizations* (1999), *International Crimes* (2003), *It's Legal but It Ain't Right* (2005), *Upperworld and Underworld in Cross-Border Crime* (2002), *Transnational Crime* (1999), *The Future of Anomie*

Theory (1997), and *Organized Crime* (1995). He is currently preparing books on the regulation of informal remittance systems and financial controls of terrorism and a legislative guide for the implementation of the UN convention against corruption.

Hal Pepinsky teaches criminal justice at Indiana University, Bloomington. His most recent book, *A Criminologist's Quest for Peace*, is available online for free use at *http://www.critcrim.org/critpapers/pepinsky-book.htm*.

Richard Quinney is Professor Emeritus, Northern Illinois University, and author of several books in critical criminology, including *The Social Reality of Crime* (1970); *Critique of Legal Order* (2002); and *Class, State, and Crime* (1980). His selected writings in criminology are collected in *Bearing Witness to Crime and Social Justice* (2000). Autobiographical sketches are included in his books *Journey to a Far Place* (1991), *For the Time Being* (1998), *Borderland* (2001), and *Where Yet the Sweet Birds Sing* (2005). He has been a Fulbright lecturer in Ireland and received the Edwin H. Sutherland award for contributions to criminological theory. He lives in Madison, Wisconsin.

Nicole Rafter is a senior research fellow at Northeastern University's College of Criminal Justice and an affiliated faculty member in Northeastern's Law, Policy and Society Program. Her recent books include *Shots in the Mirror: Crime Films and Society* (2000) and the *Encyclopedia of Women and Crime* (editor-in-chief, 2000). With Mary Gibson, she is preparing new translations of Lombroso's key criminological works. The first volume, *Criminal Woman*, was published in 2004; the second volume, *Criminal Man*, will be published in 2005. She is also preparing a new edition of her book on crime films. Rafter is a fellow of the American Society of Criminology.

Joseph H. Rankin is professor and chair of the Department of Criminal Justice at Wayne State University. He has held previous faculty appointments at Purdue University and Eastern Michigan University, where he also served as department head and interim director of the university honors program. Rankin has published widely on the association between families and delinquency. His most recent research explores the relationship between parental controls and self-reported crime among college students.

Matthew Robinson is associate professor of criminal justice at Appalachian State University. He is the author of *Why Crime? An Integrated Systems Theory of Antisocial Behavior* (2004) and *Justice Blind? Ideals and Realities of American Criminal Justice* (2005). He also co-authored *Spatial Aspects of Crime: Theory and Practice* (2004). Robinson has also published fifty other articles and is immediate past president of the Southern Criminal Justice Association. He lives in Boone, North Carolina, with his wife and two children.

Richard Rosenfeld is professor of criminology and criminal justice at the University of Missouri-St. Louis. He is a member of the National Academy of Sciences Committee on Law and Justice and the steering committee of the National Consortium on Violence Research. Rosenfeld is co-author with Steven F. Messner of *Crime and the American Dream*, third edition (2001). He has published widely on the social sources of violent crime, and his current research focuses on the effect of law enforcement interventions on trends in urban violence.

Stanton E. Samenow, Ph.D., is a clinical psychologist specializing in criminal justice and child custody matters. His office is in Alexandria, Virginia. He is author of *Inside the Criminal* Mind (2004) and *Before It's Too Late* (2001) and co-author with Samuel Yochelson, M.D., of the three-volume *The Criminal Personality* (1976, 1977, 1987). Dr. Samenow has presented onsite continuing education, staff training, and consultation throughout North America.

Robert J. Sampson is Henry Ford II Professor of the Social Sciences at Harvard University, where he was appointed in 2003. He taught at the University of Chicago for twelve years before that and spent 2002–03 at the Center for Advanced Study in the Behavioral Sciences in Stanford, California. In addition to a body of work on urban social ecology and violence, Sampson is the author (with John Laub) of *Crime in the Making: Pathways and Turning Points Through Life* (1993) and *Shared Beginnings, Divergent Lives: Delinquent Boys to Age 70* (2003), both winners of the American Society of Criminology's Distinguished Book Award.

Martin D. Schwartz is professor of sociology at Ohio University. Often with Walter DeKeseredy, he has written or edited eleven books (several up to four editions), about sixty refereed journal articles and another forty book chapters, government reports, and essays. He is co-editor of *Criminal Justice: An International Journal of Policy and Practice* and has served on the editorial boards of eleven other journals. At Ohio University, he received the Graduate Professor of the Year Award and Best Arts and Sciences Professor Award (twice), and the university research achievement award. He has won the top research award from two different divisions of the American Society of Criminology.

Christine S. Sellers is associate professor of criminology at the University of South Florida. She has published several articles testing criminological theories in journals such as *Criminology*, *Justice Quarterly*, and *Journal of Quantitative Criminology*. Her research interests also include gender differences in delinquency and intimate partner violence.

Paul B. Stretesky is an associate professor in the sociology department at Colorado State University. His publications have appeared in a number of leading journals in several disciplines, including *The Archives of Pediatrics and Adolescent Medicine*, *Rural Sociology*, *Social Problems*, *The Journal of Health and Social Behavior*, *Justice Quarterly*, *The British Journal of Criminology*, *Theoretical Criminology*, *Society and Natural Resources*, *Sociological Quarterly*, and *Social Science Quarterly*. He is currently completing work on a grant from the Environmental Protection Agency on audit policy business self-regulation.

Larry Tifft is professor of sociology at Central Michigan University and **Dennis Sullivan** is adjunct professor of criminal justice at the State University of New York-Albany. They have been collaborating on writing and activist projects since they first taught together at the University of Illinois-Chicago in 1972. In 1980, their book *The Struggle to be Human: Crime, Criminology, and Anarchism* was the first pacifist-anarchist treatise to appear on crime, punishment, and justice. This was followed by Sullivan's *The Mask of Love: Corrections in America* (1980); *Toward a Mutual Aid Alternative* and *The Punishment of Crime in Colonial New York: The Dutch Experience in Albany During the Seventeenth Century* (1997) and Tifft's *Battering of Women: The Failure of Intervention and the Case for Prevention* (1993). They are authors of *Restorative Justice: Healing the Foundations of Our Everyday Lives*, second edition (2005) and editors of *Handbook of Restorative Justice: A Global Perspective* (2005). Sullivan and Tifft founded and currently serve as editors of the *Contemporary Justice Review.* They were also instrumental in establishing the Justice Studies Association, an association of scholars, practitioners, and activists committed to restorative and social justice.

Austin T. Turk is professor of sociology at the University of California, Riverside, and was founding (interim) director of the Robert B. Presley Center for Crime and Justice Studies (1994–1995). He is a fellow (1978) and a past president (1984–1985) of the American Society of Criminology, and has served on the board of trustees (1982–1984) of the Law and Society Association and on the board of directors (1976–1986) of the Research Committee for the Sociology of Deviance and Control, International Sociological Association. He has written extensively on conflict theory; law, power, and social inequalities; and the dimensions, sources, and policing of political crime. Recent work focuses on patterns and trajectories of political violence, including terrorism.

L. Edward Wells is professor of criminal justice science at Illinois State University. His research has focused on the impact of the family as a central element of social control and on the influence of community contexts in the development of local juvenile gangs and crime problems. Recent research has focused especially on social control of crime and delinquency in smaller, less metropolitan settings. He is co-author with Ralph Weisheit and David Falcone of *Crime and Policing in Rural and Small-Town America* (1999).

Index